STARING INTO CHAOS

Also by B. G. Brander

Australia

Canary Islands

New Zealand

The River Nile

STARING INTO CHAOS

Explorations in the Decline of Western Civilization

B. G. BRANDER

SPENCE PUBLISHING COMPANY • DALLAS
1998

This book is dedicated to the memory of Oswald Spengler,

Arnold Toynbee, and Pitirim Sorokin,

whose broad vision of modern society and its future

has proved dramatically prescient.

Published in the United States by
Spence Publishing Company
501 Elm Street, Suite 450
Dallas, Texas 75202

Library of Congress Cataloging-in-Publication Data

Brander, Bruce.
Staring into chaos : explorations in the decline of Western civilization / B.G. Brander
p. cm.
Includes bibliographical references and index.
ISBN 0-9653208-5-5 (hardcover)
1. Civilization, Western. 2. Civilization—History. 3. Regression (Civilization) I. Title.
CB245.B69 1998
909'.09821'0072—dc21 97-36927

Printed in the United States of America

If the West is to go under, it will have had the pleasure of reading its own obituary, the most erudite and voluminous obituary ever penned. And no Westerner can protest that he was not warned.

Kenneth Winetrout

Contents

Part II: Oswald Spengler, The Master Doomsayer

Preface

Warnings of Decline

THIS BOOK BRINGS TOGETHER the studies and insights of many social thinkers who have warned of decline in modern Western civilization. Artists, historians, sociologists, and other observers of cultural trends have seen deterioration in the culture at least since the mid-nineteenth century.

For a long time the material progress of the West has brilliantly eclipsed their admonitions. Well into the twentieth century, the spectacular achievements of science, technology, and the production of wealth have led most people to believe our civilization has been progressing on a steady upward course and carrying the whole world with it. Except for the years immediately after the two world wars, warnings of decline from even reputable figures seemed quirky, absurd, and unduly pessimistic, when they were heard at all. Only during this century's closing decades have the progress, stability, and prestige of the West declined sufficiently for their admonitions to seem worthy of attention.

These pages explore the view that Western civilization is coming to an end, at least in the materialistic, sensate, scientific, technological, irreligious, expansionist, world-dominating form into which it has developed over the past five centuries. According to supporters of this view, the end is not coming in the future but is upon us now.

I begin this collection of warnings with words of the French poet Charles Baudelaire. An early tune-carrier of decadence, he saw the technology by which the West lives as also destroying the culture. The Russian novelist Leo Tolstoy agreed, while his contemporary and countryman Feodor Dostoyevsky saw Western civilization headed for catastrophic breakdown. Jacob Burckhardt, one of the most eminent historians of the nineteenth century, likened Europe of his time to ancient Rome in decay, a topic on which he was a noted expert. At a time when Western people were enthralled with their progress and brimming with optimism, he predicted a twentieth century of economic depressions, great wars, the waning of democracy, and the rise of totalitarian states.

Other thoughtful people who have issued warnings for the West include Alfred Nobel, for whom the peace prize is named; the humanitarian doctor Albert Schweitzer; and American historians Brooks Adams and Henry Adams, who believed that Western civilization, as Henry put it, was hurtling toward "ultimate, colossal, cosmic collapse." The literary figures Jack London, H.G. Wells, George Orwell, and Aldous Huxley also had much to say about cultural deterioration.

Yet none of them approached the intellectual scope and authority of three giants who appeared in the midst of twentieth-century events. Separately and together, they paint a broad picture of the West's disintegration as it is occurring now and will continue to occur.

The first was the German social philosopher and historian Oswald Spengler, with his well-known work, *The Decline of the West.* This large and difficult study in social philosophy traces Western culture from its rise through its decline to its ultimate collapse several hundred years from now. Next came the English historian Arnold Toynbee, with his three-million-word, twelve-volume *A Study of History.* The largest historical work ever written, and the largest book of the twentieth century, it compares Western culture with every known civilization and suggests the West is treading a well-worn downward path. The third master scholar of Western civilization's fate was the Harvard sociologist Pitirim Sorokin, with his *Social and Cultural Dynamics.* This four-volume study predicts the imminent downfall of the culture in its sensate, materialistic form and its ultimate rebirth as a culture of spiritual values.

To distill the insights of more than two-dozen thinkers into this single volume, I have treated their works in different ways. Social observers who noted signs of decline but did not analyze them deeply I mention only briefly. Where writers contributed whole books on the topic, I offer concise digests of their works. The largest part of this book condenses the three grand studies of Spengler, Toynbee, and Sorokin. I have tried to cover each from start to finish in a balanced and comprehensive way to preserve the full meaning of the original without its enormous size.

My intention in echoing these warnings of decline is not to spread pessimism or cause alarm. Certainly, admonitions like this can be disturbing, especially for people who feel content with things as they are and live in emotional dependence on the ways and leading of the culture. Such warnings, probing far and deep, can leave us feeling that the cultural ground we walk upon is collapsing beneath our feet.

Yet this book is written for more constructive purposes. First, it will serve historians and social scientists with greatly shortened versions of important works in their fields, some so extensive and demanding that their fame greatly exceeds their readership. They exist in what one wit called "a kind of highly topical obscurity."

At the same time, I hope this book will serve many general readers who feel stranded in a painful and bewildering time. Anyone who wonders about the rapid social change sweeping over the culture like a tidal wave will find in these pages abundant clarification of why changes are occurring and where they might be leading. People confused about how to respond to modern trends will appreciate the vast knowledge and profound perspectives of the authors. Conservatives who longingly recall more stable, decent, or predictable times, as well as the socially alienated who yearn for an altogether different kind of life, can find encouragement in forecasts of the world that will emerge once the present time of troubles is past.

Perhaps these pages also will lead some readers to the loftiest ideal they contain: the best recourse in disordered times is to transcend the limitations of human cultures and rise to a universal culture of truth, right, and life. If so, I shall consider this book to have been well worth the writing.

I AM GRATEFUL to many people in many places for their assistance in completing this book.

Among the institutions that graciously allowed me to use their research facilities are the University College Cork, Ireland; the University of Hawaii in Honolulu; and the University of Wisconsin-Milwaukee.

Notable among people who helped me along the way are Anthony Krzyzewski, Leola Little, Frederick G. Schmidt and Joy Schaleban Lewis, who perseveringly read and commented on early stages of the manuscript. Breton Buckley offered invaluable encouragement. The eminent American historian John Lukacs carefully checked the final manuscript and made valuable corrections.

My wife, Mary Wederath Brander, combed through the draft with an exacting eye for text errors and confusing passages. Meanwhile, our four children accepted with sweet patience my seclusion while the work was in progress.

When all that was done, Mitchell Muncy, an informed, educated, and excellent editor of the old school, immersed himself in the manuscript and was responsible for much improvement in its structure and content.

I thank them all.

PART I

The Problem of the West

I

Progress and Doubt

For the past five centuries Western civilization has thrived and expanded on the vigor and appeal of its progress—spectacular progress in geographical discovery, political ideology, scientific inquiry, technology, production of wealth, and a dazzling array of other means of enriching the life of humankind. Today the whole world lives and has its being from the fruits of Western progress, advances unparalleled in all history.

Yet anyone living in the Western world over the past few generations has been sharply aware of vast changes sweeping over the culture. These transformations, dizzyingly rapid and perhaps wholly out of control, are challenging and reshaping art and philosophy, commerce and politics, ethics and law, education, religion, and all the relationships that hold together a society of civilized people. Scholars generally agree that the tidal wave of change rarely has been equaled in the past in either magnitude or speed. These stunning upheavals leave many bewildered and anxious.

What are we to make of the grand transformations in our culture? Customs and ideals, beliefs and modes of living are disintegrating rather than integrating. Institutions and forms once firm and solid are teetering, sagging, collapsing. The prevailing tenor of the age rings less of advance than decline.

Future annals of history probably will mark the twentieth century less for triumphs of science than for the sudden collapse of the West's vast global empires. People living through the century's middle decades witnessed imperial decline unseen by any generation since the fall of ancient Rome. Seen from a historical perspective, the spectacle is breathtaking: at least ten major empires, some centuries old, crumbled away in a single generation. Meanwhile, the position of the West as the world's dominant political and economic power continues to decline, with consequences still uncertain.

In the midst of this transition, we can only wonder where such trends are leading. Do they represent a passing aberration, a temporary lull in the endless upward progress that modern Western peoples long have taken as their destiny? Or are we witnessing a kind of renaissance, a paradigm shift that will change the nature of the culture to something altogether different? Or are we coming to an end—the end of Western culture's long, splendid, soaring age of strength and high civilization?

As thoughtful people ponder the condition of the West, their views differ widely, often clashing in conflict, yet seem to carry equal weight. Many people remain confident in the culture, ignoring the negatives or giving them scant attention, while focusing more sharply on areas of continuing progress. Others regard disintegrative trends with deep unease as foreboding approaching disaster.

Science and technology continue to promise a golden age to come, a lasting expansion of the brilliant technology that continues to transform the world. At the same time these two quintessential occupations of the West conjure up ways to destroy civilization, to annihilate humankind, and perhaps to put an end to all life.

Social optimists envision scientific triumphs, universal prosperity, vast strides in human health, longer life spans, universal justice, global peace, colonies in space, and many other futuristic marvels. Social pessimists variously foresee economic dissolution, decay of health, environmental calamity, nuclear catastrophe, mass migrations, "massive population dieback," and a steel cage of tyranny reducing human beings to the level and worth of insects.

Caught between strangely wide extremes of glowing dreams and stark despair, most people feel only anxious and uncertain. We sense that something has gone wrong, that a rudder has been lost, that the civilization is adrift and unknown reefs loom ahead. We sense more than understand what is happening around us, wonder how to defend ourselves against it, hope things will come right, are braced if they do not, and have no clear notion of what we ourselves can do to help correct the culture's deviation from a sure, safe course.

Not long ago almost everyone believed that Western civilization was destined to progress continuously toward a glorious, utopian future. Today that hope is severely shaken.

Varying Views of Man's Course

For many generations Western society preached and accepted a faith in evolutionary human progress as a doctrine beyond doubt or question. Yet belief in social progress is far from universal. People of other times and places have held greatly differing views of humanity's march through time.

Ancient Greeks, for example, saw history moving in a straight line—but backward. The epic poet Homer, who lived before 700 B.C., wrote of past ages as better than his own. A more elaborated view was recorded by the farmer-poet Hesiod, who dwelled in the fertile Greek region of Boeotia probably as early as the eighth century B.C. He charted humanity's course regressively downward, from a dazzling golden age through lesser silver, bronze, and heroic ages to a base iron age that he thought to be his own.

Another view of history prevailed in Greece by the fifth and fourth centuries B.C., when Socrates schooled Plato, and he in turn instructed Aristotle. People of that time compared humanity's story to the natural cycles of the cosmos: sunrise and sunset, summer and winter, generation and decay. They saw city-states, their largest political units, following a pattern of rise and fall: from small beginnings, to strength and prosperity, then on to overweening pride and ultimate ruin.

In later centuries of ancient Greece and Rome, conceptions of man's course were mixed and inconsistent. At least one thinker, however, the Roman naturalist Pliny the Elder, who lived at the time of Christ, displayed solid faith in progress, advising, "Let no one lose hope that the ages will always grow better."

In the Europe of the Middle Ages, notions of progress were all but forgotten. The rise of Christianity brought another view of man's passage over the earth. Human history was seen as transitory and relatively unimportant, a mere interval between two periods of perfection: the Garden of Eden in the beginning, then, after the apocalypse and the last judgment, the City of God at the end. For the interim, people saw no consistent development in civilization, but only a cycle of more or less irrelevant rises and falls.

The concept of progress reappeared faintly in writings of the twelfth and thirteenth centuries. Not until the seventeenth century, however, did this smoldering notion begin to flicker in literature, philosophy, and social theories, in science and political thinking. In the eighteenth century it burst into flame, outshining and consuming other theories of man's course, in the brilliant philosophical movement known as the Enlightenment.

By far the most distinctive intellectual enterprise of modern times, led by thinkers like Voltaire, Montesquieu, and Rousseau, Hume, Paine, and Kant, the Enlightenment challenged medieval traditions by bringing forth a sweeping new credo to guide humankind. It promoted free use of reason, which it saw as a power almost without limit. It advocated the empirical method of inquiry in science. But most of all it proclaimed a doctrine of universal human progress—not a halting advance of jagged ups and downs but improvements forging a straight line steeply upward. This heady faith in progress grew and spread from that time forward, enduring, however faltering and dimming, to the present.

The Progress of the West

The great thinkers of the Enlightenment, redefining human potential, also paved the way for the culture's onrushing future. Yet the progress to come, like the concept itself, had its early beginnings long before the eighteenth century. The expulsion of Moors from Europe, daring oceanic voyages of exploration, the renaissance in learning and art, the conquest of new empires—all were signs of a culture growing in strength and confidence. The Enlightenment presaged not a wholly new trend but a continuance of one already surging forward. Yet it seemed like the dawn of a wholly new era, as the doctrine of progress took tangible form and advancements unfolded as never before in history.

Agriculture was touched by its magic first. In the eighteenth and nineteenth centuries, new knowledge and older techniques freshly applied revolutionized the growing of crops and the husbanding of animals. In mere generations the quality and scale of farming improved to an extent that matched in significance the original discovery of agriculture in the Neolithic Age. In the three decades between 1810 and 1840, farmers in Britain increased their yields of vegetable-based calories by 25 percent. At the same time, French production leaped 60 percent. In America in 1800, farmers worked 373 hours to grow and harvest a hundred bushels of wheat. By 1840, they were bringing in the same amount in 233 hours.

By the middle of the nineteenth century, the specter of famine that had stalked humankind since the beginning of history vanished completely in times of peace for all the advancing countries of the West. The final famines struck Germany and Belgium in 1846-1847 and Ireland in 1846-1848.

Close on the heels of agricultural progress, the Industrial Revolution arose, reshaping the West more than any influence since the growth of Christianity. Sources of energy never before exploited—steam, petroleum, electricity—transformed human labor, added vastly to wealth, and drastically altered social organization. In only decades, the crusade to industrialize changed the landscape of entire countries. Factories dominated towns and cities as castles and cathedrals had earlier, their smokestacks rising like the steeples of a new and provident religion. Steel tracks filigreed the land, viaducts vaulted valleys, tunnels pierced mountains, and railroad trains left horse carriages, goods caravans, and canal barges in the dust of history. Modes of travel changed in the fifty years following 1830 more than in the previous five centuries.

In the eighteenth century, the scholars known as "natural philosophers," who systematically investigated the natural world, adopted the new name "scientists." Under their guidance, the quest for knowledge surged ahead, and science acquired the status of a major new cultural institution.

Important discoveries in metallurgy multiplied machines and put iron hulls on ships. Ironwork also led building in bold new directions, first in 1851 with the Crystal Palace in England, then in 1889 with the Eiffel Tower in Paris and the first skyscraper in New York.

As electricity was harnessed, the telegraph clicked into operation in 1844, speeding messages across whole continents and spanning the Atlantic Ocean by cable in 1866. The telephone appeared, and the incandescent lamp, and the dynamo, and electroplating. An amazed society stood in awe of its rapid advance: "And now we have the phonograph," the *Illustrated London News* proclaimed in August 1878, "which machine first imprints a message and then speaks or sings it off any number of times at the operator's will." [1]

Eleven years later, electric trams were displacing horse-drawn street cars in Europe. Not long after, a twenty-two-year-old Italian student named Guglielmo Marconi invented an "electric telegraph without a wire conductor," later known simply as the wireless or radio.[2] Meanwhile, a new and growing chemical industry was producing inexpensive paper, synthetic dyes, artificial silk (rayon) made from wood pulp, photographic film, and, in 1891, color photographs.

Forecasts of future progress were all the more dazzling. In 1894, the *Illustrated London News* announced that a report by American inventor Hiram S. Maxim, who had been experimenting with a framework holding five tiers of wings and a three-hundred-horse-power engine, "furnishes trustworthy information that we are within measurable distance of the faculty of flying."[3] Not long after, a rocket-powered car invented in Germany gave people the idea that man soon might fly to the moon.

The prolific growth of science and its stunning successes inspired an all but religious faith in its ability to continue improving life. As one rhymer blithely put it:

When men of science find out something more,
We shall be happier than we were before.[4]

With agriculture yielding abundant food, industry spinning out growing quantities of goods, and science improving sanitation and medicine, the population of the West also grew enormously. During the century after 1750, France's population grew by 26 percent, the Russian population swelled 42 percent, and the number of Britons grew a staggering 70 percent. According to the reckoning of German economic historian Werner Sombart, Europe entered the nineteenth century with 180 million people and met 1914 with 420 million. Another estimate calculates that for every four Europeans in 1800 there were ten a century later.

Great cities grew along with populations. Between 1800 and 1920, the population of Paris expanded five times over. Vienna grew by more than seven times. London multiplied its population by nine, Berlin by twenty-five, Philadelphia by thirty, and New York by one hundred. Between 1870 and 1900, the number of German cities with more than 100,000 inhabitants grew from eight to forty-one. Even relatively backward European Russia saw its cities of that size increase from six to seventeen.

Urban areas measured their progress not only in population but in living conditions. Though squalid slums pocked the great cities, civic improvements appeared at every turn. Clean water, efficient sewerage, and extensive street lighting joined public libraries, attractive parks, playgrounds, and inexpensive entertainment to make metropolitan centers as early as the mid-1880s generally more healthful and pleasant than the country.

Though progress often meant material advance, social progress also underwent major change. By age-old tradition, lower classes had been counted as insignificant beneath the social weight of royalty, aristocracy, and wealthy middle classes. Now, the common man gained recognition and importance unparalleled in history.

Emancipation movements freed serfs in Russia and slaves in America. Democratic ideals arose and intensified. Trade unions bettered wages and factory conditions. Legislation slashed workdays from fifteen hours to eight. Child labor, which in some parts of Europe put youngsters to work at the age of four, was regulated and limited. Many other social reforms touched the common man's existence.

Education also progressed by great strides. Prior to the mid-1860s, most Europeans could not read. By 1900, literacy was common, as networks of publicly supported schools spread across the Western world.

Meanwhile the civilization of the West was spreading its influence around the world as no other culture ever had done before. By 1815, explorers from Portugal and Spain, the Netherlands, France, and Britain had charted almost all the earth's surface accessible by water. Adventurers continued penetrating the mysteries of unknown lands on every continent until nearly every corner of the globe was visited and mapped.

Progress in transportation opened new routes for travel and commerce. Sailing ships grew larger, faster, and safer than any in five thousand years of recorded voyaging. Steam-powered vessels performed unprecedented feats of navigation. As early as 1859, the British liner *Great Eastern* churned across the Atlantic in a record fifteen days. Meanwhile, rail lines pushed from busy seaports to remote spots on every continent, bringing businessmen and tourists into regions once closed to all but the hardiest of travelers.

The burgeoning society could not contain itself in its own lands. The waves of ancient Germanic barbarians that surged against the empire of Rome were puny compared to massive emigrations that poured out of Europe from the mid-nineteenth century onward—the largest movement of peoples in history. In only three decades, between 1870 and 1900, at least twenty-five million Europeans sailed across the seas to settle in the new worlds of North and South America, Africa, and Australia.

Along with them went their civilization, which seemed vastly superior to others in an age when many peoples lived as savages and older civilizations were despotic, stagnant, impoverished, and crumbling. Western culture gained dominance throughout the world by coercion, persuasion, and attraction. European Christianity kept pace. In the thirty years after 1870, its missionaries won some forty-one million converts overseas.

The growth of empires, for some time waning, surged ahead from 1870. Before then, not a tenth of Africa lay under European sway. By the turn of the century, Europe controlled almost the entire continent. At the same time France, the Netherlands, and Britain ruled 85 percent of Southeast Asia. Belgium, Germany, and Italy entered the drive for colonies in Africa and the Pacific. The United States and Russia expanded their borders. With India and Australia also British, South America white, and the seas dominated by European navies, Western might and culture now ruled most of the earth.

The West offered its progress to the entire world. Already the globe was united as never before. Europe's great empires were held together less by force than by mutual cooperation, as colonies, accustomed to their status and impressed by European ways, gave voluntary loyalty to their rulers. International trade, which had been mounting steadily since 1815, wove a world economy, with Western lands serving as industrial workshops and colonial areas providing raw materials. Cooperation among countries and sharing of ideas brought the Universal Postal Union of 1875; conventions to standardize copyright and patent laws; and a series of world fairs originating with the Crystal Palace Exhibition of 1851 and culminating grandly with the 1900 Paris World's Fair when thirty-nine million people came together from all over the earth.

Meanwhile, equable law and accepted customs were spreading almost everywhere. So was a common code of social order that left violence generally petty, sporadic, and rare. Citizens rested securely in their homes. Travelers moved freely, safely, and in peace, needing no passports, visas, or credentials beyond their identity as human beings. In 1887, growing world unity received a language of its own when a Polish Jew named Louis Lazarus Zamenhof introduced Esperanto—the name meaning "hopeful" in the new international tongue.

Queen Victoria's Diamond Jubilee in 1897 marked the climax of Western hope and glory. The busiest, richest, most progressive century of all time was coming to a close. The next century held unprecedented promise. Machine-made plenty would end poverty, granting everyone affluence and leisure: more food and clothing, shelter and luxuries than they possibly could consume. Sanitation and inoculation would banish disease. Education would enlighten and ennoble the masses. Progress even would extend to human evolution, with humanity attaining a near-angelic state as the fittest who survived also turned out to be the morally strongest and best.

Evolution and progress, many people believed, already had elevated Europe above war. As duels and blood feuds had waned, major armed conflict seemed unlikely among civilized peoples, who now were too intelligent, too rational and humane to engage in military strife. Any further warfare would be minor, limited to backward lands and pursued only to extend the benefits of civilization.

So accustomed were people to awesome progress that few believed it ever could falter, much less end. As the present was superior to the past, so the future was bound to be always better still. The faith in endless improvement expressed almost two millennia earlier by Pliny the Elder, was brilliantly reborn and firmly in command. Barbarian incursions had upset the ancient Roman thinker's prediction. But with a common civilization soon to blanket the globe with material abundance and happiness for all, from where could barbarians come to threaten it?

The Rise of Doubt

World War I shattered the general belief that humankind's world was approaching perfection. The shock of the cataclysmic conflict to Western culture was devastating.

As the war broke out in the summer of 1914, country after country rushed into the fray, people everywhere pouring into the streets to cheer the opportunity for gallantry and heroism. The war would be short, they assumed, over within weeks or months.

All their expectations proved wrong. Brave soldiers found few fields of glory, instead enduring an unbearable existence. They lived in trenches, caked with mud, crawling with vermin, waiting in constant dread of artillery bombardment. When their own big guns thundered to clear the way for attack, they fixed bayonets and went over the top, only to face thickets of barbed wire and murderous machine-gun fire.

Enormous armies from thirty countries balanced each other in size and strength. Total war, the first of its kind, dragged on for years. The line of trenches zigzagged all across Europe from the North Sea to the Swiss frontier. The costliest battles known to history took colossal tolls while yielding negligible gains. Along the Western Front, battle lines were locked in place for two agonizing years, swaying back and forth never more than ten miles.

When the fighting finally ended in 1918, the world stood appalled at its staggering cost. Never had a single war desolated a civilization so severely. The industrialized slaughter had taken the lives of some ten million military men. Twenty million more had been wounded. Ten million noncombatants had perished through invasion and blockade, famine, and disease. Four historic empires were wiped off the map: the German, the Austro-Hungarian, the Ottoman, and the Russian. Russia itself was writhing in the throes of horrendous revolution, with consequent political purges and massive famines.

Europe's economies groaned under crushing war debts. The years of bloodletting had depleted its human resources. The continent's global supremacy was weakened. So was its role as the world's exclusive industrial supplier, since importing countries, under pressure of shortages, were building their own factories. Still more important, the morale of the West had suffered irreparable damage. In the shadow of unprecedented carnage and devastation, how could glowing dreams of progress to perfection survive?

For many intellectuals, the catastrophe foreboded the collapse of Western civilization. Other people, less philosophically inclined, hoped the world would return to the way it was before the war. To their dismay, it changed beyond all recognition. Values and virtues built and nurtured for centuries were questioned, challenged, overthrown. Frivolous amusements, entertainment idols, fads, and frantic dances joined scanty clothing and sexual liberation to raise gnawing doubts about the culture's direction for the future. Yet even then opinions were diverging to extremes. Investors playing a surging stock market imagined that the golden millennium promised by progress had arrived. Soon, some thought, everybody could be rich.

The Roaring Twenties collapsed with the stock market crash of October 1929. A century of economic growth was thrown into reverse and the world plunged into the Great Depression. Industry everywhere ground to a halt. Men and machines stood idle. Architects, lawyers, teachers, engineers tramped the streets with office clerks and factory hands looking for any kind of work to keep themselves and their families alive. The unemployed lined up at soup kitchens and sought shelter in municipal lodgings. Men in the prime of life turned bitter and despairing. The young, threatened with a bleak future, felt demoralized and hopeless. Governments intervened with emergency programs and longer-range social and economic reforms. Gradually national economies began to revive.

By the late 1930s, it appeared that the West was lurching from one disaster to another. No sooner was the Great Depression lifting than Europe teetered on the brink of the World War II. The conflict, erupting in 1939, set staggering new precedents for human and material destruction. While World War I had been confined mainly to the European continent, the second frenzy of mass annihilation ignited much of the world into flames. The battles of the World War I generally took place on terrain evacuated by civilians. World War II revived barbaric strategies of deliberate attacks on noncombatant populations. During six years of continuous fighting, seventy million men were drawn into the struggle in Europe and Africa, Asia and the Pacific. The final death count, including civilian casualties, was roughly double that of the previous great war, approaching forty million, as nearly as estimates of carnage so stupendous can be reckoned.

At the war's end in August 1945, much of Europe lay in ruins. Large parts of the Pacific and Asia lay damaged or devastated. Nations reeled under the horrendous cost in lives, resources, wealth, and stability. The war's aftermath brought ghastly tales of inhuman horror and brutality: of concentration camps, organized torture, and, most appalling of all, the systematic extermination of approximately one-third of the world's Jewish population.

Perceptive observers saw civilization thinned to a mere veneer, with barbarism surging just beneath the surface, straining for release. People of the West felt less certain than ever about their progress and the future of their culture. All around the world doubts were rising about the civilization's claim to moral leadership.

Europe's might abroad, further weakened by the conflict, rapidly waned. The spirit of colonial unity collapsed, and the culture's great empires crumbled. The Dutch, the French, the British all fought to regain their former control in Asia, while Africa's colonial powers struggled to retain their possessions. But one by one countries claimed independence. Officially, the colonial powers cited as the reason the progress of their wards. Unofficially, Europe had lost the ability and will to govern. Meanwhile the United States waged long and costly wars to assert its influence abroad but generally failed despite its enormous might against materially inferior forces.

Along with waning global power, the prestige of the European race was beginning to suffer. The white man's culture long had been regarded not only as technically creative but also as morally high-minded, socially just, well organized, and singularly progressive. The white man himself, though not always liked, generally was respected. Yet only decades after Japanese armies paraded captured Europeans through Asian streets to prove the race was not invincible, much of that respect vanished. The times when the white man commonly was called *tuan*, or "lord," and *bwana*, which translates from Swahili as "our father," seemed increasingly remote.

Meanwhile, Western people were finding their own culture hopelessly perplexing. Its ethics and morality were steadily eroding, with nothing replacing abandoned codes but the threat of ultimate chaos or order by force. Equally perplexing was the steady atrophy of many of the culture's major institutions. Stable family life, once the central pillar of society, was diminished to the point of rarity. Religions continued losing influence. Schools failed in the goals of education. Business suffered from increasing dishonesty and lessening efficiency. Governments lost the trust of the governed as they reeled from mismanagement and scandal.

Unplanned and unexplained change at every turn touched and disrupted life everywhere. The general mood within the culture edged toward doubt and despair. The unbounded optimism of the late nineteenth century seemed as irretrievably lost as chivalry and courtly etiquette. Utopian visions that once glowed brightly for what had been called "the century of promise" now, with that century spent, looked more like mirages on the verge of evaporation. No longer did anyone anticipate social perfection or humanity's ascent to an angelic future. Equally implausible was the notion of the West spreading worldwide peace, plenty for all, and universal happiness. The placid security of earlier times had given way to general anxiety. And Western society's once-supreme confidence in progress without end was sinking into a mire of doubt and confusion.

Probing the Direction of the West

Any age of profound social crisis stimulates a surge of social thought. This was true in the time of Plato as the culture of Greece declined. It happened in the vastly changing Roman world around the time of Christ, and again among fathers of the Christian church as the Roman world collapsed in the fifth century. The twilight of Europe's Gothic Age and the dawn of the Renaissance brought another great wave of social thinking, as did the religious reformations of the sixteenth century. Now, as a new age of crisis unfolds, matching or exceeding those of the past, perceptive observers once again have been striving to understand the nature of their time.

Many thoughtful people regard our age from specialized points of view, concentrating on only limited aspects of the culture. One might focus on political theory, another on economics. A religious person will look at church or morality, a scientist at science and technology. Viewing one or another of these isolated perspectives, they come to conclusions often more varied than popular opinions. These range from scientific hopes for earthly nirvana to apocalyptic expectations of the second coming of Christ.

Generalists, who look at the framework of the culture, tend to be more balanced in their judgments. Diverse in their learning, their perspectives include science and technology, economics, religion, politics, law and ethics, the fine arts, philosophy, social relations, and other compartments of the culture. They fit the pieces into a fuller picture, only then venturing a verdict on the state of the civilization and its probable future.

Some specialists and many generalists agree that the modern age of crisis is not a short-term aberration but a fundamental, lasting, and momentous wave of change. These students see the present time as a landmark in world history, a time of dismantling and discarding weary and outworn old forms that no longer give meaning to life. Although some hesitate to make a final judgment, others declare that Western civilization, at least in the form familiar to us, is well into disintegration and decline.

Until recently, such an idea, in the popular mind, seemed inconceivable, ranking with placard-bearing madmen dressed in sheets proclaiming imminent doom on crowded city streets. Yet the modern social prophets who sound warnings of decline could not be described as eccentrics; among them are some of the most searching and brilliant thinkers of the age, social observers of the highest world standing in a multitude of fields.

They include social scientists, historians, literary figures, political and religious thinkers, and humanitarians from Russia, Germany, France, Great Britain, and America. Their moral convictions extend from deeply religious to humanist to libertine. Politically they vary from intense conservatives to revolutionaries and anarchists. Whatever their diversity, their conclusions are remarkably similar.

Many of the thinkers have worked independently, with little or no knowledge of the others. Confronting a welter of past and present events, they examined the affairs of humankind for principles and patterns that might give clearer shape to current times. The earliest among them only sensed malaise in the culture, groping for its nature and extent. As time went on and the culture's crisis grew in severity and became more clear, their assessments became surer, more explicit and extensive. Increasingly, the social analysts declared Western civilization to be advanced in old age and riddled with decay. They portrayed modern people as spiritually depleted, drained of inner energies and resources, swept along, aimless and uncaring, by tremendous forces that they had loosed but could not control.

The predictions of the observers are stark and distressing, and as far as time has told, startlingly accurate. Long before events proved their insights correct, they foretold the centralization of modern society, the rise of Russia and the subsequent dissolution of Communism, the massive uprooting of global refugees, the breakup of the family, growing crime and suicide, same-sex marriages, and apocalyptic military explosives. They saw arbitrary force replacing law, and democracy uprooted by totalitarian dictatorships. They predicted world government, the ultimate collapse of the current Western culture, and the fresh ascendance of religion as a leading cultural force.

Dealing specifically with modern Western culture, they answer many of our questions as the present world turns more violent and uncertain: How great is the likelihood that the quality of life as we have known it is declining? How long has disintegration been setting in? How far has it advanced? How severe is it already? Why is it occurring? How is it reflected in the arts, in the sciences, in social institutions? How does it affect human relations and the makeup, emotions, and behavior of individual persons? Can the disintegration be slowed? Can its effects be lessened? Can it be stopped? Can the culture be saved? If not, how can people be saved from the culture?

If collapse is to come, is it likely to be sudden, complete, cataclysmic? Or will the civilization slump away, ending—in the words of the poet T. S. Eliot—not with a bang but a whimper? Might the culture solidify in dreary petrifaction and drag on in endless senility like the ancient societies of India and China?

The works discussed in this book seek to answer these questions. Along the way, they offer a broad education in the rise, decline, and collapse of former civilizations. Then, using patterns in history as a launching point, they extrapolate Western civilization's course for a century and more ahead. Meanwhile, the studies read like grand sociological thrillers as they trace our journey through momentous cataclysms rare in the chronicles of humankind.

Nor do they stop with disintegration. No social trend is eternal. Just as civilization never has enjoyed unlimited ascent, neither can its decline go on forever. Modern humanity might be witnessing the decline of a world civilization, but, too, we might be seeing a dual transformation: the clearing away of an old social order so that fresh creative life can blossom in its place.

The more recent social prophets see beyond the abyss of decline to a promising future. Those who came earlier sensed only gathering storms. The first of these, appearing as early as the middle of the nineteenth century, penetrated the glitter of Western progress, the triumph of Western might, and the bubble of Western optimism with remarkable perception for their time. Boldly denying the spirit of their age, they began to sound the alarm.

2

The Alarm Sounds

ON JUNE 22, 1897, a magnificent procession wound through the streets of London. Row upon row of cavalry held aloft the flags of Australia, Canada, Cyprus, India, South Africa, Trinidad. Files of infantry soldiers and artillery troops marched by in uniforms of Jamaica, Borneo, Nigeria, Hong Kong, Malaya. Finally came eight cream horses drawing the four-wheeled open landau carriage of Victoria, Queen of Great Britain and Ireland, Empress of India. The procession commemorated the queen's Diamond Jubilee, marking her sixty years on the throne as the longest-reigning monarch in English history.

Never since the days of ancient Rome had a sphere of power spread as widely as the British Empire. The sun never set on its Union Jack banner unfurling and waving around the globe. Pink shapes covered the world map, denoting British domination over one-fourth of the world's terrain. The Royal Navy ruled the waves. Ports and islands strategically controlled by Britain assured safe haven, fueling, and passage for travel, commerce, and war.

Lining six miles of flower-decked streets, cheering people by the millions watched in wonder as the grand spectacle of imperial power and glory passed in review; "terrible and beautiful to behold," wrote an awestruck journalist who witnessed the pageant.[1] The splendid event exemplified Western civilization's global might and triumph. Yet even then perceptive people were feeling apprehension about the soundness and the future of the culture that underlay it.

The English poet and novelist Rudyard Kipling, detecting "a certain optimism that scared me," made his presentiments public for the occasion of the queen's jubilee.[2] The following day, the *Times* of London published his brief poem "Recessional." The lines cautioned against trusting human strength rather than the "God of our fathers." They went on to portray the splendors of the age vanishing like great cities of the ancient world. At a time when poetry was widely read and influential, Kipling's admonition impressed readers deeply. Yet, amidst the civilization's burgeoning power and success, few people could believe for long that someday it might all be "one with Nineveh and Tyre."[3]

Around the same time in the United States, Henry Adams, a noted historian and intellectual and descendant of two of the nation's presidents, also felt profoundly troubled by what he called "the superficial and self-complacent optimism which seems to veneer the surface of society."[4] "Ferocious optimism," a prominent New York editor, E. L. Godkin, called the spirit of the time, going on to speculate that the mood eventually would lead to disaster.[5] In this opinion Adams heartily concurred.[6] Meanwhile, all through the Western world, sensitive people looked toward the close of the nineteenth century with a strange anxiety that seemed to have no precise cause.

"The disposition of the times is curiously confused," wrote a German-Hungarian physician and psychologist named Max Nordau in a widely read book titled *Degeneration*, "a compound of feverish restlessness and blunted discouragement, of fearful presage and hang-dog renunciation. The prevalent feeling is that of imminent perdition and extinction. . . . The old Northern faith contained the fearsome doctrine of the Dusk of the Gods. In our days there have arisen in more highly-developed minds vague qualms about a Dusk of the Nations, in which all suns and all stars are gradually waning, and mankind with all its institutions and creations is perishing in the midst of a dying world."[7]

This apprehension came to be known as the mood of *fin-de-siècle*. The French phrase stood for not merely "end-of-century," but a whole symptomatology of social deterioration and decay.

"The *fin-de-siècle* state of mind is to-day everywhere to be met with," Nordau declared.[8]

> It means a practical emancipation from traditional discipline, which theoretically is still in force. To the voluptuary this means unbridled lewdness, the unchaining of the beast in man; to the withered heart of the egoist, disdain of all consideration for his fellow-men, the trampling under foot of all barriers which enclose brutal greed of lucre and lust of pleasure; to the contemner of the world it means the shameless ascendancy of base impulses and motives, which were, if not virtuously suppressed, at least hypocritically hidden; to the believer it means the repudiation of dogma, the negation of a super-sensuous world, the descent into flat phenomenalism; to the sensitive nature yearning for aesthetic thrills, it means the vanishing of ideals in art. . . . And to all, it means the end of an established order, which for thousands of years has satisfied logic, fettered depravity, and in every art matured something of beauty.[9]

The death of Queen Victoria on January 22, 1901, magnified the feeling that an era was drawing to a close. Meanwhile, in France and Germany, newspapers almost daily reflected suspicions of social decrepitude with articles on falling birthrates, diminishing rural populations, declining army standards and increasing incidence of suicide, insanity, cancer, nervous exhaustion, enfeebled vitality, alcoholism, and drug addiction. Nordau's book cited statistics from all across Europe showing an alarming growth of madness, crime, and suicide from 1840 onward.

The presentiment of endings persisted in the English-speaking world with the sudden and unexpected death of Queen Victoria's son, King Edward VII, in 1910. According to American historian Barbara W. Tuchman, "There was a general sense as of an anchor slipping away and of a recognized order of things gone. . . . When he died people expected times would now get worse."[10]

A year earlier, a British government official who described the world as divided "between nation and nation armed to the teeth" also had written, "The future of progress is still doubtful and precarious. Humanity at best appears as a shipwrecked crew which has taken refuge on a narrow ledge of rock beaten by wind and wave; we cannot tell how many, if any at all, will survive when the long night gives place to morning."[11]

Progress Disbelieved

As early as the middle of the nineteenth century, with progress in science and technology increasing at every turn, a mood of aimlessness and despair began to weigh upon some of the most advanced minds of Europe. The surge of progress, however dynamic, seemed to be going nowhere.

The Russian writer and religious philosopher Count Leo Tolstoy, journeying to Western Europe in 1857 and again in 1860, noted that

> today, electricity, railways and telegraphs spoil the whole world. Everyone makes these things his own. He simply cannot help making them his own. Everyone suffers in the same way, is forced to the same extent to change his way of life. All are under the necessity of betraying what is most important for their lives, the understanding of life itself, religion. Machines—to produce what? The telegraph—to dispatch what? Books, papers—to spread what kind of news? Railways—to go to whom and to what place? Millions of people herded together and subject to a supreme power—to accomplish what? Hospitals, physicians, dispensaries in order to prolong life—for what?[12]

Tolstoy disagreed with the common assumption that European civilization would redeem the world. Rather, he believed Europe would destroy itself and, in the process, corrupt Africa, India, China, and Japan by spreading and enforcing its progress and culture there as well. Meanwhile, he offered a solution to false progress: a restoration of Christianity, which once before had confronted a spiritually disintegrating society attempting to shore itself up with empty material values.

Tolstoy's contemporary and compatriot, the literary giant Feodor Dostoyevsky, saw the modern world in similar terms. Arguing against many Russians of his day who were fascinated by Western ways, he warned: "The European ant-hill built up without a church and without Christianity—for everywhere in Europe the church has lost her ideal—this ant-hill on a rotten foundation, lacking every universal and absolute, is completely undermined."[13] It was absurd for Russia to strive to catch up with Western progress, he insisted, since the whole of Western civilization was hurtling toward terrible collapse.

The French poet Charles Baudelaire hardly could be more different from the two Russian novelists who saw man's highest promise in active Christianity. Prosecuted for obscenity and blasphemy, addicted to opium and hashish, Baudelaire remains as identified with vice and depravity as with his single collection of consummately artistic poems, *Les fleurs du mal*, or "The Flowers of Evil." French art critics of the mid-nineteenth century borrowed the word "decadent" from the history of ancient Rome to characterize the work of Baudelaire and other poets of his ilk. Yet, almost thirty years before Dostoyevsky penned his indictment of Western progress, Baudelaire was saying much the same thing about the spiritual poverty of the West and its imminent consequences.

One of his many unfinished works was to be titled "The End of the World." In 1851, portions appeared under the heading *Fusées*, meaning "Rockets" and probably referring to flares that ships send up to signal an emergency.

"The world is drawing to a close," Baudelaire wrote.

> Supposing it should continue materially, would that be an existence worthy of its name and of the historical dictionary? I do not say the world would fall back into a spectral condition and the odd disorder of South American republics; nor do I say that we should return to primitive savagery and, with a rifle in our arms, hunt for food through the grass-covered ruins of our civilization. No, such adventures would still call for a certain vital energy, an echo from primordial times. We shall furnish a new example of the inexorability of the spiritual and moral laws and shall be their new victims: *we shall perish by the very thing by which we fancy that we live.* Technocracy will Americanize us, progress will starve our spirituality so far that nothing of the bloodthirsty, frivolous or unnatural dreams of the utopist will be comparable to those positive facts. I invite any thinking person to show me what is left of life. Religion! It is useless to talk about it, or to look for its remnants; it is a scandal that one takes the trouble even of denying God. Private property! It was—strictly speaking—abolished with the suppression of the right of primogeniture; yet the time will come when mankind like a revengeful cannibal will snatch the last piece from those who rightfully deemed themselves the heirs of revolutions. And even this will not be the worst. . . . Universal ruin will manifest itself not solely or particularly in political institutions or general progress or whatever else might be a proper name for it; it will be seen, above all, in the baseness of hearts. Shall I add that little left-over of sociability will hardly resist the sweeping brutality, and that the rulers, in order to hold their own and to produce a sham order, will ruthlessly resort to measures which will make us, who already are callous, shudder?[14]

Forecasts of Barbarism

Callousness, brutality, baseness of heart—the theme of the decline of Western man's spirit even while his technology triumphed blows chillingly through writings of the nineteenth century like the first flakes of an early winter storm. Men of vision everywhere saw behind the culture's glamour, wealth, and political power symptoms of inner decay and dehumanization. Some felt the frost of an approaching neobarbarian age.

In a purely theoretical sense, the eighteenth-century French philosopher Voltaire saw barbarism as a kind of recurrent necessity. Though a leading representative of the Enlightenment that proclaimed the doctrine of universal human progress, Voltaire personally held no belief in humanity's continuous upward climb. "After being extricated from one slough for a time, mankind is soon plunged into another," he grimly observed. "To ages of civilization succeed ages of barbarism; that barbarism is again expelled and again reappears; it is the regular alternation of night and day."[15]

Roughly a century later, another Frenchman, the social theorist and revolutionary anarchist Pierre Proudhon, was seeing the waning of civilization's day and the approach of a barbaric night not theoretically but specifically for European culture. He sensed an atmosphere of decay and compared it to that of ancient Rome. For the future he envisioned not only barbarism but also harsh totalitarian rule. Proudhon foresaw

> a compact democracy having the appearance of being founded on the dictatorship of the masses, but in which the masses have no more power than is necessary to ensure a general serfdom in accordance with the following precepts and principles borrowed from the old absolutism: indivisibility of public power, all-consuming centralization, systematic destruction of all individual, corporative and regional thought (regarded as disruptive), inquisitorial police. . . . We should no longer deceive ourselves. Europe is sick of thought and order; it is entering into an era of brute force and contempt of principles. . . . Then the great war of the six great powers will begin. . . . Carnage will come and the enfeeblement that will follow these bloodbaths will be terrible. We shall not live to see the work of the new age, we shall fight in the darkness; we must prepare

> ourselves to endure this life without too much sadness, by doing our duty. Let us help one another, call to one another in the gloom, and practice justice wherever opportunity offers. . . . To-day civilization is in the grip of a crisis for which one can only find a single analogy in history—that is the crisis which brought the coming of Christianity. All the traditions are worn out, all the creeds abolished; but the new programme is not yet *ready*, by which I mean that it has not yet entered the consciousness of the masses. Hence what I call *the dissolution.* This is the cruelest moment in the life of societies. . . . I am under no illusions and do not expect to wake up one morning to see the resurrection of freedom in our country, as if by a stroke of magic. . . . No, no; decay and decay for a period whose end I cannot fix and which will last for not less than one or two generations—is our lot. . . . I shall witness the evil only, I shall die in the midst of the darkness.[16]

Darkness still was gathering later in the century when the Swedish chemist and millionaire Alfred Nobel also sensed the approach of an age of violence: "one hears in the distance its hollow rumble already," the inventor of dynamite and manufacturer of explosives wrote to an aristocratic friend.[17] Only weeks later he resolved to light a lamp for the future. He wrote to the same friend, "I should like to dispose of my fortune to found a prize to be awarded every five years,"[18] to the person most substantially contributing to the peace of Europe. He believed then that the prize should endure for only three decades, "for if in thirty years society cannot be reformed we shall inevitably lapse into barbarism."[19] In 1895, a year before he died, he drew the peace prize into his will, allowing an appreciably longer period for Europe to resolve its growing problems.

A few years earlier, the German philosopher Friedrich Nietzsche also had perceived the kind of future that would develop from his century. Yet what others saw as darkness, he interpreted as an awesome new dawn. He preached a "master" morality that first would depose God, Christianity, altruism, love, and humane sympathy, then go on to incite the "superior" individual—the over-man—who would ruthlessly trample underfoot the servile masses. Openly glorifying brute might and cunning, he welcomed what others saw as fearful barbarism, believing it to be mankind's joyous path to higher evolution.

Nietzsche's impassioned and influential philosophy led to a breach with an elder friend and fellow university teacher, the deeply conservative Swiss scholar Jacob Burckhardt. One of the nineteenth-century's greatest historians, Burckhardt mapped out the basic landscape of a barbaric future as early as 1848. But far from welcoming it, as a man of high culture who embraced the best in European tradition, he loathed the vision and dreaded its materialization.

From the perspective of later times, the period of his life—from 1818 to 1897—appears to have been an era of stability, security, and freedom. Moreover, Burckhardt lived and taught in the old patrician city of Basel, where he was comfortably situated as a member of a solid and distinguished local family. Nonetheless, he felt himself to be "in a state of siege," as though his position were that of an uprooted refugee whom Europe might cease to tolerate at any moment.[20]

With a gift for visualizing history as a whole, Burckhardt believed that European traditions had been disintegrating since the French Revolution of 1789. Like the radical Proudhon, he compared the deterioration to that of the ancient Roman Empire. He foresaw "times of pauperization" putting an end to the society's burgeoning material luxury and waste. He also forecast an end to the peace that so many people of his time were assuming would last forever.[21]

Shocked by an outburst of armed conflict between France and Prussia in 1870, he wrote in a letter: "What is most serious, however, is not the present war, but the era of wars into which we have entered."[22] During that era, he predicted, Germany would fight Russia, and the same crushing end would befall Germanic military glory that Napoleon's France had suffered early in the century. He told an acquaintance, "The Hohenzollerns are digging their graves," estimating only one more generation for the Prussian dynasty that soon after fell, along with the rulers of three other empires, as a consequence of the First World War.[23]

Following the series of wars he predicted, Burckhardt believed Europe would consolidate into a single economic and military area, a kind of new Roman Empire with a central administration and peace imposed by force. The administration, however, would be nothing like the optimistic dreams of the political visionaries of his day. Everywhere he looked, Burckhardt saw omens of tyranny.

Democracy would lead not to individual liberty and responsibility, as it promised. Rather, it would bring pretentious mediocrity and despotism. Meanwhile, socialism would erect an overdeveloped governmental machine that could be taken over by any audacious demagogue. Likewise, just as the French Revolution had led logically to Napoleonic Caesarism, so would the revolutionary trend sweeping the West bring the whole society under similar dictatorships.

As early as 1849, Burckhardt wrote to a German friend: "I have no hope at all for the future. It is possible that a few half endurable decades may still be granted to us, a sort of Roman imperial time. I am of the opinion that democrats and proletarians must submit to an increasingly harsh despotism... for this fine century is designed for anything rather than true democracy."[24]

He saw the seeds of the future state in the ingenious and ruthless mechanism of Renaissance politics, which he likened to "the works of a clock."[25] The state of the future would function as a precision instrument of mass control with no regard for creative freedom for individuals or minorities. In a letter written in 1872, he described this political mechanism: "I have a premonition, which sounds like utter folly and yet which positively will not leave me: the military state must become one great factory. Those hordes of men in the great industrial centers will not be left indefinitely to their greed and want. What must logically come is a fixed and supervised stint of misery, glorified by promotions and uniforms, daily begun and ended to the sound of drums. ... Long voluntary subjection under individual *Führers* and usurpers is in prospect. People no longer believe in principles but will, periodically, probably believe in saviors. . . . For this reason authority will again raise its head in the pleasant twentieth century, and a terrible head."[26]

Burckhardt also had a clear vision of the kind of "Führers" to whom the people would look to save them: "My mental picture of the *terribles simplificateurs* who will overrun our old Europe is not a pleasant one. . . . People may not yet like to imagine a world whose rulers completely ignore law, prosperity, profitable labor and industry, credit, etc. and are then in a position to rule with absolute brutality." But "somewhere, finally, after more unmeasured violence, a real power will be formed, which will make desperately few concessions to the right to vote, popular sovereignty, material prosperity, industry, etc. For this is the inevitable end of the constitutional state when it has fallen a prey to majorities."[27]

In spite of his specific, and accurate, prophecies of economic depression, war, dictatorship, and growing barbarism in European civilization, Burckhardt was no embittered doomsayer. He did not declare the culture to be declining without hope. He had reached grim conclusions by logical reasoning and historical analogies, projecting major trends of his time into the future. But his forecasts left him neither a romantic pessimist savoring the melancholy of life in a dying civilization nor a Roman-style fugitive-philosopher retreating into his studies in despair. He continued to believe that fresh creativity can well forth suddenly and unexpectedly, bringing new life to a society and its culture. And all through his days he hoped this would happen in Europe, perhaps in the twentieth century, possibly even later.

Like Tolstoy and Dostoyevsky, he saw religion as the essential transforming element, "for without a transcendent urge which outweighs all the clamor for power and money, nothing will be of any use."[28] He personally had abandoned explicit expressions of the Christian faith. Anticipating twentieth-century neoorthodox theologians, he saw organized churches as compromising religion to remain acceptable to a world pursuing other goals. With a deep understanding of the classical age of disintegration in ancient Rome, he hoped for the rise of a new religious spirit, like that of early Christians who disdained the feast of pleasures and vices their society offered and embraced a cleansing fast of discipline, asceticism, and charity toward their fellow man.

He was sure that "the new, the great, and the liberating" could appear only in contrast to wealth, business, and power.[29] And he foresaw a time when persecuting governments "might meet with a resistance of the strangest sort from Christian minorities who would not fear even martyrdom." [30] The new spirit, he declared, "will need its martyrs. It must be a something which by its nature can keep its head above water in all catastrophes, political, economic, and otherwise."[31]

A Society Sickening

While Jacob Burckhardt foresaw impending collapse of the civilization's political and economic health, the psychologist Max Nordau detected signs of deterioration in the physical and mental condition of the society's people. His *Degeneration* was first published in 1893 in Germany. Dramatic, extreme, even somewhat sensational in tone, it created a sensation. Nordau defined the affliction named in the title as a debilitated condition of both mind and body—"*a morbid deviation from an original type*." [32] He attributed the condition to fatigue and nervous exhaustion brought on by enormous changes in life that technology and the growing speed and intensity of living had caused.

Nordau cited the observations of medical authorities that people of the time were aging faster than previous generations. "Old age encroaches upon the period of vigorous manhood," one of the authorities, Sir James Crighton-Browne, had told a university medical faculty in 1891. "Deaths due exclusively to old age are found reported now between the ages of forty-five and fifty-five. . . ." [33]

Nordau quoted an eminent oculist as saying, "My own experience, which extends now over a quarter of a century, leads me to believe that men and women, in the present day, seek the aid of spectacles at a less advanced period of life than their ancestors. . . . Previously men had recourse to spectacles at the age of fifty. The average age now is forty-five years." [34]

Likewise, dentists were noting that teeth decayed and fell out at an earlier age. Also, the general tendency toward more rapid aging showed itself in premature baldness and graying hair. "Everyone who looks round the circle of his friends and acquaintances," wrote Nordau, "will remark that the hair begins to turn gray much sooner than in former days. Most men and women show their first white hairs at the beginning of the thirties, many of them at a very much younger age. Formerly white hair was the accompaniment of the fiftieth year."[35]

Nordau affirmed that the traits of early aging "are the consequences of states of fatigue and exhaustion, and these, again, are the effect of contemporary civilization, of the vertigo and whirl of our frenzied life, the vastly increased number of sense impressions and organic reactions, and therefore of perceptions, judgments, and motor impulses, which at present are forced into a given unity of time." [36]

Leaving the topic of premature aging, Nordau moved to more serious pathological signs of human deterioration that he and other medical practitioners were observing. "We stand now in the midst of a severe mental epidemic," he wrote, "of a sort of black death of degeneration and hysteria. . . ." [37] Among the mental-emotional symptoms of degeneration, he listed: "emotionalism, or an excessive excitability . . . feebleness of perception, will, memory, judgment, as well as inattention and instability. . . ." [38]

One of the more prominent features of degeneration, Nordau cited, was egoism. This was "unanimously confirmed by all observers." He quoted other specialists: "'The degenerate neither knows nor takes interest in anything but himself,'" and he has "'only one occupation, that of satisfying his appetites.'"[39] Nordau saw the degenerate person as incapable "of attaining to the highest degree of development of the individual, namely, the freely coming out from the factitious limits of individuality, *i.e.*, altruism. As to the relation of his 'Ego' to his 'non-Ego,' the degenerate man remains a child all his life. He scarcely appreciates or even perceives the external world, and is only occupied with the organic processes in his own body. He is more than egoistical, he is an ego-maniac."[40]

Nordau made clear that not the whole of civilized humanity in his time was suffering "the mental disorder affecting modern society."[41] It was only "the upper stratum of the population of large towns,"[42] the "rich educated people"[43] and, above all, those artists, writers, and philosophers of the period who led the trends toward egoism, pessimism, licentiousness, and generally unwholesome and neurotic attitudes toward life.

Meanwhile, Nordau found the majority of people from the middle and lower classes, though somewhat affected by "moral sea-sickness,"[44] to be basically healthy and sound. Yet he saw the possibility of degeneration filtering down through the classes and blighting the entire society. He presented a hypothetical picture of life in the twentieth century should this occur.

His forecasts were based upon criminal and psychological studies, though he admittedly considered them more fanciful than probable. They included clubs catering to suicide and mutual assassination, tavernlike places serving hashish and other stupefying drugs and groups of men assigned to tranquilize citizens "when taken by a fit of nervousness."[45]

Continuing his hypothetical forecast, he described a future in which "Sexual psychopathy of every nature has become so general and so imperious that manners and laws have adapted themselves accordingly. . . . Masochists or passivists, who form the majority of men, clothe themselves in a costume which recalls, by colour and cut, feminine apparel. Women who wish to please men of this kind wear men's dress, an eyeglass, boots with spurs and riding-whip, and only show themselves in the street with a large cigar in their mouths. The demand of persons with the 'contrary' sexual sentiment that persons of the same sex can conclude a legal marriage has obtained satisfaction, seeing they have been numerous enough to elect a majority of deputies having the same tendency. Sadists, "bestials," nosophines, and necrophiles, etc., find legal opportunities to gratify their inclinations. Modesty and restraint are dead superstitions of the past, and appear only as atavism and among the inhabitants of remote villages. The lust of murder is confronted as a disease, and treated by surgical intervention, etc."[46]

Finally Nordau asked, "Will it come to this?" And he answered, "Well, no; I think not."[47] Sharing the progress-oriented mentality of his time, he believed that humanity was still far from its peak of evolution, and people of the twentieth century either would adjust themselves to a faster pace of living or sensibly discard the more oppressive aspects of modern technology.

Nordau's book attacked the leading literary and artistic figures of his age so trenchantly that it was not accepted "with complete conviction," as a reviewer for the *Times* of London put it with fine understatement.[48] Yet *Degeneration* was read, discussed, and praised around the world as an acknowledgment of a decay that many people felt to be lurking beneath the surface of Western civilization. The book continued to appear in new editions into the 1920s.

Nordau was not the only medical figure of his day to view the condition of Western society with concern and even alarm. Another was the English physician Forbes L. Winslow, founder of the British Hospital for Mental Disorders and a principal consultant in cases of criminal insanity in both Britain and the United States. In a book entitled *Recollections of Forty Years* he wrote: "On comparing the human race during the past forty years, I have no hesitation in stating that it has degenerated, and is still progressing in a downward direction. We are gradually approaching, with the decadence of youth, a near proximity to a nation of madmen. By comparing the lunacy statistics of 1809 with those of 1909, . . . an insane world is looked forward to by me with a certainty in the not far distant future."[49]

The Austrian physician and founder of psychoanalysis Sigmund Freud later confirmed the possibility of such a world. In his book *Civilization and its Discontents*, published in 1930, he showed that society and human nature can have conflicting demands, and hence that a whole society can be mentally ill.

Other psychologists have warned that a pathological society already exists. The brilliant Swiss psychiatrist and onetime colleague of Freud, Carl Gustav Jung, said modern "normalcy" is equal to mental sickness. The radical Scottish psychoanalyst R.D. Laing stated in his book *The Politics of Experience* that "The condition of alienation, of being asleep, of being unconscious, of being out of one's mind, is the condition of the normal man."[50] And the German-born psychoanalyst and social philosopher Erich Fromm explained in his book *The Sane Society* how adjustment to modern society requires people to step out of their own psychological center and thus become alienated to themselves, creating a society that functions along the lines of mass mental illness.

A number of psychological studies have amplified these opinions, finding mental-emotional disturbance afflicting 80 percent and more of the populations of specific regions studied. A spokesman for the famed Menninger psychiatric clinic of Topeka, Kansas, once ventured a more extreme estimate. When asked how large a part of the population currently suffers from some form of emotional illness, he responded, "One out of one of us."[51]

Viewing the same question from the standpoint of sociology, Harvard Professor Pitirim A. Sorokin spoke in equally extreme terms. Noting the proliferation of literature and advice about inner conflicts and general mental problems, he wrote, "All these phenomena unquestionably demonstrate that the Western world has become a sort of lunatic asylum, in charge of thousands of mental healers of all sorts. Mental abnormality tends to become Western. . . man's normal state; the lunatic asylum his normal home; some sort of psychiatrist his guardian angel."[52]

Utopia Revised

Almost from the dawn of the twentieth century, writers of serious fiction began to depict a future vastly different from the bright visions inspired by progressive technology and political idealism.

In 1907 a novel called *The Iron Heel* by American adventurer and author Jack London became the first of several literary nightmares about the approach of tyranny and the dehumanization of modern humanity. An ardent socialist, London saw powerful capitalists turning into despots—the Iron Heel that "will walk upon our faces."[53] In his tale, they consolidate their might, wipe away the middle class, and freeze the rest of the society into a rigid status order. Workers range from well-fed human cattle who have sold their souls for material security to wretched near-slaves. London has his despotic oligarchy holding back "the mighty tide of human progress" for three centuries before the ultimate triumph of socialist democracy.[54] The political details of *The Iron Heel* were colored by London's beliefs, though his basic intuition of totalitarian rule looming darkly in the future of Western culture is akin to the reckonings of Pierre Proudhon and Jacob Burckhardt.

The English author H.G. Wells held another—and far more catastrophic—vision of the future of the West. One of the most widely read and highly respected writers of his generation, Wells began his literary career late in the nineteenth century with a series of brilliant scientific thrillers. By the end of World War I, he held the position of social prophet. With his characteristically furious energy, he attempted to alert humankind to the dangerous instability of the modern world order with writings sometimes fanciful but often accurate in their predictions.

His novel *The Shape of Things to Come*, published in 1934, saw the age of Europe's predominance over world affairs to be "the outcome of an uncontrolled irregularity in growth, of economic hypertrophy in a phase of political and cultural atrophy."[55] The book sketched a fictional picture of the end of both growth and predominance as Western culture slides into total collapse.

Wells saw the world's patchwork of empires and nationalistic states as "a hollow shell in 1933."[56] He foretold that "For the British Empire there was to be no such decline and fall as happened to Rome. Instead it relaxed . . . to nothing."[57] The tale goes on to predict, by the 1960s, humanity racked by economic chaos, warfare, pestilence, and universal hunger. Then, ultimately optimistic, it has the shattered remnants unifying after 1978 in "the Modern World-State,"[58] a union "socialistic, cosmopolitan and creative. . . ."[59] Finally general prosperity returns under a dictatorship after the year 2010.

Through the 1930s, Wells plunged actively into world affairs, pushing to the center of every event that threatened to propel civilization closer to destruction. Seeking a solution to the dangerous rivalry between private and state capitalism, he interviewed both United States President Franklin D. Roosevelt and Soviet dictator Joseph Stalin. He persistently urged the people of the world to form what he called an open conspiracy against forces leading humankind to suicide. Finally, in his last days, he was overwhelmed by a deep and strange despair.

In 1945, when he was seventy-nine years old and shortly before his death, he released a thin book titled *Mind at the End of Its Tether*. It asserted with apocalyptic conviction that the end of all life was at hand. "The rotation of the earth and its annual circulation in its orbit is slowing down,"[60] he wrote, while the cosmic process "which has endured life for so long . . . has now turned against it so implacably to wipe it out."[61] Meanwhile, "the human story has already come to an end . . . *Homo sapiens*, as he has been pleased to call himself, is in his present form played out."[62] Mankind, Wells declared, held the strictly limited alternative of perishing like prehistoric creatures when their time had come or evolving hurriedly and steeply into a vastly superior being who then would see life out to its impending finish.

It appears that Wells, in this late effort, with the fate of the world weighing on his mind for so long, was projecting a foreboding of his own demise upon all earthly life. Or perhaps he had succumbed to the alarm that often comes over people who sense the horrifying implications of their culture's disintegration.

Much of modern literature, from T.S. Eliot's poem *The Waste Land* and D. H. Lawrence's novel *Women in Love* to a bevy of the most recent novels, portray society at the brink of apocalyptic crisis. Two of the classic literary prophecies never have been equaled in showing the crisis of the present resolved in a future at once grotesquely inhuman and thoroughly possible.

The first, *Brave New World* by English author Aldous Huxley, appeared in 1932. A social satire in novel form, it projected current trends toward consumerism and hedonism, conformity, and dehumanized technology some six hundred years into the future. In the new world these influences have created, all things, including human beings, are manufactured by scientific techniques patterned after Henry Ford's mass production line. Citizens bred in bottles are genetically engineered to produce the kind of people the society desires, complete with a class of morons. Further conditioning shapes attitudes, tastes, and behavior. In the infantile utopia in which all personal concerns are trivial and mindless, love is replaced by promiscuity, art by sense stimulation, and inner growth by drugged escapism. Beauty and truth are suppressed. So are religion, purpose, and meaning in life, and beyond a pragmatic point, science itself.

Huxley's futurist tale was seen as chillingly realistic in the 1930s. Events since then have made it all the more convincing. In a book called *Brave New World Revisited*, published in 1958, the author claimed that his only major prophetic fault lay in timing. He revised his estimate of the period needed to fashion such a world from six hundred years to something less than a century.

In the second classic novel of social prophecy, English writer George Orwell depicts a forbidding future closing in even sooner. *Nineteen Eighty-Four* is both the title of his work of political satire and the year it has Western society crushed under totalitarian domination. While historical prophets like Burckhardt could only sketch the basic forms of the despotism they foresaw, Orwell, as a novelist, was free to use the full palette of fiction's colors to paint in the details.

In his version of the tyrannical state to come, citizens are subject to the omnipresent dictator "Big Brother." Truncheon-wielding state police patrol the streets. Torture is as common as law enforcement. Each person lives under almost constant surveillance, with no right to privacy. All actions, feelings, and thoughts are directed by the state. The inevitable frustrations of people denied healthy human development are vented in sessions of organized hate.

Even more than *Brave New World*, Orwell's *Nineteen Eighty-Four* lodged itself in the minds of people who, from the time of the book's release in 1949, watched the society and counted the years, wondering how closely the author's forecasts would match unfolding reality. A California neuroscientist and brain researcher, Dr. David Goodman, carried this speculation into the technical realm. Studying the ability of the human mind to foresee and predict, he and two colleagues counted 137 specific prophecies in Orwell's book, some scientific and technological, others social and political. The forecasts included data banks containing personal information, think tanks in which experts plan future wars, and new physical and psychological tortures; large-scale defoliants for military use, three-dimensional art, state lotteries, and the merging of sex identities.

When the research team compiled the list in 1972, about eighty of the predictions had come true. By 1978 the tally was around one hundred. Projecting a mathematical curve line into the future, the neuroscientist estimated that Orwell's 1984 could not arrive on time unless a major social upheaval occurred to hurry it along. Yet the prophet-novelist's totalitarian nightmare seemed well on the way.

3

Visions of Decline

While social thinkers of world stature from many different fields were detecting decline in modern Western culture, others were probing deeper to explain why it was occurring. Varied in national origin, political stance, and philosophical views, they also diverged in their approach to the question. Some wished only to make sense of the baffling social changes around them. Others, acting in the spirit of their time, sought scientific laws to explain the culture's downward movement. A few offered solutions, either to save the civilization or to save people from the worst effects of decline.

A Quest for Patterns: Ernst von Lasaulx

According to nineteenth-century German philosopher and historian Ernst von Lasaulx, all high cultures follow a consistent order of development. First, a society discovers mining or some other kind of metalworking. Then it adopts shepherding and breeding livestock. Next it discovers agriculture. Then comes shipping, trade, industry, and material welfare. Later, from crafts, the arts emerge. Ultimately, the arts give birth to the sciences.

Lasaulx's scale for cultural growth was not new. It closely followed some observations by the seventeenth-century English philosopher and statesman Francis Bacon. What was new in the thinking of the German historian, whose works are almost forgotten today, was his added application of the classical Greek theory that societies follow a pattern like the cycles of nature. Along with sunrise and sunset, summer and winter, generation and decay, societies similarly rise and fall. His conception was remarkable for the time, since he lived from 1805 to 1861, when technological development was surging ahead and belief in endless progress for the West was particularly strong.

Lasaulx claimed that every culture comes into being with a specific and limited amount of vital energy, just as a person, an animal, or a plant possesses a certain maximum sum of life. The culture proceeds to live out its days in the way of an organism. It passes through stages—childhood, youth, maturity, and age—and then it dies.

In its beginning, a culture is formed from a religious creed or cult. This is the essential element in any culture's life. For awhile the religion functions as the heart of the culture's aspects and activities, issuing the lifeblood from which they grow. In time, however, the arts and sciences clamor to be free and independent. Gradually, the culture becomes less religious, more secular. As the secular mood gains strength, it begins to attack religion with rationalism and skepticism. The religion weakens steadily until the culture is hollowed out and only a framework remains. Lacking creative and vigorous religion at the core, the culture also lacks the conviction and sense of duty needed for continued existence. At that point, a barbarian invader can topple the whole grand but empty structure with ease. Such an invasion, Lasaulx pointed out, is desirable for the fresh life it brings: "At the moment at which a great people no longer possesses, as a community, a certain quantity of unused strength, a natural spring of refreshment and rejuvenation, it is near its decline, and there is no regeneration for it save by way of a barbarian influx."[1]

The political expression of a culture, Lasaulx said, normally lasts about two thousand years, first as a monarchy, then an aristocracy, followed by democracy, and finally military despotism. And where on this life cycle does modern Western culture stand? In 1856 Lasaulx wrote that European civilization was far advanced into old age. He placed his hope for a new and vital culture in the rise of a Christian Slavic civilization or perhaps one formed by European elements "beyond the Atlantic Ocean."[2]

A Scientific Law of History: Henry Adams

Professional historians, acutely aware of humanity's often grim and violent past, are better prepared than people who think mainly of the present to hear distant storms approaching. American historian Henry Adams, aided by a somewhat embittered disposition, saw Western culture of his day riddled with decay and threatened with catastrophic collapse.

A towering figure of nineteenth century intellectual life, Adams was born in 1838 into a patrician Boston family of scholars and statesmen that included United States Presidents John and John Quincy Adams. He traveled widely and frequently, served as correspondent and editor for leading journals, wrote essays, novels, and biographies and taught medieval history at what then was Harvard College. Though his eighty-year life passed through Western society's highest age of optimism, Henry Adams found nothing along the way to inspire hope.

"Decline is everywhere,"[3] he wrote in the 1890s, observing that the society was "Drifting in the dead-water of the *fin-de-siècle*—and during the last decade everyone talked and seemed to feel *fin-de-siècle*—where not a breath stirred the idle air of education or fretted the mental torpor of self-content."[4] He complained of "the total, irremediable, radical rottenness of our whole social, industrial, financial, and political system"[5] and declared, "The whole thing is one vast structure of debt and fraud."[6]

He was so far from the general faith in evolution and humankind's progress that he saw modern people not at the top of the evolutionary ladder but at the bottom as "the most advanced type of physical decadence."[7] Likewise, he believed that civilization had shown not continuous growth but constant downward movement. The test of that lay in how the word "civilization" was defined.

When the term was used to measure material improvements, then modern society decidedly had progressed. But if it was a gauge of heightened human energies and ideals, then contemporary culture obviously was degraded. Henry Adams chose the second definition. From that standpoint, the miracles of modern technology were only mistaken for progress. They amounted to humanity's drawing unprecedented sums of energy from sources outside itself, which testified to rapid exhaustion of people's inner energies and personal resources and their growing dependence upon nature's reserves to sustain and enhance their lives. Technology merely masked decline, then served to speed it along.

To Adams, modern humanity was not the equal of its barbaric ancestors. To his mind, present-day people were weaker both physically and spiritually. Also they were no wiser. They had loosed massive forces that swept them along as aimlessly as driftwood in a raging cataract. They had no idea where they were going, nor did they seem to care.

Adams thought he knew where humanity was headed. In a letter written in 1905, he stated: "At the present rate of progression since 1600, it will not need another century or half century to tip thought upside down. Law, in that case, would disappear as theory or *a priori* principle and give place to force. Morality would become police. Explosives would reach cosmic violence. Disintegration would overcome integration."[8]

Economically, he saw the world drifting unavoidably toward a socialistic order and agreed with his younger brother and fellow historian Brooks Adams that concentration of capital would invite the "Russian millennium of a centralized, despotic socialism."[9] On another occasion, he wrote to Brooks that the century ahead would witness an "ultimate, colossal, cosmic collapse."[10]

Seeing the modern world propelled by forces it did not understand toward a dangerous destination, Henry Adams took on the task of analyzing history and applying its lessons to the present. In December 1895, as president of the American Historical Association, he proposed that history might be disciplined, as so many other fields of study, into a science. If that were done, he said, it might better predict things to come. Then in 1909, he announced his discovery of a scientific law that projected historical trends from the past through the present and onward into the future.

The 'Rule of Phase Applied to History,' as he called his law, actually abandoned history and borrowed its methods from contemporary physics and mathematics. It was based upon two recent hypotheses: the rule of phase in chemistry, devised by American mathematical physicist Josiah Willard Gibbs, and the second law of thermodynamics, in which British physicist Lord William Kelvin posited that the earth's energies gradually are dissipating.

Henry Adams sought to establish "that man is a thermodynamic mechanism" and that social energy, as illustrated by historical movement, is as real as electricity and therefore subject to the laws of degradation that govern all forms of energy.[11]

At this point Adams reversed the popular idea of continuous evolutionary progress. According to his law, civilization, as an expression of social energy, had been dissipating through four phases: the religious, the mechanical, the electrical, and the ethereal. The religious phase, beginning in the mists of the past, had ended around 1600. Each successive stage had been shorter. The final, which was just beginning, would be a time of pure, abstract mathematical thought in which science would dominate the mechanics of existence and usurp the realms of philosophy, religion, and history. That phase would be the shortest of all. Adams calculated, by way of his analogy with the law of physics, that it would end in a final cataclysm possibly in 1921 or otherwise around the year 2025.

Some scholars see Adams's strenuous attempt to fit history into a scientific frame as something of an embarrassment amid the otherwise top-rate works of a brilliant mind. Yet, viewed another way, it was a bold experiment springing from an age in which science dominated the whole horizon of human knowledge and opened new vistas in almost every direction. Meanwhile, as the twentieth-century social philosopher Lewis Mumford has observed, it "buried a profound intuition of approaching disaster beneath a pseudo-scientific structure of ideas."[12]

THE LAW OF CIVILIZATION AND DECAY: BROOKS ADAMS

While Henry Adams was constructing his scientific law of history, his brother, Brooks, ten years his junior, also was seeking to explain the rise and decline of civilizations.

In a book entitled *The Law of Civilization and Decay*, first published in London in 1895, Brooks began, like Henry, with a concept of energy. He assumed that the earth was endowed with a specific sum of solar energy that was being expended, part of it by human society. Since expenditure rather than accumulation was a key to his theory, he also, like Henry, saw human history as a record of degeneration. At that point, though, Brooks departed from strict science and entered the two realms of historical philosophy and commerce.

Like Voltaire, he believed that the history of humanity shifts from barbarism to civilization and back to barbarism. Here he also joined Ernst von Lasaulx in reviving the classical Greek theory of cultures following cycles rather than progressing or retrogressing in a straight line.

In a civilization's early stages, Brooks maintained, human energy is dissipated primarily by means of fear. Such an age produces, outstandingly, military, religious, and artistic types of people. Their society is loosely organized, decentralized in structure.

As the civilization develops, it accumulates economic capital, and centralization begins to develop. At this stage, the means of dissipating energy shifts from fear to greed. Military organization gives way to economic control. With that, the seeds of the society's decay are planted.

As economic interest and competition arises, humanity is degraded. The military, religious, and artistic forms of manhood decay. Meanwhile, the economic types—the capitalist and the usurer—rise to power. As commerce grows and empires expand, the man of capital and greed gains dominance. Meanwhile, the truly productive person, especially the man of the land, sinks into debt and servitude because of low-cost foreign labor and development of commerce. The society's women also are degraded. Once powerful mothers of soldiers, they now live as parasites of the economic man, or independently as members of a biologically functionless third sex.

Eventually centralization tightens to a maximum. The society's energy is dissipated, approaching exhaustion. Its productive people have been driven to extinction. The accumulated capital also dissipates. Disintegration sets in and the society ultimately collapses. Its survivors lack the power for renewed centralization, and their territory lies fallow until a barbarian influx revives and renews their race.

Where did Brooks Adams place modern Western civilization in his cycle of rise and decline? Adopting an increasingly common comparison with ancient Rome, he believed the culture in 1895 had reached the same stage of deterioration as the classical empire in A.D. 200. He ended his volume with a melancholy observation:

> No poetry can bloom in the arid modern soil, the drama has died, and the patrons of art are no longer even conscious of shame at profaning the most sacred of ideals. . . . Decade by decade, for some four hundred years, these phenomena have grown more sharply marked in Europe, and, as consolidation [centralization] apparently nears its climax, art seems to presage approaching disintegration. The architecture, the sculpture, and the coinage of London at the close of the nineteenth century,

> when compared with those of the Paris of Saint Louis, recall the Rome of Caracalla as contrasted with the Athens of Pericles, save that we lack the stream of barbarian blood which made the Middle Ages.[13]

At a comparatively optimistic moment, his brother Henry once speculated that "we ought still to have more than two hundred years of futile and stupid stagnation."[14] But just as Henry's scientific law slashed that estimate possibly to decades, Brooks also stood aghast at the threat of imminent social collapse. And if change was racing much faster in modern times than in ancient Rome, would not the catastrophic end be that much greater?

Brooks Adams's work was read widely and generally well received. "The book is very suggestive; it presents a theory of history which must be reckoned with,"[15] said *The American Historical Review* in 1896, the year the volume was published in America. Later it came out in French and German editions. In a long review written in 1897, a young Theodore Roosevelt agreed with Adams that the contemporary observer could "recognize more than one disagreeable resemblance between the world as it is today, and the Roman world under the Empire."[16] And as late as 1943, *The Law of Civilization and Decay* still was being reissued, called then "the first extended attempt by an American to interpret the whole history of Western civilization in a truly scientific spirit."[17]

THE WEST AND RUSSIA I: NIKOLAI DANILEVSKY

Some years before Henry and Brooks Adams were searching physical science for laws of civilization, a Russian natural scientist discerned several such laws while examining the politics of Europe's relations with his homeland.

Nikolai Danilevsky came early to an interest in political matters. In 1849, shortly after receiving an advanced degree in botany from the University of St. Petersburg, he was arrested on political charges with some thirty other suspects, including the novelist Feodor Dostoyevsky. Unlike Dostoyevsky, who was sentenced to hard labor in Siberia, Danilevsky was acquitted.

Soon afterward he began a long and varied government career. Appointed first to the staffs of provincial administrators, he rose to the level of government official, serving as an economist, an engineer, and leader of a series of exploring expeditions to remote parts of the vast Russian Empire. Mainly, however, he worked as a fishery specialist, finally heading the Russian Commission of Fisheries.

Long and leisurely winters between expeditions allowed Danilevsky time for reading and reflection on a variety of topics. He also wrote prolifically. Along with many specialized publications in the fishery field, he wrote large works on economics, Darwinian evolution, political science, history, and linguistics.

Danilevsky's widely ranging knowledge led in 1869 to his major work: *Russia and Europe: A Viewpoint on the Political Relations Between the Slavic and Germano-Latin Worlds*. Published first as a series of articles in a Russian magazine, it later appeared in book form. From the start, the work attracted the attention of Russian thinkers, writers, and statesmen. Yet probably because it examined the decline of European civilization at the period when optimism was soaring, the book took seventeen years to gain wider notice in his homeland. Not until the end of World War I, almost half a century after its first publication, was it translated elsewhere. Today *Russia and Europe* still is valued by scholars of civilization, a testimony to the author's probing vision into the future.

Danilevsky began his book in a political vein, claiming Europe had shown continual hostility toward Russia. Time and again, he cited, European powers had invaded Russian soil. Europe also chronically distrusted Russia, often unjustly and even when Russia held "only the most sincere devotion to European interests."[18]

Danilevsky maintained that no rational basis existed for Europe's animosity, injustice, and distrust. The cause lay deeper, "in those unfathomed depths of tribal sympathies and antipathies which are a sort of historical instinct of peoples and lead them . . . towards a goal unknown to them."[19] These historical instincts explained why ancient Germanic tribes had blended with inhabitants of Roman Europe but clashed with Slavic groups in mutual repulsion and antagonism.

Danilevsky agreed with Russian political factions that opposed Westernization and urged union among Slavic peoples to work out their destiny apart from the West. Russia, he asserted, never had been really part of Europe. The Western countries were the territory of what he called the Germano-Latin civilization, which saw in Russia and in Slavs generally something alien to itself. Meanwhile, Russia was the center of a different culture—the Slavic culture. The country did not nourish itself from the roots of European civilization. It had not belonged to the inter-European Holy Roman Empire of Charlemagne and his successors. It had not taken on Europe's feudal system, nor had it joined the European movement for political and civic freedom that ended feudalism. Russia had accepted neither Catholicism nor Protestantism. In short, Russia had not participated in Europe's existence.

Going on to explore whether the antagonism between Europe and Russia would fade or persist in the future, Danilevsky developed a whole philosophy of history. European civilization, he maintained, was neither a standard nor a universal civilization. Universality was implied by dividing history into ancient, medieval, and modern periods. But the implication was false. Europe's culture was not the highest building block in a structure of continuous upward progress. Rather, it had developed as only one of many civilizations: each with its own ancient, middle, and later periods, each unique, complete, and perfect in its own way. Civilizations emerged, developed the creative potential inherent in their spiritual natures and geographic environments, then passed away without being continued directly by any other culture.

Danilevsky classified the great civilizations of history in chronological order. First came the Egyptian, then the Chinese.

They were followed by the Ancient Semitic, which included Assyria, Babylon, Phoenicia, and Chaldea. Next came the Hindu, then the Iranian and Hebrew. The seventh great civilization was that of Greece, followed by the Roman. Later the Neo-Semitic, or Arabic, arose, and finally the Germano-Latin, or European. To this list of ten he added the two great American civilizations of Mexico and Peru. These had not completed their normal course of life, dying suddenly at the hands of the Spanish conquistadors in the sixteenth century.

Some of these civilizations, Danilevsky noted, were transmittable in the sense that their achievements fertilized the soil of later developing cultures. The transmittable types included the Egyptian, Ancient Semitic and Hebrew, the Greek, Roman, and present-day European civilizations. Other cultures, as the Chinese and Hindu, were of a solitary kind. A whole chain of transmittable types in the West had made that part of the world more progressive than the Orient, even though the Eastern civilizations had endured almost as long as all the others put together. Yet China and India, while apparently stagnant for millennia, were not altogether so. They had developed some aspects of human existence more completely, "and thereby these solitary civilizations contributed greatly to the unfolding of the many-sided manifestations of the creative human spirit, which in itself constitutes true progress."[20]

Along with societies that grew to the level of civilization, Danilevsky cited two other classes of peoples in history.

One he called history's 'negative agencies.' These groups, which included the Huns and the Mongols, performed a destructive mission. Raging through their age like historical tornadoes, they helped failing civilizations die. They scattered the remains, then themselves disappeared. Occasionally one of these negative cultures went on to perform a constructive mission as well, building a new civilization over the ruins of the old, as did the Germanic tribes that overran the Roman Empire and the Islamic Arabs that pushed into the Middle East and across North Africa.

The final class of peoples in Danilevsky's scheme included most of the tribes that have inhabited the earth. These are 'neutral agencies' of history whose creativity, for one reason or another, has been arrested. Neither notably constructive nor destructive, they serve only as "ethnographic material," enriching civilizations that draw them in, now and then becoming an element in a rising culture, but never achieving historical importance of their own. Sometimes the peoples of a dead civilization descend to this neutral, nonhistorical level.

Returning to developing civilizations, Danilevsky outlined five main laws that apply to their existence.

The first defined an original civilization as a group of peoples speaking the same language or clearly related tongues who possess a spiritual capacity for development and a degree of growth already beyond "childhood." Of the ten great civilizations that make up practically all human history, the Egyptian and the Chinese each had a language of its own. Three others spoke related Semitic languages. The remaining five used languages of the Aryan group: Hindu, or Sanskrit, Iranian, Greek, Latin, and Teutonic.

The second law stated that a people capable of building a civilization must have political independence to do so. The Celts of Britain, who also spoke an Aryan language, never built a great civilization because they were conquered by the Romans at an early stage in their growth. Likewise, conquest and subjugation have been responsible for holding back many tribes from rising independently to a civilized level.

Danilevsky's third law maintained that the basic principles of one civilization cannot be transmitted to another. Influence in greater or lesser degrees can pass freely. But each civilization retains its own distinctive character. Thus Egyptian and Hindu cultures never diffused intact beyond their language areas. So, also, with the Chinese civilization that spread only as far as Japan, and then probably coming with peoples who migrated there from China. The Ancient Semitic civilization diffused only among peoples of Semitic origin. The same proved true of the Hebrew culture. The ancient Greeks tried to spread their culture, especially during the campaigns of the Macedonian conqueror Alexander the Great some three hundred years before Christ, which drove all the way to India. Yet their efforts invariably failed. Greek culture took root only in places like Alexandria on Egypt's Mediterranean coast, where Greek colonists maintained it. Similarly in modern times, the British established English-style schools and European scientific and cultural institutions in India, even overlaying their language upon the country's educated and official classes. Yet India, for all its cooperation, remained thoroughly Hindu instead of changing into a European offshoot.

The nearest thing to a civilizational transplant occurred when Greece passed on large parts of its culture to Rome. Yet even that was far from complete and remains in the category of influence. Wherever Romans borrowed elements of Greek culture—as they did in philosophy, ethics, and the fine arts—they turned out to be nothing more than uncreative imitators. Only when they acted as Romans and cultivated their own special talents did they soar to lofty heights, building a mighty political empire and creating the greatest system of law in history.

So while elements of one civilization can penetrate another, basic principles and the entire civilization cannot. Meanwhile, the fragments of culture that are transmitted are changed, adapted by the borrower to the highly selective organism of its civilization. Practical techniques, such as science and technology, pass most readily. They have a more or less neutral cultural value that does not alter the unique character of the adopting civilization. Things with greater cultural weight, like religion, philosophy, art, and ethics, are shaped and changed as much as necessary to put them into harmony with the civilization borrowing them.

The Russian thinker's fourth law stated that a civilization can reach its fullest and richest growth only when its peoples are diverse and remain in independent groups rather than united in a single political unit. The richest civilizations thus far, Danilevsky wrote, were those of the ancient Greeks and present-day Europeans. The former, in the city-states of Athens, Sparta, Thebes, Corinth, and other less important political centers, never came together. Far from it, their cities were warring constantly among themselves. Yet, living in cultural conjunction, they bore a mutual civilization upward to soaring heights. In the same sense, European civilization has been broadly varied in its members—as, by contrast, Egypt of the pharaohs was not. Therefore it had a chance to blossom more luxuriantly. Just as lack of this diversity held back ancient Egypt, it also is one of the main reasons many tribes have not developed their cultures into civilizations.

The author's fifth and final law dealt with the life span of civilized cultures. Any civilization, he said, can grow indefinitely. But its time of blossoming and fruit bearing in fully realized form is brief. Further, this time exhausts the culture once and for all and never can be repeated.

The growth period, which can be measured in millennia, is a preparatory time when the culture's creative forces are accumulated and organized. In the later time of fulfillment, which averages between four and six hundred years, this accumulation is rapidly and magnificently spent. An age of spending has marked European culture all through the post-medieval, or modern, period. Only then did the civilization realize fairly fully all of its creative possibilities and ideals of freedom, justice, and social and individual well-being. The spending time depletes a culture and exhausts its peoples. Then, with their cultural heritage and human creative powers gone, the civilization declines and disintegrates. Some cultures at that stage slip into dull stagnation as, for example, China did, idealizing the past in senile apathy and self-satisfaction. Others, like ancient Rome, slide into an anguished apathy of despair.

The decline of any civilization is inevitable, in Danilevsky's view. One of the principal reasons for this is the limited nature of a culture's creativity. No civilization has pushed its creative efforts into every possible field. Rather, each has followed distinctive inclinations of its own. The ancient Greeks raised the ideal of earthly beauty to unsurpassed heights. Rome specialized in political organization and law. China excelled in developing the practical and useful aspects of life. India inclined toward imagination, fantasy, and, to some degree, mysticism. The Semitic civilizations lifted religious creativity to lofty levels. The main achievement of European civilization is unparalleled development of the physical sciences. Each of these fields, however, has limits to its possibilities. When the ceiling is reached, the civilization has finished its task. It has nothing open to it then but decline and ultimate death.

According to Danilevsky's scheme, the notion of endless upward progress is invalid. Yet he does not imply that the growth and decline of civilizations is a hopeless, futile cycle, a meaningless turning of a cultural wheel, the eternal labor of a King Sisyphus rolling his boulder up Hades's hill only to have it, near the top, tumble down again. Human progress does exist, Danilevsky affirmed. But it occurs on a broader scale than nineteenth-century Europe understood. Genuine progress appears in the grand combination of all the cultures together, all creative in their special ways. As the Russian thinker put it: "The task of mankind consists in an unfolding . . . and realization, by different peoples at different periods, of all the aspects and forms of creativity that virtually or potentially underlie all humanity."[21]

Finally Danilevsky's book returns to the question of why Europe was hostile toward Russia and whether this animosity would persist or fade away with time. In addition to basic tribal incompatibilities, Europe resented Russia and Slavic peoples because European civilization lay well past its zenith, while the Slavs—the seventh Aryan language group—were perched on the verge of their most creative period. The civilization of Europe, by Danilevsky's reckoning, began its decline in the seventeenth century, though the first symptoms of serious deterioration were becoming visible only in the nineteenth century. This decline appeared in many forms: in waning creativity, in growing cynicism, in de-Christianization, and especially in a lust for power and world domination, not only in the political and economic spheres, but culturally as well. Sensing its old age and approaching dissolution, Europe felt envy and enmity toward the Russia and Slavhood that soon would bloom and thrive. Moreover, while Europe had lived as a civilization of twofold creativity, specializing in political development and the combined field of science-technology-aesthetics, the coming Russian-Slavic civilization showed signs of blossoming in all four main fields of culture: political, economic, scientific-technological-aesthetic, and religious. Mainly, though, Danilevsky predicted, it would specialize in the socio-economic field by building a new and just social and economic order.

Danilevsky, in the course of developing his theory, ventured other significant predictions. He considered the empires of Austria-Hungary and Turkey already dead and without any further reason for political existence. Half a century later, both empires fell in the aftermath of World War I. Also in the 1860s, he foresaw world power being split into two opposing camps—Europe and a Slavic federation under Russian leadership—which came to pass after World War II as Western Europe under the Atlantic Pact and Eastern Europe under Communism. He also forecast as inevitable a war between a unified Europe and a united Slavhood. Europe, he declared, would "invade Russia under the first handy pretext."[22] But federated Slavhood, with its day of glory dawning, would withstand any onslaught by semisenile Europe. It would take up the torch of creative world leadership from the exhausted civilization. Then it would bear the light forward into the future until the Slavic civilization itself aged, declined, and passed away.

THE WEST AND RUSSIA II: WALTER SCHUBART

Some seventy years after Danilevsky, amidst the vast upheavals of the twentieth century, a German scholar, Walter Schubart, also envisioned the West losing its supremacy and the East, led by Russia, rising to predominance.

Schubart, who came from the Baltic area of northern Germany, was a specialist in Slavic culture. He lived in Russia before and during the Communist Revolution of 1917 and married a Russian. A Protestant by birth, he later joined the Russian Orthodox church. Prior to World War II, he served as a professor of sociology and philosophy at the State University of Latvia in the Baltic country's capital of Riga. When the Union of Soviet Socialist Republics occupied Latvia in 1940, Schubart became a Soviet citizen. In 1941 Nazi Germany took the country and he disappeared. Nothing was heard of him after June of that year.

Schubart wrote extensively on Slavic life for periodicals in Poland, Germany, Austria, and Switzerland. Among his books, all originally written in German, was a cultural study entitled *Europa und die Seele des Ostens*—Europe and the Soul of the East—first published in 1938. Though the author remains little known outside limited scholarly circles, this work was translated into most languages of the Western world. An English-language edition appeared in America in 1950 under the title *Russia and Western Man*.

In this widely read and thought-provoking volume, Schubart joined Danilevsky in abandoning the notion of continuous upward progress and revived the idea of cyclic rhythms in culture that was held by ancient Greeks and, as well, by Buddhists, Hindus, Persians, Jews, and thinkers of ancient Mexican civilization. His theory, however, unlike Danilevsky's, saw the rise and decline of civilizations not depending entirely on the cultures themselves. Rather he detected in the course of history four different modes of life that appear, endure for a time, then pass away. Each of these modes dominates a whole era. The culture most in tune with that era rises to prominence and dominance.

One of these modes—or "prototypes," since they mark both an era and a basic type of people—he named 'Ascetic.' A person who lives in the Ascetic prototype believes all the world is illusion and error, a kind of mirage full of evil temptation. He nurtures neither hope nor desire to improve things. Instead he renounces the world altogether and devotes himself to finding the ultimate essence of reality. This attitude distinguishes Hindu culture and the neo-Platonic philosophical movement that arose in third-century Rome.

Another basic type of man—and historical era—Schubart called the 'Harmonious.' Such a person and an age view the cosmos and the world as perfect. Perfused by inner harmony, the world needs neither human guidance nor efforts to reconstruct it. It is meant to exist just as it is, an object of human meditation and love. The Harmonious person lives at peace, as one with the universe. He holds no ambition for progress nor ideas of evolution. Instead he regards the purpose of history as already fulfilled. The very ancient Greeks of Homer's day, the Chinese in the time of Confucius, and the Gothic Christians of Europe between the eleventh and sixteenth centuries are prime examples of the Harmonious man.

A third type of both man and age Schubart named the 'Heroic.' This kind of person and his era do not live at peace with the world but are set against it, as though chaos is prevailing and humanity's mission is to put things into order. The Heroic man wants to change things, to mold them according to his plans. He goes about the task as though the earth were a slave and he the master. While Ascetic and Harmonious aeons are static, the Heroic era is tense, energetic, dynamic. Ascetic and Harmonious man gaze heavenward in worship and humility. Heroic man, bursting with self-confidence, pride, and lust for power, glares earthward in enmity and malice. His nature drives him ever further from God and ever deeper into absorption with the material world. The age of ancient Rome at the height of its imperial power epitomizes this kind of time. So does the culture of Western Europe from the sixteenth century onward. Of the Heroic man, Schubart proclaims, "Secularization is his destiny, heroism his ideal, tragedy his end."[23]

The fourth and final type of man and aeon the author named the 'Messianic.' Like the Heroic man, the Messianic person dynamically strives to change the world. But he does not labor for his own advantage. He views the earth not as a slave to be tamed but as rough material in need of ennoblement and consecration. Like the Harmonious man, he loves the world—but not as it is, only as it ought to be. He does not believe, with the Harmonious man, that the purpose of the world is preaccomplished but sees his goal lying far in the future. He too enjoys deep inner harmony, but he also feels called to share that harmony, to spread his sense of completeness to the shattered world around him. So, inspired not by lust for power but by a spirit of compromise, love, and reconciliation, he does not divide in order to rule but seeks out the divided to bring them into union. He sees his fellow human beings not as competitors and enemies but as brothers. Believing himself the earthly representative of the divine order, he works to establish the Kingdom of God among all humankind. Like the Heroic man, the Messianic person is active, energetic, and dynamic. Equally so is a Messianic era. Schubart cited as examples of the character type the early Christians and most Slavic peoples.

The aims of the four prototypes are: world renunciation for the Ascetic; world harmony for the Harmonious; world domination for the Heroic; world redemption for the Messianic. All of the eras, the author suggested, are equally close to God, including the Heroic in which no gods are desired. "Like the silent periods in a melody, even the godless epochs have their part to play in the cosmic symphony. And it is only in contrast to the dark ages that the light epochs appear in their full luminosity. . . . Darkness intensifies the power of sight and enhances the desire for more light."[24]

In the cyclic movements of humanity's history, especially striking are periods of transition as one era wanes and a new one begins. The story of civilization, Schubart pointed out, holds no more thrilling spectacle. These are apocalyptic ages when people endure a break with the past so extreme that it seems the world is coming to an end. They imagine such a time has never happened before, though actually these periods are repeated throughout history.

The twentieth century is one of these cataclysmic intervals. A Heroic age has triumphed for almost five hundred years. It blossomed into a riot of progress under the lead of North Germans, Anglo-Saxons, Americans—hard men of action from northern lands who were eminently suited to the era. But uncertainty began to creep into Western culture in the eighteenth century with the ideas of the French philosopher Jean Jacques Rousseau. Gradually it grew to uneasiness, staleness, satiety. The nineteenth century was spared an awareness of approaching downfall as it reached new heights of material progress and well-being. But World War I shattered the culture's illusions of security and revealed the crisis.

Now fissures of impending collapse are appearing everywhere. Western civilization was the first to attempt to rebuild the world to human standards. Its failure shows in all directions. The exact sciences once claimed they were reducing nature to comprehensible laws. But recent inquiries of reason have loosed an uncontrollable flood of new questions, defeating reason itself and leading people back into the realm of mystery.

Humanity's attempt to rebel against disease and death equally has failed. Infectious diseases that were suppressed are being replaced by a rising incidence of other maladies: heart disease, cancer, nervous disorders. Meanwhile, where death has not received its natural due, man is stifled by his own swelling masses and threatened by shortage of food-producing land.

Western culture's intent to build a kingdom of universal well-being on earth also has miscarried. "No culture hitherto has ever expended so much energy and effort in attempting to achieve material comfort and the satisfaction of mere fleshly desires as the [Western], which has entirely disregarded the health of the soul. And no other culture has ever achieved such a degree of human misery!" [25]

The technology once expected to free man for a creative life instead has drawn him into a rhythm of its own. Autonomous and demonic, it has robbed him of his work and stripped him of power, hurling him through life like a helpless victim of evil spirits. Human organizations, rather than offering the security he hoped for, deprive him of liberty and enmesh him in arbitrariness and injustice. Likewise, economic and national policies obey their own laws without consideration for human aims. Meanwhile, uncontrolled technocracy paves the way for future wars to be as destructive and exhausting as possible.

Western culture, Schubart asserted, is yearning for self-destruction. It has begun to hate its own fading era. An apocalyptic atmosphere hangs over the earth, and the suicidal collapse of the West is unavoidable. Meanwhile, people of the West are aware of their impending downfall. They flee from solitude and reflection into work, narcotics, the crowd. They shun freedom and responsibility, preferring obedience and slavery.

Not even people of wisdom can save the culture. "The far seeing members of the human race are suffering today from the fact that their warning voices do not reach those who wield the power that molds history. The voice of wisdom is silenced by hopelessly blinded authorities. Thus—as so often before—it is once more the tragic fate of prophets to see the misfortune approaching without being able to prevent it, and it is the equally tragic destiny of the actors in the drama that they are unable to see the misfortunes they themselves are causing."[26]

In spite of approaching mass disaster, Schubart believed, the whole grand cultural movement is in full cooperation with the plan of Providence. Western society is moving toward destruction to liberate mankind for a new era now faintly dawning on the horizon of the future. The age to come, the German scholar predicted, will be a Messianic era. Embodying the spirit of compromise and reconciliation, forgiveness and love, it will resemble Europe's Middle Ages—a time that modern Western man disdains but people of the future will admire. As eras shift, so will the center of cultural predominance. It will pass from Western nations to peoples best suited to the Messianic prototype. "The leadership will be given into the hands of those who possess, as a permanent national characteristic, the tendency to other-worldliness. And these are the Slavs," Schubart attested, "in particular the Russians."[27]

As early as 1765, the German philosopher and poet Johann Gottfried von Herder spoke of Europe's outworn culture and called Russia the land of the future, seeing in its people a unique spiritual power capable of redeeming the human race. Nothing short of redemption is necessary, Schubart affirmed. "The West has endowed humanity with the most refined forms of technological development, of organization of government, and of systems of transport and communication, but it has robbed the human race of its soul. It is Russia's task to give back to mankind its soul. . . . The Russians possess the spiritual qualities required for this task, qualities that are lacking in every Western nation."[28]

First, the author forecast, "the gray misery of the Soviet period will pass, as did the black night of the Tartar yoke."[29] Marxist Communism was contrary to the nature of the Russian people. It was one more of many Western imports overlaid upon the country and ill-fitting. Proponents of Russia's Westernization committed suicide with Bolshevism, which would be cast out as the country spiritually turned away from the West and back to the East.

A second part of Russia's future task, according to Schubart, will be to serve as a bridge for East and West finally to meet, then merge in a union that the Messianic era will create. "Russia is a part of Asia, and at the same time a member of the Christian community. She is the Christian part of Asia, and in this fact lies the unique and individual quality of her historical mission. India and China have both withdrawn themselves from Western man, for whom the community of religious belief has bridged the way to Russia. That is why Russia, and Russia alone, is in a position to regenerate a mankind fallen victim to lust for power and become hardened by absorption in practical problems."[30]

The reconciliation of East and West will arise as the last major problem of the waning Heroic period and the first of the new Messianic era. The birth of a culture combining both halves of the world will become the greatest spiritual task that ever occupied the human race. It will come into focus as the central issue not only of foreign policy but also of intellectual life in Europe and Russia.

The settlement, however, will not be achieved peacefully, Schubart believed. It began in 1812, when Napoleon's *Grande Armée* of a half-million men invaded Russia, throwing the two cultures into sharp political contact and jolting the Slavic East awake. Continuing antithesis between the Slavs and Europe brought about the first World War, the author wrote. And with that conflict, as Germany's main theater of battle shifted to Eastern territory, a century of wars between East and West began.

According to Schubart, these wars will serve a cultural purpose. As one of many means of mutual interpenetration, they will provide a meeting ground for East and West. Thus will they aid the ultimate merger of the two separate worlds. The entire process, like the gradual rapprochement between ancient Germanic tribes and the peoples of the dying Roman world, could require all of five centuries to complete.

As the combined culture arises, Western nations will not cease to be important. But they will sacrifice their intellectual supremacy and cease to represent the dominant type of human being. Many Western achievements will be retained, in economics and technology, in political economy, social structure, and organization. Also both West and East will keep their individuality. Europe will not have to turn itself into a part of Russia, nor will Russia have to sell itself to the West. Instead, two original forms of spiritual being will seek to reach one another. Like man and woman, they must come together in order to be creative.

While the cultures are merging, so will the two hemispheric divisions of humankind. The result will be one world-man—the person of the Messianic future. This fusion of the mental types of East and West is no new idea, Schubart pointed out. It was seen as the only way to produce the perfect human being by such noted universal thinkers as the seventeenth-century German philosopher Gottfried Wilhelm von Leibniz and the eighteenth-century German literary titan Johann Wolfgang von Goethe. Leibniz went so far as to suggest East-West academies for intellectual exchange to advance this goal.

The need for fusion of the two types of man is clear, Schubart asserted. "The spiritual Russian needs practical qualities; the practical European is in the need of a new humanity. . . . The Russian must become more efficient, the European more virtuous."[31] Actually the merger already has begun in response to the passing of one era and the rising of another: "In Russia, a type of humanity is developing which is . . . a quite new species with an Eastern soul that has been influenced by Western culture as by a hardening process. This new type, while truly Russian, is yet heir to the eternal values of the West."[32] The proverbial Russian indolence has been replaced by energy, enthusiasm, a growing interest in work, and a sense of duty. A servile attitude common in former times has given way to awareness of the dignity of labor. Efficiency, punctuality, and precision are now highly prized qualities among the Russian people, who generally are well along in transformation of their lives.

Meanwhile, a major spiritual transformation is occurring in the West as well. A period of religious indifference is drawing to a close. Though "in the mass of contemporary mankind there is not the smallest sign of reflective thought, repentance or the ascent to a new type of humanity," a fresh religious outlook is germinating in a few receptive hearts.[33] As in past periods of similar change, a small, spiritual elite has arisen consisting of the best minds "who are repelled by the crudeness of contemporary everyday life, in which nothing of reverence, kindness or love is known and in which lawlessness and the use of force are openly acknowledged."[34] Such an elite always has gathered followers. And religion in general is gaining a new following in the West, especially among educated classes. This religious rebirth is no isolated phenomenon. Rather, it springs from a complete spiritual transformation taking place in Western humanity, whereby it is drawing closer to the spirit of the East.

Today Russia is life without form, while Europe is form without life. In one case, life has burst forth without a mold to contain it. In the other, the soul has escaped and left an empty dwelling behind. "Russia—not the present but the future—is the refreshing wine capable of renewing the exhausted life of modern humanity," Schubart wrote. "Europe is the durable vessel in which to preserve the wine. Without the solid form to keep it together the wine would be spilled over the country; without the wine that fills it the precious cup remains an empty and cold showpiece alienated from its purpose. Only when wine and cup meet can mankind most fully enjoy them."[35]

The present age, Schubart observed, often is compared to the time of ancient Rome's decline. Yet the likeness is not entirely dismal; beyond is fullness of light. The ancient period was an epoch of death and decay, but also one of Messianic promise. The twentieth century is a kindred time. "A new Apocalypse is approaching," Schubart declared, "with a Last Judgment and a Resurrection!"[36]

The Coming Middle Ages: Nikolai Berdyaev

The awesome sense of endings that pervades modern Western civilization has been interpreted in a variety of ways. As Walter Schubart theorized that the end at hand was the close of an aeonic way of life, the Spanish philosopher Miguel de Unamuno saw it as the end of two thousand years of Christianity. The Russian thinker and literary figure Dmitry Merezhkovsky believed the present age to be the termination of post-Atlantis humanity. The German social philosopher Karl Marx saw it as the end of the capitalist economic system. Another Russian thinker, Nikolai Berdyaev, took the modern age to be the conclusion of the European Renaissance.

Berdyaev, who was born in 1874 and studied at the universities of Kiev and Heidelberg, was one of the earliest supporters of Marxism in Tsarist Russia. Arrested for his political beliefs, he was banished for a time to a northern province. Later he withdrew from Marxist ideology and acquired a reputation as one of Russia's notable idealistic thinkers. He held the chair of political economy at the University of Moscow, among other positions. In 1922 he was arrested by the Soviet government and expelled from the country as an upholder of religion. He settled in Paris. There, as possibly one of the greatest mystical philosophers of the twentieth century, he directed a philosophical-religious academy. From 1900 onward he wrote many books of social science, political economy, philosophy, and ethics, most of them translated into several languages. He died in France in 1948.

As so many other modern social thinkers, Berdyaev regarded the present as an age of severest crisis. He saw the rhythm of history turning catastrophic. Western culture's foundations, once seemingly stable, he felt to be shifting like volcanic ground, and any kind of eruption, material or spiritual, was possible. Europe was spending its strength extravagantly and already was exhausted. No longer could the peoples of the West place their faith in old theories of progress that painted the future as always better, more beautiful, and more desirable than what had come before. Berdyaev, like Lasaulx and others, disclaimed notions of continual upward progress, accepting instead that societies and civilizations undergo organic processes, with periods of youth, maturity, and old age, of expansion and decay.

Again as many other social observers, Berdyaev compared the modern age to ancient Europe's classic period of decline and fall. "We are not living to-day so much at the beginning of a new world as at the end of an old one," he wrote in a book titled *The End of Our Time*. "Our age resembles that of the fall of the Roman Empire, the failure and drying-up of Graeco-Roman culture, forever the head-water of all European culture."[37] As in ancient times, day is not fading into night in quiet and peace. Instead darkness is coming with the roar of vast upheavals and ghastly calamities of a kind that leave behind the impression of irremediable ruin. Looking toward the future, the author warned, "We are entering into the realm of the unknown and the unlived, and we are entering it joylessly and without much hope."[38]

By Berdyaev's reckoning, the West rests on a foundation built in medieval times. After ancient Rome's profligate spending and depletion and the centuries of chaotic barbarism that followed, the Christian Middle Ages were not only a period of order restored. They also were a time when European peoples accumulated a great fund of inner strength. The ascetic way of living that went with the practice of Christianity led to a gathering and storing of human creative power. Knighthood and monkhood, especially, disciplined and spiritualized man, creating models of spiritual freedom and fearlessness. "Medieval ascesis was a most effective school: it tempered the human spirit superbly, and throughout all modern history European man has lived on what he gained in that schooling."[39]

At the start of the period now known as the Renaissance, this strong and controlled man with all his forces concentrated loosed his energies in a grand burst of creativity. Berdyaev considered the beginning of this age, around the thirteenth century, as the highest point in European history. It also was the origin of the modern era that now is coming to an end.

The post-medieval age was a time for man to be free, no longer curbed by external controls. He could create and live governed solely by his own reason and self-control. Yet as he progressively uprooted himself from the source of his strength, it also proved a time when the accumulated fund of vigor was spent without renewal. The period liberated man's energies but emptied him out spiritually. The further he traveled down the pathway of freedom, the more his powers deteriorated. In time, man's self-reliance led him to inner poverty. Only the remnants of Christianity, persisting in secular form, have kept him from total disintegration.

In the nineteenth century, people still were feeling the consequences of the joyous and hopeful Renaissance. By the close of that century, however, decline already was apparent. With the twentieth century, quickening decay forebode the extinction of the age. Berdyaev believed the advent of heavy machines contributed more than anything else to bring the Renaissance to an end. The Industrial Revolution—"one of the worst revolutions that has ever swept over mankind"[40]—ripped man out of the bowels of nature and disrupted the entire rhythm of his life. It snapped the organic tie that held man and nature together, turning a light-hearted and carefree alliance into unavoidable warfare. The machine conquered nature for the benefit of man, but then it ground ahead to conquer man himself. Now, at the close of the age, it is wreaking destruction upon both.

European man of today, with all his creative forces spent, stands exhausted. He is a pallid shadow of his hopeful, enthusiastic forebears who looked forward to the growth and triumph of man as a strong, free individual. Weak, empty, drained of faith, he "is tired to death and is ready to rest upon any kind of collectivism that may come; and then human individuality will vanish once and for all."[41]

With his strengths depleted, modern man cannot hope for yet another renaissance. No fresh outpouring of creative energies is possible because no fund of energy is present:

> There is good reason to believe that man's creative forces cannot be regenerated or his identity re-established except by a renewal of religious asceticism. Only such a recall to our spiritual foundations can concentrate our powers and keep our identity from coming to dust. . . . It is no good to yearn for a new kind of renaissance after such a spiritual drying-up and dilapidation, after such wanderings in the desert of life, after so deep a sundering of human identity. By an analogy we might say that we are approaching not a renaissance but the dark beginnings of a middle age, and that we have got to pass through a new civilized barbarism, undergo a new discipline, accept a new religious asceticism before we can see the first light of a new and unimaginable renaissance.[42]

In the twentieth century, which Berdyaev also regarded as a time of transition, the Russian thinker detected many signs of a new Middle Ages approaching. He saw modern people already falling into the "civilized barbarism" that first would dominate the culture, savage hordes both within and without suggesting a future much like the obscure seventh, eighth, and ninth centuries that preceded the rise of orderly Christian society. As in similar times past, the modern period is marked by visible rotting of old institutions and invisible formation of new ones. Traditional forms of government, politics, art, philosophy, intellectual life are being discarded. Taking their place are spontaneous outbursts of life, for good and for ill. Berdyaev cited the sudden appearance of Fascism as an example of a harmful outburst in the area of politics.

Another sign of the new Middle Ages taking shape is the growing desire among many people to surmount national barriers and seek the kind of universality that linked the lands and peoples of medieval Europe. Connected with this is the tendency of Christian denominations to work toward union, and parallel trends favoring a worldwide spiritual culture. The return of intellectuals to Christianity, even as the masses are being led away from religion, suggested to Berdyaev the beginning of Europe's historic medieval period when intellect played an important part within the church. Similarly, a "terrible home-sickness" that has taken hold of the larger part of mankind is another sign of an approaching new age of religion. Still another symptom is the modern revival of magic and occultism.

Yet the coming era in no way will duplicate the old medieval time. Just as the Renaissance did not actually revive the Greco-Roman age as its founders intended, but developed into a new and unique period, the coming Middle Ages also will be fresh and distinctive. A planetary way of looking at the earth is arising, so the dawning era is likely to be universal. Also Berdyaev believed that the peoples of the Orient might emerge from cultural torpor and once again join the torrent of history. Then, as Schubart predicted, the East and the West might come together.

The church will stand as the spiritual center of the age, the Russian thinker wrote as he continued sketching his outline of times to come. Religion will not function merely as a small department of culture as it does at present, but "must again become all, the force which transfigures and irradiates the whole of life from within."[43]

The overall society will be "of the people" to the highest degree, yet not in the least democratic. "Democracies are inseparable from middle-class domination and the industrial-capitalist system. The masses ordinarily are indifferent to politics, for they never have enough strength to seize power."[44] Rather, citizens in the coming age more likely will rely on councils to represent them: professional, economic, and spiritual unions that will grow to form the whole fabric of society and state. Present political scrambles after power will be stigmatized as parasitical and lacking relevance to real life. Meanwhile, strivings after various types of human equality will come to an end, and a new hierarchy will arise based on true ability and genuine spiritual aristocracy. New monarchies might appear—not the liberal, formally legitimate kind of the present, but the medieval type, with "Caesarism" as their strongest trait and their power expressed in dictatorial terms. Power, however, will not be taken as a right but as a sacred duty to be exercised in good faith under strict supervision of conscience.

The culture of the future will be rooted in the principle of work. This, instead of being felt as a burden to be shunned, will be understood as joining in the act of creation. The leisure and laziness associated with privileged classes will disappear. Meanwhile, the aim of labor will be not quantity, in which goodness or badness does not matter, but quality, which always was the Christian ideal. Workers will band together in vocational groups much like the powerful guilds of medieval times. These, unlike present political parties, will represent their real interests.

Life will become more austere, as people discard superfluous wants and abandon material showiness. The means of life, which now absorb the attention of people exclusively, will fade in importance in favor of life's purposes and ends. The idea of progress will be relinquished as concealing the true ends of living. Finally people will acquire a taste for eternity and turn once again to God—or to Satan.

Berdyaev believed that women will hold great significance in the new Middle Ages. The heightened part they play in society will have nothing to do with current emancipation movements, "the end and method of which is to reduce woman to the likeness of man by leading her along a masculine road."[45] Instead, women will find greater importance as the eternal feminine, which "is bound more closely than man to the soul of the world and its primary elemental forces. . . . Masculine culture is too rationalizing, out of touch with the mysteries of universal life: this is corrected through woman."[46]

Berdyaev felt less certain than Danilevsky and Schubart about Russia's position in the grand march of the future. He saw the country already dwelling in the new Middle Ages, with a society firmly hierarchical, dictatorial, unified, and "sacred" under Communist rule. It had, in fact, leaped directly from the old Middle Ages under the tsars to the coming medievalism. Its unification was forced, however, and therefore false. And its government, the Russian thinker charged, was not a theocracy but a satanocracy. Like Schubart, Berdyaev saw Russia as a unique blend of West and East. But he was not sure how the country would take form in regard to either itself or the rest of the world. "Our cultural traditions had always been too weak. As a result we are creating an ugly civilization, for the barbarian element in us is always strong and our will to religious transfiguration stricken with a sort of diseased vision." He concluded that the Russian soul possibly possesses a greater capacity than that of the West "for asserting its will to achieve the miracle of religious transfiguration." However, "The will of the Russian people has need of purification and tempering; and our people has a great expiation in store for it. Only then will its will to transfigure life give it the right to determine its mission in the world."[47]

Equally uncertain in Berdyaev's mind was the choice of direction people everywhere would take in shaping the new Middle Ages.

Though he preferred to speculate on the possibility of a positive society, he wrote, "I have a presentiment that an outbreak of the powers of evil is at hand."[48] The new age of religion does not necessarily mean the absolute and quantitative triumph of Christianity. It also could imply religious struggle, with deadly warfare between Christianity and anti-Christianity.

In Berdyaev's estimate, "the future is doubtful, and do not believe that we are obliged to look forward to a period of radiance and joy. The illusions of earthly happiness no longer have any hold on us, and the sense of evil becomes stronger and more acute in the middle ages: the powers of wickedness will grow and take on new forms wherewith to plague us in new ways."[49] Yet, in man's freedom of spirit and liberty to select his path, two choices remain open to him. "He can either submit himself to the highest divine principles of life and thus strengthen his personality or he can become the slave and subject of nondivine, evil, and superhuman principles. He is free to choose either path."[50]

AN ETHICAL SOLUTION: ALBERT SCHWEITZER

Dr. Albert Schweitzer, like Nikolai Berdyaev, also believed that man is free to choose. The humanitarian medical missionary and social philosopher saw the present choice as crucial: between the life and death of civilization.

Schweitzer was born in 1875 at Kayserberg in Upper Alsace, then a part of Germany and now in France. He was the eldest son of a Lutheran pastor. By the age of thirty, he was principal of the theological college at Strasbourg and a noted scholar and musicologist. Suddenly, to the dismay of friends and colleagues, he gave up his position. Announcing plans to prepare himself as a missionary to Negro peoples in Africa, he began a six-year course of medical studies.

In 1913, Schweitzer left Europe with his wife of one year, who also was a scholar and had trained as a nurse to join him in his work. They journeyed to the Gabon Province of French Equatorial Africa. There Schweitzer built a hospital, using his own funds and, aided by local people, with his own hands. Except for a period when the first World War caused the French to intern him as a German citizen, he made his home in the steaming West African jungle for the rest of his ninety years. Not only did he treat the ill and supervise every detail of his hospital. He also added to his renown as a theologian, as an authority on Johann Sebastian Bach, and as one of the great concert organists of his time. Later he gained worldwide repute as a philosopher, a recipient of the Nobel prize in 1952 and one of the most noted humanitarians of the age.

His philosophical thinking focused on human cultures, and principally on modern Western civilization. He was working with the topic as early as 1900. But not until his wartime internment did he develop his ideas in two books, the first titled *The Decay and the Restoration of Civilization* and the second, *Civilization and Ethics.* The volumes later were combined under the title *The Philosophy of Civilization.*

"We are living to-day under the sign of the collapse of civilization," Schweitzer warned at the beginning of his work.[51] He saw the culture of the West committing suicide, its people practicing a dangerous mixture of civilization and barbarism. In his view, no modern country was exempt from this condition. All the civilized nations side by side were suffering the same decadence, and all of them had sunk to the same barbaric depths.

Schweitzer laid the blame for the collapsing culture with philosophy—or an insufficiency of it in the present age. By philosophy, he meant not the uncreative history of past philosophical systems nor the hopelessly abstruse and unintelligible thinking that he found currently dominating the field. Rather, he saw the true role of philosophy as guide and guardian of the general reason, with the mission of refining and expanding upon the basic questions about life that people are pondering, or ought to be. And he noted that all through past ages the condition of civilization was linked inexorably to the philosophy that prevailed within it.

For example, ancient Romans, living with the pessimistic philosophy of resignation that Stoicism gave them, had no positive intellectual grounds for advancing their worldwide empire. Therefore they suffered decline and collapse. Conversely, Europe's eighteenth-century philosophical movement known as the Enlightenment developed a highly optimistic world outlook. This vitalized the culture and diffused valuable ideas over all the earth.

By far the most important element in civilizational philosophy, Schweitzer maintained, is ethics. All other factors, whether artistic, intellectual, or material, are secondary. Only in ethics can humanity find the driving force to create, maintain, and develop a civilized condition. The Enlightenment philosophy of modern Western culture was not only optimistic, with its goals of perfecting the individual, the society, and all humankind. It also was strongly ethical. Originally, its conception of humanity's upward progress referred even more to spiritual growth than to material advancement. This philosophy guided the thought of European peoples throughout the eighteenth and early nineteenth centuries. In the latter century, however, its ethical content broke down. People intoxicated by heady progress in discovery and invention began to neglect progress within themselves. In time, they forgot about it altogether, coming to believe that man's advancement was a matter of scientific, technical, and artistic improvement alone. At that point, Schweitzer claimed, civilization abdicated.

Since then, in an intellectual atmosphere where natural science is the only truth held acceptable, "the ethical ideas upon which civilization rests have been wandering about the world, poverty-stricken and homeless."[52] Meanwhile, the culture's balance is dangerously disturbed. More developed materially than spiritually, the West flounders about like a ship without a rudder. And philosophy, rather than offering solutions, ignores the elemental problems of the age. This leaves modern people without any guidance as the darkness of disaster gathers like an approaching storm.

The lack of direction, Schweitzer pointed out, already has led to an inhuman way of living that further contributes to the culture's suicidal drift. This unwholesome life begins when man is separated from a home and field of his own. Such a displacement, according to Schweitzer, causes serious psychical injury. The less-than-human existence continues as man is restricted to narrowly specialized work. With limited tasks that use only a fragment of his full capacities, he cannot avoid imperfect development. His skills do not grow and expand. His creative and artistic powers atrophy. To be sure, amazing productive efficiency can result from minute divisions of labor, but a stunted people is the ultimate consequence. And in modern society a limiting specialization occurs even where productivity is not the purpose. In many fields, such as education and administration, a heavy load of rules and tight supervision narrows as much as possible the scope of the work at hand, again reducing chances for personal growth.

At the same time, the spirit of the present drives people to excessive activity. It claims their toil for this and that purpose, keeping them so busy that they might not even have a chance to question what their restless sacrifices have to do with the meaning of their lives. Excessive strain leaves the many people who function more as workers than as human beings too depleted to manage their lives satisfactorily outside work. Spiritually exhausted, they are unable to invest what free time they have in self-cultivation. Instead, out of physical necessity, they collapse into idleness, forgetfulness, and diversion. Neither can they devote enough of themselves to the task of raising their children. Thus the cycle of aimless, frantic living is perpetuated in succeeding generations.

Meanwhile, public life is excessively organized. People no longer are nurtured by social institutions but subordinated to them. As a consequence, most modern people no longer think as individuals but follow the ideas of one group or another. They dare not question socially accepted views, often fearing even to bring them up in conversation. "The modern man," Schweitzer observed, "is lost in the mass in a way which is without precedent in history, and this is perhaps the most characteristic trait in him."[53] Under the thumb of the crowd, drawing from it the opinions he lives by, he becomes incapacitated to produce new ideas or use old ones freshly. Thus both real thought and its creative benefits disappear.

Leading him still deeper into inhumanity are rushed and crowded living conditions that promote mechanical, impersonal relations among people. In such circumstances, courtesy gives way to indifference. No longer are people accorded human value and dignity. Often, in fact, they are regarded as so much raw material or property, mere objects belonging to the material world. Influenced by the environment, schools have ceased to stress the duty of humanity. Meanwhile, technical achievements that allow people to kill their fellows at great distances and in enormous numbers lead them to discard any last impulse to human feeling.

"The man of to-day," Schweitzer summarized, "pursues his dark journey in a time of darkness, as one who has no freedom, no mental collectedness, no all-round development, as one who loses himself in an atmosphere of inhumanity, who surrenders his spiritual independence and his moral judgment to the organized society in which he lives, and who finds himself in every direction up against hindrances to the temper of true civilization."[54]

In spite of Schweitzer's dismal vision of a disabled humanity in a crippling society, the humanitarian thinker believed that the decadence afflicting both could be halted. Then growth from the present civilized barbarism back to true civilization could begin. He took issue with social observers who, with a concept of civilization not based upon ethics, regard signs of decay as symptoms of old age and assume that civilization, like any other natural process, must in due time reach its end. This conception, he noted, offers no recourse but to accept the causes of deterioration as natural and try to see the phenomena of advancing cultural senility as intellectually interesting.

He also questioned the idea with which these same observers console themselves that a new age, a new race, a new civilization will arise to take the place of the old. Echoing the assertion of

American historian Brooks Adams that the modern era lacks the stream of barbarian blood that made the Middle Ages, the doctor-philosopher noted: "The earth no longer has in reserve, as it had once, gifted peoples as yet unused, who can relieve us and take our place in some distant future as leaders of the spiritual life. We already know all those which the earth has to dispose of. There is not one among them which is not already taking such a part in our civilization that its spiritual fate is determined by our own. All of them, the gifted and the ungifted, the distant and the near, have felt the influence of those forces of barbarism which are at work among us. All of them are, like ourselves, diseased, and only as we recover can they recover."[55]

Therefore, said Schweitzer, modern Western man must renew his culture if civilization is not to be lost to all humankind both now and for the future. This great and vital renewal is fully possible, he explained, first by restoring the habit of individual thinking among people and then by rebuilding humane ethics—this time on a philosophical foundation that will prove sound and lasting.

The first step is every person's responsibility: to separate from the crowd. At present, relying wholly upon organizations to guide them, people are obsessed with the notion that if only the institutions of social and public life could be reformed, then everything else automatically would fall into line. They disagree on exactly how organizations might be made better. But they all believe that the failing condition of the society and its members is due to a failure of institutions. In reality, Schweitzer maintained, institutions count for very little. The future of a society depends not on how near to perfection its organizations are but on the worthiness of its individual members. The only way to rebuild society is for people to rebuild themselves. To accomplish this, the individual first must break free of the society's grasp.

Then people must begin to reflect, by themselves and together, about the meaning of life. They must form a new *Weltanschauung*—a world outlook, or theory of the universe—to guide them. Modern man still does not understand the serious consequences of living without a satisfactory philosophy of life, or with none at all. He must be stirred to elementary considerations about what he is in the world, what he intends to make of his life and how his existence needs to be given meaning and value.

Can the average person reflect that deeply? If present-day humanity is taken as the sole example of the species, doubts are justified, Schweitzer admitted. Yet, the German thinker reminded his readers that modern man, "with his diminished need of thought, is a pathological phenomenon."[56] Any judgment based upon the prevailing mental vacuity leads to a lowered conception of what man should be. Normally contemplation about the purpose of life and how best to live it is a perfectly natural feature of all men, and it needs nothing more than freedom to proceed. Yet, for modern people to break away from the mass, then develop a workable world outlook, will be difficult, Schweitzer acknowledged.

Among many barriers standing in the way are widespread habits of blind optimism and equally blind pessimism. The first arises in refusal to see that things are not alright. This is supported by lowering standards of judgment to make them seem alright. The common pessimism of the age, meanwhile, abandons all hope that humankind can advance spiritually.

Another hindrance—an extremely severe one—is the whole modern economic system. Not only does it "tend to bring up the man of to-day as a being without freedom, without self-collectedness, without independence, in short as a human being so full of deficiencies that he lacks the qualities of humanity."[57] It also leaves people, whether poor or prosperous, so unassured of economic security that they are continually preoccupied by material concerns and all other considerations seem like mere shadows by comparison.

Meanwhile, the overorganized society will do its utmost to prevent man from becoming an independent personality. "They will use every means to keep him in that condition of impersonality which suits them. They fear personality because the spirit and the truth, which they would like to muzzle, find in it a means of expressing themselves. And their power is, unfortunately, as great as their fear."[58]

The many obstacles on the path to true civilization create an atmosphere of demoralization and despair. We can well understand the men of the Greco-Roman decadence who felt paralyzed by the events of their time and, abandoning the world to its fate, withdrew into themselves. Like them, we suffer bewilderment and are tempted to live only for the day, to renounce thinking and hoping about anything beyond personal existence and to find solace in resignation.

Yet even as a horde of obstacles looms before us, recognizing that civilization is founded on some sort of world outlook and can be restored through a spiritual awakening lifts us above all difficulties. If ethics can provide sufficient standing ground amid events of the age, then modern humanity shall rebuild true civilization by establishing a workable philosophy and the convictions about life to which this will give birth.

A philosophy capable of supporting a civilization must be ethical, Schweitzer repeatedly emphasized. This provides the basis for each person to perfect his inner self. The philosophy also has to be optimistic. It must affirm, unlike some Oriental philosophies, that life holds absolute value in itself. This leads the ethical person away from a tendency to withdraw, moving him to work for the general society rather than ignore it. Throughout history, whenever ethics or life-affirming optimism advanced, so did civilization. Conversely, when they declined, civilization suffered the damage or collapse of any structure whose foundations have weakened or given way.

While past philosophies sometimes were ethical and optimistic about life to a greater or lesser degree, with corresponding benefit to the societies they influenced, none of them endured, Schweitzer explained, because they tried to find their roots in the external world—the world as modern science views it. And that world is ethically irrelevant. "If we take the world as it is, it is impossible to attribute to it a meaning in which the aims and objects of mankind and of individual men have a meaning also."[59]

Rather than beginning from external roots again, Schweitzer sought for a philosophy of life not outside man but within him. Drawing from extensive philosophical learning and a career dedicated to humanitarian work, he found the basis for both life-affirming optimism and ethics in a will to live that abides in all healthy forms of life. This will to live is self-evident, needing no explanations, no proofs. It also carries the meaning of life within itself. It holds more significance than any available knowledge of the world, and it needs no knowledge of the external world in order to function.

"The knowledge which I acquire from my will-to-live is richer than that which I win by observation of the world. . . . Why then tune down one's will-to-live to the pitch of one's knowledge of the world, or undertake the meaningless task of tuning up one's knowledge of the world to the higher pitch of one's will-to-live? The right and obvious course is to let the ideas which are given in our will-to-live be accepted as the higher and decisive kind of knowledge."[60]

The will to live leads directly to the philosophical optimism of life-affirmation. It also declares in itself the fundamental principle of ethics: "that good consists in maintaining, promoting, and enhancing life, and that destroying, injuring, and limiting life are evil."[61] To expand into a full philosophy of life, the will to live needs only to become reflective. It recognizes then that the will within oneself also exists within other living things and should be honored there equally.

The philosophy that Schweitzer evolved from these ideas he called 'reverence for life.' Its key principle, expressed simply, requires that each person accept responsibility without limit toward all things that live. A person following this precept becomes truly ethical when he willingly aids and advances all life that he is able to assist, and at the same time shrinks from injuring anything that lives or obstructing its growth and progress. "He does not ask how far this or that life deserves one's sympathy as being valuable, nor, beyond that, whether and to what degree it is capable of feeling. Life as such is sacred to him."[62]

In our relations to our fellow men, "the ethics of reverence for life throw upon us a responsibility so unlimited as to be terrifying."[63] Offering no pat rules, they compel us in each separate case to decide responsibly how much of our lives, our possessions, our rights and our happiness, our time and our rest we must devote to others and how much we may keep for ourselves.

Wealth, under this philosophy, exists as a social trust—the property of the community placed under the sovereign control of individuals—to be used not for purely individual purposes but in the service of society. Rights are not to be clung to but freely relinquished when they promote self-interest at the expense of other people's welfare and growth. Even happiness is not to be hoarded, since the happy are, by virtue of their good fortune, called upon to give much, to get off their smooth track and become "adventurers of self-devotion."[64] However much or little wealth, time, and leisure a person possesses, the philosophy of reverence for life calls upon him to constantly search his conscience for ways to be a human being for human beings.

Schweitzer's philosophy extended from relations among people to animals, insects, plants—all living things. In this way it resembles the ethical systems of some Far Eastern religions. If the suffering of an animal can be alleviated or prevented, reverence for life demands that be done. An earthworm strayed onto a barren roadway or an insect struggling in a puddle call out to be saved by the passerby who follows the life-affirming ideal. The practitioner of reverence for life tears no leaf from a tree, plucks no flower, damages no plant except under necessity.

Reverence for life, Schweitzer summarized, demands that man, with the completest possible development of his faculties and in the widest possible freedom, both material and spiritual, struggle to take a sympathetic and helpful interest in all life around him. Advancement in this way of living amounts to being ruled more and more by the longing to preserve and promote life, while becoming more and more resistant to injuring or destroying life.

By its very nature, reverence for life nurtures the ideals that create ethical civilization. It raises man to his highest value and compels him toward every kind of personal progress he can achieve. It focuses his attention outward as well, urging him to raise all humanity along with himself.

Moreover, reverence for life carries a built-in standard for assessing all progress. Any custom or social usage purporting to be moral can be measured against the standard of service to life. Thus, society no longer can foist upon its members meaningless ideals of power, passion, or nationalism, or principles of expediency or opportunism. Previous generations, Schweitzer observed, have made the great error of idealizing society as ethical, while in reality the collapse of civilization has come about through ethics being left to society. But people following the philosophy of reverence for life will permit only those policies and actions that stand consistent with the welfare of life. Regard for life and individual happiness, for sacred rights and justice, for all the claims of humanity, once more will receive full honor. Thus will the philosophy promote the restoration and advance of civilization.

According to Schweitzer, "complete civilization consists in realizing all possible progress in discovery and invention and in the arrangements of human society, and seeing that they work together for the spiritual perfecting of individuals which is the real and final object of civilization. Reverence for life is in a position to complete this conception of civilization and to build its foundations on what lies at the core of our being."[65]

Schweitzer believed that his ethical system, in order to work, had to be thought out and embraced on the level of the individual person, rather than promulgated from above and accepted by the masses in a superficial way. The renewal of civilization is possible only if ethics are grounded first in the mentality of thinking human beings. Then, transformed by a change of heart, such people can win over the crowd and spread a reviving influence to church, state, and all society.

From Dawn to Twilight

Before World War I, social thinking that painted the future not as a dawn but a twilight gained little general attention. A society dazzled with its own surging progress was not prepared for notions that its civilization was sinking into decline.

Even when well-known figures issued warnings, their admonitions were submerged by their fame for other things. Baudelaire is remembered for his poetry but not for his belief that "the world is drawing to a close." Tolstoy and Dostoyevsky, though globally renowned as masterful novelists, might surprise many people with their statements that the West has been corrupting the world and engineering its own destruction. Alfred Nobel, esteemed for his Peace prize, rarely is recalled for founding it to curb approaching violence and barbarism in the civilization. Henry Adams is remembered for his superb autobiography, *The Education of Henry Adams*, but not for his conviction that "decline is everywhere" and Western culture is rotten with decay and teetering on the verge of collapse. Albert Schweitzer's warning that "We are living to-day under the sign of the collapse of civilization," is mislaid beneath his noble reputation as Europe's great humanitarian jungle doctor.

After 1918, attitudes toward warnings of decline began to change. With the shock of the Great War and the greater one that followed, vast disillusion and disintegrating values left thoughtful people everywhere searching for explanations. Admonitions of the culture's disintegration were heeded increasingly by both scholars and the general public.

The First World War brought the German philosopher Oswald Spengler's masterwork, *The Decline of the West*. Almost immediately the book gained enormous attention. The Second World War left the world receptive to two more major studies of the West's decay: the English historian Arnold Toynbee's *A Study of History*, and the Russian-American sociologist Pitirim Sorokin's *Social and Cultural Dynamics*.

The three twentieth-century authors were in no way heirs of previous social thinkers who sought to diagnose or explain the problems of the West. Quite possibly Spengler knew little of his predecessors. Toynbee launched his study from a plan of his own. Sorokin, as a scholar, was familiar with the works of past social jeremiahs, but he built his analysis upon foundations wholly of his personal devising.

The work of all three thinkers arose intuitively from the spirit of the age. The same spirit brought them wide recognition, if not unanimous support. Most educated people since 1918 have known of Oswald Spengler and his book, even if they have not read the demanding work. Toynbee's massive study was widely known and discussed, while the historian himself became a celebrated social sage. Sorokin's endtime theories, though tailored more for scholars, were published around the world, while a brief and simple version was made available for popular consumption.

Now, in our Golden Age of material wealth and ease, as one millennium ends and another begins, an oddly apocalyptic atmosphere leaves the three works more pertinent than ever as the largest, most complete, and penetrating studies of an ailing culture and its sick society

PART II

Oswald Spengler, The Master Doomsayer

4

Spengler and Decline

THE MOST RESOUNDING PROPHET of Western culture's doom is the German philosopher-historian Oswald Spengler. His single major work, *The Decline of the West*, began to spread across a confused and shattered Europe at the close of the First World War. As a grim and somber vision of a sinking civilization, it seemed to give rational shape to a bewildering age of collapsing empires, tottering standards, failing values, and fearful signs of a new barbarism rising from humanity's depths.

Spengler's ponderous study compared the course of seven civilizations long decayed or dead with the path of modern Western culture. Within a few years of its publication, it became a worldwide best-seller. Though many decades have passed since the first appearance of *The Decline of the West*, the German thinker remains prominent throughout the world as Western civilization's master doomsayer, while his two-volume work still is printed, sold, and read with fascination by scholars and laymen alike.

OSWALD SPENGLER

Oswald Spengler was born in 1880 in the town of Blankenburg in the densely forested Harz Mountains of northern Germany. His father was a minor official in the Imperial German postal service. His mother came from a family of ballet artists. One of her sisters, successful and famous as a ballerina in Paris and Moscow, had died four years before Oswald was born, leaving Oswald's mother a moderate fortune.

In 1890 the Spengler family, now including three daughters, moved to the university city of Halle. There Oswald, attending classical high school, gained a sound grounding in Greek and Latin studies and mathematics. To a love of music probably acquired from his artistic mother, he added an interest in writing and a deep fondness for poetry. At the same time he enthusiastically discovered the works of the German literary master Goethe and the philosopher Nietzsche. All these factors later were to merge in his masterwork.

After his father's death in 1901, the legacy his mother had received enabled Oswald to go on to university, a privilege then largely reserved for upper-class families. He followed the German custom of attending several universities, spending a year at Munich and another at Berlin. He returned to Halle to complete his doctoral thesis. At all three institutions he studied ancient Greece and Rome, mathematics, and the physical sciences. In Munich he added music, and at Berlin, drama. Also, following a custom of German scholars, he made several journeys to Italy. His doctoral dissertation showed the scholastic boldness that characterized his later writings. It dealt with the surviving fragments of the works of Heraclitus, a fifth-century B.C. Greek philosopher considered the most abstruse of the thinkers before the time of Socrates. Spengler received his degree in the spring of 1904. He then wrote a second dissertation to qualify as a high school teacher, choosing as his topic "The Development of the Organ of Sight in the Higher Ranks of the Animal Kingdom."

For the next several years he taught at schools in Saarbrucken, Dusseldorf, and Hamburg. From all accounts he proved able and successful. A handsome young man with dark hair and a pointed beard, he dressed formally with high wing collars and broad cravats.

He maintained classroom discipline by the strength and dignity of his personality and taught in a manner that his students later recalled as lively and intuitive. In 1910 his mother died, leaving him an inheritance that offered modest financial independence. Soon after, he applied for a year's leave of absence to try his hand at writing.

Spengler's character and life convey a self-made quality that showed most clearly in 1911 when he moved to Munich, took up residence near the university, and embarked upon a long course of private study, reflection, and literary endeavor. He never returned to teaching. Experimenting with poetry, drama, and short stories, he wrote reviews and articles to supplement his investment income. He read voraciously in history, philosophy, and art history. He also hoped to write a book on politics.

International events spurred him forward with the book. A long-standing arms buildup in Europe, growing polarity between the age's great power blocs, and a series of crises among them reached a point of high tension in 1911. A confrontation between France and Germany over the North African Kingdom of Morocco brought the two imperial powers to the verge of war. The incident, which shook all Europe, awakened Spengler to a sweeping revelation. First, he saw massive war as both inevitable and imminent. Second, he understood the approaching conflict not as an isolated event but as part of a great historical change of phase marking the beginning of the end for the whole Western world. Finally, he believed that such wars were preordained as a natural part of a civilization's gradual breakdown.

The book he began was meant to be a limited political work entitled "Conservative and Liberal." He intended to focus on Germany in his alarm over the country's apparently careless foreign policy and the "blindness" and "criminal and suicidal optimism" he saw around him.[1] As the work developed, his broad interests and learning expanded its scope. The theme swelled from politics to the grand rhythms of human cultures. In 1912 he saw a book in a shop window about the decline of the ancient world. It inspired a new title for his own growing work: *Der Untergang des Abendlandes*, which translates literally as "The Going Under of the Evening Lands," or more faithfully to meaning as "The Sinking of the Western World." Spengler later wrote that he chose the title to counter the optimism of the period—to stress the "aspect of historical development . . . that nobody at that time was willing to see."[2] The "sinking" did not refer to a sudden cataclysmic end but rather a gradual decline as the civilization of the West completed a logical course through time. By 1914, when war erupted, the first draft of his book was done.

Spengler was called up for military service but was rejected because of a heart condition and acute nearsightedness. Meanwhile, the larger part of his funds, invested in foreign securities, stopped yielding income. Plunged into poverty, Spengler revised his manuscript with barely enough food and clothing and little heat in his lodgings. He long had suffered headaches that often grew to migraine intensity, and he endured them constantly while he wrote.

In 1917 the book was ready for publication. In the uncertain wartime business atmosphere, the large, erudite volume of historical philosophy that was difficult even for an educated person to read was rejected time and again. When it had made the rounds of most major publishers in Germany, Spengler turned to Vienna. There the book was accepted. A mere fifteen hundred copies were printed.

In the summer of 1918, only months before the German Empire collapsed, the ponderous work appeared in book shops. Six months later it was sold out. A second printing followed, then a third as the book was taken over by the old and venerable firm of C.H. Beck in Munich. By the mid-1920s, more than one hundred thousand copies of the first volume had been printed and a second volume was on its way to almost equal acceptance. Meanwhile, *The Decline of the West* was spreading around the world. Ultimately it was translated into English, French, and Spanish, Italian, Russian, and Arabic. "Never had a thick philosophical work had such a success," wrote a German commentator, "and in all reading circles, learned and uneducated, serious and snobbish."[3] Its success continued, the

Decline remaining one of the most enduring books of the twentieth century.

While World War I had nothing to do with the *Decline* except to delay its publication, the postwar atmosphere had everything to do with its unexpected popularity. Launched in a nation badly defeated, the book moved across a world sharply disillusioned in its hopes that civilization and mankind were evolving ever upward. In its gloom, confusion, and despair, the society was ready to receive a somber warning.

Spengler was catapulted from obscurity as an unknown scholar to the front ranks of the century's most influential social thinkers, a position he occupies to this day. Yet the attention he received was not always favorable. The *Decline* was praised but also condemned. In 1922 one authority on the work listed more than four hundred critics who had written commentaries about the first volume alone. The author was sufficiently affected by the reviews to rewrite and considerably modify the volume. Some of the harshest critics were academics. Spengler had little regard for professional intellectuals, and he made his feelings clear. They, in turn, attacked him and his book vehemently.

Actually, the *Decline* is a difficult work to criticize. Spengler's learning was so broad that few people were equipped to deal with more than a portion of the study. The work covers world history and politics, religion and language, mathematics, philosophy, and the arts, all the sciences, and some of the most abstruse categories of cultural thinking. All the same, both the author and his work invited argument. Though Spengler was vastly erudite, he was largely self-taught in many areas. He never held a university post nor did he have substantial academic standing. As a historian he was an amateur, untrained in the rigorous techniques of sifting materials that modern professional history requires.

By the criteria of modern scholarship, the *Decline* was too metaphysical, too dramatic, and often too poetic—criticisms that also had been leveled at Spengler's philosophical model, Nietzsche.

The author was faulted for being Teutonically oversure of himself, for boasting of a fresh vision that was not as original as he believed, for exaggeration, omission, repetitiveness, and a militaristic spirit. Yet often the same critics who condemned him for these things praised him for wide-ranging imagination, fascinating insights into historical relationships, and the resonant power of his prose at its best.

The avalanche of criticism failed to bury the *Decline*. With time, respected supporters began to emerge. The German academic figure Egon Friedell referred to Spengler as "perhaps the most powerful and vivid thinker to appear on German soil since Nietzsche."[4] The noted German historian of antiquity Eduard Meyer defended both Spengler's method of cultural comparison and his view of the present age as a period of artistic and institutional decline. "Consciously or unconsciously," Meyer wrote, "we are all oppressed by the feeling that we are decadents."[5]

Half way through the century, Harvard sociologist Pitirim A. Sorokin cited the *Decline* as "one of the most influential, controversial, and durable masterpieces of the first half of the twentieth century in the fields of social science, philosophy of history, and German philosophy."[6] And the biologist Ludwig von Bertalanffy, writing in his book *Robots, Men and Minds* almost half a century after the *Decline's* first appearance, remarked:

> The most important confirmation of any theory is in its predictions. This, then, leads to the question of our own position in history. Like it or not, make any objections you please against Spengler's intuitive and "unscientific" ways, his questionable conceptualizations, his metaphysics, dogmatism and militaristic spirit; the fact remains that his predictions, made fifty years ago and long before atomic war, the emergence of the USSR and China were even dreamt of, proved to be alarmingly correct.... It seems seldom realized that titles that have become popular slogans nowadays in American sociology, from Aldous Huxley's *Brave New World* and Orwell's *1984* to Ortega's *Revolt of the Masses*, Fromm's "sick society," Riesman's "other-directed

> man," Whyte's *Organization Man*, Hoffer's *True Believer*, are but variations on Spenglerian themes . . . . There is no use in glossing over reality with sociological, astronautical or genetic utopias. The "Decline of the West" is not a hypothesis or prophecy; it is an accomplished fact. . . .[7]

Spengler, with his financial position greatly improved, moved into an apartment overlooking Munich's Isar River and lined the walls of its three living rooms with books and a growing collection of paintings by minor Italian masters. He began to travel widely in Europe. Now in his forties, he quickly went bald and shaved his beard and mustache as well, leaving a face almost frighteningly austere with its thick eyebrows and huge dome of forehead. In spite of his forbidding appearance, personal acquaintances found him gentle and charming. His American publisher, Alfred Knopf, recorded that "he was always agreeable, friendly, and interesting . . . a big soft-spoken man with a pleasant, kindly voice." Mrs. Knopf judged him "an extremely human and considerate person—enormous in bulk, very forceful-looking, and—for a man of his stature—exceedingly easy to talk to."[8]

Generally Spengler shunned the company of fellow intellectuals, feeling more at home with common people in the Munich beer-hall atmosphere. His single close companion was a worshipful admirer employed as a reader with his German publishing house who, in later years, hearing of Spengler's death, threw himself under a tramcar.

The author, now practically a German institution, lectured all over his homeland. He was offered two university appointments, at Gottingen and Leipzig, but turned them down to concentrate on further writings. These, however, proved few and comparatively spare. He was preparing a large metaphysical work and doing a major study of the precivilized stage of social development, but only fragments appeared in print. He also engaged in politics, but here, too, his writings were not extensive. Adolf Hitler's National Socialist Party tried to gain his services as a propagandist. Spengler, who had a long meeting with Hitler in 1933, refused to aid the cause. He declared that what the national movement needed was a hero, not a heroic tenor. Eventually the Nazi government banned mention of Spengler's name in the press. During the last three years of his life, he existed under almost complete official boycott. He remained active, however, studying and publishing scholarly writings. In 1936, a few days before his fifty-sixth birthday, he died quietly in bed of a stroke.

His masterwork continues as a key to modern times, giving shape to a malaise that many people feel but few can express. Today only professional scholars, advanced students of history and the most literate of laymen read from start to finish through the thousand pages and more than half-million words that make up the *Decline*. Yet the work remains well known, enduring in what one scholar called "a kind of highly topical obscurity."[9] Nor is its topical value likely to diminish. Though the work is mainly an investigation of patterns in world history, it also credibly projects the course of Western civilization more than two hundred years beyond the twentieth century.

The Decline of the West

Spengler's study was not only history but also diagnosis and prophecy. It examines the ills of Western civilization, then predicts the culture's future with certainty. Spengler himself is seen as historian, seer of the present, and forecaster of times to come, as philosopher, political thinker, and sociologist. He also gained a following among anthropologists, notably Ruth Benedict, who modeled her classic *Patterns of Culture* about native American and South Pacific tribes on Spengler's cultural insights.

The *Decline* figures equally as a piece of modern literature. The style, though sometimes turgid and difficult, is often powerful and filled with vivid pictorial images. The author showed a fine talent for choosing personalities and incidents that bring the past to life.

In dealing with the present, the book serves as a synthesis and symbol of the age. Reflecting a society weary of upheavals, fearing more and worse catastrophes, and suspecting its own possible end, it anticipated the growingly pessimistic mood of the twentieth century.

As Henry Adams some years earlier had tried to turn history into a science on the order of physics and chemistry, Spengler approached it from the opposite direction. He dealt with the past in the manner of an artist, by intuition. He rejected the idea that history could be analyzed logically. Instead he sought to comprehend it as a gifted statesman inwardly perceives the present. "Sympathy, observation, comparison, immediate and inward certainty, intellectual *flair*," he cited, "*Now these are the means of historical research*—precisely these and no others."[10] He wished not to calculate but to see, not to dissect history but to live in it.

This intuitive approach probably led to the *Decline*'s unusual organization. Rather than proceeding from one thought to another, it leaps ahead in flashes of inspired understanding with little concern for conventional rules of deduction. The chapters seem at first to lack order. An opening chapter on mathematics is followed by several on metaphysics, which lead to chapters comparing various cultures of the world. The second volume is still more diverse, grouping chapters on the city, religious reformations, the state, money, and the machine with no apparent effort to construct a logical sequence. All the while the writing turns back to subjects discussed before, wandering in afterthought and repetition. As the study moves on, however, a logic of construction gradually comes into view. Some commentators have compared the *Decline* to a musical composition—a theme and variations played in complex counterpoint, not meant to be followed as an orderly sequence but instead experienced as a grand and balanced harmony.

Like Lasaulx, Danilevsky, Schubart, and Berdyaev, Spengler rejected the popular theory that humanity's past pursues a single straight line of steady upward progress. The division of historic periods into ancient, medieval, and modern—which assumes that present-day Western civilization is the highest point and the purpose of the past—he regarded as meaningless and egocentric. He did not believe, for example, that painting built steadily upon itself from the ancient Egyptians to the impressionists, nor social organization from the primitive lake dwellers to modern socialists, nor music from Homer to Wagner. World history is not "a sort of tapeworm industriously adding on to itself one epoch after another." Rather, it is "a picture of endless formations and transformations, of the marvelous waxing and waning of organic forms."[11] He saw all the high cultures of past and present as distinct and separate entities, no one more important than another.

In lieu of the historical chain Spengler substituted comparison, placing side by side in a universal history the eight high cultures he chose to examine. In doing so, he detected similarities in the way cultures develop, much as Ernst von Lasaulx had noted uniform progressions from mining through shepherding and on to art and science and from monarchy through aristocracy and democracy to military despotism. Spengler, however, saw many more relationships: in religion and philosophy, in science and the arts, in politics and social organization. He arranged these in a detailed pattern of rise and decline that he said applied to every high culture.

He believed this pattern was so consistent that knowledge of one culture could be used to plot the course of another. Long vanished epochs could be reconstructed by much the same method that paleontologists use when they infer the structure of prehistoric animals from single fragments of bone. By the same plan, the future of the Western, European-American civilization girdling the globe could be visualized long in advance of its unfolding.

In his scheme, the modern age, far from being the highest point on an ascending straight line, is a stage of development common to all aging cultures. Meanwhile, the future of the West is not an unlimited extension of its present ideals onward and upward for all time, but a strictly limited historical phenomenon covering a few centuries and predictable from known precedents. The culture is no different in character from those that have gone before it. And just as they passed away, so must the West decline and fall when its appointed time is fulfilled.

5

The High Cultures

CULTURES ARE ORGANISMS, Spengler declared. Each one has a life of its own, unique and real. This life goes on independent of the culture's human members, much as they have a higher life apart from the separate living cells that compose their bodies.

Spengler called his approach to cultures "morphological," a term borrowed from biology where it refers to a study of the form and structure of animals and plants. The idea of cultures as organisms, strange to many modern readers, is not new. Along with the theory that human history moves in cycles rather than in a straight line, it reaches back to antiquity in Greco-Roman, Hindu, and Chinese thought. In more recent times, Lasaulx saw organic processes in cultures. The Russian botanist Nikolai Danilevsky also approached human culture with a biological interpretation. Spengler's work only gave the idea renewed prominence. The enormous interest in his book, in fact, was the reason Danilevsky's *Russia and Europe* was revived and translated outside Russia almost half a century after its first publication.

Like all other organisms, Spengler maintained, cultures have fixed and predictable life cycles. They are born, they grow, they decay, and they die. More precisely, each culture passes through the phases of an individual person's existence, with a childhood, youth, maturity, and old age. The normal life expectancy of a culture is one thousand years. This, however, can vary considerably, just as humanity's three-score-and-ten can be cut short or extended.

So consistent are cultures one to another that their life phases have exactly the same duration. Every adolescence, every maturity, every period of decay takes an identical amount of time to occur. Nor does the similarity end there. In every culture, humankind's great creations appear, become fulfilled, and wane at the same stage of the culture's life span. This applies equally to religion, art, and politics, social life, science, economics, and other departments of culture.

To illustrate these consistencies more clearly, Spengler drew detailed charts comparing the various endeavors of humanity in several different cultures. According to the charts, architecture and painting reached peaks of development always at the same stage of every culture's life. So did mathematics, music, politics, and science. Towns always expanded into cities at precisely the same point on Spengler's graph. With equal regularity, feudal rulers vanished and democracy arose, followed by mobocracy, which in turn led to the kind of dictatorship practiced by the Roman Caesars.

Spengler's scheme was so detailed that even major events and personages could be matched from one culture to the next. Thus, Alexander the Great parallels Napoleon. The twentieth century's spate of fearsome wars is comparable to the social upheavals of the ancient Chinese "period of the Contending States" and the still earlier time when Semitic invaders known as Hyksos dominated Egypt in the second millennium before Christ. Projecting the parallel into the future, the first Roman Caesars will be matched by dictators in times soon to come.

While all cultures grow along the same basic pattern, each one possesses its own distinct identity: a personality, a style, and a singular soul that develops during the course of its life. The form this takes is determined by the way the culture views time and space. One of the German historian's most illuminating contributions to understanding cultures was his awareness that different societies think differently, that perception is not merely a matter of blank minds recording sensations. The most important way in which peoples of various cultures perceive the world separately, he explained, lies in their attitudes toward time and space—the two great categories of "extension."

Ancient Greeks, for example, saw both time and space as unextended—that is, as having bounds. Time, for them, meant primarily the present—like a point—and all-time was merely a series of such limited points. Likewise, space, for which the Greek language had no word equaling the modern Western concept of it, was felt to be similarly bounded and nonextended. Thus the Greek mentality imagined the universe as a corporeal vault, and beyond its limiting shell lay nothing.

Exactly opposed to the ancient Greek view is the Western idea of time and space: as unbounded, unlimited, infinitely extended. Seen from this viewpoint, time becomes enormous, a span of eternity. The universe, as well, becomes vast, limitless, infinite.

Still other cultures saw extension in their unique ways. Ancient Egyptians conceived of it as a long, straight path. Chinese culture pictured it as a wandering way. Societies originating in the Middle East, which Spengler lumped into a single encompassing culture, viewed it as a kind of cavern.

Each culture's unique idea of extension amounts to what the author called its 'prime symbol.' This symbol is chosen as the culture is born. Then, as a seed holds the pattern of a plant, the prime symbol determines the whole shape of the culture in every aspect of its growth. Like a master pattern, it touches every person who develops within the culture. It also finds expression in the culture's every endeavor. It gives its form to philosophy, religious cults and myths, to the governmental state, to ethical ideas, to painting, music, poetry, and drama, to the culture's special view of mathematics, and its fundamental notions of each science.

A prime symbol cannot be named or defined precisely. It can only be grasped by inner feelings, intuitively. Yet words can be helpful in evoking the necessary intuition. So with the proviso that intellectual concepts cannot represent the inconceivable, Spengler implied the prime symbols of several high cultures in words intended to be used as suggestions.

The prime symbol of ancient Greco-Roman culture he thought of as "the near, strictly limited, self-contained Body."[1] This finds a clear example in the freestanding nude Greek statue, while it also is reflected in the city-state's political organization, the concept of the atom as a miniature body and myriad other aspects of the culture.

The Middle Eastern culture, which Spengler named the Arabian, was shaped by a prime symbol that the author described as "the world as a Cavern."[2] This symbol is exemplified in church architecture of Middle Eastern origin, with its lofty domes and small ceiling windows filtering down beams of ethereal light.

The prime symbol of Western culture is "infinitely wide and infinitely profound three-dimensional Space."[3] Its influence is seen in the skyward striving of Gothic cathedrals and modern skyscrapers, in the urge to explore the world and probe the universe, in the infinite reach of modern communications.

The prime symbol of ancient Egypt, in line with its concept of extension, is best expressed as "way," or "path." Spengler relates that the Egyptians saw the soul resolutely moving down a narrow and inexorably prescribed path of life, to come at the end before judges of the dead. This one-directional way was exemplified in Egyptian architecture, in which the main element was not the single separate building but a rhythmically ordered sequence of spaces, proceeding down paths enclosed by mighty masonry, through passages and halls, arcaded courts and pillared rooms, all growing ever narrower and ultimately leading to the chamber of the dead.

Chinese culture, in accord with its idea of extension as a wandering way, took its shape from a prime symbol best expressed as "landscape." The Chinese way is not a narrow, straight path but a hither-and-thither way, and so the Chinese envisioned the soul's course through the world. This prime symbol is reflected clearly in the layout of the Chinese temple, which is not a self-contained building but a whole landscape of hills and water, trees, flowers, and stones. As the Egyptian was conducted to his god by walls of masonry, the Chinese are led on life's pilgrimage by friendly nature. Appropriately, their culture is the only one to elevate gardening to the level of a religious art.

One more prime symbol that Spengler pointed out is the Russian: "the plane without limit."[4] Its influence is hinted at in old Russian churches, their ground-hugging, hillocky roofs topped by little tentlike peaks all capped as if to suppress any further upward tendency. The prime symbol finds still clearer expression in Russian social attitudes submerging the personal ego in a horizontal brotherhood of man.

While each prime symbol guides its culture to a majestic unfolding as a unified whole, it also has a limiting effect. It tailors the culture to a unique and special pattern in all its ideas and creations. Thus, Spengler maintained, the history of humankind contains no one universal art or science, no continuous psychology, philosophy, or religion. Rather, history displays many separate expressions of each—exactly as many as there are prime symbols and high cultures.

None of these expressions are universally accepted, similarly understood, or identically interpreted everywhere at all times. In each culture, for example, the arts—architecture, sculpture, painting, music—are all distinctly different in character, predominance, composition, even in such details as prevalent colors and the type of portraiture practiced. Cultural variations continue in the matter of morality: Greco-Roman ethics have to do with attitude, Western apply to deeds, while other cultures practice ethics of compassion, of catharsis, of purgation, and liberation from ego, will, and individuality. Separate psychologies make it impossible for Western man to understand the Japanese. Nature knowledge—or natural science—differs as well from one culture to another, with no absolute physics or chemistry, but only unique forms of each that come, flourish, and pass along with their cultures. Even mathematics, the most abstract and eternal of the intellect's activities, are not universal and wholly cumulative, as commonly believed. There are as many mathematics as there are high cultures. Each civilization devises its own and has its unique understanding of what numbers mean.

Just as cultures are distinct, so did Spengler believe that they are largely isolated in separate compartments, neither transmittable to other societies nor genuinely influenced from the outside. A certain degree of borrowing is possible. But then it is not the lender who influences but the borrower who absorbs. And the acquisitions always are reshaped in the image of the receiver.

Thus, Roman law adopted in modern continental Europe is fundamentally different from the law that ancient Rome devised, which is demonstrated by several European countries with different Roman laws. Likewise, present understandings of Plato's philosophy are mainly misinterpretations of what Plato had in mind. And Christianity in modern Western culture, with its dogmas, rituals, hierarchy, and spirit, is not the same religion recognized by St. Paul and St. Augustine. Similarly, men of the Italian Renaissance did not revive Greco-Roman culture as they meant to do but only quarried from it for their own developing cultural edifice.

Yet, Spengler allowed, one culture can powerfully affect another, not in basic form but in the way the form develops. Growth can be speeded, hindered, or retarded. In fact, a culture can be killed by outside influence, as the Aztec civilization of Mexico was destroyed in the sixteenth century by assault from Western culture in the person of Hernando Cortez and his band of conquistadors. Other cultures have been misshapen by the weight of older neighbors lying massively over their land and preventing them from getting their breath and gaining self-awareness. As a case of this, Spengler cites modern Russia, a culture he saw as not yet fully born, which was stirred awake by its Western neighbor early in the eighteenth century and has suffered distortion ever since by the overwhelming pressure of Western ways. In contrast to the normal "morphosis" of cultural organisms, the author named this maldevelopment "pseudomorphosis." Yet even in this case the submerged culture is not transformed into another but retains its unique and individual form.

Not only are cultures more or less hermetically sealed against one another, they usually are also mutually incomprehensible. Each of the great cultures, Spengler said, has arrived at a secret interpretation of the world that is fully understandable only to people whose souls belong to that culture. Yet they are not entirely closed to the perception of outside observers. Intuitive thinkers sometimes can look into other cultures to a certain degree. Western man, with his far-reaching mind, is especially able to do so. Thus Spengler, and his readers who are gifted with this insight, could make excursions through the high cultures of history.

The author considered a culture to be a group of people who have made a spiritual commitment to a way of thinking, seeing, and living. The boundaries of their homelands, their physical races, their languages and religious faiths are irrelevant to that deeper unity. A culture, as a purely spiritual bond, is capable of containing an enormous diversity of peoples.

The eight high cultures that Spengler reviewed in *The Decline of the West* are not greatly different from the ten that Danilevsky examined. The disparity in their analyses lies mainly in classification—in how the various peoples and countries are grouped. For example, Danilevsky kept Greece and Rome separate, while Spengler combined them in a single culture that he called the Classical. Other cultures gaining his attention were the Babylonian, the ancient Egyptian, the Indian, and the Chinese. The Middle Eastern culture that he called the Arabian is his own original category. His list was completed with the Mayan-Aztec culture of pre-Columbian Mexico and the present Western culture of Europe and America.

As cultures are organisms, Spengler declared that world history is their biography. He did not deal equally, however, with all eight of the cultural characters in his sweeping saga. No one person could gain enough knowledge to portray the whole procession fully.

So bringing five of the cultures forward only now and then, he laid emphasis on three: the Classical, the Arabian, and the Western.

Classical Culture

The Greco-Roman culture that Spengler called the Classical lived its organic existence for somewhat more than one thousand years. Also designated throughout the *Decline* as the Apollinian culture—in reference to Apollo, god of light, music, poetry, and prophecy—it began in Greece around 1100 B.C. It was fading as a healthy and vital organism about the time of Julius Caesar and Christ.

With its here-and-now conception of space and time, the Classical culture ordered itself around the prime symbol that Spengler expressed as "the near, strictly limited, self-contained Body." The ideal example of this primary symbol—the freestanding nude Greek statue—is timeless, isolated, self-contained, standing wholly for itself, the perfect individual body. The rest of the culture's principal traits show equal aversion to distance and the movement of time, and are organized exclusively around the near and present—as so many separate bodies.

As the heavens were considered a physical vault ending with what could be seen of the sky, so was the home of the gods an actual physical place: the summit of Mount Olympus, the highest point in Greece, close to all and clearly to be seen. The gods themselves were bodily beings, not floating in the infinite but always nearby. They were seen as so present and localized that when a Greek left his country, traveling to Babylon or Egypt, he also left his space-bound gods behind and offered sacrifice to the deities of whatever place he was visiting. Religions, equally aligned with the cultural prime symbol, were not organized as universal faiths but rather in a vast number of separate bodies, or cults.

Also in accord with the symbol, Classical man looked upon his soul not as a spiritual entity but as a cosmos ordered in a group of parts. In the Greek conception of soul, will was entirely absent, probably for much the same reason that the concept of space was missing from Greek mathematics and the notion of force from Greek physics. The man of the Classical culture experienced his ego as *soma*—or body. He lacked any sense of personal unfolding or inner development. In place of inward character he substituted outward gesture.

The Classical person felt his home not as his entire country but only what was visible from the acropolis of the city where he lived, the corporeal ground upon which the city was built. Neither Plato nor Aristotle in their political writings were able to conceive of the ideal community in any other form but the *polis*—or city-state. This small, enclosed political unit was regarded as a body made up of the multiple bodies of its citizens. When the people gathered in the forum to exercise their political rights, they were a visible body in which every single body had its fellows nearby and constantly in sight. Spengler contrasts this with Western politics based upon the prime symbol of limitless space, in which mass communications take the place of the forum and the community is flung far and wide. In line with the Classical culture, Alexander the Great, whose conquests some three hundred years before Christ reached all the way from Greece to Egypt and India, originally planned his enormous empire not as a unified whole but as a sum of separate cities. Five hundred years later, the empire of Rome, even as the culture was fading, still retained a strong spirit of the near and small. One orator, Aristides, resoundingly declared that Rome had "brought together this world in the name of one city: wheresoever a man may be born in it, it is at its centre that he dwells."[5]

As the culture denied the distant and abstract, so did it lack a sense of duration. While Classical man dwelled in closed-off space, his existence was virtually timeless. He felt no continuous past or future. He lived every day and every hour for itself. All time was drowned in the present. This gave his life extraordinary intensity.

The culture had no clocks. Although sundials and water clocks had been in regular use in the older cultures of Babylonia and Egypt, Classical man had no need of them, since reckoning of time did not enter intimately into his everyday life. Nor did he have any real history. He regarded the past only as a chain of incidents—anecdotal, discontinuous, meaningless. He could not have understood present-day archaeology. Nor would it have occurred to him that a sheet of Plato's handwriting was a valuable relic, or that a fine edition of the dramas of Sophocles should be treasured away in the Acropolis. Classical writers composed brilliant accounts of contemporary events, but the distant past was transformed into myths, like the Homeric legends. One of the greatest Athenian historians, Thucydides, affirmed on the first page of his account of the Peloponnesian War between Athens and Sparta, which was fought in his time, that before then nothing of significance had happened. The wars with Persia a few decades earlier, during which the fate of Greece was threatened, already were too distant in time to matter anymore. Similarly, in the age of Aristotle, the loftiest period of Classical education, it was no longer known for a certainty if Leucippus, an important thinker of a century earlier, ever really had existed.

To the same extent, Classical man had no sense of the future. The oracle and augur foretold no distant future but dealt with particular questions of immediate bearing. Even in the matter of economics, the person of the culture lived without foresight, managing only from day to day. He thought of sources of income only when he felt a need for income, and then he drew upon them with no regard for possible future needs, even at the cost of destroying them entirely. Thus he often robbed the earth not only of its bounty but also of its capacities, while he squandered instantly any surplus. In every sense he let the future come without attempting to work on it in any way. Finally, at his death, his body was destroyed by burning, a negation of time by a means opposite to the mummification process that the Egyptian culture used to affirm time.

In the art of the Classical culture, not only the freestanding statue shows clear descent from the prime symbol "Body." To be sure, the statue accomplishes this especially well. The pure exterior lacks any personality and consequently stands detached from the viewer as a self-contained body allowing no relations. Yet the symbol can be sensed equally in Greek vase-painting, fresco, relief, architecture, drama, and dance.

Vase-painting, for example, was strongly two-dimensional, with almost no sense of depth. Nor did the scenes it depicted suggest time, no shadows showing the position of the sun, no heavens displaying stars.

As the statue was purely material, soulless body, so did the Doric temple emerge in a wholly externalized form. The Egyptians ranked columns inside a building to support the roof of a hall. The Greeks turned the architectural style inside out like a glove, placing all the columns on the exterior, leaving the interior no more than a simple cells large enough only for the statue of a deity. While the Gothic cathedral of Western culture soars, reaching for infinity, the Ionic temple hovers evenly in place. The cathedral's interior pulls upward with primeval force; the temple is laid down in majestic rest.

Classical drama, too, focused upon the bodily and external. The protagonists of the Greek playwrights Sophocles, Euripides, and Aeschylus do not unfold inwardly as a result of some kind of opposition, as principal characters in Western drama do. Rather, cast in situation tragedies, they simply endure the blind fate of the moment. Lack of inwardness was all the more intensified by stylized stage costuming, including stilt-like shoes, padded clothing, and masks.

Nature, in the eyes of Classical man, was a sum of well-ordered tangible things. Likewise, science concentrated upon matter and form. As the Greek philosopher speculated on the atom as a miniature body, so he believed optical vision to consist of the eye being penetrated by particles of the things seen. The culture's attitude toward science tended to be static and contemplative, as opposed to the Western tendency toward the active and experimental. Therefore, despite the brilliance of Classical culture, its technology was weak.

Its trireme ships were no more than glorified rowboats. Its battle catapults were not to be named in the same breath with the war engines of Assyria and China. People of the culture toyed with technical data but made no real effort to translate it to practical purposes. Spengler noted that even the steamship was discovered in principle in the Classical age, but it took the experimental, world-changing bent of Western culture to bring it to development.

In the matter of numbers, Classical man could think only in terms of the positive and concrete. His characteristic mathematics was Euclid's geometry, with its visibly limitable and tangible units—or bodies—concerned with timeless magnitudes, near and corporeal. The culture's legal system held a similar immediacy. It was a law of the day and even of the moment. Legislation covered individual cases, and once a case was settled, it thereafter ceased to be law.

Appropriately, money was thought of as magnitude, tangible, immediate, physical. Western culture's abstract bank draft would have seemed inconceivable to Classical man. The ideal form of money for the culture appeared about 650 B.C., simultaneously with the statue-body modeled in the round and the stone body of the Doric temple: a "money-body," a metal weight of beautifully impressed design—the coin. For a long time thereafter, all notions of income, capital, and debt meant not abstract figures but a sum of actual valuable objects in hand—a pile of coins. Wealth was thought to consist not of land or possessions but only of tangible, visible cash. And a man's accumulation of coins commonly was kept near his person at all times. Roman military leaders carried their entire fund of precious metal with them on campaign. Marcus Brutus and Caius Cassius, assassins of Julius Caesar, packed all the gold of Asia Minor on long mule trains to the battle of Philippi, where they were defeated by Caius Octavian and Marc Antony. One can imagine, Spengler remarked, what sort of economic operation the plunder of a camp after a battle must have been!

When Classical society expanded and ran short of precious metal, its eyes fell upon the slave—another kind of body which subsequently also was used as money. The great multitude of human beings held in bondage during the Roman age did not exist to work. Their laboring hours often were short, and many probably did not work at all. They were human stock, collected from near and far, accumulated, even loaned out in the manner of cash, and thus they answered their purpose.

In Spengler's view, the Romans were barbarians who took over Greek culture and carried it forward to its end. The beginning of that end arrived early in the Roman imperial age. By then, the Classical culture had been living for more than one thousand years. Around the time of Caesar and Christ, the Classical manner of thinking, feeling, and living was giving way to the dawn of the Middle Eastern culture that Spengler called the Arabian.

ARABIAN CULTURE

Spengler looked upon the broad Middle Eastern culture that he called the Arabian as his own discovery. "Its unity was suspected by late Arabians," he related in the *Decline*'s second volume, "but it has so entirely escaped Western historical research that not even a satisfactory name can be found for it."[6] He also referred to the culture as the Magian, after the Magi priestly caste of ancient Persia who reputedly were possessed of magic powers.

The culture took form in the broad realm of the ancient Babylonian civilization, heralded by the prophetic religions of Persians, Jews, and Chaldeans. It awoke in the decades just before the birth of Christ "in the countries between Nile and Tigris, Black Sea and South Arabia."[7] It encompassed Judaism, early Christianity, other monotheistic religions of the area, the Iranian and Syrian peoples, and the Byzantine Empire governed from Constantinople.

Yet, during the Arabian culture's first several centuries, the political power of Rome and the prestige of Greek thought stifled its spirit. The budding organism suffered what Spengler called 'pseudomorphosis,' a distorted growth in which the new way of cultural feeling could find its expression only by twisting established forms of society and art to its fresh purpose. So two ways of life dwelled side by side and intermingled: the fading civili-zation of the aged Classical world and the thwarted youth of the new Arabian culture.

Only when the Roman Empire was dead did the Magian world come into its own. In the seventh century after Christ, Islam arose in the Arabian Peninsula and washed like a tidal wave over the Middle East and across North Africa. As the true expression of the culture, it brought Magian areas and peoples at last into spiritual cohesion, also giving them the name Arab as their badge of nationality. The vital phase of this culture, by Spengler's reckoning, continued until about A.D. 1000.

The prime symbol that guided Arabian culture's unfolding can be hinted only vaguely in the language of Western man. Its best expression—the world as Cavern—does not define the plan on which the culture grew but can suggest the pattern of its unity. The man of Arabian culture felt both space and time as cavernlike. His Ptolemaic picture of the universe placed the earth at the center, surrounded by the cavernous dome of the heavens. By contrast, the modern Copernican system in which the earth loses itself in space would necessarily seem to Magian people crazy and frivolous.

Time had an equally vaultlike perspective. Rather than being restricted to the present as it was for Classical man, Magian time had both a beginning and an end. Religions of the culture, with their accounts of the world's creation and final cataclysm, express this idea vividly. Meanwhile, all events in the vault of time have a precise moment of their own, fixed and predetermined. This belief was the basis of Chaldean astrology, which presupposed all things to be written in the stars. It covered every occurrence, from the origins of the Savior to the smallest details of everyday life, in which the hurry of modern Western man would seem meaningless and unimaginable.

Life itself, to the Arabian soul, seemed like a mysterious cavern bathed in unearthly light whose rays could pierce but not dispel the surrounding darkness. "*The world of Magian mankind is filled with a fairy-tale feeling,*" Spengler asserted. "Devils and evil spirits threaten man; angels and fairies protect him. There are amulets and talismans, mysterious lands, cities, buildings, and beings, secret letters, Solomon's Seal, the Philosophers' Stone. And over all this is poured the quivering cavern-light that the spectral darkness ever threatens to swallow up."[8]

The contrast between light and darkness is central to the culture's religious view of unremitting struggle between the forces of good and evil. The battle rages equally in Persian Zoroastrianism between Ahura Mazda and Angra Mainyu, in Judaism between Yahweh and Beelzebub, in the Manichaen religion of Roman imperial times between spiritual good and evil, in Christianity between Jesus and the devil, in Mohammedanism between Allah and Eblis. Man enters this struggle at its center. For his success, the systematic reasoning of Greeks and Romans is so much useless vanity. Will, the mainstay of Western man, does not exist, replaced by resignation as expressed in the Arabic word "Islam"—or submission. Only mystical potency counts, like the substantial divine grace written of by St. Augustine some four hundred years after the birth of Christ. Meanwhile, the home of God for the Arabian culture is not a nearby mountaintop as for ancient Greeks but a distant Paradise, a magic garden somewhere in the universe.

The Magian concept of nation and home had nothing to do with geography. Among Jews, early Christians, Mohammedans, the nation was the community of cobelievers. They might look to a spiritual center—Jerusalem or Mecca—but they were bound to no specific plot of land. As Classical man belonged to his nation by virtue of citizenship, Magian peoples were linked by sacraments—circumcision for the Jews, specific forms of baptism for Persian Mandaeans and Christians. The unity of those who know the way to salvation is expressed in the Arabic word "*ijma*"—or consensus.

Ultimately, the Magian community includes the whole world-cavern, the here and the beyond, the believers and the good angels and spirits, while the political state is only a small unit of the visible part. Civil and ecclesiastical law thus become identical, a fact that makes separation of church and state in the Magian mind so much impossible nonsense.

As Classical man could not conceive of universal history, for Magian culture, both past and future are a great cosmic drama of the struggle between good and evil, God and the devil, with its culmination in the coming of the Savior.

The cavern-feeling entered strongly into Magian architecture. As the Doric temple was all exterior, religious buildings of the Arabian culture are entirely interiorized, whether the cavelike basilica of Christianity, the Mazdaist fire-temple, or the Moslem mosque. In the central dome the Magian form achieved its purest expression. The sense of closed-in space is emphasized by sparkling golden mosaics and arabesque ornamentation perfusing the cavern in the unreal, fairytale light that Westerners find so seductive in Moorish art.

The Arabian scientist was no mere contemplator, as the Greek, but an active seeker as well. He did not seek, however, as Western man does, for means of directing the world according to his will. Instead, as alchemist, he looked for magical ways to possess himself of nature's treasures without effort. As the idea of matter and form belonged especially to Classical science, the notion of substances with invisible or secret attributes is the creation of Arabian culture. Even vision, which for Classical man was effected by corporeal particles and for Western man is the detection of a force, was for Arabian thought the result of colors and shapes being conveyed in a magic and "spiritual" way to a seeing-power substance resident in the eyeball.

Early Greeks, who were able to think only in numbers that were positive and concrete, could not have stated anything about an undefined number *a* or an undenominated number three. Algebra, with its magical quality of unknown, indefinite, and negative numbers, would have been incomprehensible to the Classical mind. It was a Magian creation.

Though algebra advanced into Magian thought through a Greek named Diophantus, he was working in the third century after Christ, when the Classical feeling was giving way in every field to the strengthening young Arabian culture. Some seven centuries later, around the year 1000, this culture, well ripened and matured, also was fading, while a new one was coming into being in the colder lands to the north.

Western Culture

For Spengler, the history of Western culture does not begin, as some historians have accepted, with the political collapse of Rome in A.D. 476. He sees the five dark centuries of chaotic barbarian struggles that followed as a primitive precultural time. Only around the year 900 did the new cultural organism emerge in clear and vigorous form.

Many developments signaled it. Central Europe came together in the Germanic imperial union of the Holy Roman Empire. The social and economic system of feudalism solidified. The medieval architecture called Romanesque appeared. By the turn of the millennium, tribal peoples known as Franks, Lombards, and Visigoths were beginning to think of themselves, in the culture's characteristic style of nationhood, as Germans, Italians, Spaniards, and Frenchmen.

The culture that grew and flourished in Europe and today reaches around the world Spengler also called the Faustian. This referred to the restlessly striving Dr. Faust of German legend, whose limitless ambition led him to sell his soul to the devil for knowledge, youth, and magical powers.

In accord with the conception of time and space as unbounded, unlimited, infinite, the culture unfolded around its prime symbol of pure and limitless space. As the upward-striving Gothic cathedral powerfully exemplifies this symbol, its influence appears everywhere in the culture's development: in the modern skyscraper, in city streets laid out as straight as arrow flights into remote distances, in the sport of mountain climbing that leaves human beings alone with limitless space, in machines that produce ever more and move ever faster.

"It is the Western world-feeling," Spengler wrote, "that has produced the idea of a limitless universe of space—a space of infinite star-systems and distances that far transcends all optical possibilities—and this was a creation of the *inner* vision, incapable of all actualization through the eye, and, even as an idea, alien to and unachievable by the men of a differently-disposed Culture."[9] Arriving at this view of the universe was less a matter of discovering right facts than being able to think in a way that accepts infinity.

The word "God" rings otherwise for Western man than for people of the Classical and Arabian cultures. The Deity is not a bodily being atop a bodily mountain, nor even the stern giver of laws and powerful protector perceived by the Jews. The Western view of God evolved while the culture itself developed: from the personally present, caring, mild Father known to Gothic man, to an impersonal principle, intangible, unimaginable, working mysteriously in the infinite. "From the later days of the Renaissance onward, the notion of God has steadily approximated, in the spirit of every man of high significance, to the idea of pure endless Space."[10]

As God is seen in the West as the Infinite All, so was the old Nordic Valhalla a characteristic Western afterworld. This "hall of the slain" is located nowhere, floating in dim, remote regions, lost in the limitless, the supreme symbol of solitude with its inharmonious gods and lonely heroes.

While Christianity became a different religion for Western man from what it was for Magian peoples, the concept of the soul also was adapted to the context of the culture. For Magian man, the soul was a mysterious substance permeating the body that received the mysterious divine substance of Spirit from above. For Classical man, it was, in the last analysis, the form of his own body. For Western man, the body is the vessel of the soul, which is something inner, introspective, infinite. It also is functional throughout: it thinks, it feels, and, most outstandingly, it wills.

The power of will, which is denied in both the Classical and Indian images of the soul and relinquished in the Arabian, emerges in Western culture from the idea of time as infinite extension; will for the West has the function of linking present to future. Nowhere has the problem of free will been meditated upon more deeply or more painfully than in Western lands. Other cultures simply have not known it. To be able to will freely is the principal gift that the Western soul asks of heaven. Accordingly, the "I", the first-person, stands alone as an individual, supreme within the culture. Life becomes "fulfillment of an 'I', ethical work upon an 'I', justification of an 'I' by faith and works; respect of the neighbour 'Thou' for the sake of one's 'I' and its happiness; and, lastly and supremely, immortality of the 'I'."[11]

The Western sense of home characteristically extends far in both time and space. Even before the idea of a fatherland arose, Western communities united themselves under dynasties, feeling bound together not by place or consensus but by history. When nations came together in the culture, they were vast—considering their day and means of communication—and unparalleled in any other culture. The fatherland itself is an impalpable unity of nature, speech, climate, habits, and history—not soil but country, a region with boundaries that the individual citizen probably never has seen but nonetheless will defend and die for.

Ultimately, the West's bent toward extension—political, economic, and spiritual—was so overpowering that it overrode all geographical bounds. With no practical objective, merely for symbolic value, it strove to reach the North and South Poles. Eventually it transformed the whole world into a single colonial and economic system.

No other culture has been so deeply conscious of time and history, not even the Chinese of the Chou dynasty in the first millennium before Christ, which had a highly developed sense of eras and epochs. The Indian peoples, like the Classical, tended to live in denial of time. They had no clocks, no pure Indian astronomy, no calendar, and, therefore, no history, as far as history is the record of a conscious spiritual evolution. By contrast, Egyptian culture was acutely sensitive to the past. While not even the names of the Dorian kings of ancient Greece survive, the Egyptians preserved their history in memorials of stone and hieroglyph so purposefully that four thousand years later modern people not only can determine the names and order of their kings but also can look upon still-recognizable royal features in museums.

Western man in many regards surpasses the historical sense of the Egyptians. He knows the exact date of birth and death of every great person since the thirteenth century. His museums store up everything available representing the past. He excels in archaeology and the study of history as no other people ever have done. Meanwhile, he conceives of history dynamically, as a tense unfolding toward an aim, a linear and progressive climb leading to a goal that can be interpreted either in secular terms as an evolution toward perfection or in Christian terms as a movement toward an ultimate City of God.

In Classical and Indian cultures, centuries scarcely counted. In the West, years, hours, even minutes hold importance, a fact the Greeks and Indians of old could not have comprehended. The birth of Western culture appropriately coincided with the invention of the mechanical wheel-clock. From the year 1200 onward, clocks have been appearing on towers and belfries all over the Western landscape, ticking away the minutes day and night in a superlative expression of the culture's acute sense of time.

Printing and gunpowder belong together as two means of Western distance tactics. Both appeared at the highest point of the Gothic Age. The Reformation a century later witnessed the first fly sheets, or handbills, and the first field guns. The French Revolution brought the first tempest of pamphlets in 1788 and the first mass-fire of artillery at the village of Valmy in 1792. Since then, the printed word, produced in vast quantities and distributed over enormous areas, has paralleled explosives as an uncanny weapon. Under verbal bombardment, the intellect is so cowed that hardly anyone can gain the inner detachment necessary for clarity of mind. Thus, ironically, the abolition of censorship is linked to the most thoroughgoing slavery that ever existed. Meanwhile, the printed book is emblematic of time-infinity, and the journalistic press, of space-infinity. It follows that the West is *par excellence* a reading and writing culture.

The typical forms of Western literature are the biography and the novel that later grew out of it. Both are dynamic accounts of unfolding lives. Similarly, Western drama, unlike the Classical, pursues an inexorable logic of human becoming, of personal development. Meanwhile, Western tragic literary figures—Siegfried, Parsifal, Tristan, Hamlet, Faust—tend to be solitary, at odds with their gods and themselves, the loneliest heroes in the universe.

Spengler saw architecture as the basic art of each culture. He also perceived in religious buildings the spiritual attitude of the people who created them. For these reasons he considered the Gothic cathedral as a perfect expression of Western culture's straining upward and outward toward infinite space. The very size of churches in rural England, he noted, led one modern observer to theorize that the country must have been more populous in medieval times than in more recent days. The cathedral's exterior strives skyward in pointed arches and soaring steeples. Inside, the entire design fulfills the idea of infinite space, with upward-thrusting vaults and broad expanses of bodiless stained-glass windows that express an urge to burst forth into the boundless.

While Gothic architecture was developing as a clear expression of Western man, painting lagged behind under the influence of the old Magian tradition with its stylized human figures and solid golden backgrounds. Not until the thirteenth century did the conventional

Byzantine style begin to give way in European art. With the work of the Florentine painter Giovanni Cimabue and his noteworthy pupil Giotto, a naturalistic manner appeared with lifelike, expressive faces and the illusion of movement. From then on, painting, like literature, developed in a biographical style more appropriate to the time-feeling of the culture, the personal portrait rendering a whole lifetime in an instant. With the discovery of depth perspective, the Western space-feeling also entered pictures, backgrounds becoming distant horizons while blue-green heavens reached to infinity.

Sculpture, at the close of the Renaissance, fell out of the culture as a great art. Its intractable material could not express the Western spirit adequately. In the same way, painting, from about 1700, yielded its predominant place to instrumental music. Far more readily could music relate the contemplative vision of pure space with, as Spengler described, "bodiless realms of tone, tone-intervals, tone-seas. The orchestra swells, breaks, and ebbs, it depicts distances, lights, shadows, storms, driving clouds, lightning flashes, colours etherealized and transcendent—think of the instrumentation of Gluck and Beethoven." And finally, in the middle of the nineteenth century, "in the lonely, utterly infinitesimal tone-world" of Richard Wagner's opera *Tristan und Isolde*, musical form "frees itself from all earthly comprehensibleness. This prime feeling of a loosing . . . of the Soul in the Infinite, of a liberation from all material heaviness which the highest moments of our music always awaken, sets free also the energy of depth that is in the Faustian soul."[12]

As Classical money was static and material, money in Western culture is regarded in terms of function and force. Its creation is not the product of mining and minting but of organizing and energizing economic life. Its value lies not in its mere existence but in its effect. Money is transformed into force, and its quantity determines the intensity of its working influence. As the Classical money-symbol was the coin, the Western is the bank draft—abstract, insubstantial, reaching into distant areas.

"Our whole life is disposed dynamically, not statically," Spengler reiterated, "therefore our essentials are forces and performances, relations and capacities—organizing talents and intuitive intellects, credit, ideas, methods, energy-sources—and not mere existence of corporeal things."[13] Classical culture presents a minimum of organization, Western a maximum. Classical man, interested only in piling up tangible cash, never thought of expanding and intensifying his economic existence. Western man does this all the time through the use of credit. His thinking in money generates money. "When an organizing magnate writes down a million on paper, that million exists, for the personality as an economic centre vouches for a corresponding heightening of the economic energy."[14] Throughout Western culture, the credit of a country depends not upon any quantity of gold or silver it possesses but upon its economic capacity and political organization.

The metal coins that exist within Western culture do so only as fossils, a form carried over from Classical culture and ill-fitting. As a consequence, Western man behaves toward them much as ancient Egyptians did. Nothing resembling the coin existed in the culture of Egypt; written transfers were considered entirely sufficient. When Classical coins filtered into the country after 650 B.C., they usually were cut into pieces and reckoned by weight in the manner of wares. Similarly, precious metal coins in Western culture have been used not genuinely as money representing the standard of value but as merchandise that fluctuates in money-value. They have a price relative to national credit: the poorer a nation's credit, the higher the price of the metal.

As Western money-thinking tends toward the abstract and dynamic, so does the culture's mathematical creativity. To Classical man numbers meant magnitude; to Western man they mean relation. The mathematics of the Greeks dealt with concrete numbers; that of the West deals with functions and functional analysis. While Classical culture invented Euclidean geometry, which was a purely static mathematics of measure and tangible units, or bodies; and

Magian culture developed algebra, which held a magical quality in its unknown, indefinite, and negative numbers; so Western culture produced the calculus, which is essentially the mathematics of motion.

"The history of Western knowledge," wrote Spengler, is "one of *progressive emancipation* from Classical thought, an emancipation never willed but enforced in the depths of the unconscious. *And so the development of the new mathematics consists of a secret and finally victorious battle against the notion of magnitude.*"[15] The appearance in the nineteenth century of the non-Euclidean geometries of Karl Gauss and Georg Riemann represented a significant step in this direction. And the conception of multidimensional space that led to Einstein's theory of relativity was a culmination in the breakaway of Western mathematical thought from inherited Classical forms. Ultimately for Western culture, in accord with its prime symbol, "Numbers are images of the perfectly desensualized understanding, of pure thought, and contain their abstract validity within themselves."[16]

As the conception of matter and form belongs to the Classical view of nature, and the notion of substances with visible or secret attributes to the Magian, in Western natural science the concepts of force and mass arise. Typically, modern physics dissolves the material world into bodiless energy in the limitless void of space-time.

As Classical scientific theory was a quiet contemplation, and Magian a silent knowledge of alchemy, Western is from the outset a working hypothesis—"the very kind of thought-product," Spengler remarked, "that is meaningless to other Cultures. It is an astounding fact . . . that the idea of immediately exploiting in practice any knowledge of natural relations that may be acquired is alien to every sort of mankind except the Faustian (and those who, like Japanese, Jews, and Russians, have to-day come under the intellectual spell of its Civilization)."[17] The view that knowledge is virtue is common to many cultures, but the phrase "knowledge is power" holds meaning only to the European-American mentality.

The Western inventor and discoverer also is unique. "The primitive force of his will, the brilliance of his visions, the steely energy of his practical ponderings, must appear queer and incomprehensible to anyone at the standpoint of another Culture, but for us they are in the blood. Our whole Culture has a discoverer's soul."[18] Equally extraordinary is Western technology, which has altered the face of the earth and will leave behind traces and scars of its heyday when all else of the culture is lost and forgotten.

"This is the outward- and upward-straining life-feeling—true descendant, therefore, of the Gothic—as expressed in Goethe's Faust monologue when the steam-engine was yet young. The intoxicated soul wills to fly above space and time. An ineffable longing tempts him to indefinable horizons. Man would free himself from the earth, rise into the infinite, leave the bonds of the body, and circle in the universe of space amongst the stars."[19]

6

Culture and Civilization

Often the words "culture" and "civilization" are used interchangeably. But Oswald Spengler gave them separate definitions. Using a capital "C" for both, he employed them as special terms designating different phases in an advanced society's development.

His distinction between Culture and Civilization originally was made by the German philosopher Nietzsche. It assigns to Culture a society's period of growth, of creative activity. In Spengler's terms, this means its childhood, youth, and maturity—or spring, summer, and autumn. Civilization is the society's late and final period, its old age, its winter, its phase of declining and failing.

The time of Culture is the period of achievement. Civilization is the period when the accomplishments of Culture are elaborated theoretically, an age of tying things up, rounding them off, the fulfillment before demise. The thing-becoming is succeeded by the thing-become. Expansion is followed by rigidity, life by death.

The Culture phase is the organic period with a normal life expectancy of one thousand years. The Civilization stage can drag on for centuries longer, even for millennia.

Both stages in the history of advanced societies are, according to Spengler, natural, normal, and inevitable.

THE CULTURE PHASE

Primeval man is a ranging animal, keen and anxious in his senses, ever alert to hostile elements of nature. As hunter and shepherd, he is a plunderer of nature. With the advent of agriculture, man undergoes a deep transformation. He who digs and plows is seeking no longer to plunder but only to alter, not to take but to produce. In the act of settling on his personal plot of soil, man becomes a plantlike being—a peasant, rooted to the ground that he tills. What before was to him hostile nature now is mother earth.

So lives man of the pre-Cultural period. He possesses no history, beyond a collection of legends and sagas. He has no state, no politics, no social classes, no masses. His existence, in blood-related tribes under chieftains, is formless. Life in this condition is no more than an endless, meaningless repetition of births, struggles, and deaths. It is experienced as "just the zoological up-and-down, a planless happening without goal or cadenced march in time, wherein occurrences are many, but, in the last analysis, devoid of significance."[1]

Why, from the vast ocean of pre-Cultural peoples, does the rare and infrequent high Culture arise? Spengler states simply that the matter is a mystery not to be explained by any why or wherefore, a cosmic event like the coming of a glacial age. We know only that Cultures did indeed begin: in Egypt and Babylon around 3000 B.C.; in India about 1500 B.C.; a century later in China; around 1100 B.C. in Greece; about A.D. 1 for the Middle Eastern Magian Culture; in Western Europe around A.D. 900.

"A Culture is born," Spengler related, "in the moment when a great soul awakens out of the proto-spirituality of ever-childish humanity, and detaches itself, a form from the formless, a bounded and mortal thing from the boundless and enduring."[2] Every Culture begins in the countryside with an ordering of the common life under feudalism. At the same time, the grand architectural forms—the pyramid, the cathedral—appear on the landscape. The idea of feudalism, which has dominated all Cultural springtimes, amounts to a transition from the primitive, purely practical relationship of ruler and those who obey to a private-law relation of lord and vassal. This new affiliation rests upon an ethic of nobility, honor, and loyalty.

The peasant is not essentially part of the Culture. He is, rather, the eternal man, preceding Culture, outliving it, propagating himself from one generation to the next, limited to the soil. A dumb creature, yet possessed of dry, shrewd understanding that sticks to practical matters, he remains independent of Culture and history. He is the origin of the blood that later makes world history in the cities, and events occasionally spill his blood, but never is his inward being altered.

All effectual history begins with the primary classes, or estates—the nobility and the priesthood—forming themselves and rising above the peasantry. This separation is not based upon possessions, nor power, nor calling, nor upon any logic. Its nature is metaphysical. As an early Gothic rhyme put it:

God hath shapen lives three,
Boor and knight and priest they be.[3]

The noble of the castle is a man of hard facts, the priest of the cathedral, one of truths. The first possesses shrewdness, the second, knowledge. The one is a doer, the other a thinker. The nobility symbolizes time, the priesthood, space.

In this period, social powers are preestablished and God-given. The noble and the priest are unquestioned and beyond all criticism. Their standing imposes self-respect and also the sternest self-discipline, to the point of death if need be. They act intuitively, inspired by a sense of vocation and obligation, and their leading is surefooted and creative. Their actions, even when these involve fierce struggles, spring from a spiritual source and work to translate ideals into living realities.

The ideals of the Cultural springtime arise from religion and chivalry. The social and economic values are agrarian. The village, with its hillocky roofs and evening smoke, its wells, hedges, and beasts, lies completely fused and embedded into the countryside. Towns are still no more than peasant houses gathered around a market or crowded in the shadow of a castle or cathedral.

But gradually people of the early Culture gravitate more to the towns. To the pre-Culture man these are bizarre creations—masses of wood and stone strangely teeming with population. So deeply uneasy does he feel about them that Germanic tribesmen on the Rhine and the Danube settled only at the gates of dead Roman cities, leaving them uninhabited. Yet, what the cottage is to the peasant, the town is to Culture-man, whose history is one of growing urbanization. His politics, religion, arts, and sciences all reside within it. So, ultimately, the town takes on a spirit of its own. No longer is it a mere marketing place for the country but a higher entity that sees the country as its environs. Meanwhile, as the Culture matures, patriarchal feudalism undergoes a crisis and dissolves, replaced by the aristocratic state.

In the advancing years of the Culture phase, the state as a means of government develops and acquires strict form. In such periods, Middle Kingdom Egypt organized its centralized bureaucracy-state; ancient Greece crystallized the city-state; and Western Europe fashioned well-developed nation-states under powerful family dynasties.

In the same period, a new social class emerges: the townsman, the burgher, the bourgeois. As this third estate gains importance, its members look down on the old primary estates—"the squire" and "the parson"—as historically backward and intellectually inferior. They disdain the pristine land-economy that persists outside the town walls. They feel contempt for the countryside in general, which lies dull and unaltered, while they sense themselves to be more awake, freer, and therefore further advanced along the Culture's road.

The city, growing larger and more important, begins to defy the landscape. It contradicts nature with its silhouette of pinnacles, spires, cupolas, and high-pitched gables, which neither are nor wish to be related to anything natural. The city wants to be different from nature, something higher. The country, in the meantime, glares sulkily at the man-made creation, distrusting its intellectualized existence.

As the city breaks free of the land, religious reformation bursts forth and strives to restore spiritual faith to the purity of its early days. "In no Culture is this movement missing," Spengler stated. It occurred in ancient Egypt and in the Culture phase of ancient India. It appeared in the Greek Orphic movement of the seventh century B.C. Likewise, in Western Culture it arose with Martin Luther and the Protestant Reformation. Also, by deduction, in line with Spengler's pattern, "in the ninth century [B.C.] a corresponding epochal point must have occurred in the religious history of China," however unknown to recorded history.[4]

The closer a Culture approaches its culmination, the more virile, austere, and controlled is the structure of forms it creates for itself—forms in statecraft, in the arts, in diplomacy, in social manners. And the more assured grows its awareness of ripened creative power. Every trait of its expression is deliberate, strict, measured, marvelous in ease and self-confidence. This is illustrated equally by the sculpture of Egypt from the nineteenth century B.C., the architecture of the Magian church of Santa Sophia built in Constantinople in the sixth century A.D., and the paintings of the sixteenth-century Venetian artist Titian.

In Greece of the sixth century B.C., the philosopher-prophet Pythagoras became the center of a widespread religious brotherhood dedicated to the moral reform of society. Among the results of that Culture's puritanical enthusiasm was the destruction of the Greek colony of Sybaris in Italy, famed for wealth, luxury, and "sybaritic" living.

According to Spengler, the parallel period in the Middle Eastern Magian Culture erupted with the appearance of Mohammed and the rise of Islam in the seventh century A.D. "It is incident, and no more, that the Puritan movement for which the Magian world was ripe proceeded from a man of Mecca and not from a Monophysite [Christian] or a Jew," the author declared. Thus, he sees Islam as the puritanism of the whole group of early Middle Eastern religions. Only formally was it a new faith, while actually it was a heretical form of Eastern Christianity, as indeed it originally was regarded. "At most Islam was a new religion only to the same extent as Lutheranism was one. Actually, it was the prolongation of the great early religions. Equally, its expansion was not (as is even now imagined) a 'migration of peoples' proceeding from the Arabian Peninsula, but an onslaught of enthusiastic believers, which like an avalanche bore along with it Christians, Jews, and Mazdaists and set them at once in its front rank as fanatical Moslems. . . . The enemy of yesterday became the front-rank comrade of tomorrow."[5]

Western Culture saw its Puritanism rise up in the seventeenth century with the army of Oliver Cromwell, riding psalm-singing into battle against the forces of England's ill-fated King Charles I. Like Sybaris all over again, Shakespeare's "Merrie England" was annihilated in the span of a few years. And during the course of the century, more than a million witches were burned, alike in the Protestant north, the Catholic south, and communities in America and India. In every time and place, the late-Culture Puritan movement proved deadly earnest, sour, and pedantically intellectual. Always it lacked the profound joy, the humor of life, the quiet blissfulness found in springtime religions.

The later days of a Culture also witness geographical expansion of its power and influence. The superlative example of this was the imperialistic growth of the infinitely reaching Western Culture. Possibly the hardy voyages of the Vikings foreshadowed the West's special inclination to range far and wide. In any case, the Culture's expansion began vigorously with the Portuguese and Spanish of the fifteenth century and proceeded rapidly until people of the West girdled the globe and carried their power and ways to its most remote corners.

As a Culture enters its autumn, the state form of government rises to a climax with absolutist rule: the strict central power of XIIth-Dynasty Egypt; the eighteenth-century reign of King Frederick the Great as "benevolent despot" of Prussia; France's "Sun King," Louis XIV, who is said to have declared, "I am the state."

Shortly afterward the state form breaks up. Egypt at this stage suffered revolts and military government beginning in the eighteenth century B.C. Similarly, Greece slid into revolution in the fourth century B.C. The West experienced milestone revolutions in eighteenth-century France and America. The breakup is accompanied by dramatic military exploits, like those of Alexander the Great of ancient Greece and Napoleon in Europe twenty-one centuries later.

As the Culture phase reaches its end, the city has grown to dominate the countryside. Old agrarian values have given way to urban values. Blood ties, once important, now carry little consequence. Tradition and the sly shrewdness of the countryside have succumbed to city intellectualism. The influence of the privileged classes yields to "the people" and democracy. The power of landed property withers, superseded by the growing dictatorship of abstract money. The society is ready to enter its wintertime: the phase of Civilization.

The Civilization Phase

Civilization, as Spengler used the word, is the inevitable destiny of an advanced society, its last, most external and artificial condition. Once a Culture's aim is attained—its idea, its entire content of inner possibilities fulfilled and made actual—it suddenly hardens. It mortifies. Its blood congeals. Its creative force breaks down. The fire in the soul dies. Life is fatigued. The society experiences no more fullness but, instead, inward poverty, coldness, emptiness, an intellectual chill and void. Values built up and maintained within the Culture begin to fall away. A sweeping transvaluation, a rejection, a persistent nihilism remolds all the old forms, understands them otherwise, practices them in different ways. The society begets no more but only reinterprets—and therein lies the negative mood common to all such periods, whether the age of the Buddha in India, of Socrates in Greece, or of Rousseau, Schopenhauer, Nietzsche, and Wagner in Western society.

Everything begins to change. Religion of the heart yields to dead, abstract metaphysics or scientific irreligion. Reverence for tradition and respect for age vanish in cold, matter-of-fact practicality. Patriotism diminishes and internationalism increases, while home, race, and fatherland give way to a cosmopolitan outlook. The economic base of the fruitful earth is abandoned in favor of money. Quality succumbs to quantity, appeals for the best giving way to appeals for the most. Concern for creativity and growth is displaced by concern for comfort and luxury. Hard-earned rights are replaced by natural rights. The folk becomes the mass. Motherhood is replaced by sexuality. Social unity crumbles in social divisiveness. Ideals lose their power, and all further strivings are no more than struggles for animal advantage.

In the Culture time, life is lived as something self-evident, hardly a matter of consciousness, or it is accepted as God-willed destiny. In the Civilization stage, life becomes a problem, to be dealt with by the intellect according to "rational" or "utilitarian" criteria. The soul has abdicated and the brain rules in its place.

As the pre-Culture period was a formless time, and as people of the Culture phase lived by a sure and innate sense of style and form, the onset of Civilization sees all forms beginning to disappear again. To Doric and Gothic men, Ionic and baroque men, the whole vast structure of Cultural form—in religion, art, government, custom, knowledge, social life—came easily and instinctively. They carried it lightly, put it into practice intuitively. They had the same unstrained mastery over their Culture that Mozart enjoyed over music. With the coming of Civilization, the same forms begin to feel strange. People no longer master them but, instead, feel enslaved by them. The idea arises that forms must be overhauled or thrown off for the sake of creative freedom. Thus do they begin to disintegrate. The Civilization phase, as a historical process, consists in a progressive taking-down of forms that have become inorganic or dead. Increasingly, events cease to be predictable on the basis of form, and life is given over to incident, accident, and arbitrariness. The society returns to the formlessness of the pre-Culture time.

Early in the gray dawn of Civilization, the society also falls into a period of violent social upheaval and vicious warfare. Ancient Egypt entered its Civilization phase about 1800 B.C. A contemporary manuscript known as the Leiden Papyrus describes the conditions that ensued:

> The higher officials are displaced, the land robbed of its royalty by a few madmen, and the counsellors of the old state pay their court to upstarts; administration has ceased, documents are destroyed, all social differences abolished, the courts fallen into the hands of the mob. The noble classes go hungry and in rags, their children are battered on the wall, and their mummies torn from the grave. Mean fellows become rich and swagger in the palaces on the strength of the herds and ships that they have taken from their rightful owners. Former slave-girls become insolent and aliens lord it. Robbery and murder rule, cities are laid waste, public buildings burned down. The harvest diminishes, no one thinks now of cleanliness, births are few—and oh, that mankind might cease![6]

Chinese historians have named their parallel time, from 480 to 230 B.C., the "Period of the Contending States." It culminated with a century of unbroken warfare between mass-armies accompanied by frightful social upheavals.

For the Classical world, the Civilization phase arrived in the fourth century B.C., as Greek soul gave way to Roman intellect. Its period of contending states began when great powers were defined by two battles: that of Ipsus in Asia Minor in 301 B.C. between the generals succeeding Alexander the Great; and the Roman victory over Etruscan and Samnite peoples in Italy in 295 B.C. In succeeding wars, Rome emerged triumphant. Rome then became embroiled in battles between its own political factions until the peace of the imperium was established following the decisive victory of Julius Caesar's adopted heir, Augustus, over Antony and Cleopatra at Actium in Greece in 31 B.C.

As forms are being abandoned in the Civilization period, so are those of warfare. Battles then follow few formal rules. They are not knightly duels with fixed regulations to determine what maximum force might be employed and what conditions chivalry will permit the victor to impose. Instead they rage as ferocious clashes of infuriated men fought to the utter collapse of one side and exploited without reserve or restraint by the other. The greatest forces available are brought to the battlefield. The methods of war, which once lagged behind technology, now relentlessly draft all mechanical possibilities into their service and spur new inventions to advance the conflict. Meanwhile, the personal heroism of the thoroughbred, the ethos of the noble, and the subtle intellect of the late Culture are largely ineffectual.

The great wars between states or fearful internal revolutions of this period achieve no genuine aim. The questions at issue, regardless of the catchwords that embellish them, revolve ultimately, consciously or otherwise, around personal power and nothing more. Yet the warring does have a significant result: It speeds demolition of old forms and leaves the political way clear for the kind of absolute dictatorship known as Caesarism.

In every Civilization period, the giant city is the preponderant center of all important affairs. Spengler's narrowed definition of "Civilization" thus is soundly logical, with the term derived from the Latin word for city. Among ancient examples of the great city are Babylon, Thebes of Egyptian society, the Greek-established city of Alexandria, Rome, and Constantinople. Later came Baghdad and Samarra, Uxmal of the Mayas, and Tenochtitlan of the Aztecs. Then London, Paris, New York arose to rank prominently among great world-cities of modern times.

All existence in the Civilization phase is dominated from the megalopolis. The city gathers to itself the significant politics of the time, while the countryside no longer is consulted but only told what it is expected to desire. Tolerating nothing beside itself, the city sets about annihilating the country scene. Woods and pastures become parks. Mountains are turned into tourist viewpoints. Fountains mimic springs. Flowerbeds substitute for meadows, formal pools for ponds, clipped hedges for bushes. The city swells and overflows in all directions, destroying noble aspects of former times with clearances and rebuilding, eating into the decaying rural landscape, spreading its formless barrack-tenements relentlessly. It collects into itself the whole life of broad regions, sucking people off the land, insatiably demanding and devouring fresh streams of humanity, using up the best of them until the countryside is exhausted of vitality. Everything outside the city's boundaries is reduced to the status of insignificant provinces.

A monstrous symbol of the soulless intellect, the world-city tends to follow the artificial, mathematical, and utterly inorganic layout of the chessboard. This plan of regular rectangular blocks astounded the Greek historian Herodotus when he visited Babylon in the fifth century B.C., and, likewise, the Spanish conqueror Cortez when he gazed upon Tenochtitlan in the sixteenth century A.D. Neither does human feeling fashion the city's buildings, as in former Culture towns; rather, they are designed coldly to meet requirements of commercial enterprise.

The country-dweller, uninfluenced, suspicious, irritated, does not comprehend what is happening. He wanders, gaping helplessly, down pavements in the long, deep gorges filled with dust and strange uproar between stony houses the like of which no nature-being ever has conceived. Clothing and even faces are adjusted to the background of stone. By day, traffic of strange colors and sounds courses through the streets. By night, a new light outshines the moon. The yokel, perplexed and powerless, understands nothing and is understood by nobody. He is merely tolerated as a useful character-type for farce and as the provider of daily bread.

Meanwhile the city-dweller is gripped compulsively by the habitat. No wretchedness, no force, not even a clear vision of the madness of its development can neutralize his attraction to the demonic creation. Once the full sinful beauty of this final marvel of history has captured a victim, it never lets him go. Even disgust with its pretentiousness, weariness of its thousand-hued glitter, and the deep inner tedium that overcomes many of its residents does not set him free. He has lost the country within himself. If he tries to go back to the land, rather than regaining it he will only suffer homesickness for the stone desert he left behind. The man of the world-city can feel comfortable enough in any other world-city, since the megalopolis is also a cosmopolis lacking in any distinctive national character. But in the nearest village he will sense himself an alien.

City people bear little resemblance to the folk of old sprung from the soil. This humanity of the new order, in whom every period of decline places high hopes, is traditionless, rootless, and religionless, parasitical, unfruitful, and deeply contemptuous of the countryman. A fluid, unstable populace, they are the marketplace loungers of Alexandria and Rome and the newspaper readers of today; clever, "educated" people who think mechanically and make a cult of intellectual mediocrity; the people of theaters and places of amusement, of sports and best-sellers. They appear equally in New Empire Egypt, in Buddhist India, in Confucian China, and in the present age. The same dry intelligence reflected in Roman busts is visible in living faces of the modern American city.

The life of the giant-city dweller is made of high tensions. Hard, intensive brainwork is relieved by bodily tension in sport, by sensual straining after pleasure, by emotional straining in betting and competitions. Genuine play and *joie de vivre* no longer are comprehensible in their essence, replaced by relaxation and distraction.

When the spiritual part of man is sufficiently uprooted and the intellectual part sufficiently strained, there suddenly emerges the sterility of the Civilization-man. Though he might cling to his individual life, as a type he no longer cares to live, and the notion that his name and family might be extinguished has lost its former deep and fearful import. Marriage ceases to be a union for engendering offspring and becomes a matter of companionship, a problem of mentalities, a craft-art for the achievement of mutual understanding. Woman, who once yearned only to be Mother, now seeks emancipation. She, by choice, belongs to herself, and she is unfruitful. Instead of children, she has soul conflicts.

Children cease to happen, mainly because intellect at the peak of its intensity no longer sees any reason for their existence. "When the ordinary thought of a highly cultivated people begins to regard 'having children' as a question of *pro's* and *con's*, the great turning point has come. For Nature knows nothing of *pro* and *con*. . . . When reasons have to be put forward at all in a question of life, life itself has become questionable."[7] At that point prudent limitation of births begins. In time, general depopulation follows.

As the rise of the Culture's town added to nobility and clergy a third estate in the bourgeoisie, the Civilization's megalopolis creates a fourth estate: the urban proletariat, the Mass, the *canaille*, the mob. This social group is the absolute essence of formlessness. It rejects completely the old Culture and its ways. It persecutes with hate every aspect of form, every distinction of rank, the orderliness of property and knowledge. The Mass, as the will-less tool of ambitious leaders, demolish every remnant of the old order, striving to duplicate in the outer world the same chaos that reigns within themselves. They are new nomads who recognize no past and possess no future. They are the radical nullity whose true and only impulse is destruction.

Meanwhile, the nobility and priesthood have lost their once-dominant influence. In the social scheme they have been replaced: the noble of the castle by the businessman, the priest of the cathedral by the scientist. Likewise, property is replaced by fluid money. In the setting of the city, not only intellect but money as well celebrates its greatest and last triumph. As high intellectuality is possible only in the advanced society's Civilization phase, so only then does money becomes a preponderant force. During this period, every idea, in order to be realized, has to be put in terms of money. Once a man was wealthy because he was powerful; now he is powerful because he has money. Even intellect holds power in democratic politics only because money has installed it there.

Party politics is a purely urban phenomenon which succeeds estate politics when the city is emancipated from the country. In its early stages it belongs to intellect alone. High-minded, responsible leaders plot the course and hold the reigns. Soon, however, men discover that they can make use of constitutional rights only when they have money. Leadership then passes from moral idealists to shrewd moneymakers and unscrupulous politicians. They begin to control the voters through all the available machinery of intellectual compulsion. Public opinion becomes no more than a weapon that party leaders forge and use to swing blows at one another as they struggle for primacy by methods that the multitude neither can perceive nor understand. Elections, far from being nominations of class representatives, have become the battleground of party candidates, a field where money—and ever bigger money—intervenes. During Rome's Civilization phase, though laws limited the use of money for political purposes, election capital mounted to colossal proportions and on one occasion tied up so much available cash that interest rates rose from four to eight percent.

Where elections once functioned as peaceful revolutions in legitimate form, they turn into prearranged games staged in the name only of popular self-determination. Thus, after money has destroyed intellect, money-democracy becomes its own destroyer. A general feeling arises that the vote holds no effective rights at all. Where torrents of blood once reddened streets in all world-cities so that the great truths of democracy might be realized, now people cannot be moved, even by threat of punishment, to use their voting rights. By Julius Caesar's time in Rome, reputable people had almost ceased to take part in elections, while the Emperor

Tiberius, who ruled during the adult years of Christ, felt embittered that the most able men of his reign held aloof from politics.

Meanwhile, political theories and ideals pass away, dying not of refutation but of boredom, as people give up not on this or that theory but on belief in theory of any kind. Coming to the understanding that one power can be overthrown not by a principle but only by another power, they begin to long for the old and worthy tradition that remains alive. Weary to disgust of money-economy, they yearn for salvation by way of something real that holds honor and chivalry, nobility, unselfishness, duty.

The period of party government, Spengler claimed, covers scarcely two centuries in the life of an advanced society. Far from being a permanent achievement, it is only a transitional stage between the late Culture and full-blown Civilization. At its end, the sentiments, the popular goals, and the abstract ideals that characterize all party politics dissolve, along with the party itself as a form.

They are supplanted by private politics. Up to this time the old aristocracy, and the dictature of money with its political weapon of democracy, have stood opposed to one another. Now both are submerged. The long-prevailing power of money is swept away by the might of individual rulers for whom the great parties become mere obedient retinues. Over the centuries, the governing minority has developed steadily from that of the nobility, through that of the party, to that of the individual's following—from rule by tradition to the personal regime. As the nobility was guided by instincts and the party had a program, the following has a master in the formless omnipotence of Caesarism.

With this return of the unchecked will-to-power, history relapses into the historyless condition of pre-Culture time. Henceforth, only private histories exist, with private ambitions, private destinies, and private wars for private possession of the world. The old beat of primitive life has returned, with endless, meaningless battles for material power that differ only in inessentials from the happenings of beast-life in a jungle.

The loss of religion in the Civilization phase is directly related to the general loss of spiritual fruitfulness in Civilization-man. He continues to experience the outer world, but he no longer experiences the sacred causality in it. He learns to know it only in terms of profane, mechanical causality. The science he constructs on this basis, which seems opposed to religion, actually is only an unspiritual, intellectual extension of religion. "Always," Spengler said, "science has grown up on a religion and under all the spiritual prepossessions of that religion, and always it signifies nothing more or less than an abstract melioration of these doctrines, considered as false because less abstract."[8] All the great inventions of Western society, the author pointed out, were nearly approached by the high-hearted and happy research of early Gothic monks. For example, the thirteenth-century English Franciscan philosopher Roger Bacon meditated upon steam engines, steamships, and aircraft. Regarding this succession of science from religion, Spengler asserted, "there is no distinction between the Catholic and the Materialistic views of the world—both say the same thing in different words."[9] One speaks from the soul, the other from the brain.

Meanwhile every Culture has its own mode of spiritual extinction in an irreligious ethic of some kind. For Indian Culture it was Buddhism, which originally was not a religion "but a final and purely practical world-sentiment of tired megalopolitans who had a closed-off Culture behind them and no future before them."[10] For Classical Culture it was Stoicism, a calm and static acceptance of difficulties.

In the realm of philosophical thought, an age of reason and optimism characteristic of a late Culture is displaced by a skepticism that dissipates the world-picture of the Culture period. The same unfruitfulness in Civilization-man that results in loss of religion shows itself equally in the extinction of great formal thought, of great courtesy, of great style in all things, including the arts.

In every advanced society, the transition in the arts from Culture phase to Civilization phase consists of classicism and romanticism of one sort or another. The symptom of declining creative power appears as the artist's demand to be freed from form and proportion in order to produce something round and complete. But what is understood as freedom is in fact indiscipline. Arbitrariness and immoderation proceed to trample the conventions of centuries.

The most obvious sign of lost creativity is a taste for giganticism. In this period, size is not, as in the Gothic and pyramid styles, an expression of inward greatness, but the dissimulation of its absence. "This swaggering in specious dimensions is common to all nascent Civilizations—we find it in the Zeus altar of Pergamum, the Helios of Chares called the 'Colossus of Rhodes,' the architecture of the Roman Imperial Age, the New Empire work in Egypt, the American skyscraper of to-day."[11]

In order to forget that art is dead, people of the Civilization phase set up an art-clamor of new styles, personal peculiarities, theoretical babble, and pretentious and fashionable artists who invent new trends and successfully bluff their public. Every modern age holds change to be the same as development, and substitutes revivals and fusions of former styles for real creativity. "The fashion at Rome was now Graeco-Asiatic, now Graeco-Egyptian, now (after Praxiteles) neo-Attic. The relief of the XLXth Dynasty—the modern age in the Egyptian Culture—that covered the monstrous, meaningless, inorganic walls, statues, and columns, seems like a sheer parody of the art of the Old Kingdom."[12]

In time, even the strength to change drains away. Rameses the Great, who ruled a splendorous and luxurious Egypt in the thirteenth century B.C., appropriated to his honor buildings of former pharaohs by having their names chipped away and his own inserted. A similar consciousness of artistic impotence led the Emperor Constantine to adorn his fourth-century triumphal arch at Rome with sculptures taken from other buildings. As early as A.D. 150, Classical craftsmen were copying old masterpieces, not because these were understood and appreciated, but because no one was capable any longer of producing originals. Copy-work represented the maximum of creative power still available.

Finally in a Civilization that endures long enough, art deteriorates to endless, industrious repetition of a stock of fixed forms destitute of any deeper significance, such as one finds in Chinese, Indian and Islamic art of the present. "Pictures and fabrics, verses and vessels, furniture, dramas and musical compositions—all is pattern-work. . . . So it has been in the Last Act of all Cultures."[13]

Meanwhile, the Civilization phase tends to pursue imperialistic aims. "Life is the process of effecting possibilities," Spengler observed, "and for the brain-man there are *only extensive* possibilities." As the energy of Culture-man is directed inward, that of Civilization-man is aimed outward. Expansion becomes everything. Far from being a matter of choice or conscious will, "The expansive tendency is a doom, something daemonic and immense, which grips, forces into service, and uses up the late mankind of the world-city stage, willy-nilly, aware or unaware."[14]

During the Civilization period, occasional imitative attempts arise to revive the values, patterns, and spirit of the former Culture phase, but they all are fruitless. Meanwhile, the skepticism that follows an age of reason and optimism is replaced by a hunger for metaphysics. A new, resigned piety, sprung from tortured conscience and spiritual hunger, looks no longer for steel-bright intellectual concepts but rather for holy secrets. With the tyranny of reason long broken, men find a pathway from skepticism to what Spengler called the "second religiousness." Thereafter they dispense with proofs as so much barren and tiresome word-jugglery and desire no longer to dissect but only to believe. The deep piety of the second religiousness impressed Herodotus in the waning Egyptian society and equally has impressed modern Westerners in China, India, and Islam.

In the meantime the trend toward depopulation continues, a phenomenon that can last for centuries. Greatly diminishing population is evident in the Egyptian New Empire, especially from the XIXth Dynasty onward. In Roman society, though the empire was rich, highly developed, well organized, well ruled, and enjoyed the completest peace, populations dwindled rapidly and wholesale. Desperate marriage-and-children laws came into being as early as the rule of Augustus around the time of Christ. Large-scale adoptions, food charities for children of poor parents, and incessant importation of barbarian bands to replenish the depleted countryside proved insufficient to check the process. First Italy became empty and desolate, then North African possessions and Gaul, and finally Spain, which in the age of the early Caesars was one of the most heavily populated areas of the empire. By A.D. 193 the countryside was so sparsely settled that anyone in Italy or the provinces could take possession of untenanted land and, by bringing it under cultivation, retain it as legal property. A more spectacular example of depopulation in the Civilization phase occurred in Mayan Mexico, where within a brief period grand cities were abandoned and most of the society's people literally vanished.

Provincial cities shrivel first. Later the giant cities empty out. A long series of Classical writers from the second century B.C. onward tell of old and renowned population centers in which streets were lined with deserted and crumbling buildings, cattle grazed in forums and gymnasiums, and amphitheaters were sown fields. Rome by the fifth century A.D. held no more population than a village, though its imperial palaces were still habitable. In India, the great capital city of Pataliputra was an immense and uninhabited waste of houses when a Chinese traveler, Hsinan-tang, visited the area about A.D. 635. The city of Samarra north of Baghdad, seat of Abbasid caliphs during the ninth century, was abandoned by the tenth.

A Civilization, in Spengler's sense, can endure for hundreds and even thousands of years. Though lifeless and barren, it can remain standing like a worn-out giant of the primeval forest thrusting its decaying branches into the sky. India and China provide current examples of enormous longevity. In its dead and petrified state, however, the superannuated social body lacks all creativity and vitality. So do its people. Spengler described the human residue of a once-great advanced society as "fellah" peoples, a term long used to denote the peasants of Egypt since post-Roman times. It suggests a population stripped of its best elements, dull and dumb, without energy, direction, or destiny. Century after century their lives drag on, while barbarian war bands and young Cultures sweep over them and shed their blood. They remain passive objects, choosing slavery over self-defense or death. Thus have Babylonians, Egyptians, Chinese, and Indians been passed on through the ages from one conqueror to another.

In all very late Civilizations, social castes appear. Their establishment represents absolute finishedness, the ultimate stage in which development is succeeded by immutable hardening and fixation.

After the passing of the Culture phase, centuries are less historically important than were decades during the time of growth. This is why visitors to old Civilizations feel them to be changeless. As life was for primitive pre-Culture man, so it is again for the fellaheen peoples—"just the zoological up-and-down . . . devoid of significance."[15]

The Decline of the West

The decline of the West, in Spengler's estimation, will compare closely to the waning of the Greco-Roman world in both course and duration. Already happening around us and within us, it will continue through the first centuries of the coming millennium. Then, "the history of West-European mankind will be definitely *closed*."[16]

The West as it now prevails over the entire surface of the earth is the only advanced society still in a stage of fulfillment. As with similar aging societies of the past, its decline comprises nothing less than the problem of Civilization.

This phase of its existence was developing to full bloom as early as the first decades of the twentieth century. Yet its beginnings came considerably earlier. As the Swiss historian Jacob Burckhardt believed that European traditions had been disintegrating since the French Revolution of 1789, so did Spengler see this landmark event as the end of the West's Culture phase and the start of its Civilization phase. As he put it, the revolution marked the defeat of the organic countryside by the inorganic city. On one side of the historic frontier lay life in fullness and sureness, formed by growth from within and evolving steadily from early Gothic times to the age of Goethe and Napoleon. On the other side arises the artificial, rootless existence of the swelling modern city developing from patterns shaped by intellect.

The West's "Period of Contending States" began promptly with the Napoleonic Wars. After the Corsican leader's final defeat at Waterloo in Belgium in 1815, Europe enjoyed almost a full century with exceptionally few major wars. But the long spell of relative peace occurred only because the great powers of the world were unceasingly and massively preparing for war. At first hundreds of thousands, then millions of men stood constantly ready to march, while great naval fleets, renewed every decade, filled harbors. Nations in dispute held back from armed clashes, often at the final hour, only because they feared that the consequences would be devastating. Thus, the world powers of the time waged war without warfare, a running battle of overbidding in equipment and readiness. Yet the longer actual war was postponed, the greater grew both the means of warfare and tensions between nations. The taut control snapped with the cataclysm of 1914.

Before the end of World War I, while Spengler was writing the *Decline*, the author felt certain that the conflict was only the first of many to come. He foresaw the twentieth century unfolding not as the era of peace, progress, and democracy that people had been expecting, but as a period of imperialism, tyranny, and almost incessant wars. "It falls to us," he warned, "to live in the most trying times known to the history of a great Culture."[17] Yet in spite of the bloody century's apocalyptic atmosphere, the modern West is still young as a Civilization, Spengler indicated. Its decline will require several hundred years to reach completion.

As always in the past, the principal setting of the end phase is the world-city. Spengler rightly judged that major cities of his day were far short of full development. “I see, long after A.D. 2000,” he wrote in the second decade of the twentieth century, “cities laid out for ten to twenty million inhabitants, spread over enormous areas of country-side, with buildings that will dwarf the biggest of to-day’s and notions of traffic and communication that we should regard as fantastic to the point of madness.”[18]

Already in his lifetime he detected world-city conditions developing. The folk of former days had become the mass. And modern megalopolitan people he saw as spiritually dead: the pure intellectual, the sophist, the sensualist. Within this new raw breed simmers a period of decline’s hostility to hallowed traditions of the Culture: to nobility, privilege, dynasty, and church, to conventions in the arts and cultural limits to knowledge and science. As in the past, the unanchored brain-man of the megalopolis possesses the kind of sharp, cold intelligence that confounds the wisdom of the peasant. He also displays a newfound naturalism regarding sex and society that reaches back to primitive instincts and conditions. Equally, the Roman institution of bread and circuses have reappeared in the form of wage disputes and sporting grounds. Such symptoms, Spengler claimed, signify the definite closing down of the Culture phase and the start of an existence that is antiprovincial, late, and futureless.

Though modern Western man with his magnificent machines has established himself as lord of the earth, he obviously is not destined to keep that position. Already he is enslaved by his own machinery. The machine does the work, but it forces man to co-operate. It determines the size of his population and the arrangement of his life, and in both of those matters it leads him down a path where he can neither stand still nor turn back. Meanwhile nature becomes exhausted, and man himself sickens of machines and of his entire Civilization, longing to return to a simpler, more natural way of life. Already appearing are the world citizens, world pacifiers, and world reconcilers who in all aging societies are spiritual leaders of the fellaheen.

Modern philosophical thinking, Spengler observed, also shows signs common to periods of decline. "To-day all 'philosophy' is nothing but an inward abdication and resignation. . . . It was just the same in Roman times."[19] Rationalism is giving way to metaphysics and mysticism. Christianity, Oriental philosophies and religions, metaphysical gnosticism, occultism, and spiritualism are reviving as the second religiousness of the West gets underway.

In the political sphere, the nineteenth century was Western society's heyday of party politics, corresponding to the third century B.C. for Classical man. But, Spengler noted, by his time parliamentarianism was in full decay. As in the past, the democratic form was proving not a pinnacle of achievement but a relatively brief transition stage between the late Culture phase with its mature forms and a coming age of mighty individuals in a formless world. Already elections were degenerating into the kind of farce they became in Classical Rome, with money organizing the process in the interest of people who possessed it. When, ultimately, the politics of money grows intolerable, he predicted, mankind will choose its destiny once again by the primitive means of bloody violence.

The age of political theory for the West also is approaching its conclusion. "The great systems of Liberalism and Socialism all arose between 1750 and 1850. That of Marx. . . . has had no successor."[20] As Buddhism was the mode of spiritual extinction for the Culture of India, and Stoicism served the same function for Classical society, so Socialism is the sign of the end for the West. By "Socialism," Spengler did not mean a specific political creed. He referred, more broadly, to a way of political, economic, and ethical thinking akin to a system practiced in Old Egypt, which understands and maintains permanent economic relations, trains the individual person in his duty to society, and glorifies hard work as an affirmation of the future. As such, Socialism is a secular version of the lofty spiritual goal toward which Western society in its religious days saw itself tensely and steadily progressing.

In its final aspirations, however, Spengler predicted, modern Socialism is only building a castle in the air. "Its friends regard it as the form of the future, its enemies as a sign of downfall, and both are equally right. . . . Faustian man has nothing more to hope for in anything pertaining to the grand style of Life. Something has come to an end. The Northern soul has exhausted its inner possibilities, and of the dynamic force and insistence that had expressed itself in world-historical visions of the future—visions of millennial scope—nothing remains but the mere pressure, the passion yearning to create, the form without the content."[21]

Great art in the West equally is a thing of the past, Spengler maintained. Architecture as an organic form came to an end in the eighteenth century with the maturing of the delicate and ornate rococo style. Though the author saw the modern skyscraper as heir to the Gothic cathedral in its characteristic upward-straining urge, it is a cold and controlled expression of the Civilization phase. Portrait painting, with its biographical way of conveying the Western feeling for time, reached its highest point in the seventeenth century with the work of the Dutch artist Rembrandt van Rijn. Painting in general slipped into decline with the French impressionists in the last half of the nineteenth century. In their manner of interpreting the world, space is not experienced but cognized, not contemplated but visually seen, while landscapes, rather than being felt by the artists, are rendered as the mechanical object of physics.

Western art as a whole, in Spengler's estimation, reached its loftiest heights with eighteenth-century chamber music. Here the West's prime symbol of endless space is conveyed in fullest measure. "When one of those ineffably yearning violin-melodies wanders through the spaces expanded around it by the orchestration of Tartini or Nardini, Haydn, Mozart, or Beethoven, we know ourselves to be in the presence of an art beside which that of the Acropolis is alone worthy to be set."[22]

In music the last of the Western arts died. Spengler called Wagner's *Tristan und Isolde* the giant keystone of the society's music, a finale far stronger than that presented by impressionistic painting. It also was the decisive turning point beyond which music fell into decline. Even the later works of Wagner he saw as examples of theatricality and decadence.

Since Wagner in music and Paul Cézanne in painting, art has become nothing but impotence and falsehood: "A faked music, filled with artificial noisiness of massed instruments; a faked painting, full of idiotic, exotic and showcard effects, that every ten years or so concocts out of the form-wealth of millennia some new 'style' which is in fact no style at all since everyone does as he pleases; a lying plastic that steals from Assyria, Egypt and Mexico indifferently."[23]

The modern artist, Spengler declared, is not a creator but a mere workman. "We go through all the exhibitions, the concerts, the theatres, and find only industrious cobblers and noisy fools, who delight to produce something for the market, something that will 'catch on' with a public for whom art and music and drama have long ceased to be spiritual necessities."[24] As did failing Civilizations of old, the West today is only playing a tedious game with defunct forms to sustain the illusion that art is still alive.

The time of great mathematics for Western society also is past, by the author's reckoning. The tasks in the field for the present "are those of preserving, rounding off, refining, selection—in place of big dynamic creation, the same clever detail-work which characterized the Alexandrian mathematic of late Hellenism."[25]

Similarly, the grand creative age of Western science already lies behind. Its methods were tried out in the eighteenth century, its powers in the nineteenth. Since then, the gently sloping route of its decline has been clearly visible. Growing use of statistics in the physical sciences is putting probability and chance in the place of necessity, undermining the precision that scientific thinkers previously demanded. Likewise, the emergence of the theory of relativity, the elimination of mass, the abandonment of absolute time and space, the replacement of the atom by a complex universe of intra-atomic forces, the uncertainty principle of quantum mechanics—all these contradict basic scientific principles of former days, signifying that dissolution has begun.

Meanwhile, Spengler indicated, "savants of the calibre of Gauss and Humboldt and Helmholtz were already no more by 1900. In physics as in chemistry, in biology as in mathematics, the great masters are dead, and we are now experiencing the decrescendo of brilliant gleaners who arrange, collect and finish-off like the Alexandrian scholars of the Roman age."[26]

The history of former high cultures shows that science always is a temporary phenomenon, belonging only to the autumn and winter stages of development. Alike in the Chinese and the Indian, the Classical and the Arabian societies, the field exhausted its possibilities within a few centuries. From these precedents, a present-day observer can foresee a date when Western scientific thought will end. Two centuries of exact scientific thinking is sufficient to bring satiety. One sign that a culture has had enough is the tendency toward ever narrower, smaller, and less fruitful investigations. Spengler believed that the final advances of Western science will reach hardly beyond the twenty-first century, if they persist that long. The individual person will renounce science by laying aside his books, and the society by ceasing to produce high scientific intellects. Then the science of the West, weary from its strivings, will return to its spiritual home in the second religiousness.

One major task remains in the field: a study of the form and structure of the exact sciences. Such an endeavor would discover how all their laws, concepts, and theories are inwardly related as forms, and what they have meant in that sense during the culture's life.

Likewise, to the extent that the West continues to use types of Roman law, its greatest works of jurisprudence still lie ahead. Classical law was not an appropriate borrowing for the Western mentality. Based upon its own culture's prime symbol, it was a law pertaining to bodies: to persons, slaves, things. The Western mind, on the other hand, views all existence in dynamic terms. Persons are not bodies as much as units of force and will, while things are seen not as corporeal objects but as aims, means, and creations. Thus, Roman-style law has fallen into confusion over purely modern, wholly unembodied issues like electric power and electronic broadcasting. It also opened the legal field to great incongruities, like treating the theft of a piece of paper as an offense while the theft of an infinitely more valuable business idea written on it remained unpunishable. Legal minds of the future will have the task of bringing Western law into line with the culture's mathematics, higher physics, and general way of thinking, rebuilding it as a Western creation upon Western experience. "Our whole social, economic, and technical life is waiting to be understood, at long last, in this wise. We shall need a century and more of keenest and deepest thought to arrive at the goal."[27]

Spengler also affirmed that the West is locked irrevocably into a future of imperialism, if only because outward expansion is the sole course of action open to Civilization-man. "Hard as the half-developed Socialism of to-day is fighting against expansion, one day it will become arch-expansionist with all the vehemence of destiny."[28]

The West's "Period of Contending States" with its gigantic wars of annihilation and wrenching revolutionary upheavals will come to an end as the transition from Culture to Civilization is completed. Along with this completion, the unchained might of Caesarism will burst forth, proclaiming with arbitrary dictatorship the society's total divorce from the rule of tradition and return to thorough formlessness. As in past ages, Caesarism will overwhelm what remains of the old aristocracy, break the power of money and democracy, and entrench itself as the final political constitution of the Civilization phase. From then on, the way will be open for the energetic, politically creative individual who yearns for power and is willing to pay any price to have it. His rise can establish him personally as the destiny of an entire people, even a whole society. As armies once served nations, they now will serve him as their sole master. He might be elevated to the status of divinity, as were emperors in ancient China and Rome. His success can catapult his people almost instantly to the dizziest heights of prominence. And the incident of his death can send his retinue, his country, his empire plummeting from compact order to shattered chaos.

The rule of Caesars, however capricious, fills a definite need for its time, according to Spengler. "The mighty ones of the future may possess the earth as their private property—for the great political form of the Culture is irremediably in ruin—but it matters not, for, formless and limitless as their power may be, it has a task. And this task is the unwearying care for this world as it is, which is the very opposite of the interestedness of the money-power age, and demands high honour and conscientiousness."[29]

Though the new Caesarism still lies in the future, its precursors already are appearing. In Spengler's view, the first modern Caesar-figure was the nineteenth-century British capitalist and statesman Cecil Rhodes, who traveled to South Africa for his health and personally carved out an economic, political, and territorial empire, leaving an entire country named after himself. Spengler did not consider Adolf Hitler as a significant forerunner of the force-men to come, though he might have changed his mind had he lived to see Germany's rocketing rise and devastating collapse under the dictator's personal rule. But shortly after the *Decline*'s publication, he referred to the Russian leader Vladimir Lenin as the most important Caesar-figure since Rhodes. He also saw in the Italian dictator Benito Mussolini an ice-cold, skeptical, realistic statesman who functioned not as party leader but as lord of his country and therefore stood as another early model of Caesars soon to appear.

While the social theorist Pierre Proudhon, the philosopher Friedrich Nietzsche, the historians Ernst von Lasaulx and Jacob Burckhardt, and the novelist Jack London all preceded Spengler with visions of totalitarian government taking over the West, the *Decline* went further: It forecast exactly when modern Caesars will arise. Applying the pattern of past cultures to the future, Spengler predicted that arbitrary rule will clamp down upon the West around the year 2000. For a time thereafter, rival Caesars will struggle for supremacy, raking the landscape with wars all the more fierce for their formlessness. Then eventually one of the dictators will triumph and establish a world empire.

Meanwhile, the life of the masses in the great barrack-cities will drag on meaninglessly in a decadent mixture of refinement and brutality. And gradually the second religiousness will spread, bringing to the drab, mechanical, vulgar existence the promise of solace and salvation.

The technocracy of the West will hold together, Spengler predicted, as long as engineers keep it going. This small, quiet band—the priests of the machine—also are its destiny. Not even exhaustion of present fuel supplies poses a real problem as long as these technical pathfinders remain at work. But when recruits for the all-important vocation fail to appear, then machine industry will flicker out.

"Suppose that, in future generations, the most gifted minds were to find their soul's health more important than all the powers of this world; suppose that, under the influence of the metaphysic and mysticism that is taking the place of rationalism to-day, the very elite of intellect that is now concerned with the machine comes to be overpowered by a growing sense of its *Satanism* . . . then nothing can hinder the end of this grand drama."[30]

Within a few centuries, the author foresaw, "there will no more be a Western Culture, no more be German, English or French than there were Romans in the time of Justinian. Not that the sequence of human generations failed; it was the inner form of a people, which had put together a number of these generations as a single gesture, that was no longer there."[31]

One day, as Spengler starkly described in a book that followed the *Decline*, the West's technological splendors "will lie in fragments, *forgotten*—our railways and steamships as dead as the Roman roads and Chinese wall, our giant cities and skyscrapers in ruins like old Memphis and Babylon."[32]

Spengler believed, like Lasaulx, Nikolai Danilevsky, and, later, Walter Schubart, that the next great Culture of mankind might arise in Russia. At a time when most knowledgeable people thought of Russia as a backward province of Europe, he, again with Danilevsky, saw it as a region with a future separate from the West. Since Tsar Peter the Great in the eighteenth century, its rulers had been dazzled by the powerful influence radiating from their Western neighbors. Forcing European ways upon the country, they distorted its development into a pseudomorphosis, not only stirring awake prematurely a land still in the pre-Culture stage but also overlaying it with an ill-fitting Culture it could not comprehend.

The ease with which the Russian Revolution of 1917 swept away the country's social classes is proof in itself that the structure of nobles, merchants, small townspeople, and peasants was a mere imitation destitute of any real local meaning. Yet the regime that replaced the Westernizing Tsars offered no more than another form of pseudomorphosis. Controlled by Bolsheviks who also were Western in spirit, it followed a program thoroughly megalopolitan and "Civilized," and equally unsuited to Russia. Just as the people of the country rose up and destroyed the old Westernism in one massive upheaval, Spengler predicted that they would send the new Westernism after it in another.

Meanwhile, for today and tomorrow, the Russian will adapt himself to the still-prevailing ways of the West. He will accept as inevitable the present industrial age and live within it. Yet—along with Arabs, Japanese, Indians, and other non-European peoples—he inwardly looks upon the machine and its tyranny of wheels, cables, and rails with fear and abhorrence. And "there will come a time when he will *blot out the whole thing from his memory and his environment*, and create about himself a wholly new world, in which nothing of this Devil's technique is left."[33]

Then the Russian people will give rise to their own true nobility and clergy. Above all, they will form a fresh religion as the basis for their unfolding Culture. This will be a primitive Christianity of the Gospels, and to it the next millennium will belong.

Spengler's rich and complex tapestry of history, ideas, and insights—about Russia, Greco-Roman and Middle Eastern societies, the cultures of ancient Egypt, China, India, Mexico—offers deep intellectual excitement. Yet it was the author's analysis of Western culture and its future that aroused the highest acclaim and the bitterest denunciations from readers around the world.

Not all of his panoramic presentation of Western existence is unique and controversial. His Cultural springtime for the West closely resembles what is better known as the high Middle Ages. The summer and autumn stages that follow mesh well with times conventionally thought of as the age of absolutism and the baroque period. Even the early part of his Civilization phase remains in line with customary views of history. The French Revolution and the Napoleonic Wars generally are considered a decisive turning point in Western society. And the nineteenth century commonly is seen as a time of materialistic and skeptical philosophies and of eclecticism in art and intellectual pursuits.

But when Spengler proceeded to the twentieth century, then boldly charted the future, he shocked and alarmed many readers. Two factors proved especially disturbing: his apparent pessimism and his deterministic conviction that the West must pass through dismal and agonizing decline to inevitable death.

The charges of pessimism he denied. His conclusions may be deplorable, he admitted, but mere sentimental wishing cannot alter facts of existence. So, he argued, far from discouraging and demoralizing his readers, he was rendering them a service:

> We are civilized, not Gothic or Rococo, people; we have to reckon with the hard cold facts of a *late* life, to which the parallel is to be found not in Pericles's Athens but in Caesar's Rome. Of great painting or great music there can no longer be, for Western people, any question. Their architectural possibilities have been exhausted these hundred years. Only

> *extensive* possibilities are left to them. Yet, for a sound and vigorous generation that is filled with unlimited hopes, I fail to see that it is any disadvantage to discover betimes that some of these hopes must come to nothing. And if the hopes thus doomed should be those most dear, well, a man who is worth anything will not be dismayed. . . . The lesson, I think, would be of benefit to the coming generations, as showing them what is possible—and therefore necessary—and what is excluded from the inward potentialities of their time. . . . And I can only hope that men of the new generation may be moved by this book to devote themselves to technics instead of lyrics, the sea instead of the paint-brush, and politics instead of epistemology. Better they could not do.[34]

About his deterministic view of the future, Spengler remained unyielding. A Culture's organic life is as thoroughly immutable as that of a plant or a person. Its decline is insusceptible of modification. He warned at the close of his masterwork,

> For us . . . whom a Destiny has placed in this Culture and at this moment of its development—the moment when money is celebrating its last victories, and the Caesarism that is to succeed approaches with quiet, firm step—our direction, willed and obligatory at once, is set for us within narrow limits, and on any other terms life is not worth the living. We have not the freedom to reach to this or to that, but the freedom to do the necessary or to do nothing. And a task that historic necessity had set *will* be accomplished with the individual or against him.[35]

PART III

Arnold J. Toynbee, The Master Historian

7

Toynbee and History

When Arnold Toynbee, as a young Oxford don, came across an early copy of *The Decline of the West*, he wondered whether a grand plan of research taking shape in his mind already had been fulfilled by Oswald Spengler. As he perused the German author's work, however, he found gaps in both subject and method. Spengler, he noted, had not explained how civilizations arise from the morass of primitive conditions and had regarded their appearance only as a mystery. Also, Toynbee believed, the whole sweeping study of their history could be improved by a more scientific, empirical approach. Reassured, he went ahead with his project.

During the next forty years, he investigated every human civilization on record from earliest historic times to the present, including the least familiar ones. He examined their origins, growth, decline, and dissolution. He compared the course of more than a score of these civilizations to Western culture. Then he spread the majestic panorama of his findings over the pages of a monumental twelve-volume work entitled *A Study of History*.

Published in installments over twenty-seven years, the profound and brilliant analysis of all civilized humankind's known past, combined with Toynbee's interpretation of trends in modern Western civilization, was read by scholars the world over. Shortly after the catastrophe of World War II, intelligent laymen, anxious and perplexed about the future, also began seeking answers in its pages. In years that followed, growing attention to Toynbee's *Study* made it the most extensively discussed work of history in modern times.

ARNOLD J. TOYNBEE

Arnold Joseph Toynbee came to his project well prepared. Born in the heart of London in 1889 into a middle-class family, he was surrounded from the start by the classical writings of ancient Greece and Rome and the Bible of Christianity. His mother, one of the first women in England to earn a university degree, was a historian, and she regularly exposed her son to contemporary researches on ancient civilizations. His vocation was nurtured further by relatives who had lived through great episodes of nineteenth-century British history in distant parts of the sprawling empire. The boy's youthful interest in other times and places gained all the more stimulus from frequent visits to London's rich museums.

At the age of ten, he was sent away to boarding school. Three years later, he won a coveted scholarship to Winchester College, one of England's finest private secondary schools. Here, as he later recounted, "in the first decade of the twentieth century, we were still being given the complete humanist education of the fifteenth century Italian Renaissance."[1] He also noted that his generation was the last to receive the formal classical education that had served as the intellectual staple of Western culture for half a millennium.

Young Arnold had started to learn Latin at the age of seven and Greek at ten. By the time he entered Balliol College at Oxford under another scholarship, he was thoroughly grounded for the university's classical course in the history and thought of ancient Greece and Rome. In the years that followed, he became so steeped in the classical period that at moments of emotion he wrote verses in Greek or Latin rather than in his native English.

He took his degree in 1911. His scholarship was renewed for another year, with the instruction to spend the time abroad doing whatever he thought most useful to his future. He was planning to become a professor of ancient Greek at Oxford, where he already was appointed to a tutorial fellowship for the year 1912. So he decided to round out his education with a long visit to Italy and Greece. Traveling overland to Rome, he checked in at the British Archaeological School there and spent several weeks hiking the surrounding countryside. He then went on to a similar school at Athens and made the city his base for nine months of walking through the mainland and islands of Greece. Before those months were over, he had logged between two and three thousand miles on foot.

The master project that would occupy most of his future life began to germinate on Crete. Among the shadowy remains of the island's ancient Minoan civilization, which predated classical Greece, he came upon the ruins of a baroque country villa that had belonged to a landowner from Venice when the Italian maritime city ruled the island as a colony. The abandoned relic of the seventeenth century A.D. not far from the ruins of the seventeenth century B.C. stirred in Toynbee a powerful suggestion of cultural mortality. He reflected further that Venetian control of Crete had lasted some 450 years, which was longer than Britain's reign over any of its colonies. He found it easy to picture similar ruins heaped and strewn about his homeland at some future time.

Returning to Oxford, he married Rosalind Murray, daughter of the university's outstanding classicist Gilbert Murray, who later served as adviser for *A Study of History*. One of their two sons, Philip Toynbee, became a well-known novelist.

The outbreak of World War I brought Arnold Toynbee closer to his budding project. Teaching about Thucydides, the fifth-century B.C. Greek historian of the Peloponnesian War, he became aware of striking parallels between ancient history and modern political experiences. He asked himself, as he later recorded, "if this were the true relation between the Graeco-Roman and the Western civilizations, might not the relation between all the civilizations known to us turn out to be the same?"[2]

The World War also made his career crowded and varied, as it would remain for decades to come. Barred from military service by chronic dysentery picked up during his walks in Greece, he left his studies for five years of government work. He edited a book on Turkish atrocities against the Armenian people and did further work on Turkish affairs in the Political Intelligence Department of the British Foreign Office. At the war's end he served as a minor delegate to the Paris Peace Conference. The shock of the conflict, which had killed approximately half of his former classmates, spurred more reflection on the mortality of civilizations. In his seventh book he cited that the death of Western culture had seemed inconceivable before 1914, but "By January, 1920, the picture had changed."[3]

By 1920 Toynbee was serving as professor of Byzantine and modern Greek studies at London University. It was then he made a first attempt at his masterwork, though it proved a false start and came to nothing. Shortly afterward he traveled to Asiatic Turkey as special correspondent for the *Manchester Guardian* to cover a war between Turkey and Greece. On the way back to England aboard the Orient Express train, the thirty-three-year-old scholar, teacher, and author casually jotted on half a sheet of note paper the skeletal plan for his entire *Study of History*.

He understood that the project could not be accomplished in less than two million words—about twice the size of the eighteenth-century *History of the Decline and Fall of the Roman Empire*, which occupied Edward Gibbon for twenty years. If all went well, he could hope to complete the study only in his old age. Size and duration notwithstanding, he went ahead with it.

In 1924 Toynbee resigned as a full-time professor to accept a choice post as director of studies for a recently established Royal Institute of International Affairs, an unofficial body designed to aid the scientific study of international questions. He remained there for the next thirty-three years. He continued to lecture at London

University, where he became a research professor of international history. But his principal work involved editing and often writing annual volumes of *The Survey of International Affairs* produced by the institute. The massive interpretative report of world events that developed under his supervision was widely read and highly praised for clarity, careful research, and lucid writing.

Meanwhile he studied the histories of India, China, Japan, Mexico, and Peru in preparation for his monumental personal work. During the summers of 1927 and 1928 he expanded his first outline into detailed notes. Then, after journeying overland to the Persian Gulf, by sea to China and Japan, then back to Britain via the Trans-Siberian Railway to gain a firsthand view of the East, he felt ready to begin writing.

Simultaneous work on the *Survey* and the *Study* broadened his horizons for both tasks. His deep and far-reaching inquiries into history built a sound foundation for understanding current events. His growing fund of knowledge about the modern world enriched his historical writings. As a single example of how the two projects coincided, the 1931 *Survey* speculated on a possible "general breakdown of society." An entire section subsequently appeared almost intact in the *Study*. Toynbee later stated, "I could not, I believe, have done either piece of work if I had not been doing the other at the same time."[4]

The first three volumes of the *Study* were published in 1934 and the second three in 1939. They proved unlike any other work in the field of history.

Toynbee broke out of the narrowly specialized confines of modern "microscopic" historical research into the exhilarating grand epic of humankind's entire story. As Spengler had done before him, he also abandoned the then-common bias of history as a European phenomenon and embraced the whole world. He did not restrict himself to individual nations or races but broadened his view to entire civilizations. Also, in an age of nongeneralizing researchers whose work suggests that the past holds no rhyme or reason, Toynbee, like Spengler, detected a grand order in history. Further, working among rationalist thinkers who considered God irrelevant and sometimes viewed religion only as a primitive aberration, he put God back into the account of human societies and did careful justice to the large part religion has played in history.

With boldness unapproached by any of his colleagues and exceeding the range of even Spengler, he raised an exhaustive series of questions about human culture and society: What, precisely, is civilization? How many civilized societies are known to history? How did they begin? How did they grow? How did they end? What conclusions can present-day people draw from the immense drama of the past about the condition and the course of their own civilization? With his enormous fund of information, a prodigious memory, keen imagination, and flashes of original insight, he proceeded to answer these questions in detail.

The knowledge underlying Toynbee's *Study* is virtually without precedent. The historian moved with ease and confidence through the past of Europe, North Africa, Asia, the Americas, and many remote portions of the globe. He applied modern psychology, sociology, ethnology, and philosophy to his work. He displayed familiarity with at least half a dozen languages. He quoted liberally from Shakespeare, Goethe, and the poets Andrew Marvell, William Blake, Percy Bysshe Shelley, and George Meredith. He knew the Bible as thoroughly as most theologians. He also surveyed the other major religions of the world and many minor ones.

"The learning is miraculous, the wealth of examples and parallels overwhelming,"remarked one of his scholarly reviewers about an erudition so vast and convoluted that it left many highly educated readers wondering how one person could know so much.[5]

Toynbee's vast knowledge, however, did not save him from criticism. To the contrary, it made his work a marvelously broad intellectual target. As with Spengler's *Decline of the West*, no one authority could pass a verdict on the entire *Study of History*. Its expanse placed it beyond the reach of current scholarship. Quite simply, nobody knew enough to deal with it as a whole. At the same time, each specific area Toynbee touched upon was inhabited by specialists. Their reception of the *Study* was mixed and often unsympathetic.

Many scholars looked with suspicion on the very idea of so broad an inquiry. Outraged historians complained that Toynbee as a historian went too far by entering the realms of philosophy and theology as well. One noted critic considered Toynbee's basic assumptions questionable. Others called his hypotheses arbitrary. The validity of his scientific empiricism was challenged as he was accused of stretching and squeezing facts to fit the patterns he found in the past. Errors in detail were inevitable in the mighty scope of his work, and critics pounced upon these with a vengeance.

Philosophers challenged his frank moral judgments. Liberals took offense at his conviction that religion acts as a positive force in human development. Conservatives disliked his pacifist views on war and his belief that nationalism in the modern age is outdated and dangerous. Marxists scorned him as a purveyor of an opposing interpretation of history and a mortal foe of Communism. Jewish readers took offense at his work for ranking Judaism among remnants of dead cultures that survive as "fossils." He also was chided for romanticism and vagueness, naivete and conceit, literary long-windedness, and cumbersome style. For a time, it seemed no historian's bibliography was complete without an article criticizing Toynbee and his *Study*. Ultimately, whole volumes of collected reproaches were published.

Much of the negative commentary, especially in matters of detail, was justified. Yet Toynbee's overall edifice, in spite of the critical cannonade, continued to stand firm. Errors that seemed serious to a restricted specialist did nothing to invalidate the work as a whole, since its purpose was not to achieve detailed exactitude but to organize the scattered pieces of the entire human past. Grand generalizations that upset and confused specialists remained appropriate to Toynbee, whose view from the mountaintop was different from theirs on the plain below. When all things were considered, the *Study*'s weaknesses were far outweighed by its merits as a bold and exciting effort by an exceedingly well-informed mind to chart humankind's troubled and inspired ascent from the bog of primitivism to a fellowship between man and God.

Nor was scholarly praise lacking, even from some of Toynbee's critics. The historian was compared for his vision to the ancient world's master theologian St. Augustine, to modern philosophers Herbert Spencer and Karl Marx, to Oswald Spengler, and to Sigmund Freud. He was acclaimed for redressing the lopsided balance between the microscopic and panoramic views of history, for restoring religion to its rightful place in the human epic, for leading readers to the global perspective that present and future ages need. A dean of Princeton University proclaimed Toynbee "the ablest living historian of civilization."[6] Most commentators agreed that *A Study of History* was of major significance to historians, sociologists, and political scientists as a twentieth-century intellectual monument.

Toynbee later confessed that reading the criticisms had the "depressing effect of taking daily doses of weed-killer."[7] Yet the academic storm did not surprise him, and he weathered it philosophically, not battling the critics but choosing instead to learn what he could from them as partners in his endeavor.

With the outbreak of World War II, Toynbee again entered government service, this time as director of the Research Department of the Foreign Office. When the war ended, he again traveled to Paris as a delegate to the Peace Conference. He also went to work on ten volumes of the *Survey*, which amounted to a history of the Second World War. Meanwhile, divorced from his first wife in 1946, he married his longtime assistant in the *Survey* task, Veronica Boulter.

During the war years, the first six volumes of Toynbee's masterwork had begun to gather dust on library shelves, while their author, however familiar among professional historians, remained little known outside intellectual circles. Then, in 1947, Toynbee visited the United States on a lecture tour. A one-volume abridgment of the half-completed *Study* was timed to be released during his stay. Toynbee suddenly experienced the truth of Victor Hugo's remark about an idea whose moment has come.

The work, made more accessible in its shorter version, caught the attention of lay readers. Shaken by the war, many thoughtful people were haunted by a sense of impending social collapse and eager for an analysis of the critical errors that had sent former civilizations to destruction. The abridgment became a Book-of-the-Month-Club selection and by mail alone sold considerably more than one hundred thousand copies. Meanwhile, sales in normal retail outlets climbed toward two hundred thousand copies. Toynbee soon was a familiar name among better informed people the world over, while the *Study* became one of the best known books of its time.

Early in 1948 the author returned to America, invited by Princeton University's Institute for Advanced Studies to resume his long-delayed grand project there. Under a grant from the Rockefeller Foundation he set to work, writing in longhand with a fountain pen, following the penciled outline he had drafted in the late 1920s. He drew from fifteen notebooks he had filled with thoughts and quotations over the years, though most of the universe of data he put to paper came from a capacious mental file. After several years, he delivered volumes seven through ten of *A Study of History* to his publisher in five suitcases. They were released in 1954.

The continuation explored relationships between great empires and great religions, the tragedy of barbaric periods, the meetings of civilizations past and present, and the uniformities found in history. More thoroughly than earlier volumes it sought to explain the bewildering problems of present-day Western culture and offered a prescription for overcoming them.

Again the *Study* drew excited criticism and praise, all the more because Toynbee now was a major world figure. The general public considered him the representative historian of the age and his masterwork, the century's supreme historical achievement. Soon professional colleagues were honoring Toynbee as the founding father of modern world history and ranking him higher than the most notable universal historians of past ages: St. Augustine, who wrote in the fifth century as the Roman Empire was collapsing, and Ibn Khaldun of fourteenth-century Arabic culture.

Toynbee retired from the Royal Institute and his *Survey* tasks in the mid-1950s, but he did not stop working. Now in his mid-sixties, he produced writings on world affairs, travel, religion, history, and autobiography. He completed the *Study* with two final volumes: an atlas and gazetteer, and a large book of reconsiderations based on new historical evidence and the criticisms that had aided his labors. He then compiled a second, lavishly illustrated condensation of the entire work. In all, his list of published volumes included thirty-seven solely authored and some thirty-five coauthored, while he served as editor for three more. This output distinguishes him as one of the twentieth century's most prolific writers.

Toynbee's productivity might suggest that he spent most of his time buried in dusty library stacks and isolated behind a writing desk. Yet his life was active as well. Biographical glimpses show him working both fronts of the 1921 Greco-Turkish War . . . striding down the halls of government with a desert-robed, dagger-bearing Col. T. E. Lawrence of Arabia . . . nursing a Ford over a Balkan ox track . . . enduring a two-hour personal diatribe from Adolf Hitler . . . dining with Turkish dictator Kemal Ataturk at Ankara, President and Madame Chiang Kai-shek at Nanking, and Prime Minister Jawaharlal Nehru at Delhi.

In his later years, as a mild, dignified, white-haired figure, Toynbee became something of a public prophet, an international sage in a class with Albert Schweitzer, Bertrand Russell, and Albert Einstein. He traveled as far as Australia delivering lectures. His views were featured in major newspapers, in the *New York Times* Magazine, the *Reader's Digest,* and *Time*, while he was eulogized in *Life*, *Saturday Review,* and the *New Republic.* At the age of eighty-five, in the

1970s, he was writing that a widespread fuel shortage ultimately might lead to totalitarian governments but added hopefully that "a society that is declining materially may be ascending spiritually."[8]

Toynbee's spiritual attitude struck many people as oddly contradictory. In an autobiographical volume published when he was eighty years old, he confessed that he had become an agnostic during his student days at Oxford, and "now, more than half a century later, I am still an agnostic."[9] Yet his works are full of Christian terminology, theology, and symbolism. In the *Study* he proclaimed religion as the key purpose of history's movement and history itself as "a vision of God's creation on the move, from God its source towards God its goal."[10] He also urged upon his readers that Western civilization might be reprieved from disaster by earnest, humble, and contrite prayer. The contrast between self-proclaimed agnosticism and the religious tenor of his writings seems impossible to reconcile. Yet Toynbee also indicated that his agnostic views arose from his difficulty in accepting the beliefs of organized religion in a wholesale manner. Meanwhile, he clearly felt and embraced the principles of humankind's higher religions devoutly and with understanding. While he could not readily accept sectarian ideology, he apparently possessed a deep capacity for religious faith.

Arnold Toynbee died in October 1975 at the age of eighty-six at a nursing home in York, England, from the aftereffects of a stroke. While he held the strongest influence over informed opinion of any historian of his generation, his masterwork remains one of the wonders of the scholarly world, read by specialists and laymen alike as a major intellectual adventure.

A Study of History

The most distinctive feature of *A Study of History* is its enormous scope. Ranging over all humanity's recorded past and most of the earth's surface, the mammoth project was without precedent. Only in recent times, in fact, did such a study become possible, as Orientalists collected new knowledge about still-living civilizations of the East and archaeologists from the nineteenth century onward uncovered remains of civilizations so utterly lost that their writing was extinct and their very names forgotten.

Drawing together a vast trove of information old and new, the *Study* spans the millennia with the ease of a magic carpet, gliding from the ancient cultures of Sumer and Babylonia to the Austro-Hungarian monarchy, the United States Civil War and the twentieth century's nuclear dilemma. Despite its vast coverage of time and place, the work illuminates the past with specifics—from the Amalung leaders of the Arian Ostrogoths; to the Vlach people of the Rumelian highlands; to the Nestorian Uighur Turkish secretaries of the Mongols; to Mursil I, King of Khatti; to Nanak who founded Indian Sikhism; to Ogier Ghiselin de Busbecq, a sixteenth-century Hapsburg ambassador to the Ottoman Sultan Suleiman the Magnificent. In its erudite richness, the *Study* presumes its readers have either a scholar's foreknowledge or a handy encyclopedia.

Hardly less distinctive than its scope is the *Study*'s size. It is, as one critic observed, "the most massive work that our generation has seen or is likely to see."[11] The twelve volumes contain more than three million words, which makes the work three times the size of Gibbon's *Decline and Fall* and six times larger than Oswald Spengler's magnum opus. The great ocean of typography washes over some seven thousand pages. Indexes alone cover 412 pages. A diligent scholar meaning to complete the work can expect to give it something like six to eight months of his reading time. A more leisurely reader will be at it for over a year. One of Toynbee's major commentators suspended his normal family life and read for thirty hours and more per week through the autumn of one year into the winter of the next before he finished the ten basic volumes.

When Harvard sociologist Pitirim A. Sorokin reviewed the first six volumes, he remarked that the work "could have been compressed without losing anything in the clearness and completeness of its theory."[12] Toynbee apparently agreed, and he welcomed news of the 1947 abridgment made by English schoolmaster and author-historian David Churchill Somervell, "for my own amusement, without Mr. Toynbee's knowledge and without any idea of publication."[13] Somervell's condensation, which eventually covered volumes one through ten, trimmed their girth down to two volumes and little more than a thousand pages.

Toynbee's style, like Spengler's, varies from turgid to superb. At times the tone is pedantic. Often sentences drag on to cumbersome length, clogged with great masses of factual matter and the scrupulous qualifications of a professional historian. The author quoted sources in Latin and Greek, French and German, even Chinese and Hindustani, which sometimes he neglected to translate. Also he oddly spoke of the present as though his audience were living in the distant future, apparently confident that his work would endure through the centuries.

Toynbee admitted that his style had faults, saying he would have felt more comfortable writing in classical Greek or Latin. Yet at the *Study*'s frequent better moments, the reader can almost hear an urbane English gentleman in delightfully informal conversation. At its best, the style opens out full, supple, and splendid, as when the author, describing ancient Mayan ruins, wrote: "The forest, like some sylvan boa-constrictor, has literally swallowed them up and is now devouring them at its leisure, prising the fine-hewn close-laid stones apart with its writhing roots and tendrils."[14]

As Spengler did before him, Toynbee took on many roles in his work. He considered himself a historian—or, more precisely, a "post-modern western historian."[15] Yet his task of dealing with whole civilizations casts him more as a philosopher of history, while his comparison of their rising and falling is evocative of sociology. Toynbee has been called a literary artist who, like Irish novelist James Joyce, "took all knowledge for his playground," while his *Study* has been deemed both a prose epic and a poem in prose. He is seen, especially among scholars, as the twentieth century's leading religious historian. With his alert eye on the future, he also is declared a modern prophet.

Finally, Toynbee proved to be his own most thorough critic. He gathered more than two hundred major criticisms, including the harshest and most probing, and included them in the *Study*'s twelfth volume. Titled *Reconsiderations*, the final segment of his project is a remarkable document of humility and questing for truth. In more than seven hundred pages, Toynbee took each critique with an open mind, candidly admitting second thoughts, backtracking on some issues, adding nuances to others, and, in general, smoothing and softening the *Study*'s initially sharper lines. *Reconsiderations* chipped at his masterwork more severely than all his critics put together. Yet even after this unusual exercise in self-examination, the *Study* as a whole still stood strongly.

Toynbee departed from Spengler in his approach to humankind's story. He relied less on intuitive grasp and more on scientific method. "I do think," he wrote in a private correspondence, "that the scientific apparatus can be applied fruitfully to human affairs to some extent, e.g., where they are considerably affected by the physical environment and where it is the subconscious part of the psyche more than the will and the intellect that is in command."[16] In his efforts to contribute to a science of history, Toynbee approaches the intent of Henry Adams, though he carried it off more successfully. At the same time, Toynbee did not deny the value of intuition or artistic insight, and while he discounted Spengler's dogmatic tone, he admired the German thinker's genius and remarkable work.

In their ultimate goals, Toynbee and Spengler coincided closely. Both were system builders, workers in grand theories, investigators of the regularities, uniformities, recurrences, norms, and "laws" patterning the past. For both, the decline of the West served as their basic inspiration and theme. Believing their civilization to be in trouble, they were trying to determine how far it already had gone into decline. Each attempted to take bearings in the uncharted seas of a threatening future by tracing the voyages of other civilizations long since fulfilled.

8

Civilizations

Civilization, Toynbee pointed out, is a species of human society. Another species, seen as lower because it has not attained the civilized condition, is known generally as primitive society. Though this latter category is far larger—by one reckoning, more than 650 primitive societies exist—rarely is it dealt with by historians, but left instead to anthropologists. Midway through his work, Toynbee suggested that a third major social species might exist, one as distinct from civilization as civilization is from primitivism. This type of society is represented by the world's great religious organizations, such as Christianity, Islam, Buddhism, and Hinduism. He treated this theme further as the *Study* advanced, but the bulk of the work remains focused on civilizations past and present.

Toynbee did not adopt the verbal distinction made by Nietzsche and Spengler between "Culture" as a rising advanced society and "Civilization" as one in decline. Rather, he used "civilization" to cover all stages of a higher society's development. Also, in a literary instead of a scientific way, he employed "civilization" and "society" as synonyms.

Each civilization is a vast complex of political, artistic, and religious traits spread over large areas of territory and including great populations. At the same time, Toynbee indicated, civilizations "are wholes whose parts all cohere with one another and all affect one another reciprocally."[1] He defined the civilized condition itself in humane, even spiritual terms, "as an endeavour to create a state of society in which the whole of mankind will be able to live together in harmony, as members of a single all-inclusive family."[2]

Like many other scholars of the higher cultures, Toynbee rejected as an egocentric error the idea that past civilizations have led progressively upward to a pinnacle attained by the West in the present day. Similarly, he discarded the common diffusionist notion that history expanded as a single mighty torrent, with civilization developing in Egypt and spreading outward from there. Instead, he saw advanced societies rising separately in a half-dozen regions in Africa, Asia, Europe, and America.

Yet he also saw definite relationships between many higher cultures. Though all civilizations are unique and individual, some are linked in generations much as parents and children are. Some civilized societies die without offspring, as those of the ancient Egyptians and the Incas of the Andes. But most of them provide the germs of new higher cultures as the Minoan civilization of Crete inspired the rise of Greece and as Greco-Roman culture furnished a foundation for Western society. Beginning from the dawn of history some five to six thousand years ago, Toynbee traced three generations of civilizations to the present. All current survivors are of the third generation.

Where Nikolai Danilevsky examined ten higher cultures and Oswald Spengler classified eight, Toynbee identified and investigated about thirty. Included in his reckoning were promising cultures that abortively failed to develop. Among these was the Far Western Christian society of the early Irish Celts, which blossomed from the fourth to the twelfth centuries. Another was the Scandinavian society, an aesthetic culture resembling the classical Greek that was absorbed in the rise and spread of Christian Europe. Also in his count were several societies—as the Nomad, the Eskimo, and the Polynesian—that got off to impressive starts but were arrested in their growth and equally failed to develop.

All the more familiar higher cultures are covered in Toynbee's list: the "Sumeric" (or Sumerian), the durable "Egyptiac" which lasted three times longer than Western civilization to date, the "Sinic" of China, and the Hindu of the Indian subcontinent. Added to the tally are the somewhat lesser known ancient "Babylonic" and Hittite cultures and the present-day Orthodox Christian culture founded in the age of the Byzantine Empire and still surviving in the Middle East and Russia.

Toynbee drew together the Israelites, Phoenicians, and Philistines into a single "Syriac" society, which invented the alphabet, discovered the Atlantic Ocean, and arrived at the concept of one God. Like Spengler, he combined the Greeks and Romans into one civilization, seeing Rome as a community drawn into Greek orbit long before the age of Socrates and only long afterward rising to lead the culture to its end.

Toynbee's classification of the civilized societies of history is more complete and rigorous than any made before and offers a solid and comprehensive structure for drawing cultural comparisons. Yet for all its high polish, he never considered it final. It always was open to revision on the grounds of new archaeological evidence and fresh interpretations.

For example, some civilizations were so similar—as those of Sumeria and the later Babylonia—that Toynbee first regarded them as separate but subsequently reclassified the latter as no more than a Sumerian epilogue. At one stage the author mused that ancient Egypt might have had two distinct societies, an early and a later, each with its rise and collapse. Ultimately, however, he decided to combine them into one on the basis of similarities. After longer hesitation and led by new discoveries, he made the same decision about civilizations of mid-America, which originally he had divided triply into Mayan as a culture of the first generation and "Yucatec" and "Mexic" as societies of the second.

Ultimately, Toynbee had two different lists of civilizations, and he published both in the *Study*'s final volume of reconsiderations.[3]

He also observed that future discoveries might produce further revision. In the main, however, such classifications are meant to serve specialized scholars and have little effect upon the *Study*'s major point and purpose.

Toynbee saw Western civilization emerging from the wreckage of Hellenic Rome about A.D. 675. Today it shares the earth with four other higher cultures: the Orthodox Christian, Islam, Hindu society, and the Far Eastern civilization of China and its cultural satellites, Japan, Korea, and Vietnam. These four old neighbors, however, are so far gone into decay that, according to Toynbee, their death is a predictable certainty. The condition of the West he kept as an open question through much of his work, though he repeatedly suggested that the culture is well past its zenith.

So of the two dozen or so civilizations that were born alive and grew, most already are dead and buried. And all the survivors but one are in advanced stages of decline, while the single higher culture with any life remaining probably has one foot in the grave.

Toynbee's phases of civilization's rise and fall are similar to Spengler's seasonal analogy of spring, summer, autumn, and winter. In his words, the four main periods are genesis, growth, breakdown, and disintegration. In presenting the first as the *Study* opened, the author blazed a fresh trail into little-known historical terrain.

GENESIS

Primitive societies are static, not growing, never progressing. Yet they could not always have been so. At one time, more than three hundred thousand years ago, they must have been rising dynamically. With a greater advance than any civilization yet has made, they lifted their members from the level of subman to the condition of humanity. Thus primitive groups probably are static at present only because they were exhausted by their massive feat of growth and still are at rest.

Toynbee likened humanity's climb, initially and since then, to the ascent of a cliff. Primitive societies of today are huddled on a ledge. A drop of dizzying depths yawns below. Above, a sheer rock wall soars to heights yet unknown. Civilized societies have resumed the climb. No one can discern how high the next ledge above them is, nor even if the climbers can attain it. Any serious mistake will send them plunging to their death; many former civilizations already lie shattered on the ledge where they began. Yet once a society has started out, it cannot go back or even pause. It must continue climbing.

Out of hundreds of primitive societies, why have a few shaken off static repose to attempt the precarious climb to civilization? In times past, race was thought to be the answer, with superior races naturally rising to civilized levels. But Toynbee, displaying a considerable knowledge of anthropology, rejected this explanation. The white race of Europe and the Middle East, the brown race of India and Indonesia, the red race of the Americas, and the yellow race of Asia all have contributed independently to major civilizations.

As far back as the age of the ancient Greeks, geographic environment often has been seen as the reason for differences in culture. As a sole explanation for the rise of civilizations, that theory was discarded by Toynbee too. He disposed of it by means of an empirical test.

The fertile Nile Valley held a higher culture, as did the similarly hot, dry, and well-watered region of the Tigris and Euphrates Rivers. But the Jordan Valley, though much the same in its conditions, produced no civilized society, nor did the Rio Grande and the Colorado River in North America. Likewise, Inca peoples built a civilization on the high Andean plateau, but a comparable region in East Africa failed to generate an advanced society. Similarly, the civilization of the Mayas sprang out of tropical forests in middle America, yet equal conditions along the Amazon and Congo Rivers gave rise to no higher cultures in either place.

The fault of the race and environment theories lies in their attempt to apply the procedures of material sciences—biology and geology—to a question that is not material but spiritual. To explore that realm, Toynbee took his cue from psychology and delved into universal myths.

Throughout the misty records of mythology, he found time and again a tale of great challenge followed by great response. This occurs in the Biblical Old Testament with the encounter between the Hebrew God Yahweh and the serpent; it recurs in the later Old Testament book of Job and in the New Testament account of Christ's redemption; it appears equally in the ancient Greek tragedy *Hippolytus* written by Euripides, in the old Scandinavian Eddic poem *Voluspa*, in Goethe's drama *Faust*. Challenge upsets a static condition, while response is creative effort. In the symbolic terms of Chinese culture, the static Yin goes over to the dynamic Yang, a basic alternation seen in many ages as fundamental to the nature of the universe.

Taking this mythological clue, Toynbee applied it to the stirring of societies from static torpor to dynamic activity. He suggested that a challenge of special difficulty can spur a primitive society to an unprecedentedly effortful response and this will raise it to the level of civilization. Again using the empirical method as his test, the author began with the six civilizations that have arisen, as far as we know, directly from primitive conditions.

Ancient Egypt, he related, came into being as the latest ice age retreated. Temperate rains nurturing a verdant belt of grassland across the present-day Sahara region were shifting north to Europe, leaving northern Africa ever drier. The area's population of hunters and food gatherers, watching their livelihood wither away, had to find a different home or new ways of existing. Some migrated south into tropical country, and from all anthropological evidence, their descendants remain there today as the Dinka, Nuer, and Shilluk tribal peoples who resemble the earliest Egyptians in appearance, stature, cranial proportions, language, dress, and customs. Other peoples caught in the desertland survived by adopting a nomadic way of life. Still others bushwhacked into the virtually impenetrable jungle-swamps of the Nile Valley. Transforming the riverine wilderness into a neat pattern of ditches, embankments, and fields, they not only created the country of Egypt but also gave momentum to the vigorous ascent of a civilization.

The same conditions around the same period of time spurred the rise of the similar Sumerian culture in teeming jungle-swampland of the Tigris-Euphrates delta. This society's great civilizing struggle also was recorded in myth: The god Marduk slays the dragon Tiamat and creates the world out of her remains, symbolizing the subjection of the wilds with canals to guide the waters and drainage works to create fertile fields.

Present knowledge of the history of ancient China does not suggest the challenge that spurred higher culture there. Once again, however, it occurred along a watercourse, the Yellow River, and under conditions made all the more severe by extremes of summer heat and winter cold.

Like the Egyptian and Sumerian cultures, the Minoan civilization of ancient Crete was founded as a result of changing climate. Archaeological evidence of skull types on the island indicates that early residents came north from Africa. Their great challenge lay in overcoming the sea.

The Mayans of Guatemala and Belize took their stimulus from tangled jungles. The Inca culture centered in Peru overcame a dual challenge. The Andean plateau offered settlers a bleak climate and grudging soil, to which the residents responded by building stone retaining walls and terraces for planting. The Pacific coastland, in the meantime, is blisteringly hot, almost-rainless desert. The pioneers there devised irrigation works that collected water from Andean slopes and turned dead land into a chain of rich oases.

Not all civilizations arose solely on the stimulus of geographical challenge. Advanced societies of later generations often found much of their incitement in the stagnation of declining predecessors that, in effect, had relapsed to the static condition. For example, both the youthful Western society and Orthodox Christian culture pushed off on their voyages through history from the decaying ancient Greco-Roman civilization.

Toynbee demonstrated a variety of challenges that spurred the rise of humankind in different times and places. Difficult terrain induced high achievement in China, Greece, and the Middle East, as well as in northern Europe and America. The task of breaking in virgin ground consistently has produced more vigorous responses than life on land tamed by prior civilizations. Both Greco-Roman and Western history illustrate that sudden crushing military defeat can stimulate a people to "set their house in order" and rise again with strength redoubled like the giant Antaeus of Hellenic mythology. Peoples ranked along a hostile frontier tend to advance more readily than their sheltered neighbors. Early Ottoman Turks thrust up against the border of the Byzantine Empire, and Austrians who later guarded Europe from the Turks both illustrate this point. Social penalizations also can stimulate development. The freed slave class in ancient Rome rose to considerable power, as did conquered Christians under Ottoman rule and the long-displaced Jews who have flourished repeatedly under severe penalizations.

The challenges that lead to growth can vary widely. But contrary to a popular assumption, it is always challenge—and not lotus-land conditions—that lies at the basis of humankind's civilizations. As Cyrus the Great, King of Persia, observed some five centuries before Christ: "Soft countries . . . invariably breed soft men."[4] And hard conditions, often threatening life itself, time and again have invoked both brave responses and success much greater than anything originally intended.

Just as ease tempts people to go slack, so can a challenge be too harsh. In technical terms, "the interaction of challenge and response is subject to a 'law of diminishing returns'."[5] The aborted civilizations of early Christian Ireland and Viking Scandinavia both were cultural embryos overwhelmed by the challenge from their far more powerful and growing Western neighbor. So the most stimulating challenge lies in the mean between a deficiency of severity and an excess of it. A challenge too slight might fail to stimulate at all, while one too harsh can break a people's spirit.

Growth

Once a civilization is born, its growth is far from guaranteed. Much to the contrary, the higher cultures that Toynbee calls arrested civilizations have grown little if at all.

Polynesian peoples conquered the sea even more boldly than Minoans or Vikings, establishing themselves on isolated islands thousands of miles apart. Yet, while they overcame the challenge of the Pacific Ocean, they were left paralyzed for any further action. In their outrigger sailing canoes—as long as large modern yachts and, with a good wind, as swift as steamships—they could cross enormous distances of water. But never could they sail with reasonable safety. As a consequence, the Polynesians never rose above their environment. They remained in exact equilibrium with the ocean around them. Eventually they lost their civilizing tension, went slack, and fell into lotus-eating ease.

The culture of the Eskimos similarly was stunted by the massive challenge of the Arctic ice. The society's basic response was successful as it overcame brutally harsh conditions with marvelous ingenuity: Eskimos invented or elaborated the kayak, the harpoon, and the three-pronged salmon spear, the bird dart propelled by throwing board, the compound hunting bow, the dog sled, the snowshoe, and the igloo. But again, because the primary challenge was so great, Arctic society froze into a static condition.

The same proved true for the society of the Nomads. Like oceanic sailors or fishermen, nomadic peoples occupied regions accessible only to wanderers. Open expanses of grass and gravel, with oases for islands and a ring of settled lands for shores, the desert would support only people constantly on the move. Nomadic groups met the challenge of the regions' desiccation when they devised a mobile way of life. But their successful response also locked them at a static level. They became prisoners of climate, wholly occupied with following yearly vegetation cycles.

The arrested civilizations differ from abortive societies, like the Irish Christian and the early Scandinavian that were absorbed into Western culture before they could be born, as infantile paralysis differs from infant mortality. Arrested cultures came to birth by triumphantly meeting a great challenge. But their initial response to challenge so tied up their energies that not enough productive force was left for growth. They relapsed into a stationary state resembling the nonevolving societies of bees and ants. In terms of Toynbee's cliff analogy, they are like climbers who reach a position at which they have barely the strength to hang on but not enough to move higher. "Their posture is one of perilous immobility at high tension."[6] In this position they gradually wither away.

Two more arrested civilizations came to birth by way of human, rather than geographical, challenges. The people of the ancient city-state of Sparta met the problem of growing population on limited land by training armies and marching against fellow Greeks. But their military conquests had the effect of holding them captive as well, because when their subjects revolted, they were forced to be always on guard. The victorious society never could relax and go on to fresh challenges.

The nomadic Ottoman Turks, storming off the steppes of central Asia, conquered the aging Byzantine Empire in the fifteenth century. As masters of a wide domain of settled lands, they faced the challenge of adapting nomadic ways to sedentary conditions. They achieved this by forming a court of slaves that they used like sheep dogs to oversee peoples whom they governed as they once had herded cattle. But, like the Spartans, they too became paralyzed by their own methods. The demands of keeping control over large subject populations used up their entire fund of energies. Ultimately their system, like that of the Spartans, proved too rigid in its neglect of human nature and broke down.

The failure of the five arrested higher cultures shows that a moderate and workable challenge is ideal for the growth of civilization. Such challenges spur societies to successful response and leave enough momentum to carry cultures on through to other challenges. So civilizations grow—from one challenge to the next—from struggle to equilibrium to overbalance, in repetitive, recurrent rhythm. Toynbee, unlike Spengler, saw no reason advanced societies, once launched by challenge, could not go on growing indefinitely.

And what does growth in a civilization amount to? What is the criterion of progress for a higher culture?

Sometimes territorial expansion goes along with a society's rise. Yet, contrary to popular belief, geographical enlargement far more often accompanies decline. Ordinarily the new ground is gained by militarism, a common feature of cultural breakdown and disintegration. So while a time of conquest often is hailed as a high point in a culture, it usually is evidence of serious social disease. It is "the malady of the Reptiles, who turned huge on the eve of being surpassed by the Mammals; or the malady of Goliath who grew to gigantic stature in order to succumb to David."[7] Toynbee concluded that territorial expansion is not a criterion of civilization's progress.

Modern technological society often assumes that improved technology is a mark of growth within a culture. Evidence indicates otherwise. In many advanced societies, techniques have improved while civilization on the whole remained static or fell into decline. Conversely, techniques sometimes stayed the same as civilization in general moved either forward or backward. In short, "there is no correlation between progress in technique and progress in civilization."[8] In fact, Toynbee asserted, the material trappings of human society "are all trivialities which do not touch the heart of what we mean by a civilization in any respect. A civilization does not consist in machine-sewing or rifle-shooting or tea- and coffee- and cocoa-drinking or tobacco-smoking. It does not even consist in reading and writing or in metallurgy. . . . To equate this kind of thing with 'Civilization' with a capital 'C' is an absurdity which would be inconceivable to a cultivated mind that was either Hindu or Hellenic or Western of an earlier generation."[9]

Yet material progress can play a useful part in a higher culture's growth. It can pave the way upward by liberating people from a preoccupation with material concerns so they can live with greater potency on a higher spiritual plane.

Progress in spiritualization—or in Toynbee's term 'etherialization'—marks every growing higher culture. In a rising civilization, human endeavor is shifting all the time from external issues to internal matters, from the society's environment to its own body social, from lower to loftier spheres of being and action. Early Western civilization overcame the challenge of devastating Viking incursions, then used the breathing space it won to begin replacing its own feudal system with new relations between state and citizens. Modern society builds a high technology, then finds its next major life-or-death struggle in the spiritual realm, working out an ethical set of uses and controls for that technology. The whole process of civilization amounts to vanquishing external problems to grapple with internal ones. Increasingly dispensing with outside challenges, the society becomes its own challenger, its own environment, its own field of action. So growth in a civilization is defined not as wider boundaries or cleverer mechanical devices but as progress in the struggle for self-determination.

In no growing society is every person creative. In fact, very few people are endowed with the creative spark even in the most brilliant civilizations. The growth of any higher culture is the work not of the whole society but of individual productive personalities or, at most, creative minorities.

Ordinarily, people who inspire growth within a civilization arrive at their inspiration by withdrawing from their society for a time. The Buddha abandoned a luxurious life as son of a ruler in northern India and withdrew to asceticism before he found enlightenment. Jesus withdrew to wilderness for forty days and nights and only then returned to begin his teaching. St. Paul of Tarsus, enlightened by a vision of Christ on the road to Damascus, withdrew for three years to the desert in Arabia before he traveled to Jerusalem to meet the apostles. The same process of withdrawal and return preceded the inspired work of the Chinese sage Confucius, the early Christian saints Benedict and Gregory, and the Arabian prophet of Islam, Mohammed. Likewise, the Florentine poet Dante Alighieri, the Renaissance statesman Niccolo Machiavelli, and the modern political leaders Giuseppe Garibaldi and Vladimir Lenin passed through similar stages of withdrawal before achieving their notable accomplishments.

The act of withdrawal often is voluntary. Sometimes it is not, as in the case of Machiavelli, who was banished from his native city of Florence to his Tuscan farm, and Lenin, who spent long years in exile from his Russian homeland. Whatever its cause, the period of detachment helps the creative person realize inner powers that might have lain dormant had he not been released from the toils, habits, and restraints of his normal environment. In separation, the gifted person marshals and orders his strengths. Then he returns to apply them to his society.

How the inspired person will be received by his former peers is always uncertain. He returns to persuade the uncreative majority to follow his lead. His task is to raise their consciousness. Yet the mass of people are not only uncreative, they tend to be inert. They do not always comply with creative thinking. Great prophets, teachers, and leaders have suffered ridicule, abuse, attempts upon their lives, and death itself. Yet personal transfiguration, without the intent to inspire others, would become selfish and sterile. So usually the social genius tries to pass on his gift.

When a creative pioneer is received well enough to wield a positive influence upon his society, only a few followers take on his spirit. The mass of humankind, even with the best of leaders, still remains bogged in inertia. The only way people can be set in motion toward a goal beyond themselves is through "mimesis," or imitation.

Imitative behavior is basic to all societies. Among primitive peoples, it characteristically looks backward toward elder generations and dead ancestors. In civilizations, it looks forward, fixed on creative persons and minorities. In either instance, the rank and file follow leaders in a kind of social drill, mechanically mimicking newly acceptable aptitudes, emotions, and ideas.

What leads the masses to imitate creative growth? Quite simply, they do so because inspired leaders hold magnetic charm, a charisma that naturally attracts. The pleasant warmth of creative light radiating from the gifted minority captivates the entire society and fuses it together in voluntary unity. Nor does mimesis stop there. The allure of creativity radiates outward beyond the bounds of the society itself to uncivilized neighbors. When that happens, the alien peoples, rather than attacking the society, strive to imitate too.

A civilization beams out to rougher peoples in three distinct and separate rays: economic, political, and cultural. As long as the society is growing, these rays have equal carrying power and the frontier between civilized and uncivilized peoples becomes blurred to the point of nonexistence. Nearby barbaric neighbors soon are virtually as civilized as the higher culture's people, and the lustrous influence trails off so gradually that no one can tell precisely where it ends.

Also, as a civilization grows, it develops differentiation, both within itself and in comparison to other higher cultures. One segment of the society successfully meets a challenge, another follows behind, and still another fails altogether in its response. The longer a civilization grows, the more these internal differences in progress and character arise. Separate civilizations, meeting challenges that are entirely different, diverge from one another all the more. And again, the longer they grow, the more different they become.

The differentiation between separate societies expresses itself in many ways. As a single example, every civilization creates its own distinctive style of art. Also, as Spengler, too, observed, various societies emphasize different cultural activities. Ancient Greece held an outlook on life that was mainly aesthetic. The civilizations of India have stressed religion. Western culture has a strong bent toward mechanical inventiveness, industrial creativity, and material interests in general.

Yet differences between higher cultures, however great they become, remain no more than superficial in the grand perspective of world history. They are rather like masks worn by climbers scaling the cultural cliff, who nonetheless remain unified in every important regard. The climbers all began from the same starting point on the ledge of primitivism. And they all are struggling to attain the same unseen ledge above.

Breakdown

A civilization continues to grow until it suffers what Toynbee calls breakdown. However final the term might sound, "breakdown" as Toynbee used the word means only the first false step that sets a civilization on the road to decline. It is a blunder, a faltering, a reaching for a handhold on the rockface of the cultural cliff that breaks free and leaves the climber teetering for balance. It is the end, not of the civilization, but only of its audacious attempt at uninterrupted ascent.

Nor does breakdown imply the end of the society's accomplishments. Some of the most fruitful, illuminating, and celebrated achievements of a higher culture might occur after breakdown, and even as a consequence of it.

A civilization breaks down when it fails to answer a major challenge with a successful response. For example, Greco-Roman culture very early in its course was confronted with a need to expand its narrowly parochial city-state sovereignty to a broader inter-state society. Problems both economic and military demanded some form of union and mutual cooperation. Yet, presented with this vital challenge, it failed in its response. The city-states went to war with one another instead. The consequence was breakdown: the early beginning of a long, drawn-out end.

When a society's response to challenge proves unsuccessful, fresh challenges cease to arise and social growth ceases with them. The unmet challenge then repeats itself, again demanding a solution. Throughout the earlier part of Greco-Roman history, the need for effective political unity arose repeatedly. But city-state wars continued to devastate the society. Finally Rome, growing in might, forced a unification with a series of military knock-out blows, gathering the whole Mediterranean world into its empire. But by that time the society already was well on its way to disintegration.

Breakdown characteristically afflicted civilizations early in their history. Sumerian culture broke down before 2600 B.C., long before its final disappearance. Likewise, ancient Egypt, after a precocious youth, lost its grip on the upward cliff of growth as early as 2400 B.C. Its society failed to rise above the dead weight of pharaonic politics with its socially wasteful tomb pyramids and top-heavy, increasingly parasitic and ultimately insupportable bureaucracy. Greco-Roman civilization broke down only seven hundred years after it emerged, the turning point occurring just before the birth of Plato with the onset of the Atheno-Peloponnesian War in 431 B.C. The present civilization of China stumbled into breakdown in the last quarter of the ninth century A.D. The Orthodox Christian society of the Middle East faltered about a century later.

The danger of breakdown obviously is great for any civilization. Of all the higher cultures of past and present that have entered the growing stage, every one has broken down, except perhaps the West. And in all likelihood, Toynbee speculated, the West as well has passed this early milepost of decline.

What causes civilizations to fail in response to a major challenge, to break down? Before answering this crucial question, Toynbee disposed of several factors that commonly but wrongly have been thought to cause cultural downfall.

"One of the perennial infirmities of human beings," he began, "is to ascribe their own failure to forces that are entirely beyond their control. This mental manoeuvre is particularly attractive to sensitive minds in periods of decline and fall."[10]

Among the various deterministic theories that people have devised to explain cultural decline is the notion of "cosmic senescence." The Roman poet Lucretius, who lived at the time of Julius Caesar, advanced this then-common theory to account for social decay that philosophers deplored but could not find a way to halt. Some three centuries later, St. Cyprian, the Christian bishop of the city of Carthage on the North African coast, also embraced the notion. In terms reminiscent of H.G. Wells's final warning of earthly demise, Cyprian wrote:

> You ought to be aware that the age is now senile. It has not now the stamina that used to make it upstanding, nor the vigour and robustness that used to make it strong. This truth is proclaimed . . . by the World itself, which testifies to its own decline by giving manifold concrete evidences of the process of decay. There is a diminution in the winter rains that give nourishment to the seeds in the earth, and in the summer heats that ripen the harvests. The springs have less freshness and the autumns less fecundity. The mountains, disembowelled and worn out, yield a lower output of marble; the mines, exhausted, furnish a smaller stock of the precious metals: the veins are impoverished, and they shrink daily. There is a decrease and deficiency of farmers in the fields, of sailors on the sea, of soldiers in the barracks, of honesty in the marketplace, of justice in court, of concord in friendship, of skill in technique, of strictness in morals. . . . Anything that is near its end and is verging towards its decline and fall is bound to dwindle. . . . This loss of strength and loss of stature must end, at last, in annihilation.[11]

Time has ruled against the Roman version of cosmic senescence. So has modern science. While physicists lately have adopted a theory of their own along the same lines, envisioning the universe running down as matter gradually is transformed into radiation, they project that the cosmos has at least two thousand million years to go. So however it might be declining, civilizations both past and present are free from the effects.

Toynbee disagreed also with Oswald Spengler's deterministic theory that cultures are living organisms and therefore naturally doomed to age and die. He saw a society as the common ground between the fields of action of its individual members. While he noted definite patterns in the course of higher cultures, he did not accept decline as inevitable.

He disagreed, too, with the old idea that civilization exerts a degrading influence upon people, leading them regressively downward with each passing generation. Brooks Adams assumed this in *The Law of Civilization and Decay* when he referred to barbarian blood as the factor that restored Europe after the collapse of Rome. And the Roman poet Horace made the same assumption some nineteen hundred years earlier when he wrote:

Degenerate sires' degenerate seed,
We'll soon beget a fourth-rate breed.[12]

The reasoning that civilization debilitates people, Toynbee pointed out, mistakes an effect of social decline for a cause. Members of a deteriorating society might seem like cripples or pygmies in comparison to their forefathers. But the reason is not biological. Rather, it lies with the degenerate society blocking its people from developing their faculties.

Toynbee also rejected the cyclic theory of human society that prevailed in the days of Plato that envisioned cultures rising and waning as necessarily as the sun and the moon, the seasons, and organic life. This idea, which arose out of ancient Babylonian astronomical discoveries, lacks the support of more sophisticated evidence.

With deterministic causes of breakdown brushed aside, the author also discarded the notions that civilizations can be destroyed by alien incursion or sudden loss of technical expertise. Just as geographical expansion and improved technology are no criteria of genuine cultural growth, neither does territorial contraction nor diminishing technique cause decline.

An alien attack against a healthily growing civilization will not wipe it out but stimulate it to further growth. Only when a society is in decline can an enemy contribute to its demise. Thus Germanic barbarians did not destroy Greco-Roman civilization; they merely administered its coup de grace. And the civilizations of the Aztecs in Mexico and the Incas in Peru were not wrecked by Spanish conquistadors; they had broken down long before the Spaniards arrived and were only finished off prematurely by the invaders.

Likewise, the deterioration of Roman roads that once laced Western Europe was not a cause of the society's decline but one of its consequences. And a crucial abandonment of the ancient irrigation system in the Tigris-Euphrates delta between the seventh and thirteenth centuries A.D. did not cause the decay of the Syriac civilization but, rather, resulted from it.

So how do civilizations die, if not by the hand of nature, the violence of enemies, or technological failure? Toynbee's answer points to a kind of suicide. They are betrayed not by outside factors but by what is false within.

This self-betrayal begins with the same faculty that launched the society into growth: the trait of mimesis, or imitation. Mimesis proved the only means for the otherwise inert majority to follow inspired leaders, since inspiration rarely is transferable directly. Yet leaders cannot be relied upon to remain creative. The danger always exists that they will relax and become infected with the same hypnotized mimesis of their followers, tending blindly to accept established ways.

Christ pointed to the damaging effect of putting new, actively fermenting wine into old wineskins, which causes the skins to burst and the wine to be lost. Toynbee applied this metaphor to the danger of pouring new social forces into old institutions. Ideally, the appearance of dynamic new aptitudes, emotions, and ideas should spur reconstruction of the whole set of a society's institutions to keep them working together in smooth and balanced harmony. In a growing society readjustment always is going on, bringing up to date the more flagrant anachronisms. But when change in institutions proves inadequate, the new wine of fresh social forces threatens to burst the institutions with its ferment. If this happens, the rupture amounts to a revolution. This sort of explosion—a delayed catching up—announces that further growth will be increasingly hazardous. If, on the other hand, the institutions hold firm in spite of straining pressure for change, the fresh social forces are stifled altogether. And this indicates that breakdown has occurred.

Creative minorities sometimes fall into fatal inertia by resting on their laurels. They achieve success, take up pride, and soon are creating no more—a case of the self-satisfied climber ceasing to strive and losing his grip.

Or the leaders might cling to old institutions that have outlived their usefulness, imagining them to be permanently adequate. In such a way did ancient Egyptians cling to their oppressive government of pharaoh and cumbersome bureaucracy and Greco-Roman peoples adhere to the city-state long after the swelling size of their society left it no longer workable as a political unit.

A once-inventive leadership might rely too long upon established techniques, again resting on laurels. The history of warfare is full of instances in which victors of one age become victims in the next because their techniques of combat were superseded by the methods of an enemy. Modern leaders of industry likewise are notable for idolizing obsolescent methods that once made fortunes in the past but since have been supplanted.

By far the commonest cause of breakdown has been fratricidal warfare between states failing to end conflict soon enough by expanding government from parochial to universal. This problem, Toynbee repeatedly pointed out, has been challenging the culture of the West for some time and continues to loom as the gravest challenge of the present.

Finally, breakdown also can spring from victory itself. Either military or spiritual triumph can catapult the victor to downfall when success emboldens him to pursue inordinate goals and expectations.

Whatever form failed creativity might take, it also leads the society to failure in self-determination. A civilization fallen into bondage to an idol of its own making—whether past successes, hallowed institutions, revered techniques or militarism—forfeits freedom of choice. Its institutions, not changing in unison, slip out of harmony. Then the masses become aware that their leaders have gone static—that the blind are leading the blind. In pained disillusion, they abandon their former ready allegiance and withdraw their mimesis. With the loss of creativity and consequent disunity, the civilization no longer is setting its own course.

Just as progress in self-determination was the ultimate criterion of growth, so is loss of self-determination, rather than any outside factors, the ultimate criterion of a culture's breakdown. A broken-down civilization, its grip lost on the cliff-face of growth, begins an anguished skid into its final phase: a centuries-long disintegration.

Disintegration

A civilization that has lost its creativity and broken down finds the harmony of its growth period cracking in several directions. Discord and conflict erupt between states, between social classes, and in the individual souls of the society's people.

The most spectacular symptom of disintegration is a series of violent and vicious wars breaking out among the society's separate political units. Toynbee refers to this season of suicidal statecraft as the civilization's "time of troubles," a term that originated in Russian history. The Chinese called their time of troubles *chan kwo*—"the [period of] contending states"—which is the historical designation Oswald Spengler adopted to describe the bloodstained centuries that mark the bleak dawn of his Civilizational wintertime. Neither term adequately expresses the horror of the succession of wars that eat away at the margins of ordinary life until the society lies prostrate and exhausted by savage and wanton destruction. The

Sumerian and Egyptian cultures, ancient Greece and Rome, the civilizations of China and India, the advanced societies of Peru and Mexico, and the civilization of the Middle East all passed through this devastating stage of decline.

Another trait of disintegrating civilization is a conflict along class lines between leaders and the led. This social split, absent during periods of growth, appears at the moment of breakdown and distinctly signals a culture's decay. It cracks the already warring states into three more hostile segments: the "dominant minority," the "internal proletariat," and the "external proletariat." The first is what becomes of the once-creative ruling class. The second two are the followers: native and adopted citizens, and barbarian peoples outside the culture who have been happily absorbing its influence.

The once-creative minority of the growth period not only has lost its way but also has lost the magnetic attraction it held for its followers. Yet rarely will it consent to losing its superior position. The class has ceased to merit power and privilege but is not willing to give them up. So as failing rulers see disillusioned subjects withdrawing voluntary mimesis, they begin to use force to keep the masses under their control. The one-time prophets become drill sergeants, the former guides, masters. The greater their failure, the more their force increases.

The word "proletariat" Toynbee expanded from its present narrow meaning denoting the industrial working class. He used it to embrace all the peoples alienated within a declining civilization.

The internal proletariat of Greco-Roman society was made up of citizens socially ruined by political and economic upheavals. It also included conquered peoples and slaves. In any given civilization, this class also can contain a former aristocracy displaced from heritage and tradition. Equally it includes Spengler's megalopolitan mass-man uprooted from the countryside. All such people have been wrenched away from familiar habits of living at ease in a growing society. They suffer the torture of being thrust out of a once-stable condition. They have lost their sense of home and wander forlornly in a spiritual wilderness. Their civilization has turned strange and alien. They no longer feel any real share in it. Whatever their former position in the once-growing culture, they all end up in a kind of underground. They no longer belong spiritually to the society in which they live physically. They are in the social order but not of it.

The internal proletariat, though not admiring and imitating bankrupt rulers, dwells under increasingly oppressive bondage to them. Perhaps rarely can power be used without being abused, but tenure of power by a ruling class that lacks ability to lead is automatically an abuse. Gradually people become aware that they have souls of their own, and they make up their minds to save them. They begin to revolt against their servitude.

The internal proletariat continues to live with the dominant minority despite the widening moral gulf between the two factions. The external proletariat, on the other hand, can make a cleaner break with the rulers. In times when the attractive harmony of growth lulled barbarians on the margins of the civilization into accord, they peacefully absorbed its beneficent influence and willingly carried the civilization further into the hinterlands. With the catastrophe of breakdown, all this changes. The external peoples find themselves facing domineering, ugly, and menacing leaders. They no longer are charmed but repelled. Instead of willing subjects and converts, they become enemies violently resisting incorporation. Meanwhile, the vague and borderless margin around the civilization that once conducted the culture now contracts and stiffens. It becomes a rigid frontier. As the once-peaceable barbarians beyond the frontier relapse into their natural ferocity, they hurl themselves against it in attack.

As the blessings of civilization increasingly turn to curses, people do not completely lack creativity. They lose opportunity for creative action in the stifling atmosphere of decline, but they still retain a capacity for it. The dominant minority, the internal proletariat, and the external proletariat all manage to produce something of note.

The dominant minority's characteristic social types are the militarist and the exploiter. They do little but drain the society. Meanwhile, the failed rulers perform prodigies of sterilization upon new recruits to their barren esprit de corps. Yet some members of the class manage to escape impotence.

A few independent thinkers in times of disintegration produce philosophical systems that become intellectual monuments for all ages. A golden chain of creative philosophers extended through the broken-down Greco-Roman civilization all the way from Socrates in the fifth century B.C. to the Alexandrian thinker Plotinus in the third century A.D. Similarly did the decline of ancient Indian civilization yield Buddhism, and the wane of ancient China produce Confucius and the wisdom of the Tao.

More important to the disintegrating society itself is a second major creation of the dominant minority: the universal state.

When the fratricidal wars of the time of troubles have enfeebled or eliminated most contenders, one of the survivors hurls the final knock-out blow. The victor of the civilization's last great internal war is left alone with all the remaining power. This city or nation establishes an imperium, a world empire. The political and administrative state is universal not so much geographically but psychologically, in that it blankets the whole effective world of the civilization.

Not all declining civilizations have created a universal state, but most of them have done so. Sumerians set up their universal state around 2300 B.C., and Egyptians in 2070 B.C. They were followed by the Minoans of Crete in 1750 B.C., the ancient Indians in 322 B.C. and the ancient Chinese in 221 B.C. The battle of Actium in 31 B.C. knocked out Antony and Cleopatra and installed for Greco-Roman civilization the vast despotism of the Caesars. The same general pattern of self-destructive warfare ending in universal states has continued since then.

With unification by force, the declining civilization gains a reprieve. The universal state, imposed as a panacea for the time of troubles, is an effort to check disintegration and even defy it. It succeeds in conserving the society's wasting energies and preserving the outward form of culture, even though all real vitality is gone.

Meanwhile, people of the universal state, desperately weary of generations of mad-dog militarism, welcome the final victor and its rule. Accustomed to agony, they see peace at any price as a blessing. As one writer in Rome testified in the second century A.D.:

> At a moment when the states of the World were already laid out on the funeral pyre as the victims of their own fratricidal strife and turmoil, they were all at once presented with the [Roman] dominion and straightway came to life again. . . . [They] can only marvel at their present well-being. They are like sleepers awakened who have come to themselves and now dismiss from their thoughts the dreams that obsessed them only a moment ago. They no longer find it credible that there were ever such things as wars. . . . The entire Inhabited World now keeps perpetual holiday. . . . So that the only people who still need pity for the good things that they are missing are those outside your empire—if there are any such people left....[13]

The end of times of troubles and the advent of peace often brought such profound relief that founders of world empires were worshipped as gods. Even a universal state imposed by an alien nation is accepted with resignation and gratitude when a society's own dominant minority no longer is capable of building a unified empire. History reveals not only a *Pax Romana* but also a *Pax Mongolica* in China, a *Pax Ottomanica* in the deteriorating Orthodox Christian civilization of the Middle East, and, later, a *Pax Britannica* in the disintegrating society of India.

With the passage of time, alien universal states tend to lose the support of their subjects. A world empire ruled by one of its own, on the other hand, gains increasing acceptance regardless of its merits and ultimately is taken as the only possible framework for life.

World states carry decided benefits for their peoples. Beyond the initial advantage of peace, they provide military protection, a universal language, a swift and efficient transportation network, a unified monetary system, and a standard set of laws, weights, and measures. Numberless and usually anonymous civil servants and soldiers partly atone for misdeeds of predators among the dominant minority by serving often faithfully and sometimes very well. For many generations the society can bask in the pale sunshine of an Indian summer, enjoying a final repose before the dark age of anarchy looming in a barbaric future.

People of a universal state believe their empire will last forever. Their faith, however understandable in its early days, often endures beyond all reason even when the society is crumbling around their ears. The Gallic poet Rutilius Namatianus defiantly asserted the immortality of Rome after the city had been sacked by the barbarian war band of Alaric the Visigoth and only decades before the last of the puppet emperors was pushed off his throne by the Germanic chieftain Odoacer.

Invariably the universal state is only a temporary shelter in the wilderness of disintegration. Its goal never rises beyond mere conservation. It is a holding action, an effort to peg the civilization at one stage of development, a striving not for growth but only for a status quo. It is passive, archaistic, and negative in every regard. A dull, anticreative, trancelike existence neither restores what has perished nor prevents the gradual collapse of what survives.

A universal state can endure for a long time. In fact, tenacious clinging to life is one of its most conspicuous features. But its clenched grip on existence never represents genuine vitality. It is the obstinacy of the aged who refuse to die. And gradually, within its imposing armor of power and size, the imperium rots away until nothing is left to support its ponderous shell. At last the moribund universal state crumbles, proving itself to be civilization's last stage before extinction.

While the dominant minority is walling itself within its universal state, the internal proletariat is beginning a creation far greater and much longer lasting.

The people's first concern when their society lurches into disintegration is to break free from a former spiritual home now turned into a prison. Naturally creative personalities among them, finding no scope for their abilities within the social establishment, put their energies to work organizing opposition to the failed leaders. They lead the internal proletariat's secession.

Some organize open revolts, repaying injustice with resentment, fear with hatred, violence with violence. Desperate and cold-blooded proletarian outbreaks flared in Egypt against the final dynasty of transplanted Greeks; in a series of Jewish insurrections against the world state of the Caesars; and in Italy when the escaped slave-gladiator Spartacus raged up and down the countryside defying the Roman wolf in his own lair. But the disciples of violence invariably fail in their aims. As they live by the sword, so do they perish by it. Their cause, however justifiable, dies with them.

After time and much travail, the internal proletariat discovers the only sure way out of the City of Destruction that their society has become: the path to what St. Augustine in the dying days of Rome called the City of God. So begins the grandest creative act of the disintegration phase: a higher religion, leading to a universal church.

All the world's major religions are traceable to waning civilizations, whether Buddhism, Hinduism, or Persian Zoroastrianism, Judaism, Christianity, or Islam. Judaism arose step by step from a whole series of decaying societies. Abraham emerged from the endtime of Sumer; from the breakdown of Egypt came Moses; from the Syriac civilization's time of troubles sprang the religion's loftiest prophetic expressions.

A low point for society tends always to become a high point for religion. In a time of disintegration, a church deals better than other institutions with the psychic storms lashing the social landscape.

Just as physically challenging environments stimulate material achievement, so do spiritually difficult circumstances spur spiritual growth and attainment.

Thus did people of the Roman world abandon rationalism for faith and make the change with open eyes and enthusiasm. In the frustrating stagnation of their universal state, the church of Jesus Christ opened broad new channels for pent-up energies that the society no longer could liberate or put to good use. Higher religions rising from failing cultures absorb landslides of talent and ability matching the extent and speed of their civilization's demise. Even art, though long dead in a fading higher culture, flourishes anew within the rising religions.

Perhaps because a society's original religion is identified with the disintegrating order, a proletariat seeking spiritual revelation usually looks to alien sources. Egypt's worship of Osiris, god of the underworld, appears to be traceable to the Sumerian worship of the god Tammuz. China and Japan adopted Buddhism from India and much later came close to accepting Catholic Christianity from the West. Disintegrating Rome imported a whole assortment of exotic religions: the cult of the goddess Isis from Egypt; the worship of the mother of gods, Cybele, that originated in the Hittite civilization of Asia Minor; the Middle Eastern religion of Christianity; and Persian Mithraism, which was Christianity's more widespread competitor as late as the second century.

No matter where a universal church comes from, its transplanted roots find nourishment all over the decaying society. Capital cities become the centers for the flow of religious currents—a fact suggested by the words "pagan," which comes from the Latin *paganus*, or country dweller, and "heathen," or man of the heath. The universal state's elaborate communications network—the master institution that enables its existence—carries the religion rapidly from place to place. The Roman universal state provided a further legacy to the early Christian church: Latin as its language; Rome's imperial plan of territorial administration for its bishoprics; and the empire's hierarchical organization for its structure. The universal state, initially set up to preserve a dying society, is doomed from the start, but it greatly aids the growth of a religion and church that endure long after it is gone.

Just as, in the midst of stifling decay, a society's rulers create a universal state and its internal proletariat a universal church, so does the barbarian external proletariat achieve significant creations.

In days of growth when the outside peoples revered and imitated the civilization, they tended to accept the culture as a whole along with its political and economic ways. But once a society breaks down, it begins to radiate unequally. Its customs and ideas—the essence of the civilization—lose their magnetic charm. Meanwhile, political and economic influences reach out stronger than ever, since disintegrating societies typically struggle for political power and economic might.

The outsiders continue to imitate the political and economic features. But they no longer mimic to become one with the society. They want its methods and techniques, instead, to arm themselves against it. With the passage of time, almost all contact between the civilization and its outsiders fades, except for trade and warfare. And trade diminishes while wars increase.

The war bands of the barbarians become themselves a kind of creation. They serve a historic purpose, aiding the society's dissolution like vultures speeding the disappearance of a carcass. As they rage across the landscape, they also forge a chain of bloody exploits into a heroic age. From momentary triumphs the heroes emerge: Greece's Achilles, France's Roland, England's Beowulf. Their legends, too, become lasting creations—the folk sagas and epic poems that spring from all heroic ages.

The schisms breaking up a disintegrating civilization are not limited to fratricidal wars that lead to a universal state and the split between rulers and followers that results in a universal church and barbarian war bands. This visible strife is only a reflection of the turmoil within human souls. The inward schism breaking up people often proves more painful than outward troubles. Toynbee found the same soul-fractures in every decaying society.

As a failing culture closes down channels to creative living, many people turn to one of two inward alternatives: abandon or self-control. Those who choose abandon throw off moral laws and plunge into momentary appetites and aversions. People who go the way of self-control discipline their passions and embrace asceticism. Both groups claim they are going back to nature, one by yielding to natural promptings, the other by mastering them. The first of these alternatives is passive in character, the second active. Neither is creative.

Two alternatives also arise in social behavior, replacing mimesis when the culture's old ways no longer work. The passive option is to drop out of the society. The dropout, or truant, believes the cause he is called upon to serve no longer worth his service. He responds by stepping backward, out of the social ranks. The active course is a courageous stepping forward in martyrdom of one kind or another, breaking free of the burdensome culture by pursuing a lofty ideal. Roman philosophers who cultivated stoic detachment were intellectual martyrs. More spiritually potent—and literally martyred—were Christians who chose execution rather than betray their faith.

Another pair of schisms of the soul splits people on the plane of inner feeling. Again this occurs in every age of disintegration. Some people are afflicted with a passive sense of drift. One of the most painful tribulations of decline, it leaves them feeling their lives are out of their control, ruled by irrational chance or invincible necessity. The society, the world, the universe—each seems like a ship without a rudder hopelessly tossed about by circumstance or fate. On the active level, the moral defeat of the routed soul is felt as a personal failure to control the self properly. People accepting this alternative are shocked into a sense of sin by their social structure caving in around them. The prophets of Israel and Judah offer classic examples of this leaning of the soul. Groaning beneath the yoke of Assyrian captors, they blamed their condition not on circumstance but on their own sinfulness, a feat of spiritual heroism that ultimately led them to strength. As the passive sense of drift acts as an opiate lulling people to accept the evils around them, the sense of sin is a stimulus. The sinner, seeing his suffering caused not by things outside himself and beyond his control but by flaws within himself, seeks salvation in God's purposes and opens his soul to God's grace.

In days when a civilization is growing, it shows a strong sense of style, a unique set of forms distinguishing it from other cultures. This style appears in the manners and customs of its social classes; in architecture, literature, and graphic arts; in language, philosophy, and religion. People of decline lose this distinct style, the once-sharp outlines of their culture blurring away. Their social feelings turn, again, to one of two substitutes. The passive replacement for lost cultural style Toynbee called a sense of promiscuity. The active substitute is a vision of universal unity.

Promiscuity in manners and customs flows two ways between social classes. First, the dominant minority, which has joined the uncreative majority in fact, now joins them in behavior as well. Rulers take pains to mimic vulgar lower-class behavior. They also mimic the external proletariat, eventually meeting them in a common barbarism. Meanwhile both proletariats gradually draw the leaders into their ranks.

Histories of decline are full of examples of this cultural promiscuity. Ancient Rome's emperors, despite their godly status, often imitated people of lower rank. As early as the first century of the empire, Nero was setting himself up as a music hall *artiste*; his dying words were, "What an artist the world is losing in me!" Generations later, in the gathering gloom of the second century's end, the Emperor Commodus, a vulgar, vain man especially proud of his physique, brushed aside imperial duties to amuse himself as an amateur gladiator. Not long afterward, Caracalla, normally haughty and full of pride, would discard the dignity of rank among his troops and, neglecting the responsibilities of a general, encourage familiarity and imitate the dress and demeanor of the common soldier.

In a similar way did the Roman ruling class take on traits of barbarians. Though wars often flared between the empire and Germanic tribes along its borders, Romans also met barbarians under other circumstances. The crystallized frontier never stopped all commerce, entrepreneurs and adventurers regularly passing back and forth. Also Rome hired bands of outsiders to fight as mercenary troops. Talented Germans, for their part, often were eager to enter Roman service. The Visigothic leaders Alaric and Atawulf held no fonder ambition than high imperial command. At first barbarians accepted by Rome tended to imitate ways of the civilization. Hired soldiers adopted Roman names along with their appointments. But around the middle of the fourth century, it seems Germans began to keep their native names. Meanwhile, around the year 380, the Emperor Gratian, with inverted snobbery, affected the barbarian style of dress and became a devotee of German field sports. Within another century Romans were enlisting in the war bands of barbarian chieftains. The father of the last Roman emperor worked for a time as secretary to Attila the Hun. Soon after, Romans and barbarians were meeting on cultural par. Their ways of life had become indistinguishable—in favor of the barbarians. Meanwhile, native-born Romans were beginning to assume German names, speeding a cultural absorption that ultimately became complete.

The same loss of sensitivity to form that leads the upper class to aspire downward also diminishes fine arts in a disintegrating culture. In such a period, the arts diffuse rapidly and widely, but they lose the distinctiveness of style that marks aesthetic quality, taking on either vulgar or barbaric influences. Typically, highbrows of ancient Greece, after their society's breakdown, bewailed cheap trends debasing their music. Meanwhile, drama was torn from serious theater and hawked up and down the civilized world as crassly commercial entertainment. Architecture during times of decline decomposes to florid decadence. And all the arts, including literature, assume a standardized, composite style.

Language joins behavior and art in both promiscuity and debasement. Nations potent in commerce or war spread their language to other lands, throwing local distinctiveness of speech into confusion. At the same time, the dominant languages pay for their diffusion in a loss of former subtlety and fineness.

Disintegration also leads to fusion of philosophies and religions. Philosophical systems that once competed meet and merge. Religions that formerly were rivals fuse in syncretisms. Finally the upper class's philosophy meets the religion sprung from the lower class. It comes out distinctly the loser. Some of its features might be absorbed by religion, as the language of Hellenic philosophy was adopted to express the Christian creed. But philosophy ultimately dies, while faith endures.

It is the society's weaker souls who succumb to cultural promiscuity as their own culture loses sharp outlines. People of greater spiritual strength respond the opposite way. They see beyond the shifting trappings of culture a vision of eternal unity. This sense is what leads to universal states. It also can lead to an awareness that the brotherhood of man presupposes the fatherhood of God. Alexander the Great is said to have reached that conclusion. So did the Roman Stoic philosopher Epictetus at the same time St. Paul was spreading the unifying gospel of Jesus.

Some people caught in decline make up their minds to escape it altogether, to flee from the intolerable into an alternative world. All declining cultures suggest four common pathways of escape. Toynbee calls them archaism, futurism, detachment, and transfiguration. Three are dead ends. Only the fourth offers genuine refuge.

The archaist attempts to put back the clock, to reverse the flow of the society's life. The past beckons like a cozy home from which people have strayed into the present wilderness. The archaist tries to relieve his pain by going back to some happier time, a period more longed for and idealized the further it is in the past. Reconstruction of a vanished age might be attempted by reviving a style of art or architecture. Archaists might work to bring back a dead or dying language, as nationalist groups have done with Irish Gaelic, Norwegian, Turkish, Greek, and Hebrew. Religious archaists might revive a system of worship, as the Japanese restored the native primitive religion of Shinto in the eighteenth and nineteenth cen-turies. Italian Fascists of the twentieth century claimed to be restoring the political and economic regime of their country's medieval city-states. Germany's Nazis built an archaistic cult around imagined virtues of Teutonic barbarians.

All the efforts of archaists prove futile. If they ignore the present in their struggle to revive the past, the flow of life shatters their brittle construction. If they incorporate the present into their plan, their restoration becomes a sham.

Souls at bay who fail in the passive way of archaism often react by negating the present and attempting to leap into the future. Futurism tries to deal with an intolerable present by cutting it short. As archaists seek escape to what the society might have been, futurists flee toward what it might become.

A common gesture of futurists is radical change in dress. Young Jewish priests of the second century B.C., attempting to abandon their traditional society and leap into the up-to-date world dominated by Greek ways, adopted a broad-brimmed felt hat worn by Hellenic rulers of many Middle-Eastern states. The seventeenth-century Tsar Peter the Great, founder of modern Russia, included in a sweeping plan of futurization a law requiring men to shave their beards. He also banned long-sleeved, ankle-length caftan robes previously worn in Muscovy. A Turkish law of 1925 made Western-style hats with brims compulsory for males, as did decrees of the same period in Iran and Afghanistan. Similarly many non-Western people today switch their dress in an effort to leap from their native past into a Westernized future. Such changes tend to be only a beginning; a Jewish priest who dons a foreign brim-hat soon will be seeing his religion as old-fashioned and unenlightened.

In the political sphere, futurism might obliterate old geographical boundaries, dissolve sects or parties, even liquidate whole social classes. Book burnings are a classic expression of futurist sentiment, annihilating past and present. The method was practiced by Chinese in the third century B.C., by Arabs of the seventh century A.D. who burned the famed thousand-year-old library of Alexandria in Egypt, and by advocates of the millennial reich of Adolf Hitler.

Yet as a backward leap in time proves a barren effort, so is futurism's imaginary world to come unattainable. Both are utopias in the word's literal Greek meaning—nowheres.

The third common escape from an unbearable present is a passive act of philosophical detachment. Its disciples abandon the society altogether and withdraw into the fortress of their souls. This was the way of Greco-Roman Stoic philosophers, who worked to purge themselves of passions and self-indulgences until they were steeled against either pleasure or pain. The Greek thinker Zeno founded Stoicism in the third century B.C., which still enjoyed high prestige in the second century A.D. under one of its most notable practitioners, the Roman Emperor Marcus Aurelius. While Stoics were seeking invulnerability, the Epicurians of a parallel movement of detachment pursued imperturbability. In Asia, disciples of the Gautama Buddha, withdrawing from a disintegrating Indic society, pursued detachment all the further to its logical goal of self-annihilation.

The moral and intellectual achievements of detachment often are imposing. But they ultimately prove a dead end. Detachment casts out evils and weakening passions, but it also ejects humane compassion and love. As the Hindu Bhagavadgita scriptures teach: "The man whose every motion is void of love and purpose, whose works are burned away by the fire of knowledge, the enlightened call 'learned'. The learned grieve not for them whose lives are fled nor for them whose lives are not fled."[14] Similarly, the Roman Stoic Seneca who lived at the time of Christ considered pity a mental illness and declared that a sage does not succumb to such diseases. His countryman and contemporary, the Stoic philosopher Epictetus, advised: "If you are kissing a child of yours . . . never put your imagination unreservedly into the act and never give your emotion free rein, but curb it and check it. . . . Indeed, there is no harm in accompanying the act of kissing the child by whispering over him: 'To-morrow you will die.'"[15]

Detachment is a wholly negative course. It is withdrawal without return. Its adherents manage to shake the dust of the City of Destruction off their feet, but from that point they have nowhere else to go. Escape has become an end in itself rather than a means to something greater.

While the first three common avenues of flight from a disintegrating civilization end in life-negating sterility and failure, the fourth path—transfiguration—is an open way. This leads upward to a life that transcends the world.

Transfiguration bears some similarities to detachment. Both depart from the decaying society's dismal atmosphere of decline by a change in spiritual clime. Also both move into an otherworldly existence that is genuine. But where detachment is passive and negative in character, transfiguration is active in its nature and positive in its goals.

People pursuing transfiguration regard the detached soul's retreat into serenity as an act not completed. They see Nirvana not as a journey's end but only as a way station along the route. When they find serenity they give it up, willingly accepting renewed discomfort in compassion and love for their fellow men. They are practicing not planned withdrawal but a pilgrimage inspired by faith. Rather than excluding the world, they transcend earthly life without ceasing to include it in their activities. Their goal is the Kingdom of God. Though this reaches into eternity, it also interpenetrates the present and calls its citizens not to detachment but to service in the here and now.

Transfiguration is the action of the soul that produced the world's great religions. It might not halt a society's disintegration. But it can provide impetus for an entirely new cultural blossoming, as Christianity arose out of dying Rome to become the chrysalis for the new life of Western civilization.

Just as many people in an age of decline seek personal salvation in archaism or futurism, detachment or transfiguration, so does the society as a whole look for salvation from its leaders. A failing culture is on the defensive. As a time of growth has creative personalities answering major challenges to society with successful responses, leaders in a period of disintegration are called on to hold ground in a rearguard action. They often assume desperate and heroic roles. Some strive to save the society. Others do what they can to save people from the society.

Saviors who refuse to despair of the present rise out of the dominant minority. They lead a forlorn effort to convert the society's rout into renewed advance. Their instrument of salvation is the sword. The classic saviors by the sword are the captains and princes who establish universal states. Often they appear successful. But their triumphs are temporary, only slowing decay, and, sooner or later, eroding into total failure.

Other saviors rule out trying to salvage the culture's situation. These lead their followers down one of the four pathways of personal escape from decline. There are archaist saviors and futurist saviors. Both inevitably fail in their intentions. Often, in utter frustration, they take up the sword and attempt revolution.

The savior-by-detachment was proposed by Plato, who said kings should be philosophers as well. Yet, historically, philosopher-kings have met only failure. Among them were Marcus Aurelius and the Indian Emperor Asoka, who was converted to Buddhism in the third century B.C. Like other philosopher-kings through the ages, both proved incapable of saving their societies from disintegration. The creation of ruling philosophers or philosophical rulers is intrinsically faulty. Philosophy's detachment is incompatible with the force that political action demands, while the moment the philosopher-king draws the sword, he proclaims failure to maintain his own position.

The final savior appears as a saving god. All the world tells of demigods born of human mothers by superhuman fathers who strove to lighten the load of men and died for their efforts. Tammuz died for the Sumerian world and Zagreus for Minoan society of Crete. Attis perished for Hittite peoples, as Adonis did for the Syriac world and Balder for early Scandinavians. The dying savior-god's earliest appearance can be traced to the spirit of vegetation, born for humanity in springtime and dying every autumn that humanity might live.

Yet dying gods did not necessarily perish willingly and with loving purpose. Gradually, those with flawed motives slipped into antiquity, leaving only one who chose to suffer that man might have life and have it in abundance. As the mighty and varied throng of saviors who failed in their efforts fades into the shadows of the past, Jesus Christ alone remains, filling the entire horizon.

Civilizations regularly end with their only remaining vestige embodied in a church that has risen out of their ruin. But not all declining societies complete disintegration promptly. Just as newly born civilizations can fail to grow and live in arrested condition, so can higher cultures that have broken down linger in a state of arrested decay, petrified—or as Oswald Spengler put it, like worn out giants of the forest thrusting their decaying branches into the sky.

A prime example of a petrified society is that of ancient Egypt. Little more than a quarter of its life span was spent in vigorous growth. Then, breaking down, it skidded along the normal course of disintegration, with its time of troubles, its universal state, then a period of chaos that Toynbee named the barbarian interregnum. At this point, Egyptian civilization had existed for some two thousand years. Rather than ceasing at its apparently appointed time, the society suddenly came back together and flowed on for another two thousand years. The last major traces of Egypt as a living civilization were obliterated only with the end of Roman dominion in the fifth century A.D. Yet the latter half of the society's history hardly can be considered a time of vital life. It was a life-in-death with the culture paralyzed and inert in a kind of social concrete that took two millennia to weather away.

Recent centuries in China provide a closer example of long-petrified civilization. Toynbee quoted the nineteenth-century historian Lord Thomas Macaulay describing China's rigidified culture persisting in "a tottering, drivelling, paralytic longevity . . . where, during many centuries, nothing has been learned or unlearned; where government, where education, where the whole system of life, is a ceremony; where knowledge forgets to increase and multiply, and, like the talent buried in the earth or the pound wrapped up in the napkin, experiences neither waste nor augmentation."[16]

In a final observation about the dynamics of the rise and fall of civilizations, Toynbee pointed out that the pattern of decline is remarkably fixed and regular. As societies in growth become increasingly different from each other, the mark of disintegrating cultures is standardization. For example, a broken-down civilization always splits into the same three conflicting social classes—the dominant minority, the internal proletariat, and the external proletariat. Also, the creative products of these classes always are the same: philosophies and universal states for the first, higher religions that aim to be embodied in universal churches for the second, and barbarian war bands that rage through heroic ages for alienated outsiders. Likewise, the various psychological schisms that wrack the souls of people of decline recur always in exactly the same form.

Nor does the rigid lockstep of decline end there. Toynbee also found a tendency for civilizations to decay in regular rhythm. Never do they fall into ruin in an uninterrupted downward slide. Rather, they decline in waves, in an undulating slope of rout and rally. The time of troubles in the first major rout. Its end in a universal state is a rally. The collapse of this state in an age of barbarism is the final major rout. Also, Toynbee noted, each main beat tends to have a smaller rout and rally in between. Though the number of beats is in no way invariable, three and a half is the common formula.

This number marks decline in Sumerian culture, in the society of ancient China, in Greco-Roman civilization, in the later Orthodox

Christian society, and in other higher cultures as well. So consistent has the rhythm proved that Toynbee suggested it might be used to peg Western culture and forecast the civilization's future. This task of locating and forecasting he also undertook at considerable length in his *Study*. But first he looked at the grim barbaric age that follows the fall of civilizations and precedes the rise of the next higher culture to follow.

BEYOND CIVILIZATION

While a disintegrating civilization endures, its armed frontier is a dam holding back the flood of hostile barbarians. The greatest ambition of the tribal bands is to break through the border. Time works in their favor. Defending the fronter only weakens the civilized society. The cost of troops and arms puts growing strain upon its economy and the constant threat adds a wearing burden of anxiety.

For the barbarians the border wars, far from being a burden, are an opportunity. They long since have given up the peaceful arts of their primitive forebears, trading the plow for the sword. Plunder is their major means of support. Neither are wars an anxiety for them but, rather, an exhilaration. As strife grows, it whets their appetite for more. Gradually, as they trade their goods for the weapons of the civiization and learn its military techniques in skirmishes and raids, the pressure they exert increases.

While the gates of the society are battered from without, the enemy also works from within. Waning civilizations commonly enlist foreigners to aid their defense. In Rome's later days Germanic warriors greatly bolstered the empire's forces. Also, because the society's debilitating atmosphere had left all but its most extraordinary members unable to do more than follow a routine, talented outsiders were brought in to help sustain Roman institutions. Increasingly, notable figures came from barbarian ranks, with sophisticated Germans often rising to high office.

As hired soldiers fight for the society, they learn about its strategies and weaknesses. Inevitably this intelligence leaks across the frontier. From such information, ome's enemies concluded that its body politic was grossly mismanaged and invited attack. Meanwhile, aliens working in the state, after a time of service, see tempting opportunities to wrest power from their masters. What is commonly dated as the fall of Rome in A.D. 476 marks the occasion when the mercenary chieftain Odoacer of the Heruli tribe snatched the Western empire for himsef, deposing and pensioning off the last Roman emperor.

When the dam of the frontier finally bursts, the civilized world falls into havoc. For the barbarians the breach is a thrilling experience. Their ancestors have battered the border for generations only to retreat in frustration. Now an apparently boundless horizon of wealth and power is opened. They rush into what seems an enchanted land of infinte possibilities.

But their invasion proves a disaster for everyone—most of all for the barbarians themselves. As long as the frontier endured, it served the tribesmen as a form of discipline, replacing the restraints of primitive custom they lost when they come into contact with the civilization. Now nothing shields the warriors from the destructive forces within themselves. Loosed from all controls, they run amok over the land.

Amid the derelict leavings of a civilized culture, the invaders are unable to appreciate that "sackers of cities," as Homeric barbarians called themselves, are strong only to destroy. Both more sophisticated and more brutal than their primitive forebears who were unaffected by civilization, they leave a broad swath of atrocities in their wake. Their unrestrained triumphs debase them all the more. In the days when they could do no worse than launch sporadic border raids, their orgies of consuming loot were temporary and tempered by the ordeal of defending themselves against punitive expeditions. Now that cities and estates, towns and treasuries all are theirs for the taking, their overindulgence goes on far longer and proves more demoralizing than ever.

The heroic age lurches ahead in criminal outrage, while its vulture-heroes carve the corpse of the civilization's universal state into kingdoms. These domains are not actual creations but merely the obverse side of the empire's fall. With politics parodying the defunct Caesarism in irresponsible kingships resting on military prestige, each state amounts to nothing more than a band of adventurers pledging personal loyalty to a warlord. Inevitably, the gangs of armed desperadoes prove morally unfit to govern previously civilized communities. Their rule is a combination of despotism and revolution. Winning strategies in their internecine struggles for existence mix cunning and treachery with vindictiveness, persistence, and implacability. The barbarians, incapable of creating social institutions, create moral slums and immense suffering.

Barbarian bands often have risen to seeming omnipotence. But typically their fate is sensational, sudden collapse. The Huns, who after two thousand years remain famous for brutal might, plunged into decline after the death of their warlord leader Attila. Likewise did the Vandals fade into eclipse when their chieftain Genseric died.

The final social and political failure of the barbarians is strikingly complete. They prove hardly more than teeming maggots in the carcass of the dead higher culture, surviving no longer than it takes for the putrefying corpse to dissolve into clean elements. Then they perish in a frenzy of mutual destruction, relieving the world of their pandemonium and leaving a happy ending for everybody but themselves.

Their age takes on its heroic cast from sagas and epic poems that transform their sordid history into immortal romance. Yet even these poems show heroes living evil lives and dying cruel deaths. Finally, what is their heavenly Valhalla but an otherworld slum of turbulent fighting and riotous feasting?

The master-myth of all heroic ages suggests that barbarians attempt to come to grips with their destructive impulses. This ubiquitous tale tells of a hero's battle with a monster for a treasure withheld from humankind. Thus, the ancient Greek Perseus decapitates the Gorgon, Beowulf fights Grendel, and Siegfried overcomes the dragon. If this myth, in its many versions, can be taken as a mental projection, it describes a struggle in the barbarian's soul for the rescue of his rational will. Yet the struggle fails, and the barbarians tumble into oblivion.

As the bonfires of the heroic age burn out, an age of darkness develops. Yet this period, however grim, brings fresh buds of creation. In the fullness of time, new life bursts forth to clothe fertile ash fields with tender shoots of green. The dark age proves the darkness before another dawn.

In many ways the entire process of decline works out to what Toynbee called 'palingenesia'—recurrence of birth. Social schisms of the disintegration phase lead to new creations: the universal state, the universal church, and barbarian war bands. Schisms of the soul find their palingenesia in the personal renewal of transfiguration. Finally, the savage and wanton destruction of barbaric ages clears the way for the creation of new civilized society.

In this welter of life and tempest of action Toynbee detected an elemental rhythm: the alternating beat of Yin and Yang, whose variations are challenge-and-response, withdrawal-and-return, rout-and-rally, schism-and-palingenesia. It is the song of creation, in which destruction enters not as discord but as completed harmony. "Creation would not be creative," Toynbee asserted, "if it did not swallow up all things in itself, including its own opposite."[17]

Some philosophies describe the cycle of life embodied in this elemental rhythm as an endless and futile wheel of existence. But Toynbee saw in the turning of the wheel more than vain repetition. His palingenesia is renewal of birth not merely of things that went before but of better and higher things with each revolution.

The loftier rebirth, however, is not a progress of civilizations, each leading higher in an evolutionary way. To be sure, advanced societies—when one leads to another—are involved in turning creation's wheel. Early Minoan civilization was the parent of Greco-

Roman culture. And the universal church that sprang from Rome's decline preserved a precious germ of life that burst forth in double blossom in the Orthodox Christian civilization and the culture of the West. In fact, all five advanced societies existing today emerged from universal churches that sprang from previous disintegrating cultures. Nonetheless, civilizations follow no plan of progress from one generation to the next. Rather, they tend to grow separately, distinctly, each one of itself.

In Toynbee's view, the progress of the ages is found not in civilization but in religion. Though churches have served as wombs for higher cultures, the essential link of service between the two proceeds the other way. Civilizations exist to foster the growth of religion.

The first-generation civilizations—such as grew up in Sumer and Egypt, Minoan Crete, India, and China—developed rudimentary higher religions. When these early cultures passed away, most of them gave rise to new ones in the same general regions. But the advanced societies of the second generation did not come into existence to perform any achievements of their own, nor to reproduce their own kind in a third generation. They appeared and developed solely to provide an opportunity for full-fledged higher religions to grow on the inspiration of the earlier models of worship.

Thus, civilizatios serve as stepping stones for progressive revelation of religious insight. Their decline, then, is not a total tragedy when it ministers to the birth of higher religion. To the contrary, an advanced society fulfills its function by providing for religious growth. When its death produces a living church, the end is not disaster but a proper conclusion to the story.

This becomes clear in the light of Toynbee's theory that universalchurches are a distinct and substantially higher species of human society. The lowest species, primitive culture, often offers a life that the seventeenth-century English political theoristThomas Hobbes described as "solitary, poore, nasty, brutish, and short."[18] Civilized society improves upon that. The great relgions show the way to elevate the human condition yet another step.

"The distinguishing mark of the churches," wrote Toynbee, "was that they all had as a member the One True God. This human fellowship with the One True Go, which had been approached in the primitive religions and had been attained in the higher religions, gave to these societies certain virtues not to be found in primitive societies or civilizations."[19]

Perhaps most urgently, fellowship with God gives man power to overcome the discord that otherwise rents the fabric of his life on every social level and lately has been threatening to wipe him off the earth. Secondly, divine fellowship presents an explanation of life not as an idiot's tale signifying nothing but as willing participation in a masterplan that lends divine value and meaning to human existence. Finally, a close link with Divinity removes the lethal flaw of mimesis, which brings down civilizations when leaders cease to inspire and resort to force and followers secede and sunder the society. In the City of God, mimesis is transferred from fallible human leaders to the source of all human creativity, God Himself.

It might be hoped that in som future time one or more of the major churches will supersede civilization as the prevailing form of human society. Considering the grand sweep of humankind's past, such a progression seems in no way unlikely. Compared with perhaps three hundred thousand years of primitive societies, civilizations, with hardly six thousand years behind them, are creations of yesterday. Churches embodying the higher religions are less than half as old as the oldest civilization.

An upward movement to a godly society also seems clearly desirable. Higher religions and their churches prove a far more fitting vehicle than either primitive society or civilization for aiding people in their pilgrims' progress toward the loftiest goals of human endeavor.

So Toynbee's view of history in the end becomes a 'theodicy,' a justification of the ways of God with humankind. And humanity's movement through time becomes purposive, combining the ancient cyclic theory of history with the modern idea of progress. The perpetual turning of the cultural wheel is not vain repetition if, with each revolution, it carries the vehicle of religion nearer to its heavenly goal.

This wedding of the cyclic and progressive theories agrees with the Judeo-Christian Bible's approach to history. There churches are cast as protagonists, and civilizations are interpreted not in terms of their own destinies but for their effects upon religion. The blend of the two theories also provides for the eschatology of the Christian and Islamic faiths, which puts the end of history with the coming of God's kingdom.

"And, if we ask ourselves why the descending movement in the revolution of the wheel of Civilization should be the sovereign means of carrying the chariot of Rligion forward and upward," Toynbee concluded, "we shall find our answer in the truth that Religion is a spiritual activity, and that spiritual progress is subject to a 'law' proclaimed by Aeschylus in the . . . words [we learn by suffering], and by the author of the Bible's Epistle to the Hebrews in the verse: 'Whom the Lord loveth He chasteneth, and scourgeth every son whom He receiveth.'"[20]

9

Prospects for the West

"We cannot say for certain that our doom is at hand;" wrote Toynbee in his *Study*, "and yet we have no warrant for assuming that it is not."[1] The circumstances of Western civilization are plainly precarious, he cautioned. Yet dogmatic pessimism is not justified. On the other hand, neither is dogmatic optimism.

In such equivocal terms the master historian repeatedly treated the prospects of the West as an open question. Though he kept an anxious eye on the future, he disavowed any intent to prophesy. His *Study* was an attempt to take bearings, but he refused to make it the basis for predictions. He was willing only to analyze and speculate.

On the surface, a large part of his analysis takes fairly conventional form. The preeminent problem facing modern civilization is to get rid of war before war gets rid of everything else. Thus far the society has found no solution for this menacing issue. Meanwhile the problem has grown to supremely lethal proportions as former religious restraints have slipped away, political ideologies have made rivalries more bitter, and brilliant technology conjures up increasingly destructive weapons.

To counter these grim omens, Toynbee pointed out that the West has major spiritual triumphs to its credit. Since the start of history, slavery and war have acted upon civilization like twin cancers. Western culture's unprecedented abolition of slavery suggests that the society might possibly win out over war as well. Meanwhile, the culture has made promising headway in forcing a navigable passage between abusive economic individualism and totalitarian economic controls. Under the impetus of democracy, mass education has given humanity new hope—if its recipients can rise above the unscrupulous and self-seeking commercial and political interests that strive to exploit the opened minds of the masses.

Hardly less important than the problem of war are questions of technology, class conflict, and employment. Economic inequality remains a serious issue between social classes and between various regions of the earth. Conceivably, material production could rise enough to satisfy the needs and demands of all the world. But this could occur only at the cost of limiting human freedoms: regimenting workers in factories and fields and restricting procreation. Since the dawn of the Industrial Revolution, the freedom of workers has been giving way to growing regimentation. Trade unions were organized to defend members against the oppressive trend, but they ended up enforcing regimentation of their own. In the meantime, the once-free business entrepreneur is regimented and robotized in impersonal corporate collectives. Business people who manage to remain independent find their scope progressively constricted by limitations on private enterprise. As a consequence of diminishing freedoms, the productive spirit that built the industrial age is waning. Workers on some levels have been turning against work itself. This poses the question of whether industrial technology, lacking the driving spirit that brought it into being, can endure in health and strength.

The problem of class conflict is finding different solutions in different sectors of the world. North Americans, trying to retain private enterprise, sought to lessen the breach between management and labor by raising the social and economic standards of workers to middle-class level. The Soviet Union banned private enterprise, liquidated the middle class, and eliminated formal class distinctions altogether. At the same time, the Soviets promoted the Communist ethos as a substitute religion, which attracted peoples all over the earth as a way to rise above petty personal aims to an inspiring mission. Western Europe worked for social harmony by methods more moderate than either the American's or the Soviet's, combining private enterprise with government regimentation in the interests of social justice.

Another major problem is the ancient tendency among peasant peoples to reproduce to the limits their subsistence allows. The introduction of maize, sweet potatoes, and peanuts into China in the sixteenth century, Toynbee cited, fostered growth in population from 63,599,541, according to a census of 1578, to an estimated 108,300,000 in 1661. Since then the Chinese population has been growing geometrically, reaching some 600,000,000 by the middle of the twentieth century and exceeding 1,000,000,000 well before the year 2000. Contemporary figures for India, Indonesia, and other areas of the globe tell a similar story. With present technology, science, and hygiene, what can be expected if populations continue to grow unabated?

This issue amounts to a clash between freedom from want and freedom to beget. The conflict could develop along geographical lines between Westernized and non-Westernized countries. The former would choose maximum material standards of living. The latter would continue breeding freely, at the same time feeling that the West should part with luxuries to save them from starvation.

For the future of the West, another foreseeable problem is constructive use of widespread leisure. Ancient Rome experienced far less general ease than seems in store for modern peoples, yet its relaxed challenges turned into a social and personal dilemma.

"One of the cancers of the spiritual life in souls born into the present generation," wrote a commentator in Rome's imperial age, "is the low spiritual tension in which all but a few chosen spirits among us pass their days. In our work and in our recreation alike our only objective is popularity and enjoyment. We feel no concern to win the true spiritual treasure that is to be found in putting one's heart into what one is doing and in winning a recognition that is truly worth having."[2]

In 1605, the philosopher and statesman Francis Bacon remarked on a similar trend beginning to develop in Western society: "For as it has been well observed, that the arts which flourish in times while virtue is in growth, are military; and while virtue is in state, are liberal; and while virtue is in declination, are voluptuary: so I doubt that this age of the World is somewhat upon the descent of the wheel. With arts voluptuary I couple practices joculary; for the deceiving of the senses is one of the pleasures of the senses."[3]

Toynbee, noting a continued descent in Western culture from one-time heroism to modern-day frivolity, remarked that "practices joculary" describes much of leisure in the age of automobiles, radio, and television. Bribed with pleasures and entertainment, people have sold their souls and ended up in the kind of spiritual wilderness that Plato disdained as a "Commonwealth of Swine." The guests invited to the banquet of Circe the enchantress are finding, as in the days of Ulysses, that they soon are penned in Circe's sty. The question now is whether they are going to wallow there indefinitely.

The West in Disintegration?

While much of Toynbee's analysis of the modern world rests upon more or less conventional themes, he did not end there. His background hardly would allow him to remain confined to normal contemporary thinking.

During his long life, he personally observed changes that altered the world out of all prior recognition, most of all transforming the position of the West. As a boy of eight, he watched the triumphant procession of Queen Victoria's Diamond Jubilee marking the zenith of Western splendor and might. He recalled vividly the Victorian faith that the world would remain safe and sane forever, that science was a modernized version of salvation, that an earthly paradise awaited humankind around the next corner of technological progress. He was an adult earning his living when the doctrine of progress and human perfectibility that had prevailed in the culture since the seventeenth century heard its death knell in the war of 1914. He lived well beyond that pivotal conflict to witness the fall of three historic European dynasties, a second cataclysmic fratricidal war, and the sudden withering to nothing of the West's far-flung empires. In addition to witnessing the end of an age, he amassed more learning about the world's past than probably anyone before or since, then brought his enormous erudition to life with worldwide travels.

With this extensive background, Toynbee cast his vision of modern Western culture beyond customary limits. Throughout his monumental *Study*, he often paused to reflect on the society and its likely future in the light of his historical findings.

The rise of the modern West, he pointed out, can be traced to unprecedented technological advances. This has given the society ascendancy over all humankind for some three centuries. Since World War I, however, the culture has been losing this ascendancy rapidly, not only in technology but militarily, politically, and economically. The problem of the West is that it has not been morally equal to its technology. In this sense, "Western Civilization has displayed not only a bright side but a dark one, and . . . in our time this dark side has been darker than the darkest stain on the pages of Western history in the Middle Ages."[4] By the time Toynbee completed his *Study* in 1961, he could declare that the West's world leadership was passing away.

But has Western civilization broken down, in the strict sense of the *Study*? Is it careening along the rocky road of disintegration? Toynbee remained reluctant to pass final judgment on these questions. Yet the culture of the West, he pointed out, seems in no way immune to the fate of every other civilization known to have existed. With that in mind, he declared that the society shows authentic symptoms of breakdown and disintegration.

The initial faltering of breakdown might have occurred as early as the sixteenth century with the wars of religion that erupted over Europe and raged for the next hundred years. The fanatical conflicts were succeeded in the eighteenth century by equally fanatical and far larger wars of nationalism that began with the age of Napoleon and continue to the present. Fitting these events into the patterns of the past, "if we in our generation were to permit ourselves to judge by the purely subjective criterion of our own feeling about our own age, the best judges would probably declare that our 'time of troubles' had undoubtedly descended upon us."[5] Further, that time appears to be already far advanced.

And what of disintegration? How far has the culture declined? Clearly it has not yet attained a universal state. Therefore its disintegration cannot be far along. Still, of the many traits of decline, a considerable number already have appeared.

Schism between states is obvious as the West burns up its achievements and resources in warfare. The society faces the same crucial challenge of political union that defeated ancient Greco-Roman civilization and so far is responding in the same suicidal way. Schism between classes also is present, with unmistakable traces of a dominant minority, an internal proletariat, and an external proletariat.

As modern rulers substitute lost creative spirit with various degrees and forms of force, their internal proletariat now extends worldwide. Due largely to technology, the West has added to its indigenous peoples no less than ten disintegrating civilizations and almost all the world's surviving primitive societies. Some have been conscripted forcibly. Others, like the Japanese and the former Soviet states, adopted Westernization of their own accord and on their own terms, joining the culture's comity of nations as equals rather than dependents or poor relations.

The spread of Western ways remains superficial, touching mainly technological and economic life, with no comparable transmission politically or culturally. Also, historical precedent suggests it might be only temporary. For the present, however, Western civilization makes up a Great Society within which all the nations of the earth have come and lodged. The West's internal proletariat includes almost all the living generation of humankind.

The modern external proletariat, on the other hand, is small to the point of extinction. The great hordes of barbarians that menaced the civilizations of Europe for some three thousand years were absorbed into Christendom or wiped off the face of the earth by the close of the fourteenth century. In Toynbee's generation only tiny pockets of barbarism survived in distant corners of the earth like Arabia and Afghanistan. Yet barbarism has been reemerging, not at the society's fringes but in its midst. Even before the Nazis of Germany glorified barbarism and the Fascists of Italy joined them, one twentieth century commentator noted: "Ancient civilizations were destroyed by imported barbarians; we breed our own."[6]

Some of the personal schisms of the soul that fragment people of disintegration now are splintering members of modern Western society.

The move toward abandon that leads people who feel barred from creative living to discard moral law and devote themselves to appetite is commonplace today. The converse side of that trend, however—the move toward ascetic self-control—has not appeared substantially yet.

The social truant who feels that the causes of his society are not worth serving has been long present in the society of the West. But just as it might be too early for ascetics to arise in any great number, there seems little present trend toward abandon's opposite of martyrdom in either the philosophical or literal meaning of the term.

The painful sense of drift that many people suffer when their culture is crumbling beneath their feet is a normal feature of modern Western life. But its counterpart—a sense of sin—though well known to the society through higher religions, most people presently go out of their way to avoid.

The loss of a firm cultural style and its replacement by a sense of promiscuity is a well established fact today. It appears especially in social manners and in the arts. Members of the dominant minority take pains to disguise their upper-class condition, adopting proletarian or vulgarized dress, behavior, and tastes. In the meantime, art, the most sensitive indicator of cultural change, has been eagerly abandoning its distinctive Western style. This is true in music, painting, sculpture, and other media, and "is manifestly the consequence of some kind of spiritual breakdown in our Western Civilization."[7]

In disintegrating cultures of other eras, traditional artistic styles were thought to be distasteful because they were associated with what remained of a dead and rotting past. Thus did Byzantine architects of the sixth century A.D., in building Constantinople's great church of Santa Sophia, turn away from the old Greco-Roman style to the difficult and previously unaccomplished task of crowning a cruciform building with a circular dome. In the modern Western world, where resources of creativity apparently have run dry, art alternately has descended into vulgarism and reached out to exotic barbarism for fresh inspiration.

Archaists of the present have attempted to turn back the cultural clock not only with Fascist politics, Nazi glorification of Teutonic barbarism, and the restoration of archaic languages. They also, until recently, filled the field of architecture with revivals of outdated forms. Meanwhile, the society finds futurists in political, economic, and scientific materialists who negate the present with ideological flights into imaginary ages yet to come.

THE COMING UNIVERSAL STATE

Assuming the West's time of troubles is far advanced and disintegration has set in, the next step for the culture is a universal state. For the first time in history, such a state would be not only psychological but truly universal. Foreshadowed by modern communications, it would envelope the entire earth.

As so it shall, Toynbee believed. A single government uniting the whole world is inevitable—and in the fairly near future. In past societies, as the time of troubles rose to catastrophic climax, a tide of desire for political union mounted to a flood. Such a flood of longing for a world order is mounting today, swelled all the more by the unprecedented dangers of nuclear war. "Unlike our forebears, we in our generation feel from the depths of our hearts that a *Pax Oecumenica* is now a crying need. We live in daily dread of a catastrophe which, we fear, may overtake us if the problem of meeting this need is left unsolved much longer."[8]

Germans during World War II rightly sensed that the society was ripe for unification, and Hitler himself reportedly said that a *Pax Teutonica* was the only practical means of bringing wars to an end. The failure of the Nazis to gather together a modern universal state was due to clumsy tactical errors but not to any mistake in their diagnosis of the mood of the age.

In Toynbee's time, the great powers of the world were reduced from eight in the late nineteenth century to only two: the United States and the Union of Soviet Socialist Republics. These were the last survivors of the West's time of troubles. True to the pattern of the past, they stood irreconcilably confronting one another as though preparing for the final knockout blow that would leave only one survivor to govern. As the region of Flanders in Belgium and France served the culture as a general battleground from the fifteenth century onward, in the twentieth century the whole of Western Europe seemed marked for that role.

Though Toynbee could not foresee the collapse of Communism and the dissolution of the Soviet empire, he acknowledged that today, with atomic weapons generally available, the final blow could come from anywhere, and "the knock-out blow might knock out not only the antagonist but also the victor, the referee, the boxing-ring, and all the spectators."[9] Even if nuclear catastrophe proved less than complete, would not the agonies of the conflict turn the survivors savage?

World unity is made feasible already by a skillfully assembled technological earthly paradise. But the kind of union that would leave the world intact is hampered by a political fools' paradise. The problem is the parochial state. The nation once was understood in the West as a useful piece of social machinery meriting the same conscientious but basically unenthusiastic duty now paid to county councils and city governments. In modern times, however, the nation-state has become an object of devotion and worship on the order of a pagan idol. Nationalism is the unavowed religion of most Western peoples today. This same false religion has brought fourteen to sixteen past civilizations to destruction. Given modern means of warfare, nationalism now constitutes a death wish for the West.

What the culture needs to avert the seemingly tragic fate that awaits it is a fresh solution for the time of troubles. The first concern should be to accomplish the perilous transit to a single ecumenical power without war. "What we are looking for is a free consent of free peoples to dwell together in unity, and to make, uncoerced, the far-reaching adjustments and concessions without which this ideal cannot be realized in practice."[10]

At the close of the religious wars in the middle of the seventeenth century, the West saw a notable lull in fanatical hostilities. Now, Toynbee advised, "we may and must pray that a reprieve which God has granted to our society once will not be refused if we ask for it again in a humble spirit and with a contrite heart."[11]

At the moment, the new and necessary political form that could unite the world is not in sight. Whatever it may be, it will not derive from any worshipper of the parliamentary system. Nor is it likely to grow out of the United Nations organization with its awkward constitutional makeup. More appropriate as a political matrix is the Commonwealth of Nations inaugurated by Britain, the former Russian soviet system, or the federal principle of the United States.

Whatever its governmental form, Toynbee was certain that world unity is on the way. It might come in slow and painful recovery from nuclear disaster, assuming that destruction is not complete and irremediable. It might occur peacefully by way of human accord. But no matter how, no matter where the ruler, all humanity will be unified. This unity under a single power will be an accomplished fact, Toynbee once predicted in a speech, as early as the opening years of the twenty-first century.

In past civilizations, the universal state only slowed the pace of decline while inhibiting substantial human growth within the society's framework. It was the Indian summer before wintertime, the long, peaceful coma before death. And so it also could be for Western culture. Toynbee asserted that the society might stiffen by imperceptible degrees into totalitarian petrifaction, turning even more rigid than other petrified cultures because its rulers would hold greater power through science. In any case, the universal state predictably is the final phase before total collapse and an ensuing dark age of barbaric anarchy.

Must the West look forward to trancelike somnolence before agonizing dismemberment? Not necessarily, Toynbee believed. "I am a pessimist," he admitted during a magazine interview in 1967, "in the sense that I think we can see very clearly the ways in which people did wreck a number of civilizations."[12] Yet the fact that all other civilizations either have perished or now are perishing does not somehow oblige the West to go the same way. The experience of higher cultures over a mere six thousand years of time's grand sweep, however consistently grim, establishes no strong precedent. Toynbee did not agree with Oswald Spengler that a society's life span is fixed and its demise "obligatory and insusceptible of modification." Doom, in Toynbee's view, is no more automatic than growth.

"I disbelieve in predestination," he said in a 1948 radio debate with Dutch historian Pieter Geyl programmed by the British Broadcasting Corporation, "and am at the opposite pole, on that question, from the famous German philosopher Spengler."[13] In the pages of his *Study* he declared, "It may be that Death the Leveller will lay his icy hand on our civilization also. But we are not confronted with any *Saeva Necessitas*. . . . The divine spark of creative power is still alive in us, and, if we have the grace to kindle it into flame, then the stars in their courses cannot defeat our efforts to attain the goal of human endeavour."[14]

The society might find, after all, a middle course between the two deadly extremes of devastating warfare between parochial states and peace imposed by a military knockout blow that lays waste to much of the culture. Success in passing through this pair of clashing jaws that has crushed every previous civilization might propel Western culture up the cultural cliff to a lofty, unseen ledge never before attained.

But it will not be political engineering that propels humanity's upward climb. What is needed is the spiritual redemption of souls. Disintegration of a society is nothing less than a symptom of spiritual disease among its people. The fate of the West will be decided not only by the course of man's relations with his fellow man, but also by his relationship with himself and, above all, with God, his savior. The plane on which the decisive battle is likely to be fought is neither military nor social, neither economic nor intellectual, but religious.

Religion: Restoration or Purpose

Toynbee held no illusions about the condition of religion in modern Western society. He regarded Christianity, already long on the wane, as so atrophied that he had long before referred to the society as "post-Christian" and "ex-Christian." He went on to compare the state of religion in the West to that in ancient Rome before Christianity. He also understood the difficulties of refilling a spiritual vacuum that some three centuries of religious deterioration have hollowed in Western hearts.

Yet he believed religious renascence possible and perhaps already on the way. And he speculated that the civilization, after trying to stand without God and failing, might be saved by its ancestral church. The modern dominant minority has done its best to de-Christianize life. But now the once-bright prospects of neopagan leaders have dimmed in the aftermath of debilitating war, and the sap of life again is flowing through the branches of Western Christianity.

A religious restoration, in Toynbee's view, could provide the age's most critical answers. Science has raised enormous moral problems about which, in its own limitations, it has nothing to say. To solve them, humankind must seek communion with the spiritual power who governs the universe. Also, the vast structure of a world government, which it is modern man's task to build, cannot be based securely upon the rubble foundation of economic interests. The unity of humankind is possible only with participation from God. And the only society capable of embracing the whole of humankind is the superhuman City of God.

What if Western civilization is not saved? If it is to die as all the others, what then could be its purpose according to Toynbee's scheme? Would it not appear, along with its contemporary civilizations of the third generation, to be not an advancement from the society from which it had its beginnings but a regression? Would it not seem a mere vain repetition of the heathen "from the standpoint of an observer who saw the guide-line of History in a progressive increase in the provision of spiritual opportunities for human souls in transit through This World?"[15] Yet even considering Western culture's possible demise, Toynbee found purpose for the civilization in an overall plan of human progress. It might provide a worldwide meeting ground for all the higher religions, bringing their adherents to see the unity of their basic values and beliefs.

As a scholar of religion as well as civilization, Toynbee concluded that the great historic religions and philosophies, however exclusive-minded many of them have been, all are partial revelations of the truth in one or another of its aspects. The four surviving higher religions, which he listed as Christianity, Islam, Hinduism, and Mahayana Buddhism, not only hold closer affinity than do present civilizations but actually are four variations on a single theme. Though they currently exist as competitors, in reality they are complementary; and "if all the four components of this heavenly music of the spheres could be audible on Earth simultaneously, and with equal clarity, to one pair of human ears, the happy hearer would find himself listening, not to a discord, but to a harmony."[16]

While the modern West brews the world's cultures together in a single technological, economic, and political crucible, so can the major religions meet and, to some extent, merge. In such a union they would not lose their diversity. Their differences are necessary, Toynbee judged, because the religions and their principal sects are attuned to particular psychological types. They would continue to exist distinctly but in choral harmony, all fulfilling their common purpose by enabling every human being of every mental type to enter into communion with God.

Toynbee believed that Christianity could initiate reconciliation of the world's great faiths, then go on to carry the mutual theme. Taking that role, Christianity would not retain its present cultural forms. Rather, it would draw inspiration from the other religions, just as in the failing days of Rome it assimilated the best of that time's various philosophies and religions. As the world flows together, descendants of the present generation will become heirs not only of Plato, Jesus, and St. Paul, but also of Confucius, Lao-Tse, and the Buddha.

And so, even if a new Caesar's empire arises in the West, then inevitably falls after a normal life span of a few hundred years, one can imagine "Christianity then being left as the heir of all the philosophies from Ikhnaton's to Hegel's and of all the higher religions as far back as the ever-latent worship of a Mother and her Son, who had started their travels along the King's Highway under the names of Ishtar and Tammuz."[17]

If indeed such a terrestrial communion of saints comes about and replaces multiple civilizations and diverse religions with a single Church Militant, will it create a kingdom of heaven on earth? This question arises inevitably at a time when the aim of most secular ideologies is a variety of earthly paradise.

Toynbee's answer was a definite no. The nature of man gives him innate capacity for evil as well as for good. The establishment of a worldwide Church Militant would not purge him of original sin. Though the world is a province of the Kingdom of God, it is a rebellious province, and by the nature of things always will remain that way.

PART IV

Pitirim A. Sorokin, The Master Analyst

10

Sorokin and the Crisis of the West

If Oswald Spengler and Arnold Toynbee were social thinkers whose time had come, the Russian-born sociologist Pitirim A. Sorokin was considerably ahead of his time. As a university instructor at the tsarist capital of Petrograd during the First World War and a prominent figure in the Russian Revolution, Sorokin early in his career saw that modern civilization was not evolving toward the earthly paradise that nineteenth-century social optimists had expected. Later, as an exile in America, he concluded that the culture of the West was suffering a crisis of massive proportions and all-encompassing importance. As chairman of Harvard University's sociology department, he organized an unprecedented analysis of cultural trends throughout the whole of Europe's history. His inquiry investigated the fine arts, philosophy, ethics and law, science, and technology, and the various social relationships that knit together a civilized people. After a decade of labor, he released a four-volume study that sought to explain the crisis of the West and forecast where the culture is likely to be heading in the future.

The study, titled *Social and Cultural Dynamics*, offered dire warnings for times immediately ahead, but also held out cause for hope. Sorokin believed that Western culture is not necessarily dying but is passing through a momentous change of phase out of materialism and into a more spiritual existence.

For much of his life, Sorokin held a position of global eminence among sociologists. He continues to be seen as one of the intellectual titans of the twentieth century. Yet throughout his long and remarkably productive career, his pioneering study of Western culture hovered in the rarefied atmosphere of work well in advance of its day. Widely noted, it was not as widely read. Penetratingly critical of present modes of living, it often met resentment from adherents of the status quo.

As the century wore on, the study's many predictions began to unfold. Yet when Sorokin died in 1968, it still awaited a new generation of sociologists to carry forward his inquiry into the culture and its likely fate.

PITIRIM A. SOROKIN

The story of Pitirim Alexandrovich Sorokin is extraordinary even for an age of violent social and personal upheaval. It reaches from the northern frontiers of the tsarist Russian Empire in the late nineteenth century to the pinnacle of the American academic world in the mid-twentieth century. It cast its subject in a bizarre variety of roles: wandering artisan, seminary student, farmhand, factory worker, revolutionist, editor, political prisoner, and teacher at several universities. Sorokin was jailed three times by the tsarist government and three times by the Communist regime that succeeded it. He founded departments of sociology at Leningrad, the stronghold of Communism, and at Harvard, the bastion of capitalism.

His life began in the Komi region of northern Russia, where he was born in the obscure village of Turya in 1889, nine years after Spengler and the same year as Toynbee, one of three sons of a Russian craftsman and an illiterate peasant woman. He later recalled the area as a northern paradise of boundless forests and flowery meadows, of crystal lakes and rivers, of sharp, clean air and brilliant sunlight, of endless expanses of winter snow where villages seemed like tiny islands in a vast white ocean.

The people of the land lived a relatively primitive existence, farming and hunting, fishing, trapping, and lumbering. They were peasants but never had known serfdom, traditionally managing their own affairs by village self-government. Land was held in common and periodically redistributed among villagers on the basis of family size. Community leadership was limited to the roles of Russian Orthodox clergyman, mayor, teacher, medical practitioner, policeman, and clerk. Significant inequalities—political, economic, or social—did not exist. Komi morality was based upon the Christian commandments and the principle of mutual aid, and the people largely practiced what they preached. Homes had no locks because there were no thieves. Serious crimes were nearly unknown, and even minor breaches of law were infrequent.

When Pitirim was three years old, his mother died. His younger brother went to live with a maternal aunt. He and his elder brother remained with their father, learning his trade as "master of golden, silver and ikon ornamental works."

The father and his sons traveled from village to village. Their work involved painting and decorating churches and renovating ceremonial objects. The outdoor life was robust and exhilarating but also hard. Often the artisans went underfed and insufficiently clothed against bitter winters.

Young Pitirim picked up basic education from his father and brother and from a peasant woman who taught children in one of the villages. When the family remained in one place long enough, the boys enrolled temporarily in school. Meanwhile, Pitirim was befriended by clergymen and teachers, who encouraged him to learn and lent him books. He read voraciously among works of Pushkin, Tolstoy, Dostoyevsky, translations of Charles Dickens and Mark Twain, books of history and natural science, collections of fairy tales, epics, and lives of the saints. He was spellbound with the stories of the saints, and in time he became a lay preacher for peasant gatherings on long winter evenings.

The boys' father was affectionate toward his sons, skillful in his work, and exacting as a teacher of his craft. But at his wife's death, he had taken up heavy drinking. During frequent bouts of drunkenness he grew depressed, ill-tempered, sometimes violent. Once, when Pitirim was ten years old and his brother fourteen, his father fell into a rage and struck at them both with a hammer. The boys left him, setting out to work on their own. They never again saw their father, who died the following year.

With the elder brother acting as business manager, the pair wandered the Komi countryside.

When Pitirim was twelve, his life took a decisive turn. The boys were working at a village called Gam, where a new advanced elementary school was opening. Entrance examinations were a public event, and Pitirim curiously joined a crowd of peasants to watch the testing. Hearing some of the questions, he found them easy to answer. Impulsively, he volunteered to be tested too. He passed the examination with grades so high that he was offered a scholarship of five rubles, which paid for his room and board for a full academic year. He proved the school's brightest student. His scholarship was extended for two more years. During summer vacations, he resumed work with his brother or traveled to the village of an aunt and uncle to help on their land as a farmhand. At the age of fourteen he graduated from the Gam school.

Teachers and education officials, impressed with his abilities, helped him gain a scholarship to Khrenovo Teachers' Seminary some distance away in Kostroma Province. Such seminaries, operated by the Russian Orthodox church, trained both teachers and priests and were one of the few avenues for advancement for talented peasant and artisan youths. The future Russian dictator Joseph Stalin had started up the same ladder some years earlier. Traditionally, both he and Sorokin would have ended up as clergymen or village schoolmen.

During the early years of the century, Russian schools simmered as hotbeds of revolutionary excitement. Sorokin, as Stalin before him, became caught up in the political fervor. He joined the Social Revolutionary party, an idealistic faction less based upon materialism than the Social Democrats of the Marxists. As once he had preached religion, he now began to spread the message of revolt among students, peasants, and factory workers. Shortly before his eighteenth birthday, tsarist police arrested him at a revolutionary meeting. Again like Stalin, he was expelled from school for political activities.

Prison turned out to be another kind of school for young Sorokin. With sympathetic guards, political prisoners visited from cell to cell, reading and discussing the writings of notable political thinkers. After four months, Sorokin emerged a professional revolutionist.

He began an underground existence as "Comrade Ivan." He instructed political groups, produced subversive leaflets, and organized secret meetings for thousands of workers in wooded areas on the outskirts of industrial cities. He narrowly escaped police traps and once was fired upon by mounted Cossack troops. After several months, the stress and hardship undermined his health. With police on his trail he fled to Komi country, where he worked on the land and regained his vitality.

With no prospects for education or employment in regions where he was known, he traveled to St. Petersburg, a week's journey away by river steamer and train. There he found work as a tutor and began attending night school to qualify himself for university. Meanwhile, he further educated himself in libraries, museums, concert halls, and theaters, in literary and artistic groups, and political and philosophical societies. In 1909, after two years of poverty and toil, he gained entry by sheer merit to the newly opened Psycho-Neurological Institute where he could study sociology under distinguished leaders in the field.

In 1910, to avoid being drafted into the army, Sorokin transferred to the state-operated University of St. Petersburg where he could gain exemption. He studied under outstanding professors, including pioneer physiologist and Nobel prize winner Ivan Pavlov. He continued to maintain a brilliant scholastic record, but he could not stay out of political trouble. He was arrested for revolutionary activities in 1911 and again in 1913. Now he profited all the more from imprisonment. Meeting thieves, murderers, and rapists on their own ground, he gathered original material for his first book, *Crime and Punishment, Service and Reward*, which was published during his third year at university. In 1914 he graduated with highest honors, a reputation as a rising young scholar, and a four-year stipend to prepare himself for professorship.

In half the period of his stipend, a record time, he earned a magister's degree in criminal law approximately equal to an American doctorate. This entitled him to teach at the university as a *privat-docent*, or lecturer. In March of 1917 he was ready to submit a thesis for a still higher degree available in the Russian system when the country's seething politics erupted in full-scale revolution.

The outbreak threw the nation into chaos. Sorokin set aside his academic work and plunged into the revolutionary cause. He worked as a newspaper organizer and editor. He addressed crowds with moderate socialist leader Alexander Kerensky and author Maxim Gorki. He also debated the extreme Bolsheviks Vladimir Lenin and Leon Trotsky. Offered three appointments in an early provisional government, he accepted the post of secretary to the newly chosen Premier Kerensky. He also served as a member of the Russian Constitutional Assembly. In the midst of the revolutionary furor, he married Elena Petrovna Baratynskaya, a fellow student who later distinguished herself as a biologist.

In November 1917, Lenin and his supporters overthrew the Kerensky government at gunpoint. Sorokin, who had campaigned incessantly against the radical Bolsheviks, found himself in a dangerous position, but he boldly continued to edit his moderate newspaper. Early in 1918 he was arrested, falsely accused of making an attempt on Lenin's life. He spent fifty-seven days in jail before another prominent revolutionist gained his release.

Sorokin persisted in anti-Bolshevik activities, openly editing an opposition newspaper and covertly helping organize an anti-Bolshevist revolt. The revolt failed. With a price on his head, he went into hiding. Wandering from village to village, he found shelter with peasants. Soon, even that grew too dangerous, and he plunged into wild forestland with a fellow conspirator. For weeks they trudged through wilderness, wearing bark shoes, supplementing meager rations with game, mushrooms, and berries. With the onset of winter and the disappearance of edible vegetation, the pair abandoned their flight and split up. Sorokin entered a town and turned himself in to authorities. He was imprisoned under sentence of death.

Each day he expected execution as prisoners around him were taken away at midnight and shot. Six weeks later an article appeared in the *Pravda* newspaper favoring him as an intellectual who could benefit the country. Lenin himself had written the article. Soon afterward the Communist leader personally ordered his release.

Sorokin returned to his university and resumed work despite bitter privation blighting the country. During the next three years, he established a department of sociology, published five books, and won his higher degree. He also continued to oppose Lenin's Communists. Eventually the Russian leader publicly branded Sorokin "our implacable enemy." Once again he was in danger of arrest. Taking advantage of bureaucratic confusion, he traveled to the new capital city of Moscow where he was less known and acquired a passport for exile. He left the country with his wife in September 1922, wearing a suit donated by the American Relief Administration and a pair of shoes given him by a scientist, carrying only fifty rubles in his pocket. A week later, in Berlin, he learned that had he not departed he would have been executed.

Free from the Bolshevist nightmare in which both of his brothers, his uncle and aunt, and many friends had been killed, Sorokin began piecing together a new life. President Thomas Masaryk of Czechoslovakia invited him to come there as a guest of the republic. In Prague he was offered a university appointment. During the next nine months, he taught, published two more books, and served as editor of a sociological journal. His activities attracted the attention of international scholars, and he was asked to give a series of lectures in America. He spent some time at New York state's Vassar College, then visited the universities of Illinois and Wisconsin. Ultimately, he was offered a full professorship at the University of Minnesota in Minneapolis.

Finally settled in a country that delighted them both, Sorokin and his wife built busy and productive lives. During the next six years, Elena gained her doctorate degree in botany and began teaching at Minneapolis's twin city of St. Paul. Sorokin meanwhile quickly established himself as a leader in what was then a rapidly burgeoning discipline, publishing five major works of sociology. Any one of them could have served as a scholar's main contribution to learning. Together they exceeded the average sociologist's lifetime output.

"I feel certain that within two or three years you will have opportunity to occupy a high position in some one of our leading universities," an academic friend wrote to Sorokin in 1928.[1] Less than two years later he was invited to establish a department of sociology at Harvard University. He assumed the post in 1930. Between then and his retirement in 1959, the department grew into a major center for the social sciences. Many of the outstanding sociologists of the century were either colleagues working under his direction or graduate students in his classes.

Sorokin's students saw him as stern, fiery, and colorful. Tall and slender with brown hair and eyes, he spoke rapidly, intensely, dramatically. Blunt and extroverted, he made up for what he lacked in grace with a physical vigor that people found astonishing, breaking chalks in assaults against blackboards, devastatingly attacking works of academic colleagues with whom he disagreed. "In Sorokin's courses, no one ever went away neutral," recalled a Princeton University sociologist who studied under the ex-revolutionist. "People either loved him or hated him."[2]

According to one of his close friends, Sorokin possessed a photoscopic memory.[3] Fed by prodigious reading, this gave him an encyclopedic knowledge of the social sciences and far greater general learning than one mind usually can master. In terms of quantity alone, no sociologist of past or present has approached his productivity. Sorokin wrote thirty-four major works consisting of more than forty separate volumes. He also published over five hundred articles, papers, and reviews. His works were reviewed not only in professional journals but also in such general-audience periodicals as *Saturday Review*, *New Republic*, the *Boston Transcript*, and the *New York Times*. They have gone through more than forty translations into every major language on earth. More than two dozen books and scores of treatises have been written about his ideas.

No single formula can assess his writings. He dealt with the sociology of science, of war, of law and ethics. He examined rural and urban principles, psychological theories, the American sex revolution, the philosophy of history, and the use of sociological measurements. As a pioneer in sociology, he virtually founded a half-dozen areas of study, including the sociology of political revolution, of calamity, of cultural morphology, and of social mobility and stratification. Some of his works became classics in their field. His *Contemporary Sociological Theories*, first published in 1928, still is used in universities all over the world. In the 1970s, an Ohio State University sociologist wrote that Sorokin's *Social Mobility*, often considered a masterpiece, possessed a striking modernity even though the book had been published more than forty years earlier.[4]

Sorokin's productive vigor alarmed at least one of his colleagues, who feared he might kill himself with overwork. Yet Sorokin did not feel unduly burdened. He thought of his research and writing as recreation and usually worked on them at home in early mornings and evenings. At the same time, he and his wife enjoyed concerts, social events, camping, and fishing, while Sorokin took up mountain climbing as well. The couple raised two sons, both of whom became scientists. Sorokin still found time to nurture a prize-winning flower garden that was featured in national magazines and attracted thousands of visitors annually to his home in Winchester, Massachusetts.

Sorokin's standing as one of the masterminds of the age is demonstrated most powerfully by the four-volume *Social and Cultural Dynamics.* Generally considered his greatest work, the study is a complete sociological analysis of the history—and probable future—of the Western world. Conceived while he was still at Minnesota, it probably is the grandest research effort ever undertaken by a sociologist. At first Sorokin felt some doubt that the far-reaching task could be accomplished. But when he arrived at Harvard, the university offered him $10,000 in grant money for the work. Sorokin gained the assistance of a team of specialists, among them eminent scholars, in America and Europe. They helped him investigate the history of painting, sculpture, architecture, music, and literature, religion, philosophy, science, economics, ethics, and the other principal fields of human affairs that make up civilized culture.

As research material poured in from his aides, he often wondered if the book's swelling size would be acceptable to a publisher. Yet he had decided at the start that he would rather fail in a grand undertaking than not attempt it at all. So year after year he continued to amass data and work it into written form.

The title he chose, however technical-sounding, expresses no more than a plain fact of life vividly and violently apparent to nearly every person living in the twentieth century. *Social and Cultural Dynamics* means, simply, social and cultural change. And change, among people and their way of living, is what the work is about.

Like Toynbee, Sorokin was a panoramic thinker. He overlooked lesser ripples of change in history, examining grand tidal transformations when changes in ideas, ideals, and beliefs, in standards of conduct, and methods of government sweep over an entire culture and leave its people shaken, bewildered, and gravely fearful of the future. Only a few periods of such shattering change have occurred in the history of any society. In the twenty-five hundred years or so of Europe's recorded past, the end of the Gothic Age was one of these periods and, before that, the collapse of Rome. Sorokin believed the present age to be equally momentous.

As he showed the modern crisis of the West to be far more serious than most people realize, he diagnosed current ways of living as pathological and decadent. He went on to describe the culture's self-destruction. Yet he was not without hope. He foresaw, beyond decline, a creative age when the spirit of humankind once more would soar to grand heights. For the meanwhile, he prescribed ways for people to ease their path through the painful transition.

The first three volumes of *Social and Cultural Dynamics* appeared in 1937. The work gained immediate notice all over the world. Never before had so many questions been answered about the nature of human culture and of cultural change. Hundreds of magazines and newspapers carried articles, reviews, and editorials about the work's ideas, while scholars wrote their reactions in professional journals. With time, the commentary mounted to a sizable literature.

The criticisms varied widely. Some were scornful, ridiculing. Others praised *Dynamics* as the greatest sociological work of the century. Some called Sorokin dogmatic. Others pointed out that he specifically avoided that fault by carefully qualifying his generalizations. Strictly scientific colleagues condemned him for being "philosophic." His defenders lauded Sorokin's unique blend of science and philosophy and hailed him as one of the foremost social philosophers of the age. Many sociologists dismissed him as a grand theorist, while other scholars commended his monumental and unprecedented collection of detailed empirical data. Not a few of his colleagues accused him of a "stratospheric mentality." Sorokin answered: "Those good people fall just a little short of saying that I am crazy. . . . The fact is that they don't always like the truths I tell them—truths that I have a duty to tell them because this is the reason for my being a teacher."[5]

His forecasts of wars, revolutions, and social disintegration disturbed many people in a decade still optimistic that the world was becoming more rational, humane, and peaceful. Other people praised him for squarely facing the issues of the age, even their most terrible aspects, while still not succumbing to a fashionable despair.

Sorokin enjoyed the applause. The opposition, for the most part, seemed not to trouble him. Not courting academic favor, seeking the patronage of foundations, or trying to gain the good graces of publishers, he said what he thought "regardless of whether the results are pleasant or unpleasant to this or that group."[6] Meanwhile, he gloried in disputes, blasting his opponents, as the gentle and polite Toynbee put it, "from bow to stern with the kind of broadside that used to be fired by ships of the line carrying one hundred guns."[7] All in all, Sorokin felt content with the reaction to *Dynamics*, observing, "it was similar to the reception given an overwhelming majority of the great works in the history of social thought."[8]

The final volume of *Dynamics* was published in 1941. Meanwhile, one of Sorokin's most fearful predictions was coming true: war in Europe spread around the world. That year he was invited to deliver a series of public lectures at Boston's Lowell Institute. He presented the ideas from *Dynamics* and drew a record audience.

Soon afterward, a modified version of the lectures was published in book form as *The Crisis of Our Age*. The *New York Times* hailed the volume as "a genuinely great book. . . . that will leave its mark upon our time as few have ever done,"[9] while the *Chicago Daily News*, with extravagant enthusiasm, called it a "literary thunderbolt" beside which "all other books pale into insignificance."[10] In its first four years, *The Crisis of Our Age* went through nine editions in North America alone. Ultimately it was republished in Great Britain and New Zealand and translated into German, Dutch, Norwegian, and Finnish, Spanish, Portuguese, Czech, and Japanese, among other languages. Sorokin gained special attention in India, where he was compared to ancient sages and credited with reviving eternal truths in a modern formulation of scientific accuracy and thoroughness.

In 1957, two decades after the original publication of *Social and Cultural Dynamics*, Sorokin released a one-volume abridgment of the study to make it available to a larger audience of both scholars and laymen. This was issued in English and Spanish editions. In the 1960s, the four-volume version was reissued in English, Spanish, and Italian.

Though *Dynamics* and its ideas have diffused broadly, the full import of Sorokin's masterwork, according to leading authorities, has yet to be realized. This is due equally to academic conservatism and the inevitable time lag that holds back the development of new ideas. *Dynamics* has been judged a turning point in the course of social thought, but its insights have not yet reached the average university professor, much less the average man and woman. In the view of a major scholar of Sorokin's, *Dynamics* still can "irrigate many arid zones of the sociological world, and indeed in the world of history, education, aesthetics, law, government and elsewhere."[11]

The completion of *Dynamics* found Sorokin in mid-career. In 1942, after twelve years as chairman of Harvard's sociology department, he requested to be relieved of the post so he could spend more time with research and writing. The disasters he had predicted for Western society were proving worse than he had imagined, and he threw himself into further work with the ideas of *Dynamics*, hoping this might help alleviate tragedies still to come. Studying the effects of wars, revolutions, famines, and epidemics, he wrote *Man and Society in Calamity*. Still in the early 1940s he was working on *Russia and the United States*, which warned against abandoning cooperation between the two countries for mutually harmful rivalry.

Sorokin, never an ivory-tower scholar, was becoming an intellectual activist involved with the dangers of the human situation. As World War II ended and the nations of the earth, in relief and renewed hope, began to piece themselves together again, he remained deeply disturbed. The conflict had killed some forty million people and revealed the depths of human depravity. Now the world faced the new menace of the atomic bomb. Sorokin dismissed the customary prescriptions for modern problems, whether political, governmental, scientific, economic, or educational. He saw only one clear solution. Any reform measures, in order to be effective, had to be "reinforced by notable altruization of persons, groups, institutions, and culture."[12]

As a scientist, he warned a cynical society that nothing would curb its impulse toward self-destruction except what great religions preached as generous, selfless, all-giving, creative love. He knew that many people would scoff at an idea so apparently impracticable. Yet he saw no other alternative to world-encompassing disaster.

Probing into the topic of altruistic love, he found it largely neglected by modern science. Sociology and psychology regarded hatred, violence, crime, and mental disorder as legitimate areas for study, but they tended to dismiss as pointless speculation an inquiry into unselfish love. Sorokin, in turn, dismissed this attitude as one more instance of a sickly society's obsession with the pathological aspects of life. Convinced that the scientific study of love was likely to become an important area for future research, he went to work on the subject.

He was planning to study independently and alone. But a well-known philanthropist, the pharmaceutical manufacturer Eli Lilly, offered him a grant for the project that eventually totaled $145,000. By then, Sorokin held a leading position among the world's sociologists, and Lilly considered him "one of the few scholars who could fruitfully study the problems of the moral and mental regeneration of today's confused and largely demoralized humanity. . . ."[13] In 1949 Sorokin used the grant to establish the Harvard Research Center in Creative Altruism.

Giving half his time to classes and seminars, he spent the other half on the work of the center, seeking ways to lead individual persons, social groups, institutions, and cultures to be less egocentric and selfish and more altruistic and humanly creative. Soon publications began to flow from the center. They started with *Reconstruction of Humanity* and proceeded with *Altruistic Love*, a sociological profile of some forty-six hundred Christian saints and five hundred living American "good neighbors." More publications came as he withdrew from teaching duties in 1955, continuing through the years to his full retirement from Harvard at the end of 1959. Attracting worldwide attention, the works were released in more than a score of languages.

Though now in his seventies, Sorokin enjoyed good health and remained busy. Offered other university posts in America and abroad, he declined in order to pursue what he called "the paramount tasks of our age: the prevention of a new threatening world catastrophe and the building of a new, nobler, and more creative order in the human universe."[14] Continuing to study and write, he also lectured widely at the request of universities and governments.

By this time, honors were coming upon Sorokin thick and fast. He had received an honorary degree from the Mexican National University. The Belgian and Romanian Academies of Art elected him to membership, as did several American and foreign scientific societies. In 1961, a group of European scholars unanimously elected him president of the International Society for Comparative Study of Civilizations. Traveling to Salzburg, Austria, for the society's meeting, he spent many hours with Arnold Toynbee and came away impressed with the British historian's integrity, sincerity, and kindness. In 1964, despite his seventy-five years, Sorokin was elected president of the seventy-eight-hundred-member American Sociological Association.

Only one honor remained beyond his grasp. Sorokin always wanted to return to Russia and be received at his home university in what was now Leningrad. Yet the alternative to his banishment had been a death sentence, so he would not travel to the country without personal authorization from its premier. The invitation never came, and early in 1967 a respiratory problem he was suffering was diagnosed as lung cancer. He was given one year to live.

Through his final months, more professional honors poured in from all over the world. Then, in the first weeks of 1968, after Sorokin had lived in exile from his native land for more than forty-five years, the University of Leningrad organized a "Sorokin Festival" of lectures, papers, and round-table discussions. Days after this event, on February 10, Sorokin died.

In the years since, scholars have continued to acclaim him as a front-rank creative genius and one of the most fruitful thinkers of the twentieth century. His social thought has been classed with that of Auguste Comte and Karl Marx. Some experts predict that his ideas will have a long-term influence similar to the social writings of St. Augustine in the fifth century, Thomas Aquinas in the thirteenth, and Voltaire in the eighteenth. The London *Times*, in its obituary on Sorokin, credited him with touching off a revolution in the humanities comparable to that of Albert Einstein's in physics. In a tribute written in the 1970s, Arnold Toynbee forecast that "no future student of human affairs will be able to by-pass Sorokin's work. The future student may be a disciple or he may be a dissenter, but in either capacity his encounter with Sorokin will be a major event in his own progress."[15]

Social and Cultural Dynamics

Sorokin focused mainly upon European cultures in his monumental study of social and cultural change for professional reasons. As a sociological scientist, he needed hard data. The Greco-Roman and Western cultures offered fuller and more accurate records than other historic cultures. *Dynamics* also draws from the histories of Egypt, Babylon, and the Hindu, Chinese, and Arabic cultures. Yet the work was not meant to be universal, applying with certainty only to cultures born in European regions.

He would have preferred to extend his study over a greater span of time, since it deals with long-term fluctuations—the great tidal waves of historic change. Yet, again for professional reasons, he confined it mainly to a period from around 600 B.C. to the twentieth century. Earlier historical records he found too vague for scientific use, but in the twenty-five fairly well documented centuries that he selected, Sorokin found sufficient reliable information for his work.

He also found enough major waves of change in that time span to suggest a strong pattern. Pattern, above all, was what he was seeking. Like Spengler and Toynbee, he hoped to assemble the jigsaw puzzle of the past into a recognizable picture that would reveal the meaning history held for the present and the future.

While Toynbee embraced the whole history of civilized mankind, Sorokin analyzed Western cultures more intensively than anybody before or since. *Dynamics* includes virtually all the significant cultural creations of ancient Greece and Rome and the succeeding Western culture. These range from the music of Terpander dating back some eight hundred years before the time of Christ to the richly spiritual Gregorian plain chant of medieval days and on to the crashing symphonies of Richard Wagner. The philosophy of Plato appears with the writings of the Roman Empire saints Augustine and Jerome and the sixteenth-century works of Martin Luther and Francis Bacon. In a similar manner, the paintings of Giotto and Piero della Francesca are arranged with Isaac Newton's theory of light, the works of the Roman poet Juvenal, totalitarian rule in the Byzantine state, and the literature of seventeenth-century Spain. Each element of culture forms a thread in a rich and all-inclusive tapestry of human affairs.

Sorokin's study extends over somewhat less than three thousand pages. Though not half the girth of Toynbee's magnum opus, the four volumes of *Dynamics* also have proved too awesome in bulk for any but serious professional scholars of culture. The author's abridgment of the work cut it down to little more than seven hundred pages that any intelligent and interested reader could peruse with pleasure and fascination.

Sorokin's style of writing eases the task. Though thoroughly a scholar, he had no patience with obscurity or jargon. His choice of words is precise, his phrasing, vigorous and clear. The overall effect is eminently readable prose. At times he used technical terms to sharpen precision or deepen insight. Thus, in the work's early pages, the reader learns about 'cultural congeries,' 'causal integration,' and 'logico-meaningful unity.' Yet Sorokin always explained his special language, while his central ideas are easy to grasp. As did Spengler and Toynbee, Sorokin overrode conventional academic barriers that divide one area of learning from another. He worked at once as a sociologist, historian, psychologist, logician, and philosopher.

In his approach to human cultures, he diverged from Spengler and agreed with Toynbee that intuition should give way to modern science's empirical method of investigation. Following this course, *Dynamics* became the greatest single fact-finding expedition ever to probe into history.

Under Sorokin's direction, scholarly aides on two continents classified into categories more than one hundred thousand works of art. The intention was to deal with literally every painting and every sculpture known from each European country involved in the study for every art period over twenty-five hundred years. This enormous quantitative effort ended with a list of great and minor artists and sources of research filling fifty-eight columns of small print in one of *Dynamics*' appendices—a list including every Western European artist known to history.

Another research team worked with philosophical thinkers. Their list fills seventy-eight pages of double columns. Details of wars and revolutions throughout European history fill seventy-eight similar pages. The staggering labor also produced vast mounds of data on architecture, literature and music, science and technology, ethics and law.

As material came to hand, Sorokin organized it toward logical conclusions. To ensure objectivity, his aides had not been told the purpose of their research. Thus, Sorokin was in no danger of picking facts to validate his theories. He simply took what he was given, setting out to bend or break theory on the rock of evidence and retain only what survived.

In the manner of a social scientist, he first turned the factual material into statistics and graphs. Hundreds of pages of figures and charts in his finished work drench the reader in quantitative data as they trace numerically Europe's main surges of cultural change. Sorokin's use of the statistical method to chart such qualitative topics as philosophy and art was a pioneering effort that left him open to criticism. Yet he anticipated that. All through *Dynamics* he cautioned against strict reliance on the numerical calculations. Surviving information sometimes was incomplete. Errors could occur in any attempt to count and measure. Yet, he pointed out, even considering possible errors, his scientific method was an improvement on previous historical estimates and guesswork about the same topics. Also, minuscule mistakes in detail would not substantially mar the broad picture his research was painting.

In addition to tracing the major changes in Europe's cultures and suggesting how they follow patterns, *Dynamics* also investigates the role of values in history. It explores ideas, ideals, and beliefs that have prevailed in various periods of the past. It shows how values shape all humanity's principal activities. Finally, it indicates how a shift in basic human values triggers each major wave of cultural change.

Sorokin's investigation of values opens doors to a fresh understanding of higher cultures. The study shows how values link all the fine arts, then relate them to philosophy, science, economics, and the other main pursuits of humanity. Through perception of values we can comprehend societies utterly foreign to our own and fathom the standards by which they see and judge themselves. The medium of values also can help researchers reconstruct the shape of cultures long forgotten using only a few artifacts of art or texts of writing, accomplishing this in an even more precise manner than Oswald Spengler proposed in *The Decline of the West.*

Most importantly, *Social and Cultural Dynamics* means to help people of the present understand their own confusing time and then go on to reveal a vision of a vastly different age already dawning.

THE GRAND CHANGES OF CULTURE

Sorokin's study does not focus upon "civilizations." That term proved too vague and varied for scientific use. A civilization, as thought of by historians, might be organized around language, like the culture of ancient Greece. Or it might be better defined by a region, as that of ancient Egypt. Civilizations also are held together by territory, state and citizenship, religion and customs, arts, values, and numberless other factors that people hold in common.

Amid such variation, a sociologist can find no way to pin down the term for precise investigation. To complicate matters more, every civilization contains a multitude of factors not especially related to its dominant identity: from imported religions to contradictory philosophies and alien modes of dress on outlying borders, to toys and tools and foods also common in other cultures, and work occupations pursued universally. So a "civilization," to the mind of a sociologist, far from making up a cultural unity, is only a vast and complex dump of related and unrelated factors.

Sorokin, rather than examining this "species of society," as Toynbee thought of it, dispensed with the concept altogether. He turned, instead, to another way of looking at cultures. He first took principal cultural "systems," as the fine arts, philosophy, ethics, and social relationships. Then he traced how these systems are linked to one another in what he called 'cultural supersystems.'

A 'supersystem,' by Sorokin's definition, is the largest of all cultural unities. All the systems that comprise it are interlocked in a general way, reflecting the same basic factor of value, which might be spirituality, for example, or materialism. When the parts of a supersystem change, they all change more or less together. The fine arts shift along with philosophical thinking, while ethical ideals make the same transition. So does the way social institutions deal with people, whether generously, in a family way, or through voluntary contracts, or by compulsion. A supersystem amounts to a whole way of life. It is a master pattern, a frame that holds together all the major elements of culture.

The histories of Greece, Rome, and modern Western civilization have unfolded under two profoundly different types of supersystems, two very different ways of life. Each of these has possessed "its own mentality; its own system of truth and knowledge; its own philosophy and *Weltanschauung*; its own type of religion and standards of 'holiness'; its own system of right and wrong; its own forms of art and literature; its own mores, laws, code of conduct; its own predominant forms of social relationships; its own economic and political organization; and, finally, its own type of *human personality*, with a peculiar mentality and conduct."[16]

These two different ways of life do not reflect progress, with the latest one better than the older, in the way social thinkers of the recent past assumed cultural change to occur. Rather, they come and go and come again, in a recurring, cyclic way. Each one appears, and for several hundred years develops its potential. Then, its creative possibilities exhausted, it disintegrates, making way for a new revival of the other.

Sometimes the end of a supersystem's reign marks the collapse of a civilization, as when materially oriented Rome declined and crumbled. At other times a supersystem's passing is apparent only as a great change of phase, as when the pious Gothic Age of Europe yielded to the materialistic period that has prevailed since then.

The supersystem—or phase of culture—by which medieval Europe lived Sorokin named the 'ideational.' A word with seventeenth-century origins, ideational refers to ideas about things not immediately present to the senses. An ideational phase is typically an Age of the Gods. Its culture, in theological terms, is one of the spirit rather than of the flesh. Very ancient Greece before the time of Socrates is another time and place in which this phase of culture reigned. Its prevalence in India today forms much of the West's general impression of that country as spiritual.

People of an ideational culture think of reality not as something to be perceived by the senses. To the contrary, the essence of reality is to be detected only in a spiritual way, whether they call this reality God, the Eternal Spirit, Brahma, Tao, or Nirvana. The main concerns in ideational life revolve around such concepts as soul and mind, the Devil, good and evil, justice and conscience, consciousness and salvation. Knowledge is sought through inner experience: divine inspiration, intuition, revelation, mystical union with God, meditation, ecstasy, and trance. In an ideational period theology is the queen of sciences, while natural science, as its opposite, tends to stagnate or regress.

In ideational culture, the main human values are spiritual. Such things as money and power, fame and prestige, comfort, pleasure, and happiness are unimportant and often regarded as threats to peace of mind and ultimate salvation of the soul. True values are nonmaterial, absolute and everlasting treasures laid up in heaven. The ideational age knows what Jesus meant when he said, "My kingdom is not of this world."

Ideational people fulfill their needs by turning away from the world to the things of God. They reach for satisfaction not from outside themselves, but from within. They seek to better their lives not by changing their environment, but by modifying themselves. They may renounce possessions and voluntarily embrace privation in matters of food, clothing, shelter, sex. They seek to control appetites, passions, emotions. At the same time they perform sacred duties, render service to God and their fellows, abide by categorical moral obligations, and meet whatever other spiritual requirements they perceive to exist.

Sorokin identified two types of ideational mentality: the ascetic and the active. The ascetic is the most extreme. The ascetic sees the world as mere illusion, a kind of waking dream, unstable and transient, a veil of appearances concealing the true, divine reality. Fleeing that world, he withdraws from active life, reasoning that "only fools attempt to write on waves." He seeks to throw off the illusion of personality and become absorbed in the absolute, eternal God. The ascetic ideational mentality has prevailed in the Hindu and Buddhist faiths, in Jainism, Taoism, early Christianity, and Islamic Sufism. It also arose among Stoics, Cynics and other philosophical groups of ancient Greece and Rome.

The active ideationalist, on the other hand, lives more on the material plane. He agrees with the ascetic on basic principles. But rather than withdrawing from the world, he works to change its ways. Often he becomes deeply involved in earthly affairs. He is the builder and maintainer of religious organizations. His mission is to reach out to others and secure their salvation along with his own. Active ideationalists have appeared in the Buddhist religion and the Sufist movement. St. Paul and the other Christian Apostles represent this mode of life.

The culture that prevailed in the days of ancient Rome was very different. It could be called materialistic-minded, as opposed to spiritual-minded. But Sorokin, as he did with ideational culture, chose a broader, more inclusive term. He named it the 'sensate' supersystem, or way of life. As the word suggests, the sensate phase of culture is preoccupied generally with things experienced through the senses.

A sensate period at its best and noblest is an age of humankind exalted. As it ripens with the passage of time it turns into a sensuous age of the flesh. This way of living has held sway at different stages in the history of ancient Egypt, Minoan Crete, Greece, India, and China. It has reigned in Western civilization since the Renaissance.

People who live the sensate way think of reality largely as something perceived by the physical senses. Whatever can be seen, heard, touched, smelled, or tasted is certain to exist. The actuality of anything else is doubtful, if not utterly absurd, unless it somehow can be proved by empirical means. Logical reasoning is accepted provisionally into the frame of sensate thought, especially in the form of mathematics. But even the best-reasoned theory remains doubtful until it can be tested and verified by sensory facts.

In a sensate culture the natural sciences are likely to flourish as the prime means of inquiring into reality, since they deal exclusively with the material world. Technology, too, in such a setting expands in scope and influence as a result of the culture's concern with externals. Theology and metaphysical thought necessarily wane in a sensate culture, since its people characteristically adopt an agnostic attitude toward everything not directly accessible to the senses. Meanwhile, soul, mind, and other entities reflecting the inward side of people are materialized and mechanized until the human being, in concept, is reduced to hardly more than an ape with a complicated brain.

Values in a sensate period are increasingly secular and worldly. It is an age of utilitarian pursuits, of searching for happiness, of hedonistic pleasures, and ever-growing sensual needs. Sensate people, involved in appetites and wants, yearn for a busy, rich, glamorous life. They seek to fill their cup to the brim with sense experiences of every kind, then drink it to the dregs. Their morality either ignores or mocks spiritual values. It denigrates absolutes, clinging to the relative and shifting to facilitate a quest for utility and pleasure and to avoid discomfort and pain.

Sensate people conceive of the self as inseparable from the body. Therefore they perceive their needs as largely carnal. Their lives are a restless search for food, drink, clothing, shelter, sexual pleasure, and general physical comfort. Maximum satisfaction of desires is regarded as the best way of living. Material wealth is the surest means of satisfaction. In a sensate society, money means everything: material goods, power, prestige, fame, and, its people assume, lasting happiness. Money, then, becomes the principal object of ambition. When wealth fails, force becomes the social arbiter and the basis for pleasurable living.

Time is particularly important to sensate people. Rather than dwelling with eternal absolutes, they live in a world of constant change: of progress and evolution, perhaps, or decline and entropy. As ideational people wish to be serene, the sensate person is dynamic. He is rushed, even frenzied, always conscious of the hour. With his keen sense of time, sensate man becomes civilization's master historian, recording great collections of data on the past that ideational man would think of as unimportant.

Sorokin distinguished between different types of sensate mentalities and people. All of them seek to exploit the outside world as their means of fulfillment, but they go about it in different ways.

The active sensate personality strives to control and modify the world. He might transform a landscape, build a corporation, establish a city, or struggle for political power. The most prominent incarnations of this type are history's great conquerors and empire builders, the tamers of wilderness, the founders of mighty fortunes.

The passive sensate person wishes to modify neither himself nor his surroundings. He wants only to feed upon the world in the manner of a parasite. He holds no real moral values, except those expressed in the ancient mottos "Wine, women, and song!" and "Eat, drink, and be merry!" or, in modern days, by much of commercial advertising. The passive sensate person conceives of the self as virtually identical with organs of sensual pleasure—the stomach and genitals. Regarding the past as lost and the future as uncertain, he seeks to glean only what pleasures he can find in the moment. Such people appear in practically all societies but are especially common in a sensate age.

The cynical sensate personality strives to fulfill his wants by duplicity, hypocrisy, and lies. He readjusts his values to suit the circumstance. He changes his colors to match the social fabric. Thereby can he gain society's rewards. Such people also appear in every culture, including the ideational. Unlike other sensate types, they operate covertly, and never have they developed any system of philosophy or prominent social class.

The ideational and sensate ways of life are drastically opposed to one another. Their values are closely knit within their own supersystems but totally and irreconcilably at variance.

The sensate person views the life of the spirit as superstition and ignorant delusion, if not outright mental aberration. He takes for granted that his way of living must appeal to everyone, and he tries to draw everybody into it by persuasion, pleading, argument, or ridicule. How anyone could choose ideational values is beyond his understanding. They seem to him repugnant, fearsome, a violation of life.

Sensate people assume that the ideational mentality existed in history only as an abnormal episode. Actually, however, the mode of living has been widespread, persistent, and highly influential. It has shaped the minds of hundreds of millions of people in both the Oriental and Occidental worlds. In European history, the two opposing systems balance out fairly closely, though ideational culture has reigned somewhat longer.

Sensate people also typically imagine ideational ages to be dark, dreary, and mysterious—retarded periods when human beings lacked the knowledge and development to be more sensate.

In reality, ideational cultures—whether of ancient Greece, of Europe's Middle Ages, of Byzantium, or India—provided deeply satisfying lives for the vast majority of their people. In turn, ideational peoples have viewed sensate ways as error, heresy, and blasphemy. Medieval Europeans, for a full thousand years, regarded classical Rome as the devil's own creation. From the ideational standpoint, sensate people are reckless and foolish for allowing themselves to become dependent upon material things that can vanish in a moment and leave them in a state of personal and social collapse. Ideational people see the sensate way of life as insecure and hazardous, as well as ugly and corruptive.

Because the two ways of living are so different, neither can be seen clearly nor judged accurately by the standards of the other. Each exists as a self-contained paradigm. They stand at opposite poles, contradictory and mutually exclusive. Most people living under either culture type remain prisoners within their own set of values, blind to the opposing set, wholly uncomprehending of its morals and manners, its art, music, and literature, its economic life, and its basic philosophical views. Only by accepting each culture on its own terms can a person gain some understanding of both.

Probably no culture ever set itself completely at one pole or the other, just as few individual persons live purely ideational or purely sensate lives. Each supersystem only predominates, with contradictory examples of its opposite existing at the same time. In sociological terms, a total culture never is integrated completely. Some cultures, in fact, are so mixed that they have no integrity at all. They function only as odd collections of illogical and conflicting values and behavior, all grating together without rhyme or harmony.

Now and then in the course of history, another kind of mixture comes to pass, a wonderfully harmonious meeting and merging of ideational and sensate ways of life. This integration amounts to a third cultural supersystem. Sorokin named it the 'idealistic' phase. The word describes the way the supersystem views the world—in the light of lofty ideals. In later works, Sorokin renamed this type of culture 'integral,' a term that better suggests how it integrates all the basic cultural values.

The integral way of life is a middle course that recognizes and honors both the spiritual and physical sides of humanity. Always, however, it remains stronger in transcendental values of the spirit, which give the culture its idealistic tone. It regards reality mainly as something to be uncovered by intellectual reasoning, though it also accepts intuitive revelation and perceptions of the senses. All the roads to truth are deemed real, none dismissed as illusory. Thus the integral mentality embraces reality in all its fullness as a manifold infinity.

The integral person does not renounce the world, nor does he revel in its pleasures. Rather, he seeks to use what the world provides for the greater glory and advancement of the human spirit. To this end he works both to modify himself inwardly and to alter his external surroundings. And he finds fulfillment in both spiritual and worldly ways.

In the history of Europe the integral culture has developed only as a short-lived, transitory phase. It appeared when ideational culture went into decline and sensate culture began to rise. At these junctures, for perhaps 150 years, the two ways of life came together in an inwardly consistent balance. Such an integration occurred in Greece during the fifth and fourth centuries before Christ. Another arose in Western Europe around the twelfth to the fourteenth centuries, between the Christian age of faith and the full development of the sensate Renaissance.

Integral ages proved strikingly productive in terms of sheer cultural quality. Human creativity, hovering between the two main culture types, could draw upon both. Its people were not yet cut off from ideational inspiration. At the same time they were discovering the noblest aspects of sensate reality. The integral period in Greece was the age of the great philosophers Socrates, Plato, and Aristotle; the time of the statesman Pericles, who raised Athens to its golden age; the moment when the architectural masterpiece of the Parthenon was conceived. Western Europe's integral epoch shone as a period of similar vitality when St. Thomas Aquinas and the Scholastic philosophers were blending the thought of ancient Greece into Christian doctrine and splendid cathedrals were appearing like the Bible wrought in stone. Some historians have ranked this age as the highest point in Western civilization.

As the three supersystems—and especially the main two—vary greatly in their general cast of thought, are they etched with equal sharpness in the day-to-day behavior of their people? Probing into this question in a separate section of his study, Sorokin found the people of the various cultures to be not as far apart in conduct as in mental attitudes.

Elementary biological needs have a strong leveling effect, grounding everyone in sensate living to some degree. Regardless of mental persuasion, people must eat and drink, build shelters and work, reproduce and defend themselves. So the tug of natural necessity holds ideational society lower than its loftiest aspirations, leaving it somewhat closer to the sensate position. Even in regard to more voluntary matters, ideational standards are harder to follow than the sensate path of less resistance. Thus, normal human weakness adds to the factors that prevent ideational society from developing a kingdom of saints, bringing ideational and sensate periods that much nearer. Sorokin determined by statistical research that in the purest of ideational societies, at least half the people of historical note have led lives largely in a sensate way, regardless of any higher ideals and intentions. Likewise in other epochs, all three modes of behavior existed side by side to some extent. Never does personal conduct fully match a society's aspirations.

All the same, the prevailing phase of culture wields powerful effects upon behavior. Each type, when it predominates, inevitably gathers a majority to many of its ways. Also the differences that exist between mentality and conduct are largely biological, and even these yield to social influence prescribing how and how often physical needs will be met. Meanwhile, the culture powerfully conditions other aspects of behavior.

For instance, an ideational society will spend enormous efforts erecting cathedrals, while a sensate society will put the same labor into building theaters and arenas. Ideational artists chisel statues of saints, while sensate sculptors carve works depicting sensual love. Ideational people stress preaching of religion, while sensate people promote utilitarian information. An ideational culture draws able people to the priesthood, while a sensate culture trains up leaders for commerce. All things considered, though conduct often falls short of ideals, the two always remain in logical accord.

Meanwhile, Sorokin agreed with Toynbee that the tone of a culture is set by a minority whom the masses imitate. As Toynbee called the guides the creative or dominant minority, Sorokin refers to them as the "bearers" of culture. Always they are small in number. Sorokin calculated through his study that out of billions of people who have inhabited the earth since records of man's past began, those of any historic significance do not total more than two hundred thousand.

Sorokin's supersystems, even more clearly than the broader civilizations that Spengler and Toynbee studied, rise, decline, and fall with relentless certainty. None can last forever. All must change and pass away. Change is a built-in consequence of social systems working as going concerns. A law of existence, change applies to forms of culture just as it does to living and inorganic things. Sorokin determined, along with Spengler and Toynbee, that a culture's course of change lies inherent within it. Outside forces can influence: aiding or hindering, speeding or retarding, sometimes even crushing development. But the life course of a culture is set down in its essentials when the culture is born. Just as an acorn holds the pattern for an oak tree, a culture's destiny awaits from within.

The rate of change differs for the different supersystems. It moves slowly for ideational cultures, faster in sensate phases, fastest of all in a sensate culture's overripe period. Yet whatever the pace, sooner or later every culture collides with its inward limits. As Sorokin observed in a scholarly paper a decade before *Dynamics* appeared, "no social process ever continues endlessly in one direction."[17] The end of a culture comes from the system working out its inner nature, unfolding its particular view of truth to logical conclusions.

No culture possesses all the truth, complete and infinite. If it did, its members would attain the omniscience of God. Each system is only partly true, and therefore also partly false, partly adequate and partly inadequate for maintaining human life and society.

As a supersystem develops, its valid portion tends to decrease while its false part increases. Rising to dominance, each culture type promotes its own side of truth at the expense of the others. Eventually it tries to force the others out, to secure a monopoly. Meanwhile, the error in the system, unchecked by the other approaches to truth, expands in both degree and influence. As soon as the false part of the culture begins to outweigh the valid part, the error turns lethal.

In the ideational way of life, for example, restrictions upon physical needs can go only so far before people start to oppose them. As privations grow, demands of the body become hard to manage, then, at least for the average person, irresistible. The European Middle Ages came to a natural end when repression of the physical side of life proved intolerable for many people. This set the cultural pendulum swinging in the sensate direction.

Sensate culture at its final limits defeats itself all the more. As its fleshly values are carried to extremes, they betray their own intent. The more sensate desires are satisfied, the more they increase, leaving satisfaction always beyond reach, generating only frustration. When sensate pleasures are freed from all restraints, they end up jading the senses, causing satiation, boredom, unendurable dissatisfaction. The tale of Rome's later days grumbles and laments about the barrenness of life, as does any account of an overripe sensate phase.

A society built upon premises turned false to human needs sinks by its own dead weight into ignorance, hollowness of values, and uncreativeness. Its blight does not disease the whole culture evenly and at once. Its various regions move the same general way, but some deteriorate faster than others. Likewise the various cultural compartments decline unevenly: perhaps the arts declining before economics, or ethics preceding technology. Sooner or later, however, the sickness spreads everywhere, and the system is revealed as increasingly empty, powerless, disorderly, and base.

When a failing culture's potential is worked out fully and its creative fund is exhausted, it continues to dominate for a time. But no longer does it reign by grace and attraction, ruling instead through inertia, fraud, coercion, and pseudo-values. A way of life that people once found satisfying turns sterile and poisonous. The society has only three alternatives for its future. It can fall into stagnation and serve as raw material for other, more creative cultures. It can perish completely. Or it can revive another system of truth and reality.

"In this way," Sorokin wrote, "the dominant system prepares its own downfall and paves the way for the ascendance and domination of one of the rival systems of truth and reality, which is, under the circumstances, more true and valid than the outworn and degenerated dominant system." Thus the recurrence of ideational, integral, and sensate systems of truth and their corresponding phases of culture "becomes not only comprehensible but logically and factually inevitable."[18]

The time when phases of culture are shifting is an especially difficult time to be alive. Nothing is secure. Everything is changing, the major parts of culture and its details as well. The familiar system of social control, which once seemed unshakable, is breaking down and collapsing. The coming system is not yet in sight, leaving the future an uncertain void. The whole society wallows in confusion. Moral anarchy reigns. Social chaos sets free the bestial side of humanity. Warfare increases and devastates the land. The only authorities are force and fraud.

When an ideational or an integral culture passes away, it leaves a heritage of humane values that moderates the period of distress. The end of a sensate age has none of this. Decadent sensate people long since have abandoned higher ethics. Their collapse becomes the worst of all times as they fall prey to their own demoralized condition.

Yet, like the supersystems themselves, the agonizing times between culture phases cannot last forever. Just when hope seems dead, the bleak misery of the chaotic night meets the dawn of a rising new culture and faith blossoms anew. Dark forebodings give way to bright assurance, and people are refreshed and renewed with the joy of life.

By Sorokin's analysis, history is no tale of continuous progress. Yet neither is it a mechanical cycle rumbling through the millennia in dull repetition. History repeats itself, to be sure, as the three supersystems unfold one after another. But never does it duplicate itself. Each ideational or integral or sensate phase of culture develops as a fresh and original variation on its master theme. History, then, is a process ever old and ever new as the cycle rolls on in a pattern of creative recurrence. Sorokin saw the rhythm of recurring supersystems in cultures around the world: Chinese, Hindu, Arabic, and others. Yet, with the care that governs his study, he declined to claim the rhythm as universal, confining his conclusions only to European cultures.

In Europe's recorded history, the movement of the three grand culture phases begins with a sensate age on the Mediterranean island of Crete. Since the disappearance of Crete's bronze-age civilization, Europe has seen two revolutions of the total cycle.

The culture of Crete, known as the Minoan for its mythical King Minos, also influenced regions on the mainland of Greece, like the city of Mycenae. Minoan society soared to a golden age around 1600 B.C. The center of their civilization, Knossos, was Europe's first big city, with as many as eighty thousand people. The palace of the ruler, the earliest known example of real architecture in the northern Mediterranean, was splendid, graceful, as large as London's Buckingham Palace. The domain around it reveled in riches and lived in elegant debauchery. Then, suddenly, the culture died—no one knows how. This marked the end of Europe's first sensate age.

An ideational phase followed, beginning in Greece around 1000 B.C. This was the age of the poets Hesiod and Homer. After some five hundred years, Greece's superb integral period blossomed. It reigned only briefly, then was superseded by a long sensate age extending from around the fourth century B.C. until the fall of Rome in the fifth century A.D.

From about the time of Jesus Christ, sensate trends were in decline, while fresh ideational trends were on the rise. The latter grew, took control, and established a monopoly between the sixth and the twelfth centuries. Then, from the twelfth to the fourteenth centuries, another brief integral period came and went. This was succeeded, finally, by the brilliant sensate age that left the West master of the world. Though that same sensate period lingers today, from every indication it is weakening and drawing to a close.

II

Changes in the Arts

Sorokin began testing his theory of the rise and fall of the three grand culture phases with his vast investigations into the arts. He and his aides in Europe and America explored the fine arts of ancient Greece and Rome, medieval Europe and Byzantium, England, France, the Netherlands, Italy and Spain, Germany and Austria, Czechoslovakia and Russia, and, finally, the Islamic world.

Drawing their data from encyclopedias, histories of art, and museum catalogs, from art journals, scholarly monographs, and other reference sources, the researchers listed art works by the scores of thousands. They classified each item according to its traits, whether ideational, integral, or sensate. Then Sorokin compared changes in the arts to the changes of cultural mentality he perceived over the ages. The two moved in unison, and he had no trouble identifying the three main types of art. Just as phases of culture have distinctive traits, so the arts they produce possess different forms and purposes.

Painting and Sculpture

Ideational painting and sculpture show what is thought of today as "primitive" technique. Simple means are used to create simple effects.

Figures tend to face plainly to thc front. Perspective is flat or altogether absent. Compositions lack unity. Beautifying trimmings or accessories are spare. In overall effect, the art is non-naturalistic.

Ideational art, speaking for its culture, represents a nonvisual world of transcendental realities lying beyond both reason and the senses. Its subjects are spiritual: Almighty God, the Divine Christ, the blessed Madonna, inspired apostles and saints, and, generally, the realm of intangible spiritual values. Often the visible appearance of a work bears no resemblance to its actual topic. A dove, for example, as pictured by early Christians, stood for the Holy Spirit. Likewise, anchors, olive branches, and other abstractions also suggest religious and mystical ideas. The art of an ideational culture is a visible symbol of invisible values. Even when it departs from symbolic style and turns to naturalistic methods, it continues to deal with nonempirical subjects, as paradise, the inferno, the last judgment, the *Pieta,* and allegorized ideas like virtue, vice, patience, and temperance.

Devoted almost wholly to religious themes, ideational art produces little portraiture, few landscapes or historical scenes, few views of daily life, and no comic caricature. Nude human figures are rare, and where nudity appears, it is nonsensual and nonerotic. In its inner nature, ideational art is static, quiet, and serene. Equally, it resists change, an attribute that matches its values, which are absolute, unchanging, universal, and eternal and therefore call for no shifts of fashion.

Ideational art gives rise to no connoisseurs, no aestheticism, no professionalism. Nor do artists seek credit for their creations. Often they labor in collective groups, and rarely will an individual fix his name to a painting or statue. Striving for neither mortal fame nor profit, toiling only for the glory of God, most ideational artists, along with their works, remain anonymous.

Art in an ideational age is regarded as part of religion. Spiritual leaders might go to great lengths to preserve its ascetic tone and cleanse it of all elements suggesting sensuous enjoyment. At various times, stained-glass windows, an artistic crucifix, and in one monastic order, all painting and carving have been banned as vain and dangerous things that could flatter curious eyes and charm weak souls. Expelling beauty for its own sake, however, does not detract from the quality of ideational art, which has been rich in great creations.

Sometimes it is difficult to classify a work as either ideational or sensate. At various times and places, the two basic styles have been mixed and impure. The mixture that occurs in idealistic, or integral, ages, however, draws them together in superbly harmonious balance. This merger of the two styles merits the name "idealistic" because it transforms visual reality into images inspired by lofty ideals. Like the idealistic age itself, the style emerges at a cultural crossroad, when an ideational period in decline meets a sensate period on the rise and they blend in sound organic union. The art, as the culture, still is firmly grounded in the old ideational values. But it also brings to life the noblest and purest elements of sensate beauty.

In technique, integral art approaches perfection. Figures no longer are portrayed frontally. Statues come to life. The means of execution remain moderate but are used to marvelous effect. Though visual in form, the art continues, in the ideational tradition, to ignore the vulgar, the debasing, the ugly, the immoral, the eccentric. If something base appears in a work, it does so only to serve as a contrast to exalted ideals. Commonplace people, landscapes, and scenery, the petty events of daily life are relegated to the background, if they are included at all.

The main subject matter of integral art is noble, sublime, beautiful. People are shown as idealized types. Mortals look like young gods, infants seem mature, women appear sexless and athletic, and the aged are strong and perfect. Scenes and events are portrayed not for themselves but as allegories of positive principles and values. Details of dress and scenery reflect the artist's native land, but topics are universal in significance. If the values of the culture are religious, they are profoundly so, and the art depicts deities, doctrines, beliefs, and great events in sacred history.

Unlike ideational art, however, the works of an integral age are not all about religion. They can represent nontranscendental, fully empirical subjects, such as heroic human figures and noble or virtuous deeds. Nudity in integral art appears as neither ascetic nor sensual but, rather, in the abstract and, again, in idealized form. Overall, the works remain free of sensuality despite introduction of sensate elements. Sense-gratification is not their objective, and things sexual, seductive, tempting, frivolous, and merely pretty find no place in the style.

People of an integral age regard art mainly as a means of teaching social values. It serves as an agent of religion or moral and civic principles. In spite of this basically nonaesthetic motive, the period produces some of the greatest aesthetic achievements of all time.

Like ideational art, the works of the idealistic integral period are static in their nature. Ideals are eternal, without change or movement. Therefore, art representing them is quiet, serene, beyond agitation. Also like ideational art, the integral style changes slowly as it unfolds in development.

Critics of art, formerly absent, emerge in the integral age, though they tend to make judgments in terms of religion and ethics as much as by aesthetic standards. Professional artists, also previously absent, appear as leaders overseeing communal artistic activities. The workers, however, continue to remain anonymous, and appropriately so, since their products express not their personalities but values of the general community. As a consequence, the architects of some of ancient Greece's greatest buildings and many of Europe's grand medieval cathedrals are utterly lost to the annals of history.

In the same way an integral age serves as a bridge between the two main culture phases, so does integral art provide a middle ground between the austere ideational style and its opposite, the sensate form of art. In the sensate style, techniques become elaborate, complex, highly skilled, often showy. They are designed to impress, even to stun viewers. The means used to produce sensate art are varied and enormous in scope. Often a work's mere size—its hugeness—passes for quality; the bigger a statue or building, the better it is thought to be.

Sensate art takes its subjects mainly from the secular world. Concerned with neither gods nor heroes, it concentrates on the commonplace and empirical: specific persons, tangible objects, actual scenes and occurrences. It is the art of the personal portrait, of landscape for its own sake, of historical events, of the normal daily living. While integral art deifies mortals, sensate works turn deities and heroes into ordinary people. The style draws humanity away from the realm of the spirit and into the world of the flesh. It lowers the lofty, debases the noble, deflates and debunks the grand and virtuous. All subjects are seen from an earthly point of view: as pretty, stunning, romantic, effective, sensational, salable. Nudity abounds in sensate art and generally is sexual, voluptuous, seductive. As sensate culture develops and enters its overripe stage, the topics of its art turn picaresque and perverse, vulgar, ugly and evil, macabre, pathological, disgusting.

The sensate style is intensely visual, realistic, and naturalistic. Imitating nature and empirical reality, it strives to create the illusion of life itself. In modern Western culture, sensate art reached its extremes in the late nineteenth century with the impressionistic works of artists like Claude Monet, Edgar Degas, and Pierre Auguste Renoir. In theory as well as in practice, the only reality they sought to paint was the visual appearance of their subjects. They meant to catch nothing but a momentary, fugitive, changing glimpse of what they saw—even to the point of its not mattering what they painted. Another example of matured sensate art is the photograph, which freezes an instant of time exactly as it was.

A significant technique of sensate art is described by the German word "*malerisch*." Translatable only roughly, as "painterly," it applies equally to painting and sculpture and, in a lesser degree, to architecture. While ideational art tends to render objects in sharp outline and distinct from their surroundings, the malerisch technique portrays the physical world more as it appears to the human eye, as a patchwork of light and shade, shapes and colors. It merges subjects imperceptibly into their surroundings as, for example, in the early sensate paintings of Peter Paul Rubens and Rembrandt van Rijn.

As ideational and integral art are static in their inner nature, sensate art is vividly, even violently dynamic. The phenomena of the sensate world is always changing. Light and shadow vary, color and form shift in ceaseless flux. Human subjects, too, show incessant variation. The art must be dynamic simply to follow its subjects. Equally is sensate art charged with emotion: passion and sorrow, suffering and fear, agony, comedy, drama. It also changes constantly in fashions, styles, and modes, which come and go in ever-faster tempo.

Sensate artists try to follow no traditional or conventional forms. Dislodged from both state and "school," they end up all going separate ways, each striving to create an individual style. Their individualism is augmented by general absence of universal social values. Ultimately their works express only themselves and their personal values, which may or may not be shared more broadly. Far from choosing anonymity, sensate artists sign and copyright everything they produce. Their work is inseparable from their personal identity.

Sensate artists are thoroughly professional. Flocking around them are professional critics, connoisseurs, aesthetes, and collectors. The sensate public absorbs art education, while aesthetic discussions and evaluations are popular and common. As art once sought to glorify God and advance his kingdom on earth, now it is mainly for refined sensate enjoyment. Works are valued for the pleasure they afford, the amusement, the entertainment. With the arts freed from both religious and civic obligations, art for art's sake becomes an aesthetic creed. Yet this freedom is no more than an illusion. Art is delivered to other masters—the rich, the powerful, the audience, the market. Finally, in spite of stimulus from broad attention, education, and freedom from convention, the quality of sensate art does not rise above standards set in ideational and integral phases of culture.

In the nineteenth century, most people assumed that the arts had followed civilization in steady upward progress. Their own art, with its highly developed visual techniques, was taken as the all-time peak of aesthetic achievement. Meanwhile, any work not technically brilliant, including that of ideational cultures, was placed in the scheme of aesthetic evolution both before and below the visual style. Lumped together, such works were labeled "primitive" in the belief that their creators lacked the skill to render objects realistically.

According to Sorokin, artists of an ideational phase neglect to cultivate the skills needed to reproduce objects in a visual manner because their works are not meant to imitate visual reality. Meanwhile, sensate people develop visual techniques, not because they are more clever or advanced, but because of how they perceive the world and seek to portray it.

Sorokin found ideational and sensate styles of art in the history of Egypt, India, China, Persia and other regions of the world in which civilizations flourished. Similarly did integral art, with its fine blend of symbolism, allegory, and naturalism, appear at different times in the Orient, especially in Confucian China, as well as in the cultures of the West. The styles also appeared at other levels of culture. Ideational art, with its strong symbolic content, has arisen in the Melanesian islands of the South Pacific, in the jungles of Guyana, and in the desertland of the Zuni Indians of New Mexico. Conversely, cave paintings in France dating from paleolithic times show distinct visual traits, as do rock paintings of the Bushmen people in southern Africa.

In the history of Europe, all three styles recur from as far back as archaeologists can probe. The record begins with sensate art on Crete before 1000 B.C. Artists of the island and their cultural relatives in centers like Mycenae on the mainland of Greece chose as their subjects ordinary people, slender and voluptuous women, landscapes, and scenes from daily life. Their renderings of animals and human figures reveal precise knowledge of anatomy and a high degree of visual skill. Picturesque and dynamic, dramatic and sensual, Creto-Mycenaean sensate art endured until the civilization's mysterious end.

After that, the art of Greece gradually turned ideational. It found subjects in religion and mythology while style became formal and conventional. This trend continued for several hundred years. Not until the sixth century B.C. did traces of visualism reappear. A century later, with the ideational phase declining and a new sensate stream on the rise, the two met and merged, producing the sublime integral art of Greece. The works of Phidias and other master sculptors of this unexcelled age combined the highest moral aspirations with superb control of materials. Equally did painting soar to lofty heights, the artist Polygnotus representing the period at its best. In both sculpture and painting, human figures were strongly athletic, gracefully clothed, dignified, serene, and imperturbable. They displayed the classic "Greek profile," reflecting an ideal. In general tone, the culture's integral art was religious, patriotic, educational, and moralizing.

Typically, however, its time was short. After the Peloponnesian War of 431 to 404 B.C., Greece fell into hopeless decline. As Plato pondered ways to bring about regeneration, religion waned, morality weakened, and propriety of conduct disappeared. Meanwhile, sensate art swelled in influence, overwhelming the idealistic style that had lifted Greece to its highest aesthetic level.

The conquests of Alexander the Great in the fourth century B.C. extended the field of Greek influence into Africa and Asia, and sensate art developed in many centers: at Alexandria in Egypt, on the island of Rhodes in the Aegean Sea, at Pergamum in Asia Minor, and elsewhere within the broadened realm of Hellenistic culture.

By then art was strongly visual and sensate in every way. Women, once depicted as robust and athletic, now were portrayed as sensual and erotic. Men became smooth-shaven and effeminate. No longer were babies ideally mature but, instead, simply infantile. The aged lost their strength and looked senile. Figures of gods were replaced by biographical portraits, while heroes were displaced by everyday people and low, pathological, and criminal types.

Even perennial subjects of Greek art changed appearance with the change in culture phases. The god of love, Eros, born out of Chaos, was a virile young figure in the fifth century B.C., but by sensate days looked like just another of the boy-loves of the period. Aphrodite, goddess of fertility, chaste and vigorous in the idealistic age, was by Hellenistic times soft, naked, and voluptuous. Dionysus, the god of fertility, formerly bearded and garbed, became in sensate art youthful, effeminate, and nude.

Nudity increased during the transition from ideational to sensate styles; garments slipped from shoulder to waist, then eventually vanished. Meanwhile, aesthetic quality yielded to quantity in size. Colossalism reared up everywhere, from the Asia Minor city of Halicarnassus with its huge white marble tomb of Mausolus—the original mausoleum—to Rhodes with its great bronze statue known as the Colossus looming above the island's harbor.

Romans of the fifth and fourth centuries B.C. were no strangers to the art of Greece. During that period, the southern half of Italy and the island of Sicily lay under Greek rule. But the Romans, in an ideational phase of their own, spurned Greek sensate culture. Not until around the close of the second century B.C. did the alien ways invade Roman society in strength. Staunch upholders of the old republic, like Cato the Censor, defended native traditions. But the splendor of Greek heritage proved overwhelming. Rome's own integral phase was cut short, and spontaneous growth of Roman art came to an end. For most of the civilization's remaining history—from the first century B.C. to the fourth century A.D.—art was imitative and predominantly visual. Again techniques became highly developed, subjects were emotional and sensual, and renderings tended toward complexity and emotionalism.

Around the start of the fourth century, something seemingly catastrophic happened to the art of Roman culture. Any layman can see it: the skills and high technique of preceding times vanished, the style turned "primitive," and artists either lost or abandoned all ability to reproduce anatomy, to create true-to-life images, to capture personal traits in the subjects they portrayed.

According to Sorokin, the startling change represents not artistic decay but cultural transition. Reacting against the declining sensate life and its waning creativity, artists deliberately abandoned sensate goals and transferred their allegiance to the new way of life then arising.

Since the birth of Christianity, a tiny rivulet of ideational art had been trickling through Roman culture. The catacombs outside the gates of Rome, used by Christians for burial and refuge, were filled with frescoes showing doves, crosses, anchors, fish, and other symbols of invisible and transcendental values. To the surprise of intellectuals in the Greco-Roman world, Christianity rapidly grew as a major social force. With it, ideational art also grew. By the end of the fifth century—and of Roman civilization—symbolic art again held dominance, ushering in the European Middle Ages.

The pagan art of Rome, reacting to the same change of culture, also had been turning ideational. But along the way it was engulfed in the Christian tide, and religious art gained a virtual monopoly. Once more the fine arts stood aloof from mere pleasure and enjoyment, just as they had in post-Minoan Greece. Pure, innocent, and tender, radiating peace and serenity, they again concentrated almost wholly on otherworldly subjects.

Some twenty-five years before Sorokin wrote *Dynamics*, a distinguished European art historian, Waldemar Deonna, noted many traits that medieval art shared with works of ideational Greece. Both ages, he observed, used "primitive" technique. Both neglected perspective and unity of composition. Both portrayed human figures with triangular heads, a placid smile, and ears, nose, hair, and beard similarly formed.

This symbolic art prevailed in Christian Europe for some seven centuries. The first suggestion of a visual revival appeared in Charlemagne's time in the ninth century. Yet the ebb of the medieval ideational stream and the rise of a new sensate tide did not become pronounced for another three hundred years. Then, once again, the two opposing styles met and blended. And again they produced a sublime integral period, still rooted in transcendental values but reaching out anew to embrace the sensory world.

Centered on the thirteenth century, medieval idealistic art combined lofty ideals with the noblest of earthly beauty. Its works show strong similarities to those of the parallel age in ancient Greece. Technique is superb, human figures are idealized, and works appear convincing without arousing emotional disturbance. People are portrayed as serene in posture, expression, and gesture. The art's overall effect is calm and undynamic, lacking in sentiment, and allowing no disorder. Art for art's sake is not its motive; works are created for the glory of God and express the society's collective ideals. As in the golden age of Greece, artists generally remain anonymous.

As the grand cycle of phases in art moved through the centuries of Europe's history, the whole society did not move precisely in unison. Some countries surged ahead while others lagged behind. Similarly, some forms of art preceded others. Sculpture led painting on occasion, while painting sometimes developed ahead of music. Yet Europe, as a cultural continent, moved together in a general way. All of its regions and all of its arts proceeded, at whatever different paces, in the same direction.

The integral period for Europe, as that of ancient Greece, proved short. The highest point of its painting and sculpture already lay behind by the thirteenth century's end.

The next two hundred years proved a time of transition from waning idealism to a new sensate visualism. "Virtually all the traits of the transitional period from Idealism to Visualism, which we saw in the Greek art of the fourth century B.C., are repeated, in a new setting and under different conditions," Sorokin observed.[1] The stream of religious art narrowed in favor of secular tributaries. Secular art turned everyday and common, depicting burgomasters, soldiers, merchants, and beggars, the kitchen and the tavern, fish and game, landscapes and farms. Art took on complexity, emotion, dynamic agitation. As mortals previously had been idealized as gods, now gods again were demoted to mortal form. "Lifelike" became the highest word of praise: In ancient Greece the painter Zeuxis was said to have rendered a grape so realistically that a bird tried to eat it; in sixteenth-century Italy the painter Giorgio Vasari claimed to have rendered a strawberry plant so accurately that a peacock pecked at the fruit.

With cultural change proceeding only gradually, the Middle Ages and their ideational ways had not altogether vanished in the sixteenth century. But by then the spirit of the Renaissance was stronger, displacing old hopes for celestial felicity with a new search for terrestrial happiness. Art lost its grip on heaven and fell solidly to earth. The art of humility, suffering, and sorrow, of resignation and the quest for God's guidance was replaced by a sensate art that the seventeenth-century scientist and religious philosopher Blaise Pascal defined as "concupiscence of eyes, concupiscence of flesh and lust of life."[2] At that point, religious and secular art diverged into two separate streams, religious works narrowing to the lesser rivulet.

The late sixteenth century brought fervent reaction against the growing sensate trend. The Council of Trent, spelling out general reforms within the Catholic church, also led to tighter moral control over painting and sculpture. In the secular field, academies of art came into being and imposed academic rules to bring the arts back to classical idealism.

But the sensate advance defied restraints. Visualism continued to grow. Religious art failed to regain its untroubled faith, instead joining the dispute between Catholicism and Protestantism and turning political and propagandist. Also, in stark contrast to the integral style, it fell into an emotionalism that seems nearly pathological. The tortures and sufferings of martyrs were depicted in horrifying detail. Saints experiencing ecstasies and visions were convulsed in expression and posture. Death was portrayed frequently and morbidly. In its form, religious art became less linear and more malerisch. In mood it turned ever more dynamic, at the same time becoming showy to the point of theatricality. The broader current of secular art followed similar trends, springing as it did from the same cultural mentality.

The spread of the baroque style in the seventeenth century brought still greater extravagance to the arts. The movement was luxurious and sumptuous, pagan and dynamic, sensual and sexual, pompous, artificial, illusionistic, and, again, theatrical. Its eighteenth-century offshoot was the more delicate rococo style. Now cupids and nymphs, shepherds and pastorals, and a highly artificial return-to-nature theme suggested a society weary and enfeebled.

Meanwhile, as in sensate Greece and Rome, artists ceased to lead community projects, instead working alone as individuals. They also turned professional, striving after wealth, popularity, and proximity to power. Connoisseurs and critics came into being, along with discussions of the arts and a literature devoted to their problems.

As the art of the Roman world from around the time of Christ imitated earlier styles and changed fashions with increasing frequency, so European sensate art from the fourteenth century onward resurrected and discarded past forms with accelerating speed. Various attempts to revive classicism and other former trends never resulted in true duplications. Rather, they created new variations of the current visual movement, catching outward traits of past periods but failing to grasp their inner spirit. At times the results turned incongruous, as when important people were portrayed draped in Roman togas or naked. Meanwhile, as the baroque style and academism endured for almost a century, the rococo period and the classic revival that followed each lasted hardly more than fifty years. The second quarter of the nineteenth century gave rise to a romantic movement that was outmoded within twenty-five years. Several other currents sprang into existence in an atmosphere of growing aesthetic anarchy. One of these developed into impressionism, which ruled the final decades of the nineteenth century.

Impressionistic art brought the modern sensate phase to its end. The style is the last and greatest development of European visualism. Not even photography and motion pictures—born at the same time and from the same cultural trend—surpass the visual purity of late nineteenth-century art. Deliberately mindless, espousing no ideals, blandly lacking in significant content, impressionistic works depict nothing more than the shallowest surface of things. They are malerisch to extremes, eschewing fixed linear form and constant color, since in nature, forms and colors change incessantly from one moment to the next. The style saw all the world as a brief and fugitive visual impression, a view of material reality so thinly superficial that its subjects tend to evaporate into near nothingness.

So just as the sensate phase of culture as a whole ends in self-defeat, its art fosters self-annihilation. When "the whole of reality has been reduced by Visualism to the mere passing impression, to the momentary appearance," wrote Sorokin, "the reality amounts to mere illusion and mirage, to self-deceit and dreaming."[3] Again, the time has come for another revolution of the ever-old, ever-new wheel of human culture.

The twentieth century saw a sharp break with visualism. The only open path for art to take veered off in the opposite direction.

While transition from ideational culture to sensate produces man's highest achievements in art, change the other way does not produce a similarly triumphant middle period. The grand idealistic phases are reserved only for people emerging from the life of the spirit to a dawning sensory age. When a society is moving the other direction, both its people and its art plunge into confusion. Artists, rebelliously searching for something different, create only culturally impure, incoherent, queer, freakish forms of antivisualism.

Many distinct currents of art mark the twentieth century: from futurism, constructivism, and expressionism to cubism, symbolism, and neoprimitivism. In their mutual aversion to rendering objects as they appear to the eye, all these movements and others like them represent a major landmark in Western art. But their quest for a nonsensory side of reality remains as yet unfulfilled. They are symptomatic of a search for something akin to the ideational style, in that they try to render visions of the mind rather than of the eye. Yet the symbols they produce remain intensely sensate. They do not stand for anything nonmaterial and transcendental. To the contrary, much of twentieth century art is more materialistic than the purest visualism.

For a single example, the cubism of Pablo Picasso depicts objects in the form of cubes in order to render them three-dimensionally, as the eye cannot see but, rather, as the mind conceives. The intention is ideational. Yet the subjects chosen are purely material, empirical, and, therefore, sensate. The rendering turns out to be superlatively sensate, depicting fully the subject's material spaciousness, solidity, and weight.

In many other ways, twentieth century art, though often ideational in form, remains highly sensate in both content and intent. Prior to the fourteenth century, some 96 percent of all art was religious; the same figure applies in reverse to modern times, 96 percent of recent art being secular in character. Art continues as dynamic and emotional. Daily life remains a favorite topic, with emphasis on the lower side of human existence. Landscapes are still common. Satire is popular. Nudity and eroticism abound. A frequent confusion of "more" with "better" and a stress on quantity over quality suggest a tendency toward colossalism. The number of art galleries and art schools in a region, the size of buildings devoted to art, the breadth of murals, and the physical mass of sculptures often are taken as gauges of aesthetic achievement. Meanwhile, artists, detached from even "schools," are individualistic to the point of wishing to seem odd, extravagant, queer. They also are thoroughly professional, working mainly to earn a living and gain fame and popularity.

For the present, modern art and artists are locked into an uncertain interim space. They have lost the past and, as yet, have no vision of the future. They rebel against the overripe and rotten sensate culture with its overly developed sensate view of reality. But a new view of reality eludes them. Until the sensate phase gives way for a cultural rebirth, the fine arts, like lost children, can only wander homeless and confused.

Architecture

Architecture, according to Sorokin's researches, followed the same trends as painting and sculpture in the course of Europe's history. The major buildings of ancient Greece prior to the fifth century B.C. were wholly ideational in purpose and form. Luxury and beauty were reserved for the gods. Accordingly, all grand structures of the time were temples rather than civic buildings or residences for the rich and powerful. Architecture followed the simple Doric order, named for the Dorian people who invaded Greece around 1100 B.C. and established themselves at Sparta and on Crete in the wake of the collapsed Creto-Mycenaean sensate culture. The austere style probably is best known for its plain and simple columns—pure, organic elements of structure with nothing suggesting ornament or decoration. The rest of the buildings were equally free of showy elaboration, their major parts perfectly fulfilling basic structural functions. Builders of the day had no taste for glittering materials such as gold, silver, or gems. Also their structures were modest in size. Early Greek artists found beauty in neither material richness nor grandeur but in simplicity and grace of proportion. Their edifices are static, solid, enduring, built for eternity. Standing independent of the landscape, they impress a viewer as definite, clear, and complete.

As time went on, the Doric order gave way to the somewhat more elaborate Ionic style. Named after the Ionian Greek people who colonized a coastal strip of Asia Minor, the order is distinguished by spiral volutes ornamenting the capitals that crown its columns. In the fifth century B.C., the Greek integral phase of culture burst into flower, and the Parthenon arose on the Acropolis of Athens as the period's finest architectural achievement. Dedicated as a temple to Athena, goddess of wisdom and guardian of Athens, the edifice displays marvelous harmony of ideational otherworldliness and sensate beauty. Its columns are Doric while other features take on greater visual appeal. It is larger than earlier temples, and its structure includes ornamental decoration. One sculptured frieze above the ranks of columns, depicting a religious procession, wound around the building in a continuous band 525 feet long.

The sensate period of ancient Greece created the Corinthian order of architecture. Named for the Greek city of Corinth, a wealthy, cultured, and mighty sea power, the style is noted for rich decoration of its capitals. Appearing around the start of the fourth century B.C., the ostentatious order was joined by other sensate traits in architecture. "Luxury, love of the colossal, and grandiose, pompousness, and theatrical display, the very things Greek art had once avoided, now appeared," Sorokin quoted specialists in art.[4] No longer was the architectural horizon dominated by religious structures. Side by side with temples rose grand civic buildings, triumphal arches, private mansions, palaces of rulers, theaters, and other edifices designed to serve secular life on a growing scale of magnificence.

Greek sensate trends were carried forward in Roman architecture. The buildings of Rome, founded entirely on Greek forms, became all the more profuse and exuberant, gradually rising to a climax of visualism. Columns lost structural significance, turning into mere decorations. Ionic and Corinthian orders were combined to produce more elaborate composite capitals. Temples, baths, and palaces grew to enormous proportions, splendid, rich, luxurious, and regal. With minor fluctuations, this lavish sensate style endured until around the fourth century after Christ.

Greco-Roman architecture never ended absolutely. Nor was the ideational Christian style that replaced it a wholly new beginning. The basilicas of Europe and the dome-style churches of the Eastern Roman Empire both were based upon inherited traditions and techniques. But their purpose and nature were entirely different. Once again religious buildings towered above civic structures and homes of the rich. And again architectural meaning and worth rested not upon appearance but symbolic significance. Many Western churches took the shape of a cross, not for the sake of pleasing design but to signify Christ's crucifixion. Eastern Christian churches often were roofed with one large central dome surrounded by four smaller cupolas, again not for visual effect but to symbolize Jesus and the four evangelists.

As in the Greek ideational age, exteriors were simple and plain. The church of Santa Sophia, erected between 532 and 537 by the Emperor Justinian in Rome's eastern capital of Constantinople, stands as a powerful example of a building that cut its space from its surroundings with simple, functional design. The massive masterpiece of Byzantine architecture is virtually devoid of exterior decoration. In contrast, the interior is brilliantly rich, another trait of ideational buildings, which resemble a person modestly clothed but harboring within a pure and harmonious soul. Judged as a whole, early Christian architecture "is a self-sufficient style, amply providing the early Church with buildings beautiful in themselves and even finer in their complete fulfillment of the needs for which they were designed."[5]

The Romanesque style, a thoroughly medieval form, was developed in Western Europe. It created exteriors all the more austere. Even columns were moved inside and used no longer as ornaments but, as in ancient Greece, for basic structural support. The style's builders at the same time lavished great attention on interior architectural beauty—not for the pleasure of man but to the glory of God.

Ideational buildings dominated Western architecture until the eleventh century. Then a new visual tide began to rise. It appeared in structures like the cathedral of Pisa with its baptistery and 180-foot bell tower best known for its lean. Columns were shifted outside again, once more used as ornaments. General complication increased, along with picturesqueness and other decorative effects.

The integral phase of European culture ushered in the Gothic architectural style. It appeared in the twelfth and thirteenth centuries with splendid balance of ideational and visual features. Gothic cathedrals, graceful and soaring, represent pure idealistic art, as do painting and sculpture from the same cultural period. The lofty roofs and spires of buildings for religion—cathedrals, parish churches, monasteries, convents, chapels—etched cities of Europe against the horizon until the fifteenth century. But as the sensate trend increased, skylines changed. Town halls, palaces, and commercial buildings gained both social importance and physical grandeur. Meanwhile, Gothic architecture adopted flamboyant lacy decoration, exhausting its aesthetic resources in the sixteenth century.

With the Renaissance, architecture for the first time in history looked backward rather than ahead. Overthrowing the supremacy of Gothic style, it self-consciously resurrected ancient classical traditions. Once again structure receded in significance, while facade and trimming gained principal importance. Columns, pilasters, and entablatures were put to use in the old Roman way, not as essential supports but for embellishment, while the ornamental patterns of antiquity returned in their more visual forms.

Baroque architecture came next among sensate movements. Possibly a direct continuation of late, flamboyant Gothic, it emphasized visual show. It strove for effect by arranging light and shadow, quested for theatrical impressions, labored for contrast and illusion of movement, strained for the colossal. Rich decoration was pushed to new extremes, with gold, painted colors, polychrome marble, sculpture, and pictures all exploited to advance the visual mania of the period. On the heels of the baroque came the rococo style. More visual still, this futile movement reduced architecture almost wholly to puerile decoration, creating toyland buildings, confectioners' sweets in stone.

The late eighteenth century brought a neoclassic reaction. But just as in the painting and sculpture of the time, the architectural style proved no more than an exchange of one kind of visualism for another. The nineteenth century saw several brief revivals: waves of romanticism and classicism, a return of Gothic and Renaissance styles. All of them showed intensely visual traits, with a passion for size, decoration, and outward appearance. Devoid of symbolism, they were purely sensual, aiming for convenience of use and pleasure for the eye. According to Sorokin, twentieth century architecture—notably the skyscraper—possibly represents a radical new departure, a movement toward a fresh ideational phase. Its buildings show a tendency toward structural simplicity, which possibly constitutes an antivisual reaction similar to that taking place in painting and sculpture. Many buildings conceived in the late twentieth century display these trends even more intensely, with austerity of line joined by grace of form.

As yet, however, modern architecture is far from ideational. Almost all its creations serve secular purposes as office buildings, stores, theaters, and banks, while religious structures generally are overshadowed to the point of being lost. Recent buildings make no attempt to symbolize any transcendental reality. Often they reveal the passion for colossal proportions typical of an overripe sensate age. And rather than arising as the natural outflow of spontaneous creativity, they are designed to use real estate efficiently and gain for their owners maximum revenues. It remains to be seen whether modern building styles represent only a reaction to the past or are harbingers of a coming ideational age.

Music

From the whole span of time between the dawn of history and Europe's Middle Ages, hardly a single note of music has survived. To trace the course of music in ancient Greece and Rome, Sorokin turned to literature surviving from the period. Then he carried his researches through medieval times to the twentieth century. The overall results revealed changes in music paralleling those in painting, sculpture, and architecture.

Evidence suggests that the music of Greece following the collapse of Creto-Mycenaean culture was mainly ideational. It served not pleasure but symbolized grand ideas, much in the manner of modern national anthems. Its subjects were the gods, their activities and relations with man. This is suggested by terms describing music in its classic period in ancient Greece from the end of the eighth century B.C. to the beginning of the sixth. For example, "nome" referred to a religious chant honoring the god of a province. "Dithyramb" meant a lyric hymn to the god Dionysus. "Paean" was a chant to the god Apollo. "Prosody" referred to chants of religious processions moving to a temple.

Temples, altars, and religious theaters were sites for musical performance. Far from mere entertainment, these events ranked among the most important functions of religious and state authorities. They were so sacred that strangers and noncitizens were not allowed to attend.

Administering officials also controlled and censored music. Any transgression of its formal rules was considered sacrilegious. As late as the fourth century B.C., the orator Demosthenes demanded death as a penalty for unlawful interference with a person overseeing a festival chorus. During the two hundred years before that, the philosophers Pythagoras, Plato, and Aristotle, understanding music as a potent influence on mind and character, had given much thought to the art as a means of moral education. For the same reason, and about the same time, the ethical teacher Confucius was composing and selecting the music to be played in China.

In ancient Greece many thousands of people attended ceremonies in which music played a part. Typically for an ideational age, the means of producing it remained spare and simple. A chorus might consist of only sixteen voices, while twenty-four was deemed maximum. As with other arts in such a period, music was a collective affair. Composers pursued neither personal ambition nor commercial returns, regarding their work as a religious and civic duty. In presentations, the central role went not to a single performer but to the massed chorus.

As in most times and places, the prevailing form of music was not the only kind that existed. Aristotle wrote of another type that made pleasure its goal, placing it in a class with sleep, wine, and dancing. But religious and symbolic ideational music dominated the field until around the end of the fifth century B.C.

As the ideational culture neared its end of dominance, meeting and merging with the rising sensate phase, a marvelous integral music developed in Greece. Balancing religious and artistic motifs to near perfection, this stage of the art was associated with the poetry and drama of such immortal figures as Aeschylus, Pindar, and Sophocles.

Integral music did not last long, as sensate trends grew quickly. While the power of the gods in theatrical works was giving way to mere destiny, the sacred character of music yielded to pleasing the ear. Music turned profane and sensual, more showy and rendered by more complicated means. A noted artist named Phrynis, with his following of pupils, worked for strong effects, stunning contrasts, and deliberate technical difficulties. His disciple, Timothy, transformed the dithyramb into a piece of bravura designed to display the talents of the virtuoso. Thinkers like Aristophanes and Plato denounced these innovations as corrupt, but the changes were welcomed by the general public of the day.

For topics of music, gods and human heroes were replaced by the common man. Love and sex became major themes. The old purity of style was lost, as was a mood of serenity, displaced by a mixture of styles and tricks and growing passion and emotionality. Instruments gained complexity and were used in mounting numbers. Huge private buildings were raised for performances. Monstrous concerts featured artists by the thousands. The makers of music, at one time priests and later moral leaders, now were professionals, their personal interests protected by trade unions like the "Dionysiac Associations of Artists of Ionia and Hellespont." Often these interests proved considerable. The producers of an important sensate pleasure, musicians earned fame and riches as idols of half-hysterical audiences and fans.

The music of very early Rome seems to have been mainly ideational. Before it could develop very much, however, Greek sensate music flooded the Roman world. Conservative groups made several attempts to resist the invasion, but to no avail. From the second century B.C. onward, Romans imitated the music of Greece and carried it forward in a crude and inartistic way.

Music was popular throughout Roman society, from emperors like Nero with his fiddle all the way down the classes. Children received musical training. Successful artists were friends of the powerful and rich. Critics turned out texts and compendiums, crushing some talents, making stars of others. Aesthetic theories circulated and heated discussions raged, bringing music to the avid attention that surrounds all the arts in any sensate age.

Instruments continued growing in size and complexity. Everything else about music grew as well, as colossalism transformed the art. Some theaters seated up to forty thousand people. In one play a thousand mules pranced about the stage. Concerts featured a hundred blaring trumpets, accompanying thousands of actors and acrobats. "Not being able to make it beautiful," wrote Pliny the Elder around the time of Christ, "they made it rich."[6] In time, Romans hardly enjoyed music for its own sake, so preoccupied were they with the size of orchestras, the volume of sound, and novel performances. Thus did they carry sensate music, along with the rest of their culture, to its end-point of decadence.

Early Christians rejected the elaborate music. They deliberately set about to purify the art, to strip away sensual embellishments, at the same time drawing from Greco-Hebrew sources for a music of their own. What evolved was a wholly different musical expression, in line with an opposite way of thought and life: the simple, austere, unaccompanied singing known as plain chant. By A.D. 400, the eight-century reign of Greco-Roman sensate music was over. Ideational music of the Christian church had taken its place. This religious form of music remained dominant in Europe for the next nine hundred years.

Judged by sensate standards, plain chant is hardly music at all. It pays no attention to measure. It indicates no tempo. It lacks soft-to-loud modulations. It gives little heed to what is thought of as "expression." It uses neither harmony nor polyphony. It holds little respect for words and their rhythmic disposition: on occasion, as many as 332 notes were loaded on a single verbal syllable. In its total effect, medieval plain chant offers doubtful enjoyment for the ear.

As in ideational Greece, however, music in Europe's Middle Ages was not meant to be enjoyed. It was a music of people who wished significance to be sensed inwardly through sound, like communion of the soul with God. As St. Augustine wrote in the fifth century, "I am moved, not with the singing, but with the things sung."[7]

Assessed by ideational standards, Christian plain chant represents perhaps the purest and most conspicuous known example of music composed for the spiritual side of people. First in the Ambrosian chant, which originated at Milan in the fourth century A.D., then in the Gregorian classical improvement from sixth and seventh century Rome, the music used the smallest and simplest technical means. Instruments were excluded from the church. Only human voices were allowed. These, in artless unison, sang melodies almost always contained within a single octave. At the time of St. Gregory, who assumed the office of pope in A.D. 590, the number of voices used in plain chant was only seven. Many centuries later, in all the luxury of the papal Sistine Chapel, the total had grown to hardly more than thirty-seven.

As all ideational music, the plain chant is pure in its inner self-consistency, stripped of anything not strictly belonging to its structure. An audible sign of inaudible values too great to be merely individual, it made music once more a collective endeavor. Authorship again was irrelevant, since the end result was not displayed as handiwork or vended as merchandise but offered to God. Nor did the music need aesthetic theorizers, critics, or professional appraisers, since it was not meant to be valued by aesthetic standards. Instead, as in ancient Greece, it fell under religious censors who ensured that it conveyed the transcendental values that all art was meant to express.

Gregorian chant consisted of roughly three hundred introits and communions, one hundred graduals, one hundred alleluias, twenty tracts, and one hundred offertories. All are pervaded with a spirit of gentleness, humility, and resignation. All possess the same ethereal, static, and timeless quality. Up to the end of the eleventh century, the music of the church remained virtually the only grand music taught and known.

But then a new sensate stream began to well up in music as in the other arts. It started with poctic songs of the troubadours of southern France and upper Italy, the trouveres of northern France and the minnesingers of German lands. These poet-musicians re-introduced instrumental accompaniment and added technical embellishments long barred from music of the church. The subjects they sang of—mainly sentiment and romantic love—were wholly of the world. Yet in other regards they did not stray far from their immediate cultural heritage. They dealt with romance only as chaste and noble idealism, while they retained many musical techniques of the recent past.

From the thirteenth century onward, music added one elaboration after another, gaining richness and sensate beauty. Polyphony developed, as did measure. Counterpoint emerged, reaching a golden age of its own by the fifteenth century. A broad variety of rhythms was conceived. Then came harmony and soft-to-loud intensity. The use of chromatics, consonance, and dissonance soared toward perfection. Music gained ever more expressiveness. Instrumental works expanded, were improved, were blended with voice. The size of orchestras and choruses swelled. Visual color and motion were added in opera and ballet.

The exquisite balance of ideational traits with rising sensate trends came later for music than for other Western arts. Rather than appearing in the thirteenth century, the superlative achievements of integral music developed only with the sixteenth century. They resounded then in a rare burst of glory. Master-composers like Giovanni Palestrina, Johann Sebastian Bach, and George Frideric Handel, Wolfgang Amadeus Mozart and Ludwig van Beethoven expressed sensate beauty at its purest, noblest, and richest. Western culture's period of idealistic music endured almost to the start of the nineteenth century. Only after that did a thoroughly sensate music finally gain predominance.

The sensate stream had been developing long before, however. The art form took on theatricality with the advent of opera in the sixteenth century and religious oratorio in the seventeenth. Just as colossalism inflated the arts of Greece and Rome, so did it bring its effect to Western European music.

In 1607, Claudio Monteverdi's opera *Orpheus* was scored for about thirty instruments. Orchestras performing the music of Bach and other composers of his period usually were the same size. But with the advent of the nineteenth century, the number of performers swelled enormously. The orchestra for Hector Berlioz's *Fantastic Symphony* of 1830 exceeded a hundred instruments. The number grew still larger for Richard Wagner's *Die Götterdämmerung*, Anton Bruckner's *Eighth Symphony*, Gustav Mahler's *First Symphony*, and Richard Strauss's *Heldenleben*. For Strauss's *Electra*, Mahler's *Fifth Symphony* and *Eighth Symphony*, Arnold Schönberg's *Gurrelieder*, and Igor Stravinsky's *Le Sacre du printemps*, instrumentation rose to 120 pieces and more. Equally did increased size come to choruses, stages, and buildings used for musical performances. The tendency toward expansion also influenced more intimate music, with the scale of tonality widening in range, with greater polytonality, sharper contrasts, an expanding scale of dissonance, and a swelling variety of chromatics, timbres, rhythms, and tempos.

The texture of music, in the meantime, took on increasing complication. The classic works of Europe are accessible to any ordinary orchestra. But much modern music taxes to the limit the best and most accomplished orchestras. Modern composers often labor long and hard to manufacture technical difficulties. At the same time, elaborate technique often takes the place of creative genius—a trait, Sorokin noted, that signals decadence in any field.

As always in sensate art, the subject matter of music has descended in stages from the divine and heroic to the commonplace and mediocre. Twentieth-century composers pursue this trend with music about the railroad, the factory, football, and city noises, among other everyday subjects. Comedy, another product of a sensate age, entered Western Europe's music early in the form of sixteenth-century *opera buffa*. Its popularity has grown since. The increasing change and novelty that sensate art demands show in picturesque and exotic works like *Salome*, *Aida*, and *Coppelia*, *Île de Calypso*, *Salammbo*, and *L'Africaine*. In other instances, music seeks the new and different in striking, extreme, or monstrous subjects and effects.

Western culture's sensate music also has increased in drama, pathos, and emotionalism in general. Sentimental love especially pervades its themes. So does sentimental sadness. A study by Sorokin on the use of major and minor keys revealed significant rise in the number of serious compositions written in the dolorous minor key as modern sensate culture developed. In the sixteenth century, the minor key was thought of as something painful and abnormal. By the time of Bach a century or so later, the minor key was close to the major in frequency of use. Since then it has grown more common.

As in the Greco-Roman sensate age, music in modern times has ceased to be a collective endeavor. Instead it is the product of highly professional individuals who grasp at wealth and fame with marketable compositions. Significantly, professional unions for musicians like those of ancient Greece and Rome also have reappeared.

Finally, music again is a major concern in the society. Once more children receive music education. Schools, clubs, private institutions, and governments all advance the art. Music critics, music discussions, and music journals flourish. As in the previous sensate age, however, the great number of people drawn to the art has not increased the number of musical masterpieces.

Sensate music apparently reached its modern peak in the works of Richard Wagner and other romantic composers of the nineteenth century. Since then it has shown symptoms of disorganization, degeneration, and demoralization. In spite of gigantic technical achievements, present-day music is anarchic and impotent.

Many composers of the twentieth century have turned away from purely sensate music. As if staging a revolt similar to that of modernists in painting, they turn away from the sensate goal of pleasure and look for something else, though exactly what they have not yet discovered. Whether their works signify only another turn in the old sensate stream or a rising new ideational tide remains for the future to see. But until sensate music gives way to ideationalism, it is doomed to express—albeit with the most complex and brilliant techniques—inner emptiness.

Literature and Criticism

Literature also rode the tide of change from ideational to sensate as the two supersystems alternated in the course of Europe's history. Though literature of both types seems to have existed in every culture and at every age, differences appear in purity and proportion, and usually one kind predominated over the other.

The writings of the very ancient Greeks were mainly ideational. Practically inseparable from music, the literature was symbolic in significance and religious in character. Before the fourth century B.C., Greeks read the *Iliad* and *Odyssey* of Homer not as entertaining stories or works of art but as religious, moral, and educational texts. The same was true of the works of Hesiod and the Orphic literature, along with Doric choral lyric in religious nomes, dithyrambs, paeans, prosodies, and threnodies.

As the ideational current of ancient Greece waned and met the rising sensate stream, the greatest literary masters of the culture arose. The lyric poet Pindar and the tragic poets Aeschylus and

Sophocles mark the culture's integral period, which reached its midpoint in the fifth century B.C.

Many modern scholars have expressed surprise that Greece bred virtually no literary critics before the time of Plato. Some have guessed that the Greeks had no feeling for beauty until after the Peloponnesian War, despite many great works in all the arts that the culture produced before then. Sorokin solved the mystery when he demonstrated that in ideational ages, religious and moral censors take the place of critics. Criticism written by Plato and his best-known pupil, Aristotle, represents a kind of transitional stage between ideational censors and thoroughly sensate critics. Plato, in the last quarter of thc fifth century B.C., admonished artists who failed to teach lofty values, calling them "drones" and regarding them a danger to society. Aristotle also valued art in ethical terms.

From the time of Aristotle's most famous pupil, Alexander the Great, literature and criticism took on traits of a ripening sensate age. Religion ceased to be the leading topic as secular subjects gained ground. Gods and heroes were brought down to mortal status, while common, vulgar, and subsocial characters increasingly populated literary works. Symbolism practically disappeared in favor of precise and detailed realism. Tragedy gave way to comedy and satire. Bucolic and pastoral poetry arose. Sensual and erotic themes gained popularity.

Artists mimicked old forms with revivals, especially from the third century B.C. onward, placing living patrons and potentates in the roles of the old gods and heroes in whom no one any longer believed. Poetry turned pedantic and sterile. One poet named Aratos set to verse a textbook on astronomy, while another named Nikandros did the same with a medical text. Still others, like a poet named Lykophoron, sought as their supreme aesthetic goal to compose lines in the shape of visual objects—an ax, for example, or an altar, or wings.

Aesthetic criticism grew as a profession, bringing labored discussions on grammar, etymology, the meaning of poems, and aesthetic techniques. Art education, art appreciation, and art fashions rapidly developed. The literati also became thorough professionals, cultivating individual mannerisms and preening their vanity. In the course of time, as always in a ripening sensate age, art for art's sake defeated its own purpose, turning ever more futile and uncreative.

The earliest literature of ancient Rome was mainly ideational and idealistic, though it never reached the heights attained in Greece. Around the close of the second century B.C., the irresistible invasion of Greek influence forced the rise of a Roman sensate stream. This brought Rome a literary integral phase around the first century B.C., marked by such writers as Virgil, Livy, Sallust, and Cicero, Seneca, Varro, and Cato. This idealistic period lasted until the early part of the first century A.D.

At the same time a lesser sensate stream was maintained by writers like Horace, Catullus, and Ovid. It grew rapidly, and, by the end of Nero's reign in A.D. 68, Roman society was becoming highly aesthetic, as the works of Seneca the Younger, Juvenal, Martial, and other writers show. Literary discussions were indispensable at supper gatherings of Rome's upper class. Women took an avid interest in art, and literary salons appeared. Literary novelties excited whole cities. Artists drew groups of enthused admirers. Everyone seems to have aspired to be a professional artist or writer, while the bookish aesthete became a popular role. Pliny the Younger, who coined the formula "The bigger the better," tells of being stationed at the nets in a bore hunting party with pencil and notebook in hand. Meanwhile, language turned polished and bombastic, with writers, typically for a sensate age, demanding broad freedom of expression.

For all the freedom and in spite of the furious pursuit of inspiration, the most flourishing centuries of the Roman Empire produced no great or durable literature. Sensate art, carried to extremes, dried up the culture's creative springs. Some Romans themselves realized this, lamenting, as one put it, "the world-wide bareness that pervades our life."[8] By the fifth century, the sensate wave in Greco-Roman literature had worn itself out.

Meanwhile, as in all the arts, an ideational tide had been advancing. Christian thinkers who led it saw pagan literature as spiritually dangerous and even stupid. They replaced it with commentaries on sacred books, biographies of saints, religious poems, and translations of writers like Bede, Crosius, Boethius, and St. Gregory. For seven or eight hundred years after the collapse of Rome, almost all writing of any consequence in Italy, Germany, France, and England pursued religious themes. The rare exceptions were heroic poems, like the German *Hildebrandslied* and the English *Beowulf*, both produced in the ninth century.

As all other ideational art, the period's literature was highly symbolic. Symbolism and allegory were fundamental categories of thought, dominating all thinking and writing of the early Middle Ages. As a result, the Fathers of the Church, whether dealing with the Bible or with pagan works such as those of Cicero and Virgil, were occupied largely with finding hidden meanings. Language, as all else, was an imperfect symbolic expression of the transcendental kingdom of God.

Appropriately to an ideational age, criticism vanished, along with attention to literary techniques. Modern scholars have attributed the absence of medieval criticism variously to "the fetters of religious dogma," "the age, being one of intellectual childhood," and "the prevailing ignorance of much that was best in the teaching of antiquity."[9] But again Sorokin cites the spirit of the time as the single reason for lack or criticism; the sole criteria of beauty and art were religious and moral.

In the thirteenth and fourteenth centuries, the proportion of religious writings fell from approximately 95 percent to somewhere closer to half that amount. The medieval ideational age was declining and a new sensate phase of culture was on the rise, producing an enormous increase in secular writing. Yet the literature of this transitional time, typically integral in nature, was positive in values, moral in tone, heroic, ennobling, and suffused with religious spirit. Among the period's more outstanding works were the German

Rolandslied and *Nibelungenlied*; the English Arthurian legends, and William Langland's *The Vision Concerning Piers Plowman*; the French *Tristan et Iseult* and *Roman de la Rose*; and the works of Italy's Dante Alighieri, including the age's supreme masterpiece, the *Divine Comedy*.

The *Roman de la Rose*, one of the greatest and most popular works of the time, demonstrates the change from ascetic ideational attitudes to the newly sensate state of mind. The poem was written in the thirteenth century in two parts by two authors, one working somewhat later than the other. Its topic, typical of rising sensate feelings, was romantic love. The first part of its twenty-two thousand lines, composed by Guillaume de Lorris, follows the adventures of a youth seeking to pluck the rose of love in a noble, decent, sublime, and delicate allegory. It adheres strictly to the chivalric code glorifying womanhood and lofty ideals. The second part, written by Jean de Meung, gives romantic love a fleshier face and satirically attacks chastity, the clergy, nobility, royalty, monastic orders, and other social ideals and institutions of the age. Meung's cynical advice for success in romance is: Have "a great heavy purse."[10]

At the same time, other sensate traits invaded literature. Divorce, almost absent in writings before the twelfth century, began to be presented as a solution to unhappy marriage. Economic problems, also nonexistent in works before the twelfth century, started the ascent that ultimately brought them to prominence in modern literature. Duty, inviolable in ideational periods, began to be excused away where conditions were difficult. Descriptions of landscape and nature appeared, as did topics from history and everyday life. In emotional tone, literature lost the simplicity and calm of ideational times, taking on animation and the sadness that always marks a time of cultural transition. Collective and anonymous authorship gave way to individual writers, all possessively signing their creations.

Symbolism that formerly reflected God's kingdom softened to allegorical personifications of worldly matters, like Sir and Madame Wealth, Dame Leisure, Frankness, Love, Beauty, Purity, Liberty, Reason, and Shame. As the sensate age advanced, a chain would be completed, from symbolism to allegory and on to sensory realism. Finally, Western Europe's integral age brought literary criticism in writings of the mystical theologian Meister Eckhart of Germany and St. Thomas Aquinas and Dante Alighieri of Italy.

The English poet Geoffrey Chaucer might be thought of as opening the sensate age for European literature with his *Canterbury Tales* completed in 1387. In the century that followed, religious writings fell to some 20 to 25 percent of the culture's literary output, even then often taking a form no more sanctified than current religious disputes. Sensate works began to dominate the field.

Now almost all the values of former times—the clergy, piety, scripture, chastity—were targets for literature's ridicule and denunciation. So they have remained ever since, from Francois Rabelais's sixteenth-century satire *Gargantua*, to Jean Baptiste Moliere's seventeenth-century comedies, to Francois de Voltaire's eighteenth-century *La Pucelle*, through the iconoclastic writings of the nineteenth century and on to the morally nihilistic literature of the twentieth century. Numberless works great and slight tore the past to pieces, assembling a thoroughly sensate modern age.

Love continued its descent from the heavenly heights of ideational times and the chivalric level that followed to the earthy ground of sexual pleasure, and that often tainted with cruelty and perversion. Literature's heroes slid downward apace. Once the grand gallery had included God Almighty, the Madonna, the apostles, great saints. Later it substituted brave and noble knights performing grandly heroic deeds. With the end of the sixteenth century, chivalric romances disappeared. Rabelais's *Gargantua* and *Pantagruel* and Miguel de Cervantes's *Don Quixote de la Mancha* mocked heroic values. Meanwhile, literature brought forward a common run of people to fill the heroes' place. Merchants, servants, artisans, and courtiers inhabited writings for a time, followed by rogues, failures, derelicts, criminals, and whores.

The ripened sensate mentality of today, seeing human beings as no more than physical objects moved by instincts, reflexes, and drives, virtually disallows any attempt to raise them above the animal level. Genuine heroes are all but banned from literature and all but impossible for authors to create. Their replacements are at best mediocre people of a wholly unheroic kind and at worst a motley crowd of perverse, debased, diseased, and pathological types.

Satire and irony were among the tools that sent values into decline. Early satirical literature rarely attacked fundamental tenets, content with making fun of the sillier side of life: the gluttony of a clergyman, the aged wedding the young, a chaperon's shortsightedness, or the hardships of an adventurous lover. As literature developed through the eighteenth, nineteenth, and twentieth centuries, it assailed ever greater things until it was poisoning the culture's basic values. At present, Sorokin observed, "there is nothing left which has not been slandered, ridiculed, and debased by it. Religion, God, the saints, the Virgin, angels, devils, sacraments, Paradise, Inferno, the Credo, the State, the Government, aristocracy, nobility, talent, genius, sacrifice, altruism, marriage, the family, asceticism, idealism, chastity, faithfulness, loyalty, science, philosophy, moral duty, property, order, truth, beauty, righteousness, man himself—everything and everybody is . . . defiled."[11]

Another aspect of Europe's sensate literature was the reappearance of comedy. In ideational times, comedy did not exist in great works. It emerged only with the integral period, and then both rare and mild. But with the fifteenth and sixteenth centuries, comedy grew first on the Spanish stage, then in literary works of other countries.

From the fourteenth century, the concept of duty atrophied in literature. More and more, obligation yielded to comfort as, through the years, authors endorsed neglect of religious, moral, civic, and familial duty. Also, as the sensate age advanced, literature took on emotional tones. In contrast to ideational works, which recount plainly and serenely events as momentous as the earth's creation or as tragic as the sufferings of Christ, writings from the fourteenth century onward grew in passion, pathos, and general emotionality. Today, the thoroughly ripened sensate culture exploits every means to stimulate emotion, to impress, to make impact, to cultivate sensation.

Along with emotionalism, sensate literature is full of change, its fundamental forms shifting with increasing speed. From the fifteenth to the seventeenth centuries, the main form of literary works changed roughly every sixty to eighty years. Thus unfolded the heroic epic, the chivalric romance, the pastoral *roman*, the picaresque story, the heroic or classical drama, and the tragedy. Still shorter are periods of the sentimental novel, the mystery, and other modern forms. Now change races, with current best-sellers that have their heyday lasting only weeks. With the rise of the best-seller, literature finds its colossalism. Quality as a criterion fades, while the number of copies sold becomes a gauge of greatness.

Criticism in the modern sensate age has grown from its modest beginnings with Eckhart, Aquinas, and Dante. By 1600, criticism was a recognized department of literature. Academies established to govern literature, especially in France, formulated codes of aesthetic criticism that were rational, sensible, moderate, even scientific. Still slightly touched by integral values, the rules reigned into the eighteenth century. The importance of critical writing in the culture is affirmed by the literary standing of such figures as Joseph Addison, Samuel Johnson, Friedrich Schiller, Denis Diderot, and Johann Wolfgang von Goethe, all notable for critical opinions. In more recent times, critics again are full professionals, filling journals with reviews and articles, wielding great power in art and literature, making and breaking literary talents.

Lately, however, art criticism has been losing prestige. Best-sellers no longer are made as much by critics as literary hucksters promoting bookish wares through mass advertising and public relations. Also since the end of the nineteenth century, the literary field has seen criticism of critics. This ranges from Tolstoy's sarcastic castigation of critical judgments in his treatise on aesthetics, *What Is Art?*, to manifestoes of arch-modernists who assail as outmoded present critical currents. The attack on criticism is a clear symptom of a crisis in the field. It has been joined by attacks on sensate literature in general. Dissident schools—as symbolists, futurists, and surrealists—have staged full-scale rebellions against sensate realism.

Yet as literary rebels bring to their revolt against sensate trends some sensate traits of their own, so do critics of criticism lack a coherent positive program. In this sense, the rebellion of both groups matches revolt in the other arts. As in Roman culture of the third and fourth centuries when art began to pass from overripe sensate to new ideational, revolt is growing. Yet prospects for the future remain clouded.

12

Shifting Certainties

IT MIGHT SEEM STRANGE that a standard of truth can exist other than the one belonging to our own time and culture. Yet what is generally accepted as truth in religion, philosophy, and science always depends upon cultural mentality. As Sorokin revealed three basic mentalities underlying the three supersystems of culture, so he demonstrated three basic forms of truth.

The truth of faith fits an ideational culture. Its focus rests on matters beyond reason and the senses: on God, angels, spirits, and the devil, on the soul, salvation, and immortality, on sin, redemption, and resurrection, on hell and paradise. People living by this form of truth are concerned mainly with matters of religion. They ponder such questions as whether angels use demons as messengers and whether the pains of hell are proportionate to sins committed. Things of the world they regard only incidentally, and then merely as visible signs of the invisible realm of the spirit, as symbols of transcendent reality.

The supreme discipline for the study of truth in an ideational age is theology. Philosophy and the natural sciences are either incidental or irrelevant. The truth that is revealed is deemed absolute. The only accepted proof is divinely revealed scripture. Other revelations—or, in less theological language, inspirations or intuitions—are tested by distinguishing whether they come from the same divine source. Purely logical reasoning and perception of the five physical senses play only a subsidiary part in determining what is true and false. And scripture remains the final test; anything that contradicts holy writ is rejected as invalid, heretical, or blasphemous. As the fine arts indicate, symbols are used to express this truth that is inaccessible to graphic realism.

Idealistic, or integral, culture embraces a truth of reason. This view of reality is concerned with both transcendental things and things of the world, though the realm of the spirit takes precedence. Truth is studied in an integral period by logical reasoning and exploring the empirical world with the science of the age. The findings of both methods usually come together in a rationalistic philosophy, like that of Plato and Aristotle in ancient Greece, of Albertus Magnus and St. Thomas Aquinas in Europe's thirteenth century, and of philosophers of ancient India who based their thinking on the Hindu scripture of the Vedas. People of an integral period use dialectic and deduction for the exposition of truth. Its validity is tested by logical reasoning coupled with testimony of the physical senses. To these is added the ultimate authority of sacred writings and other revelations. Truth is established when all three tests agree.

In a sensate culture, truth of the senses gains overwhelming favor. The focus of attention turns at such a time mainly to the empirical world. So intense does this concentration become that anything not readily reducible to material form might be virtually ignored. For example, thoughts, feelings, and values are dealt with by dwelling upon their external effects in the manner of modern behaviorist psychologists, while their nonmaterial aspects are likely to be disregarded. Meanwhile, transcendental truth is declared irrelevant, unknowable, or nonexistent.

The natural sciences are the supreme discipline for the study of truth in a sensate age. Their influence grows so overpowering that even philosophy mimics scientific ways while theology tries to concoct scientific religion. Sensate people use inductive reasoning for the exposition of truth, with special emphasis upon the experimental method. Truth is validated mainly by reference to the testimony of the senses. This is supplemented by logical reasoning, especially in the form of mathematics, though findings of reason remain provisional until proved by sensory evidence. If reason is contradicted by facts, it is flatly and summarily rejected. The truth of faith is valued as little in a sensate age as the truth of the senses is in an ideational period. In many instances, it is viewed as mere superstition.

To follow the three types of truth through the history of Europe, Sorokin broke them down into six main currents of epistemology, the study of the nature and grounds of human knowledge. These currents are: rationalism, mysticism, and fideism; empiricism, skepticism, and criticism.

The first three are varieties of ideational truth. Rationalism, in its more pronounced religious form, is the same as the truth of faith. It draws its verities from revelation, with reason given a secondary role yet still held more valid than evidence of the senses. Mysticism is a more esoteric kind of the truth of faith. Stressing visions, trances, and ecstasies as the main means of gaining revelation, it requires special training for mastery and sometimes is nonrational or antirational. Fideism is the third truth of faith. Emphasizing volition, it results in belief by sheer act of will.

Rationalism, as a philosophical viewpoint, has a second side that fits the in-between integral age. Known as idealistic rationalism, it grants the major role in discerning truth to reason and intellect. It also allows more authority to the senses than religious rationalism does. At the same time, it leaves the final word, at least nominally, with the authority of faith. Thus, idealistic rationalism blends all three cultural ways of seeking truth.

Empiricism is the principal basis for truth in a sensate age. This view maintains that the source of all perception rests in the physical senses. Logical reasoning it regards merely as a mental activity springing from sense perceptions.

Sensate truth, by its nature, does not allow the certainty afforded by the truth of faith. On the testimony of the senses themselves, it must remain unsure. Perception, after all, varies from person to person. It differs from the sighted to the blind, from hearers to the deaf—and also, probably, from one creature to another as, for example, from a person to an ant. Therefore, the real empirical world cannot be viewed with certitude and might even be seen as inaccessible. At times this built-in uncertainty crystallizes, turning into the purely negative system of thought known as skepticism. A phantom of lost certitude, skepticism methodically doubts the possibility of any valid knowledge.

The final philosophical category, criticism, also is known as agnosticism. A mixture of rationalism, empiricism, and skepticism, it functions as a diluted form of the last of these currents of thought. Agnosticism emerged in the modern sensate age mainly through the eighteenth-century works of the Scottish philosopher David Hume and the German thinker Immanuel Kant. It contends that only the empirical world is accessible to knowledge, while transcendental reality—whether it exists or not—is inaccessible and does not have to be known. At the same time, it accepts the evidence both of the senses and of rational thought, trying to tie them together and make them mutually conditioned.

Changes in Accepted Truth

With the various branches of philosophy finely defined, Sorokin and his aides launched another massive statistical exercise. They listed hundreds of thinkers from about 600 B.C. to the present century, then placed them into the six categories. When the tally was arranged in a table by twenty-year periods, two major conclusions came clear.

First, a currently popular belief that human thought progressed from faith to reason or empiricism is a misconception. To be sure, during the past five centuries the truth of faith has lost ground and sensate truth has gained. But this is not a constant trend for all time. The shift is only part of a fluctuation of the three basic forms of truth that rise and fall in turn through Europe's history.

The second conclusion of Sorokin's analysis is that systems of truth have joined the arts in the same grand revolution: from ideational to integral to sensate. When the very ancient Greeks were producing ideational sculpture and painting, sacred music and literature, and Doric architecture, their predominant mentality was religious rationalism. The period was one of faith and certitude, of quiet serenity and untroubled simplicity. After 460 B.C., in the time of Socrates, Phidias, and the Parthenon, empiricism entered a notable rise. This led to a brief reign of idealistic rationalism, when the truths of faith, reason, and the senses blended in harmonious combination, balanced and free of extremes. Then, from the third century B.C. onward, rationalism of both kinds receded while empiricism advanced. At the same time, in an atmosphere of cultural decline, the desperate form of ideational truth—fideism—flourished. So did the negative kind of sensate truth, skepticism.

The Romans picked up this trend from the Greeks around the first century B.C., carrying it forward. Though outwardly victorious against its rivals, Rome suffered wrenching internal disorders and general demoralization among its people. Even at better moments, the society sometimes suffered a nameless unease, which foreboded the decline of its sensate way of life. In the social climate, many people fell into cynical and nihilistic skepticism and sensualism.

The mental distress of the Roman world launched European philosophical thought on its second cycle of the three culture phases. Early Christians broke away from the truth of the senses, embracing ideational truth, a move made by many pagan thinkers as well. This renunciation of the external world was not a choice taken in serenity. Large numbers of people in Rome's imperial age felt so bereft of hope that they believed the end of the world was at hand—not only Christians but also Jews, Gnostics, Roman Stoics, neo-Platonists, and neo-Pythagoreans. Thus the desperate varieties of the truth of faith ruled: mysticism, which typically appears as a reaction to skepticism; and fideism, which enables people with little capacity for inner faith to believe by force of will.

Only after the fifth century A.D., when the old Roman sensate society was all but dead, did religious rationalism reappear and become the dominant form of ideational truth. This serene and confident system of unquestioning belief held a philosophical monopoly for the next six to seven hundred years.

The late eleventh to the fourteenth centuries in Europe saw the reappearance of empirical truth. Also, an idealistic rationalism similar to that of Greece's integral period took a leading position. This was the age of the Scholastic philosophers, which spread through the whole of Western Europe in the persons of thinkers like Robert Grosseteste in England, Albertus Magnus in southern Germany, and St. Thomas Aquinas in Italy. Merging the thought of the Greco-Roman world with that of the fathers of the church, it blended at the same time the truth of faith with that of reason and the senses.

Toward the latter half of the fourteenth century, the medieval age of faith was slipping away and the integral age had run its brief course of 150 years or so. Meanwhile, the coming sensate phase of culture had not yet taken shape. The consequence of this philosophical interim was mental, moral, and social confusion. Fitting a time of instability, skepticism and fideism reappeared, and mysticism grew enormously as wars, the black plague, and other tragedies besieged a bewildered population.

Only with the end of the fifteenth century, amid the debris of the former crumbling systems, did empirical science and discoveries grow, and with them the promise of a new phase of culture. Desperate and esoteric mysticism subsided, and a sound and balanced empiricism gained strength. Writings of this period are full of confidence, pride, and the intoxication of a fresh cultural springtime:

"Our century has more history in its hundred years," attested the Italian Renaissance philosopher Tommaso Campanella, "than had the whole world in the previous four thousand years." The

English thinker and statesman Francis Bacon added, "No age hath been more happy in liberty of enquiry than this." And the German philosopher and mathematician Gottfried Wilhelm von Leibniz exulted, "We have raised up a truly philosophical age, in which the deepest recesses of nature are laid open, in which splendid arts, noble aids to convenient living, a supply of innumerable instruments and machines, and even the hidden secrets of our bodies are discovered; not to mention the new light daily thrown upon antiquity."[1]

As early Christian thinkers had dismissed Greco-Roman intellectuals as "deceivers and babblers," so now did the empirical truth of science make war against the religious truth of faith.[2] A celebrated seventeenth-century French bishop, Jacques Bossuet, complained that scientists were "denying the work of creation and that of redemption, annihilating hell, abolishing immortality, stripping Christianity of all its mysteries, and changing it into a philosophical sect agreeable to sense."[3]

Along with growing empiricism and its science came skepticism, the inevitable shadow of insecure sensate thought. This intellectual current began with the sixteenth century and persists to the present. In the eighteenth century, Hume and Kant added a rivulet of criticism, or agnosticism, that swelled to its present flow as the most powerful current of thought besides empiricism. To counter the doubts of skepticism, the willed faith of fideism arose and has equaled it, more or less, in power. Yet the mainstream of thought for the past four centuries has been the great torrent of empiricism, which swelled steadily until, at the start of the twentieth century, it reached a level unprecedented in all history.

Ideally, in Sorokin's estimate, the three basic forms of truth—of faith, of reason, and of the senses—should not battle one another but cooperate and supplement each other. People and cultures that limit themselves to one view of truth needlessly impoverish their outlook. Far better if intuitive insight, logical reasoning, and empirical sensing were combined, each serving as a check to the other, each contributing to a mutual fund of awareness. Thus could humankind, though finite by nature, come nearer to the manifold richness of absolute truth. In practice, however, each system required the last word for itself and eventually struggled to be the only word. Then, gaining the coveted monopoly, each misled and jeopardized life to the extent that each in turn perished as victim of its own narrow-mindedness.

Though a lasting balance of the three modes of truth never has been established, Sorokin discovered they come near to balancing in their overall influence through the ages. Over twenty-five hundred years of European history, the truth of faith proved the most powerful current. The truth of the senses followed closely. Lastly, by small margin, followed the truth of reason.

In the present age, the truth of the senses is struggling for complete monopoly as science seeks to exterminate all remnants of the other systems of truth. Modern people believe less in nonsensory sources of truth, in reason, in thought itself, than people of almost any other age. The truth of faith is seen as superstition, reason, as speculation, while empirical science takes the place of both.

As in an age of faith the name of God is everywhere, now is science on the minds and lips of everyone, from scientists themselves to scholars, salesmen, and quacks. As the pulpit once stood at the center of intellectual life, the laboratory now holds that position. The very word "scientific" carries the authority that "orthodox" does in a religious age, while "unscientific" is parallel to "heretical."

While the truth of faith tends to spiritualize everything, the modern mentality tries to materialize everything. Ever since "social physics" was created in the seventeenth century to study spiritual, cultural, and other nonmaterial topics in the same way that physics studies matter, science has been working to apply physicochemical and mathematical methods to psychology, sociology, history, religion, culture, and art. Thought is dismissed as a random shot. Technique is all important. Science insists upon quantitative measures even of things that cannot be measured, such as spiritual phenomena, the human soul, intelligence, mind, and other clearly qualitative factors.

With science functioning as a cult, widespread opinion has judged it the only valid form of truth, assuming that the other varieties soon would be eliminated as vestiges of antique ignorance. Many scholars and scientists, especially in the nineteenth century, expected empiricism to grow bigger and better forever.

Yet the edifice of science is undermined by strong currents of skepticism and criticism. These steadily erode belief in truth of the senses, suggesting a growing crisis in the system. As, at the end of the Middle Ages, confidence in the truth of faith faded, so now modern society's trust in science is on the wane. As early as the first half of the twentieth century, many truths of the social sciences well supported by empirical data were summarily thrust aside when the Communist, Fascist, and Nazi political parties proclaimed their dogmas of faith.

Meanwhile, Sorokin's statistical evidence indicates the rate of progress in the natural sciences dropping off in recent times. This suggests a condition of fatigue. Science also has been turning away from its own empirical and materialistic stand to a position less sensate than it held in preceding centuries. Its once-solid world of matter already has dissolved. Now matter is seen as condensed energy that gradually dematerializes into radiation. The atom is shattered into a scattering of nonmaterial, cryptic, arcane, and enigmatic elementary particles. The testimony of the senses is replaced by fanciful quantum jumps, by Heisenberg's principle of uncertainty, by mere chance relationships. Similar transformations are taking place in the biological, psychological, and social sciences. As a consequence of becoming far less sensate and empiricist than it was in the nineteenth century, Sorokin wrote "science itself in its immanent course has brought us to something very indefinite, very nebulous, quite uncertain, conditional, relativistic, and illusionistic. A similar illusionism we met in the modern art. We shall see that in other compartments of the present-day culture a similar illusionism is also paramount."[4]

Further, science has been contradicting itself increasingly. Yesterday's "generally accepted" theories are dislodged by those of today, which are likely to be discredited tomorrow. Such rapid change in the system of truth and knowledge creates all the more insecurity in modern people and incertitude in the system itself. Finally, the ingenious instruments of warfare devised by science now threaten to destroy a large part of humankind, civilization, and science itself. This strange apocalyptic triumph grows all the more possible with the continued withering of nonscientific value systems involving reason, decency, altruism, virtue, sin, and other nonempirical criteria.

These consequences of overgrown empirical science are enough to slow or even stop its further development and call forth a revival of one of the other forms of truth. Just as the Middle Ages with its truth of faith did not fix once and for all its approach to reality, neither has the modern age with its sensate science determined it for all time to come. Growing uncertainty is inevitable, a built-in feature of the empirical system of thought. And as uncertainty grows, Sorokin foresaw, "the truth of senses can easily give way to a truth of faith."[5] An event that momentous would start a whole new cycle in the cultural history of Europe.

Once Sorokin had traced accepted truth through the ages, he turned his attention to other facets of thought. Focusing on several "first principles"—or fundamental ideas—of philosophy, he determined by his detailed research how they have fared since they initially were discussed in ancient Greece.

First he chose the opposing concepts of idealism and materialism. Idealism claims that ultimate reality is spiritual, a concept prevailing during ideational periods in history. A less religious, more dialectical form of idealism arises during integral phases of culture. Materialism, on the other hand, is linked closely to the truth of the senses and sensate ages. This philosophical view holds that ultimate reality is matter and spiritual phenomena are only a manifestation of it resulting from the motion of particles of matter.

In European history from 580 B.C. to the present century, the idealistic current of thought has been almost four times as prevalent as the materialistic system. In fact, never has materialism gained a clearly dominant position. "It seems," wrote Sorokin, "that a considerable proportion of idealism is a prime requisite for the durable existence of society. This implication is reinforced by a study of the character of the periods in which the tide of materialism rose. It almost always occurred before or during crises, hard times, social disintegration, demoralization, and other phenomena of this kind."[6]

A strong current of materialism is evident in present tendencies to interpret humanity, culture, and history in a mechanistic, materialistic, and economic fashion and at the same time to discard idealistic, divine, and spiritual aspects of humanity and culture. This trend, a reflection of an overripe sensate mentality, is likely to provoke a fresh reaction of idealism in times ahead.

A second pair of fundamental ideas that Sorokin examined underlies many scientific, philosophical, religious, and ethical theories. These are the twin notions of eternalism and temporalism, or permanency and change, or being and becoming. Eternalism regards ultimate reality as unchangeable being. Any apparent change is either secondary or illusory. Temporalism, or the ideology of becoming, sees reality as incessant change, a never-ceasing flux in which every moment differs from every other. Any apparent permanency is only becoming moving at a slow pace.

Eternalism is closely associated with ideational culture. The predominant view of Brahmanic India and Chinese Taoism, it also characterized several European philosophical systems, such as those of the ancient Greek teacher Parmenides and the founder of Stoicism, Zeno. In later times, formulas for God or ultimate reality often were expressed in terms of unchangeable being.

Temporalism, or the philosophy of becoming, is allied with sensate culture. Like its opposite, it has appeared throughout history: from the days of the ancient Greek philosopher Heraclitus, to the nineteenth century in works of the German philosopher Georg Wilhelm Hegel, and into the twentieth century in writings of the British thinker Alfred North Whitehead and countless contemporary university teachers and journalists who stress the impermanence of existence.

The difficulty of supporting either of these views to the total exclusion of the other has led to many blends, or equilibrium theories. Plato and the medieval Scholastic philosophers, for example, allotted being to the ultimate or supreme reality, while becoming was attributed to the empirical world of sense perceptions, with its change and process, generation and corruption, beginnings and endings.

This philosophical issue, far from floating only in lofty thought, wields influence all through human culture and daily living. For instance, ages when eternalism is more dominant turn to tradition as a guide for living, while periods of temporalism discard unchanging tradition for ever-changing fashion. Likewise, an eternalistic age has a blurred sense of time, with past, present, and future running together in people's minds. History, as the present age knows it, does not exist in such a period. The ideational and eternalistic Hindu culture, for example, advanced considerably in the fields of mathematics, astronomy, and other branches of endeavor yet remained incapable of compiling a coherent history of itself. The same deficiency characterized the heroic period of Greece and the European Middle Ages. As a consequence, history in the modern sense of the word did not exist in Greece until the days of Herodotus in the fifth century B.C. Likewise, it did not reemerge in Western European culture until the fourteenth century, when people of a dawning sensate age, again immersed in time, felt a need to record the sequence of events and replace legend with factual accuracy.

The most recent trends in modern Western culture covered by Sorokin's research showed marked decline in eternalism, a small influence of equilibrium theories, and a sharp rise in temporalistic mentality. This means thinkers of the present age credit lasting aspects of reality less and temporary qualities more. This shows in the society's manner of thinking and living, in which everything is seen to be constantly changing and slipping away. Nothing has solidity, certainty, or permanence. The laws of science, turned conditional and relativistic, liquefy and flow out of the hands that grasped them. Boundaries between true and untrue, right and wrong, good and bad, beautiful and ugly lose firmness and fixity. The whole world shifts, changes, and dissolves, eerie and phantasmagoric.

Time, felt as limited and evasive, is urgently important. "It is not incidental," Sorokin remarked, "that the mechanical clock was invented in the early stages of the rising tide of the temporalistic mentality. . . ," and that the device was perfected in the form of portable timepieces and now "we cannot live without a watch."[7]

A tendency to live largely for the present is another symptom of an overbalanced temporalistic mentality. Sacrificing for the future seems undesirable. Pressures mount to do and acquire things quickly —a notion strange to an ideational mind. In politics, finance, social life, and pleasure, people influenced by sensate temporalism look mainly for immediate effects, paying little heed to long-term consequences.

Meanwhile, the tempo of life and social change move ever faster. With a torrent of changing fashions come changing styles in art, changing models in cars, changing cities, changing economic and political structures, changing sweethearts, marriage partners, theories, morals, beliefs—all changing with little regard for whether the changes are beneficial or harmful for human welfare. Swept up in the furor of flux, people find no time to catch their breath and take stock of where they are and where they want to go. They sense little stability, nothing certain or secure. The ultimate result of such a life is fatigue and exhaustion.

As human maladjustments grow, the temporalistic culture charges ahead, turning ever more deadly and, along the way, grinding its own values into relativistic dust. In this way it devours itself, preparing its own destruction, which will leave the way open for the rise of a fresh eternalistic age with its unhurried life, quiet contemplation, serenity, peace, and repose.

From 600 B.C. to the present century, eternalism has wielded by far the strongest influence on European cultures. Almost 30 percent weaker was temporalism. Equilibrium of the two ideas runs a close third in their total effect.

An inescapable problem of philosophy that Sorokin covered next is the age-old opposition of realism and nominalism. Realism asserts that general categories—such as society, man, horse, star—possess a reality above and beyond any single object that the categories name. The general ideas are not fictions invented by the mind but exist as the very essence of reality. Nominalism opposes this, contending that only single objects exist and universals are illusions caused by false association. People believe they have general ideas only because they are deluded by names. Philosophers of this school argue that it is useless to look for any generic reality behind the names—or *nomina*—and thus they were called nominalists.

A kind of compromise between the two opposing theories creates a blend of both. Known as conceptualism, it agrees with nominalism that the objective world holds only single objects. For example, there is no such thing as "horse" as a universal essence; there are only separate animals somewhat similar but in no way identical. At the same time, conceptualism allows that general concepts exist validly in the mind. As people perceive similar objects, these are transformed into universal notions that substitute for each single object compared.

An age of the truth of faith, which looks beyond and above sense perceptions to eternal verities, accepts realism and its living categories as the answer to this philosophical issue. Conversely, a period governed by the truth of the senses sides with nominalism, since through the senses only single objects, and not categories, are perceived. The compromise of conceptualism is associated with the truth of reason that arises in integral periods. Thus, once again Sorokin's study shows that human truth—or rather, perception of truth—is very much a sociological issue and can be understood only by considering the culture in which it prevails.

The terms realism and nominalism originated during the Middle Ages, but the problem began with the conscious thought of man. Since the days of ancient Greece, realism has reigned as by far the most powerful current. Perhaps curiously, the weight of nominalism and conceptualism combined comes close to balancing it.

The question of realism versus nominalism arises, consciously or not, whenever a general concept is stated in science, mathematics, or any other field. Sorokin's study illustrates how it applies to the basic social problem of society versus the individual. Is society a real entity more valuable than the sum of its members, for which members rightfully can be sacrificed? Or is it no more than a word describing a kind of public utility, valuable only as it helps the individual have a richer life and realize his self-seeking impulses?

Realists of ideational ages have accepted the first conclusion, known in philosophical terms as universalism. They see society—or the state, the church, or any other major social group—as a supreme value far greater than a collection of individuals. Nominalists in sensate times disagree, saying society, the state, the church are no more than the sum of their members and apart from that have no true reality. Their stand is known philosophically as singularism.

Both sides have extreme adherents. Stricter universalists claim society has its own organic life. The individual is merely a part of the whole, like a toe or a finger of the human body. He is embraced by society and permeated by it and has no autonomous existence. His worth, in terms of ethics, is much less than the value of the society as a whole. Strict singularists, on the other hand, conceive of society in an atomistic way. They regard the individual as the only social reality and the supreme ethical value. Society exists only for the individual's safety, liberty, comfort, happiness, pleasure. Extreme singularism is upheld especially by moral individualists, anarchists, and hedonists, whom it suits in different ways. Both currents of thought also have moderate degrees, even to near compromise, in which social and individual interests become different aspects of the same basic value.

In very ancient Greece and medieval times, universalism dominated people's minds, while singularism hardly existed as a mode of thinking. Only with the fifth century B.C. did singularism arise for the ancient world, and only in the fourteenth century for Western culture. It reached its latter-day peak in the eighteenth and nineteenth centuries, when the individual stood triumphant. Over the course of Europe's history, universalism is by far the strongest current, its influence almost twice that of singularism. This suggests that a prevalence of universalism is needed for the cohesion and solidarity that sustains a lasting social system.

In spite of the strong singularism that set the tone of the past two centuries, universalism more recently has shown a slight but unmistakable rise. All through the Western world the state has grown in power, nullifying individual freedoms, imposing dictatorships, establishing a creeping totalitarian rule even in countries that pride themselves on being democratic. The growth of the totalitarian form of universalism Sorokin interpreted as part of the general revolt against sensate culture that erupted in the twentieth century.

The opposition of realism and nominalism also affects the field of law. Life, liberty, and property often have depended upon how this question was decided. The issue in the legal field hinges on the juridical personality—the corporation and the institution, both of which are treated as units or single persons.

Is a legal body of this kind something real, existing of itself over and above its members? Philosophical realists of an age of faith say it is. In the early Christian church everything Christian was seen to be united and dissolved in God. Many recent representatives of the Germanic School in jurisprudence similarly held that corporations and institutions are real organisms, partly corporeal and partly psychological. The attitude also emerges in the common notions of "group interests" and "public opinion," as well as among soldiers loyal to a military regiment or backers of a football team. In every case the corporate body is seen to possess an identity independent from its members.

Legal theory in a sensate age generally considers the juridical personality as no more than a convenient fiction, created artificially for practical needs and treated as a real unity while in actual fact it is not. This view was held in imperial Rome. It arose again in Europe around the thirteenth century. Softened by a strain of conceptualism, it prevailed through the nineteenth century.

Since then, however, political thought has turned against the nominalist position, giving greater emphasis to the powers and rights of the collective body at the expense of the individual. Sorokin compared the clumsy notions of collectives and the corporate state developed by Communists and Fascists to the cubist movement in art. While neither political group produced satisfactory doctrines, their attempts represent a fumbling revolt against the sensate nominalism still prevailing.

One more philosophical conclusion that Sorokin found varying with changes of culture involves determinism versus indeterminism. The theory of determinism claims that humanity and the world are causally conditioned; everything is the product of a cause, including actions of human beings, who have no free will, no power to shape their destiny. Indeterminism says causal relationships are not invariable, and people possesses free will to one extent or another.

Few philosophical issues involve so many vital interests as this question. Theologians, educators, lawyers, politicians, scientists, and social reformers all must have an answer, consciously or otherwise, to guide their activities. Answers come in many shadings, from extreme pronouncements to assorted compromises and blends. Sorokin and his aides sorted through a list of thinkers covering twenty-five hundred years and filling seven pages of small print in an appendix, placing them on opposite sides of the question.

Results showed determinism a philosophy of sensate cultures, such as those of ancient Rome and the present Western European age. Indeterminism, with its belief in free will, comes with an age of faith and held monopolistic sway in Europe from the sixth to the thirteenth centuries. In-between integral ages are marked by a mixture of the two, like the "indeterministic-determinism" of fifth century B.C. Greece and thirteenth-century Europe that saw Destiny or God in control of the universe.

The mid-nineteenth century was a period of iron determinism, when cause and effect were linked inexorably and unavoidably. Sorokin noted a decline in this belief between 1880 and the second half of the twentieth century. In physical science, rigid determinism softened to mere probability, while psychology and sociology have been replacing causality with "voluntaristic decision," "immanent self-direction," and "free will." Sorokin saw this movement of thought as one more sign of a modern reaction against sensate life and one more indication of growing cultural revolution.

The final first principle of philosophy that Sorokin traced in Europe's history deals with the course the world is pursuing through time. Is there such a thing as continuous progress—cosmic, biological, and social—or continuous retrogression? One view, the linear, says there is, at times upholding progress and at other times decline. An opposite view, the cyclic, says changes occur in a roundabout manner, with the present in some way repeating the past and the future coming around to resemble the present. A third, mixed category includes the belief that history moves in a trendlessly undulating way.

A society's answer to this question has a lot to do with how it sees the world and life. For example, nineteenth-century Western culture held an unquestioningly linear view: humanity was progressing steadily upward in freedom, democracy, wealth, and moral excellence. Charles Darwin's theory of evolution, first published in 1859, extended the linear idea into biology, setting the course of how thousands of specific problems in the subject were resolved. Likewise, the social sciences developed countless theories of linear social evolution where things are seen rising in stages toward ultimate perfection. Sociology, economics, history, political science, and even theology manufactured hypotheses of progress: from amoeba to man, from ignorance to science, from instinct to reason, from disorder to order, from poverty to wealth, from fetishism to monotheism, from inequality to equality, from promiscuity to monogamy (or the reverse), from despotism to liberty.

However convinced the Victorians were of evolutionary progress; or the Greeks soon after the fall of ancient Crete in a straight-down retrogression; or medieval Christians in a trendless pilgrimage through a valley of the shadow between the beatific Garden of Eden and the shining City of God—these ideas also are symptomatic of phases of culture.

Generally, cyclic theories are favored in ideational cultures. India provides a strong example in the Hindu theory of four successive ages in which the world is created, then dissolved, only to be recreated, the whole process reflecting inner transformations of the ultimate spiritual reality known as Brahma. The ancient Chinese philosophical idea of the eternal rhythm of Yin and Yang—of negative and positive, of fall and rise of dynasties, of depression and prosperity, war and peace, decay and blossoming—is another cyclic theory with its roots in ideational culture.

Progressive linear theories are associated generally with times of rising sensate culture. Thus did they begin to appear in Western Europe around the twelfth century, growing rapidly from the seventeenth century onward.

Since the close of the nineteenth century, the general belief in progress has diminished. Evolutionism increasingly draws criticism. The social sciences have all but abandoned theories of societies advancing in a uniform sequence of stages. Economists no longer chart stages of economic development, turning their attention instead to fluctuations, oscillations, and cycles. So it goes in almost all the social sciences, from anthropology to sociology and law, from psychology to ethics to history and social philosophy.

Nietzsche's theory of eternal cycles, which he proudly proclaimed in the nineteenth century, revived an ancient principle in an age ready to question continuous progress. The great success of Oswald Spengler's *The Decline of the West* in the twentieth century is another indication of growing modern interest in nonlinear concepts of social and cultural change. This trend, Sorokin noted, is yet another sign of the general revolt against overripe sensate culture.

Changes in Science

The grand transformations that sweep over cultures from one age to the next bring equally vast changes in the field of natural science. Sorokin and his colleagues tallied up the number of inventions and discoveries in eight major scientific fields from 3500 B.C. to the present century. They investigated mathematics and astronomy, biology and medicine, chemistry, physics, geology, and technology.

The exhaustive survey disproved the notion, common in the nineteenth century and still persisting, that invention and discovery progress steadily in the history of a society. Rather, scientific innovations rise and fall with the phases of culture, at times advancing rapidly, at other times slowing or stagnating.

Logically, an ideational age is a time when science should slacken or regress, since an age of faith has little interest in improving the material world. Sorokin's data bore this out. Conversely, invention and discovery are likely to flourish in a sensate age, when attention shifts from spiritual growth to worldly attainment. The data confirmed this as well. Though the past four or five centuries have brought unprecedented growth to science, this trend cannot be expected to go on endlessly and appears to be approaching a conclusion.

Not only does interest and development in science change with the phases of culture, so do some basic principles governing the field. The way thinkers view cause and effect shifts substantially. Conceptions of time, space, and number also change. General scientific theories fluctuate broadly, including theories about atoms, living matter, and light.

Both the ideational and sensate cultures allow for the existence of causes, or reasons, for phenomena. But what those causes are and where they should be looked for are issues on which the types of culture differ profoundly.

The ideational mentality looks for cause in the transcendental realm behind or above the illusionary world of the senses. The only real cause behind anything for ancient Greeks was Destiny, the gods, and other higher agents; for ideational Chinese, Tao, or the Principle of Order; and for Christians of the Middle Ages, Almighty God. Under such a system, cause is not always expected to be followed by the same effect. The First Cause—whether Destiny, Brahma, Tao, or God—can remove at will any "laws" or "uniformities" and replace them with different relationships. Always the will of God remains inscrutable.

The sensate outlook does not seek beyond perceptions of the senses for explanation of cause. While God might be hallowed in an early sensate age, He is seen only as a nominal ruler by scientific scholars, who turn their attention to immediately observable links of cause and effect. Also such links are expected to be firm, a given cause always followed by the same effect.

Thinkers of in-between integral ages look for cause in both the transcendental and empirical domains. That approach reigned in Greece of the fifth and fourth centuries B.C. and was reproduced in Western Europe of the thirteenth and fourteenth centuries A.D.

The sensate notion of causality grew in European thought from the fifteenth century onward. By the nineteenth century, the ideational conception was all but driven from the field. At its very moment of triumph, however, sensate causality showed signs of serious weakness, the once-necessary link between cause and effect deteriorating rapidly to mere probable association. This development led to the present being declared the age of 'causal catastrophe' in physics. Similar trends pervade the psychosocial sciences. Modern attempts to base all knowledge upon theories of probability dissolve the boundary line between causal and incidental, science and nonscience, truth and falsehood. Reality turns liquid, unsure, a fantasy—all of which suggests antisensate revolt and the approach of a new ideational or integral conception of cause and effect.

Ideas about time also vary with the phases of culture. In an ideational age, time tends to be absolute and qualitative. It often expresses divine activity and is marked in enormous spans. A day in the life of the supreme deity Brahma, for example, was reckoned by Hindu thinkers to extend 4,320,000 mortal years. For very ancient Greeks, time manifested the activities of the titan Cronus, the supreme god Zeus, or other transcendental beings. The Greeks also marked time in extremely long periods, like the Golden, Silver, Bronze, and Iron Ages that measured the creative and destructive acts of Cronus or Zeus upon the life of mankind. The early Christian thinker St. Augustine saw time to be something created with the world as an act of the eternal God. If the human mind were given to know all things past and future, he posited, it would see no various times, or all time would be equivalent to eternity. Because time in an ideational age is linked to eternity, past, present, and future blur together, and no chronology is kept for worldly events.

Sensate time is entirely of the world. It is strictly quantitative, marking motion, duration, and succession in man's earthly existence—whether daily schedules, length of journeys, or years of life. Measurement of time in a sensate age tends to be precise and mechanical, accomplished by clocks and similar instruments. Divisions of time are short—shortening, in fact, as sensate culture ripens. Past and future fade while the present is reduced to ever-shorter, rushing, fleeting moments—from hours to minutes to seconds to mere fragments of seconds. Ultimately this concept of time must destroy itself. In the present age, reactions already have arisen against the sensate notion of time. The French philosopher Henri Bergson declared that the true nature of time is duration in terms of life experience as opposed to a mathematically clocked measurement. The four-dimensional space-time continuum of German-American physicist Albert Einstein is another expression of an antisensate attitude toward time.

Ideational space, like the culture's view of time, has nothing to do with measurements. These would serve no purpose in a spiritual society, which thinks of space as a way to show relationships—between God and angels, for example, or paradise and the inferno. Where is God? In sensate terms, this question cannot be answered. God is nowhere in particular, and everywhere. God is in heaven—not the sensory sky, but high above everything else.

Better suited to a sensate age is the three-dimensional space of classical mechanics. It satisfies the culture's desire to fix situation, adjacency, extension, size, and volume for material bodies. It falls down, however, when sensate people forget its limitations and try hopelessly to locate everything in one or another objective place. Where, after all, is mind, or thought, or values? Where is Homer's *Iliad*? Where is Plato's system of philosophy, or Beethoven's music? Such questions reflect back, though somewhat imperfectly, to ideational space, which requires for mind neither brain nor glands, for values neither region nor particular people, for literature and music no specific book and no tangible score.

Like time and space, the concept of number also differs between the kinds of cultures. The sensate mentality generally thinks of numbers in terms of quantity and magnitude. They are used for counting or comparing quantities with a standard unit. And, logically, larger numbers always are greater than smaller ones.

The ideational mind, on the other hand, often assigns specific qualities to certain numbers and their relationships. The Hesiodic calendar of ancient Greece marked lucky and unlucky days: unpropitious was the sixth day of the month for the birth of a female child, the thirteenth for sowing, the sixteenth for planting; among good days were the fourth for marriage and the ninth for begetting or giving birth. In historic China, the number 3 could be construed as greater in significance than 8. In other ideational systems, different numbers could be equal in their qualitative value, while equal numbers—say, 8 times 9, and 6 times 12—could be unequal even though they both add up to 72. The importance and mysterious power of specific numbers—such as 3, 7, 9, 13, 81—were universally accepted in Babylon and China, in ancient Greece and Rome, by

Hinduism, Judaism, Christianity, and Islam. Finally, Greco-Roman philosophers recognized a mystical connection between numbers, music, and the harmony of the universe.

The theory of atoms is linked historically with materialistic thought, and thus with sensate ages. In ancient Greek tradition 'atomical philosophy' first appeared as the idea of a Phoenician thinker named Mochus, who is held to have lived in the pre-Trojan era. But not until the fifth century B.C. did atomic theory become widespread, promulgated by the Atomistic School under the philosopher Leucippus and later the materialist thinker Democritus. Then the atom was conceived to be a tiny particle, imperceptible to the senses, indivisible and indestructible. Such particles, in constant motion, combined to make up the universe. The theory also included the concept of a void, or genuine vacuum.

Atomic theory was discussed in Greece and Rome intermittently until around A.D. 200. Then it disappeared for almost a thousand years. In twelfth century Europe it began a slow revival, but found no significant acceptance until the time of the Italian scientific scholar Galileo Galilei and the French materialist thinker Pierre Gassendi in the seventeenth century. In the eighteenth century the atom was believed to possess inherent forces. Since that time its one-time billiard-ball solidity has yielded to a modern electrical structure. Now smashed into scores of perplexing particles and declared only a concentrated form of energy, the dematerialized atom appears to be dissolving into a new revolution of cultural thought.

What is the nature of life? Do living things function solely on a material level? Are they no more than dynamic structures subject to physicochemical principles, with no intervention from anything that cannot be investigated by physics and chemistry? The biological theory of mechanism claims that to be true. The theory of vitalism, on the other hand, though coming in many varieties, always maintains that living things are animated by a nonmaterial property above and beyond physicochemical forces. Thus are living organisms inherently different from nonliving matter. Sorokin found the theory of vitalism to go hand in hand with ideational culture. Mechanism prevails in sensate times. Sorokin also noted that in the twentieth century vitalism has staged something of a revival.

Through the ages, light has been interpreted scientifically in several different ways. Before the sixth century B.C., the nature of light was not an issue of importance. This attitude is common to ideational ages. Questions about light arose only with the integral period of the fifth and fourth centuries B.C., when three competing theories were proposed. The philosophers Empedocles and Plato maintained that light emanates from the eye—the visual ray theory. Leucippus and Democritus of the Atomistic School believed tiny particles flow constantly from the surface of physical bodies, and these impress themselves upon the eye to produce images—the corpuscular theory. Aristotle rejected both these ideas, claiming light was an impulse propagated through a diaphanous medium—the wave theory.

The corpuscular and wave theories are associated with the sensate phase of culture. The visual ray theory is linked to ideational culture, when the question arose at all among its thinkers. St. Augustine in the early centuries of Christianity held a similarly inward conception, saying the soul viewed the outer world through the eyes as through a window. As in the integral days of Greece, the question of light gained importance in Europe of the thirteenth and fourteenth centuries. And again, all three answers appeared, striking a near balance. The rise of European sensate culture forced the visual ray theory into the shadows, leaning toward the more materialistic wave and corpuscular theories. From the sixteenth century onward, the latter two alternated in predominance. In the nineteenth century the wave theory gained a strong edge. But then, early in the twentieth century, the corpuscular theory reappeared. "For the present we have to work on both theories," the English physicist Sir William Henry Bragg noted wryly. "On Mondays, Wednesdays and Fridays we use the wave theory; on Tuesdays, Thursdays and Saturdays we think in streams of flying energy quanta or corpuscles."[8]

Theories about humankind, culture, and social phenomena that make up the social sciences also fluctuate with the types of supersystems. In a sensate age, social studies turn materialistic in choice of subjects, in content, and in method. Meanwhile, they are blind to nonmaterial issues, seeing them as eerie, ignorant, and superstitious. In an ideational age, sensate social views seem perverse, heretical, blasphemous. As in other matters, each type of culture is irrevocably locked into its own paradigm.

In addition to the principles of science that Sorokin traced through the ages, many others, he observed, depend for their acceptance on the phase of culture in force. The last word in science of one age is discredited as inadequate or erroneous by the next, according to the basic system of truth that prevails. Yet, Sorokin added, "Insistence on such a relativity of scientific theories does not mean skepticism on my part. It simply means that the full and complete truth is . . . possibly accessible only to the Divine Mind. We can grasp but its approximation."[9]

13

Shifting Human Bonds

WITH THE GRAND TRANSITIONS in the arts and philosophy, similar changes also take place in the way people and their groupings relate to one another. This is true in the realm of ethics and law, in the social bonds that link people in their daily lives, and to a far lesser extent, in wars and revolutions.

CHANGES IN ETHICS AND LAW

Sorokin and his colleagues found cultural shifts in ethics and law in a study of hundreds of ethical writers from 600 B.C. to the present century. The moral system that rules in ideational periods Sorokin called the "ethics of principles." Seen to emanate from God or other transcendental sources, the system is absolute, firm, never subject to relativity or expediency. Its purpose has nothing to do with utility, happiness, comfort, or pleasure. It serves only to bring followers closer to the source of all values—to lead them to truth, goodness, beauty, to save their souls, to unite them with divinity—regardless of whether or not this also leads to further earthly advantage.

The Greeks before the time of Socrates held to such an ethic. Expounded by thinkers like Pythagoras and Hesiod and literary figures like Aeschylus, Pindar, and Sophocles, the system was regarded as sacred and neither doubted nor questioned. The gods were seen to punish all violations, including those accidental or unwitting. Never was this strictness thought of as unjust. The ethic, as absolute, had to be sustained, and punishment followed violation as necessarily as pain follows injury.

An ethic of principles also reigned in Western Europe from the fifth through the fifteenth centuries. Again, mere happiness was of no concern, and life lived according to the system was disciplined and ascetic. Moral commands were handed down from God, intended to draw people to him. Yet one great difference marked the medieval ethic of principles. Some ideational cultures have rules that are stern to the point of harshness and inhumanity, but European Christendom upheld a uniquely benign moral standard. Sorokin aptly named this the "ethics of love," since its loftiest value was the infinite benevolence of a loving God, the love exemplified on earth by Jesus and great saints, and the altruism aspired to by all faithful Christians.

The ethical shift during the integral age that settled over ancient Greece was reflected in the views of the philosophers Plato and Aristotle, the dramatist Euripides, and the historian Thucydides. Their moral systems remained rooted in the transcendental realm of the gods. But now divine will was scrutinized, sometimes questioned or protested. The main rules of ethics remained divine and absolute, but secondary principles were left to human reason and accepted as relative and subject to change. Equally significant, the age allowed concern for people's happiness on earth—a happiness regarded not as pleasure but, rather, as a consequence of living in accord with the divine side of human nature. This same high-level happiness as befitting God's people appeared again in the ethical ideals of thirteenth-century Europe. "It is not incidental," Sorokin pointed out, "that the Platonized Aristotelian system of ethics is the ethics of St. Thomas, Albertus Magnus, Dante, and of many other Scholastics."[1] Both the period of Plato and that of Thomas Aquinas were ushering in new sensate cultural ages.

Sensate ethics are strictly manmade, with no reference or relation to divine principle. Sorokin called them the "ethics of happiness." The aim of such a system is to increase the sum of human satisfaction in terms of utility, comfort, or pleasure. Necessarily, the system is relative and changing. As circumstances alter, so must the ethics, since rules that serve happiness in one situation might not serve it in another.

The ethic of happiness can exist on a variety of levels. It might take into account long-range interests and appeal to the loftiest ideals of humanity. This view represents the theory known as eudaemonism, which seeks personal well-being through a life governed by reason. Or the ethic might be based upon the principle of utilitarianism, stressing the means of gaining happiness rather than defining exactly what happiness is. According to this view, whatever proves useful for creating happiness is a positive value. Sensate ethics also can be founded upon primitive hedonism, with the pleasure of the moment as life's supreme objective. This happiness, sensual and carnal, emphasizes neither continuance of pleasure nor any other long-term goal.

The various types of sensate ethics can be applied either narrowly or broadly in society. A single individual can make his own happiness the overriding concern, with no regard for any effect upon others. Less egoistically, a person's focus might widen to family or even nation. Conceivably, it could include all humankind.

The sensate ethic of happiness appeared in moral writings in the latter half of the fifth century B.C. Rising to dominance in Greece and then in Rome, it remained prominent until the time of Christ, attesting to the overall sensate character of the age. Also while the ethical system ripened, eudaemonistic theories gave way to utilitarian ideas and hedonistic motives. The ethic entered decline with the advent of the Christian era. It finally disappeared in the fifth century, when ethics of principles and love replaced it in writings of the day.

At the end of a thousand-year reign of the ethic of principles in Western Europe, the sensate system again burst forth in the fifteenth century. The happiness ethic reappeared in all its forms, increasing suddenly and greatly, first as a noble eudaemonism, then in more earthy utilitarian and hedonistic strains. By the seventeenth century, sensate economics, as an offshoot of the ethic, was the highest of all social values, leaving religious values far behind. As the English evangelist John Wesley observed in the century that followed, "I fear, wherever riches have increased, the essence of religion has decreased in the same proportion."[2] Not only did economics reign supreme, they also served as the criterion for judging other values, including those moral and religious. The American statesman Benjamin Franklin made this point succinctly, writing, "Honesty is useful because it assures credit; so are punctuality, industry, frugality, and that is the reason they are virtues."[3]

The present age, Sorokin maintained, wallows in a high tide of the ethic of happiness. "Most of the Sensate systems have become more sensual, more relative, more earthly, and more carnal than, for instance, they were during the greater part of their Graeco-Roman history."[4] Almost all ethical values are reduced to the levels of bodily comfort and enjoyment. The society's dominant moral motive is utilitarianism, while hedonism rules the public mentality. The quest for money is obsessive, with people turning into profit everything from success in sports to notoriety in crime, from scientific fame to religion to politics, and on to the birth of quintuplets and the death of a loved one. Almost all values are relative, to the verge of moral anarchy. This gives rise to the rule of force, which shows up at every social level, from coercion of one person by another or of individuals by various groups to international coercion by means of massive military buildups.

Such an excessively developed sensate morality can only destroy itself. No clear sign of reaction against it has appeared yet. But, Sorokin observed, "we all feel sharply enough the 'carnal inconveniency' of overripe Sensate morality: it has robbed us of our security of life, of our comfort, of our sensate well-being, of our position, of our self-respect, of our dignity, of almost everything."[5]

Meanwhile, if the rule of force increases, it will make benign social life all but impossible. Thus sensate morality logically must go into decline and a fresh ethic of principles arise.

Sorokin noted that in Europe's history the ethic of principles, including that of love, has exerted more than double the influence of the ethic of happiness. This suggests that social existence in order to continue demands substantial self-sacrifice and altruism. He also emphasized that actual behavior within a society does not always coincide with ethical ideals. Yet, the system in force does represent the society's major aspirations and strongly colors the conduct of the general population.

An even clearer picture of moral mentality is a society's code of laws. Down through history law codes, too, both criminal and penal, have reflected the changes of phase in Europe's cultures.

The law of ideational times includes crimes and punishments uniquely its own. Blasphemy, sacrilege, and heresy rank prominent among crimes against religion. Also condemned and severely punished are many actions that the ethic of happiness, from its narrowly utilitarian or hedonistic standpoint, would consider harmless and even desirable—for example, acts in the area of sexual relations. Penalties unique to ideational law include interdiction, imposition of anathema, and deprivation of Christian burial.

Sensate law tends to eliminate most crimes against religion and strictly ideational values. It then goes on to emphasize crimes against bodily comfort and property values, allowing special protection for the governing class.

The amount and severity of punishment generally differ little between the types of culture. Ideational law is somewhat more severe, since it encourages higher moral conduct. But severity depends less upon the kind of culture than how thoroughly the culture phase is settled and crystallized. When either phase is deeply rooted, punishments tend to be mild and moderate. When a culture is less settled, for whatever reasons, penalties increase.

An ideational culture just coming into being finds more-than-usual strictness necessary. Taking over from a disintegrated sensate order, it inherits skepticism governing public mentality, hedonism ruling general conduct, appetites raging, and personalities demoralized and disordered. Under such conditions, stern legal curbs are needed to control passions and engraft disciplines. Legal penalties rise again when either an ideational or a sensate system begins to fall apart. The harshest laws of all clamp down when a sensate society plunges into crisis. A revolution, for example, in sensate society can shatter all stability, as moral and religious controls, already weak, crumble completely. Then sensate law turns outrageously rude, operating blindly and cruelly, fostering torture and butchery of everyone deemed an enemy of the ruling group.

Changes in Social Relationships

To explore social relationships in European history, Sorokin defined three basic ties that hold people together: the familistic bond, the freely agreed contract, and coercive compulsion. These, separately and mixed, embrace practically all human relationships.

The familylike tie need not be confined to blood relatives, just as it does not always occur between them. It is best represented by the unreserved bond between a truly loving mother and her child or the mutual devotion in a sound and harmonious family. But friends can build the same kind of relationship. It also can form the pattern for larger groups, as traditionally it has for religious organizations.

The "familistic bond" brings people together in all the most important aspects of their lives. They are united organically, trading "I" for "we," sharing joys and sorrows, successes and failures, health and illness, prosperity and poverty. They aid, sustain, and support one another without reservation or limit—not because they must or by formal agreement or for ultimate personal gain, but spontaneously, generously, because the fate of one is felt as the welfare of the other. The sacrifice of self that often is needed to maintain familistic relations is neither begrudged nor resented but accepted as a privilege. The giver functions as a part serving the whole, and the more that is given, the more satisfaction arises from the gift.

The "contractual tie" is more limited in both extent and duration. It might create strong solidarity between the contracting parties. But a provision of "no more and no less" persists throughout the relationship, and the bond readily remains an egoistic bargain intended mainly for personal gain or advantage. The parties are important to one another, but less in their own right than as instruments of utility, profit, or enjoyment. They might even be personally indifferent toward each other, remaining strangers or behaving as antagonists. The contractual bond is summed up best by a classic Roman formula: "Give to be given, serve to be served."[6]

Contractual ties make up a large part of social relationships, from agreements between employer and employee, owner and tenant, and buyer and seller, to links involving state, school, church, and family. To be genuine, the bond implies the freedom of both parties to enter the association or not as they choose. If one is less than free—as, for example, an impoverished worker needing a job at all costs—the relationship moves toward compulsion.

The "compulsory relationship" operates mainly as a one-way agreement. The dominant party, whether conqueror or despot, sergeant, master, policeman, boss, or extortionist, sets the terms and wields the power to enforce them. The parties often feel little concern for the welfare of the other and sometimes are blatantly antagonistic. They might remain strangers, their inner lives closed, lacking even a desire to bridge the gap between them. Compulsory ties range from various forms of physical and mental exploitation to many socially accepted relations in the workings of law, political states, and military groups. They also can range from infrequent and weak to constant and tyrannical, torturous, or annihilative.

With these three basic kinds of relationship defined, Sorokin returned to his analysis of European culture. Focusing mainly on France and Germany and beginning with the eighth century A.D., he studied states, the church, and military forces, the family, urban communes, and occupational groups such as guilds and labor unions. To these he added the main organized social classes, including seigniors, vassals, and serfs.

Over the course of time in Europe, the blending of the three relationships has fluctuated greatly. This change, fundamental to the workings of society, "is much more important, and indicates a much greater revolution, than any change of... political or economic structure."[7] It clearly has followed the shifts from ideational to sensate ways of life.

From around the time of Charlemagne in the eighth century to the days of Thomas Aquinas in the thirteenth century, the familistic relationship prevailed in medieval society. *Fidelitas*—loyalty—held social groups together, from paternalistic ties between king and dutiful subjects, to familylike bonds between great warriors and youths admitted to their armies, to relationships within the church in which all men were brethren and popes addressed monarchs as "good children" and "dearly beloved sons." The society was thought of as one body and one mind, a kind of *corpus mysticum*.

Compulsory relationships also ruled in the society, though to a lesser degree. These served mainly to bind unfree serfs to the free strata of society. Compulsion also played a significant part in military organization. Meanwhile, serfs maintained familistic relations between themselves. Early medieval "companions in arms" also were modeled along the familistic pattern.

Western Europe's in-between integral phase brought a weakening of the familistic bond and the beginning of a more contractual society. For a time, all three forms of relationship worked in synthesis, with the familistic tie still prevailing. The waning of that bond, however, threw the society into confusion and disorder. Socially, as in every other regard, this period proved a turning point in Western European culture.

In following centuries, compulsory ties pulled the society together. At the same time, contractual bonds gained ground, while familistic links continued to deteriorate. From the late eighteenth century, compulsory relationships decreased, replaced by contractual ties, which are more in accord with the individualistic sensate mentality. The nineteenth century and the fourteen years following that led to the First World War proved a high point for contractual relationships. Sensate man, then balanced and settled, preferred to bargain rather than to fight and was willing to live and let live with his neighbor. Toward the close of this period, however, areas of former freedom fell under the domination of various private and public power groups—the press, political organizations, and wage-bargaining factions among them. In these groups, contractual liberties continued to exist in outward form while diminishing in actual fact.

Since World War I, contractualism has fallen into drastic decline. The form became all the more an empty shell as governments and citizens took to dishonoring agreements for one-way advantage. What could replace the defrauded system? In an atmosphere of expediency, in which people hold neither God's commands nor their own word as binding, the only remaining social bond is force. Thus compulsory relationships have grown throughout the West and around the world. They appear most powerfully in authoritarian and totalitarian states but pervade every other area of society as well. This trend has ground forward not only under Fascists, Nazis, and Communists but thrives also in socialistic and democratic countries in which, though freedom still is talked of in the way of slogans, the snare of force pulls ever tighter. Among cultural creations likely to be strangled is the capitalist economic system, which is built upon contractual relations.

Yet compulsion hardly can become the fabric of a lasting social future. Rather, it reflects a temporary interval, control by force again arising in a period of social transition and unrest. This defines present rulers not as builders of the future but grave-diggers for the past, burying the structures of a once-noble but now decayed contractual order. The Fascists, the Communists, and other force-groups are groping, much like artists of the day, for something to replace the waning sensate system. For the moment, they achieve pseudosolidarity, a collectivist order of manipulated people and mechanical social forces, soulless, compassionless, devoid of altruism and genuine solidarity. As it seems likely that a fresh ideational or integral mentality soon will arise, so can we expect a resurgence of familistic ties.

From general social relations, Sorokin moved to ideational and sensate modes of government.

In ideational cultures, the government and all leadership—intellectual, moral, and social—fall to groups that uphold ideational values. This excludes the merely rich, the physically mighty, the economic and political organizers. Instead, supreme authority and prestige rest with a theocracy—with priests, elders, lamas, the Brahman caste—whoever represents the society's spiritual foundations. Even when a secular ruler occupies the throne, he remains under the dominion of religious authority. In a theocratic system, laws are absolute and thought of as handed down from a divine source. Supernatural factors play a large part in enforcement, such as trial by ordeal, expiation of crimes, and excommunication. Education in the culture is theological. And oracles, prophets, saints, or seers find significant place in the political structure.

Sensate culture, conversely, chooses for its leaders the kind of people who advance sensory values: organizers of prosperity and guarantors of physical safety and security. These might be the wealthy, the military class, empire builders, economic moguls, scientists who harness the material side of nature, clever politicians or machinating schemers, even unscrupulous social manipulators or powerful criminal bosses.

Integral phases of culture chose a mixture of both main governmental forms, adding to theocracy a secular element. Europe around the thirteenth century, for example, gave powers long vested in the papacy to emerging national rulers and aristocracies.

In the present, overripe sensate period, power ostensibly is based upon "the will of the people," "the proletariat," and similar public sources. In reality, it goes to the rich or whoever controls the society's coercive forces. Meanwhile, governing generally is viewed as a cynical and unscrupulous game full of hypocrisy, lying, partiality, and factionalism, with one unprincipled power group striving to overcome another. This is true in all societies, whether communist, socialist, democratic, liberal, or conservative.

It seems hardly possible that this trend can continue without provoking a general reaction. Revolts already are common. The alliance of the rich and the sensate aristocracy, which governed through the nineteenth century, today is discredited, and both have lost much power. Sensate socialist, labor, and radical groups have been tried and found wanting. Sensate totalitarian systems have undermined themselves and lost their prestige, relying for survival on either raw force or revision of their principles. Unrespected, impotent, and incapable, sensate rule is approaching an end. A shift toward either integral or ideational government is likely.

An important part of social relationships in general and a vital aspect of government is the degree of liberty afforded individual persons. Without reflection, many people might believe only one kind of freedom exists—freedom from restraint or coercion by external force. Yet Sorokin discerned two forms of liberty and two ways to achieve it. One is linked with ideational thinking, the other with the sensate mentality.

Freedom, in its essence, amounts to having desires met. Therefore, people can seek freedom by increasing the means of satisfaction. But they also can gain it by reducing or eliminating their desires.

Ideational culture chooses the latter. The Cynics and Stoics of ancient Greece and Rome, the Brahmans, Buddhists, and Taoists of Asia, the Christians of medieval Europe all cultivated freedom in this manner. "Freedom is not gained by satisfying, but by restraining, our desires," they instructed.[8] They extolled self-sufficiency, inner freedom of the soul, liberty in God. The ideational mentality has little interest in political and civil rights, in governmental guarantees of freedoms, in liberties set down in constitutional form.

Chinese Taoist writings state simply, "the best government is that which governs least."[9] Christians could dismiss the whole issue with Jesus's words: "My kingdom is not of this world." To the ideational mind, freedom gained by catering to desire is equal to living on the brink of slavery, risking the withdrawal of capricious material conditions.

The sensate way of thinking, conversely, regards ideational freedom as no freedom at all. Perfect sensate liberty is the right to do whatever one pleases, while freedom comes from acquiring the means of satisfying ever-expanding sensate desires.

The quest for sensate freedom in Western Europe began around the thirteenth century, with philosophical theories of liberty and legal instruments like the English Magna Carta, which in 1215 guaranteed freedoms for barons and subjects. As time went on, the struggle for freedom spread, encompassing free cities, the bourgeoisie, lower classes, religion, the press, speech, and public meetings. Declarations, constitutions, charters, and laws guaranteed liberties in varying degrees all through Western culture. The movement grew until the outbreak of the First World War.

Either form of freedom can go only so far before reaching built-in limits. Ideational liberty prepares its own decline when society is restricted more than it can tolerate. Then the method of freedom loses charm and prestige, and either the pendulum swings back toward the sensate or the society faces extinction. From this understanding, Sorokin reasoned that Pacific-island peoples who died off in great numbers after encountering European culture were victims less of imported diseases than of disheartenment from alien restrictions on their ways of living. Sensate freedom similarly must give way when appetites expand beyond means of satisfaction. That leaves some people trapped in frustrating want. Others, jaded and perverse, persist in the kind of gratification that debilitates themselves and threatens to ruin the society. Thus does the acquisitive form of liberty lose its appeal. Then limits upon freedom are felt as an advantage, even necessary, for social survival.

Such limits have been tightening upon Western culture since the end of the nineteenth century. Communist regimes, dismissing liberties as bourgeois, abandoned them. Fascism, Nazism, and other dictatorships, though espousing different political theories, followed their lead. Western democracies, though fighting costly wars in the name of freedom, end up diminishing their own freedom. To date, sensate liberty is lost; the present can be seen only as a period of transition, with any future form of freedom not yet in sight.

From his study of freedom, Sorokin proceeded to a survey of totalitarian and laissez faire governments in history.

Totalitarian rule, though recently resurgent, is as old as history. At various times it dominated ancient Egypt, China, India, and Persia, classical Greece and Rome, Peru of the Incas, ancient Mexico, Islamic lands, and several local regions in medieval Europe. It reappeared in eighteenth-century Europe with the absolutist states of King Louis XIV of France, King Frederick the Great of Prussia, and Empress Maria Theresa of Austria. Also throughout history, government control has clamped down temporarily with what amounted to totalitarian rule to deal with short-term emergencies, such as wars, famines, and severe economic crises.

These various instances of dense state controls often dropped like a net upon the lives of people. During wars and famines in ancient Egypt, the whole economic life was nationalized. Economic disorganization during the culture's final dynasty led to a universal socialistic order. Similarly China, with frequent famines, consistently maintained a high level of government control over economic production, distribution, and consumption. In ancient Rome from the time of the Emperor Diocletian near the end of the third century A.D., totalitarian rule gripped the empire like a vice. Private commerce was abolished almost completely, the state becoming virtually the only business corporation, while the population became its slaves. Money economics was replaced by a "natural economy" ration system that distributed produce, with great inequality, among various classes. From that time on, the empire ran like a massive factory. Inefficient and unproductive, it was held together only by tyrannical compulsion until its collapse some two centuries later.

Medieval European culture, by contrast, maintained notably loose state systems. With much social control shifted to the church, the feudal state was weak and generally impotent. The decline of feudalism brought the nation-state and growth of governmental power. Though this relaxed in the nineteenth century with a strong swing toward laissez-faire freedom, it began to tighten at the century's end with state regulation of business, industry, and labor. Since World War I, government control has soared stratospherically throughout the Western world.

As a general rule, Sorokin pointed out, ideational societies foster weak states, placing social control largely with religious bodies. Though these often rule firmly, their authority is not felt as a limitation of freedom. As familistic orders, they tend to use power for the welfare of the ruled who accept and support them. The secular totalitarian state, on the other hand, logically belongs to the sensate phase of culture. Coercive rather than familistic, it tends to be repressive and unpopular. Present-day states of this kind Sorokin saw as transitional governments that either must turn familistic or ultimately will be overthrown.

Sorokin completed his examination of peaceful changes in society with a survey of economic fluctuations. To collect information covering the subject from 600 B.C. to the present century, he enlisted the aid of five other scholars. When the necessary data was amassed and analyzed, he found that, "The economics of an Ideational society are fundamentally different from those of the Sensate society."[10]

The two main types of culture have altogether different mentalities toward basic economic values, theories of capital, and the place of wealth in the total value system. They differ also in details, like profit and pricing, interest and usury, property and ownership, alms and bequests.

Generally, ideational economies function at a relatively austere level. This was true in Greece before the age of Socrates and equally so in Europe of the Middle Ages. In both cultures, material wealth was viewed with indifference or disdain. Christ warned of the difficulty rich people have entering the kingdom of God, an admonition echoed in ideational Hindu and Taoist writings. As a consequence of this negative attitude toward wealth, ideational societies do relatively little to improve economic conditions. At the same time, they encourage many activities that are economically unsound, such as raising grand cathedrals, supporting monasteries, tithing income to the church, and sustaining missionary work. In spite of the general view toward wealth, however, leaders of the culture—the priestly class and landed aristocracy—rise economically as well as socially because of their position.

In an integral phase of culture, prosperity tends to grow to historic peaks. Moreover, all social classes, including craftsmen, laborers, and peasants, share its benefits. The general economic level around 1300, along with the prosperity of most social classes, was rarely equaled and never greatly exceeded until the nineteenth and twentieth centuries. The reason for the period's material well-being and its unusually equal distribution of wealth lie in the meeting of both major phases of culture. The rising sensate state of mind brings heightened economic efficiency. Meanwhile, ideational principles still strongly in force inhibit the wasteful social clashes that often interfere with production of wealth in a less idealistic, more developed sensate age. The same principles lead to familylike sharing of good fortune.

Sensate societies become relatively rich largely because wealth ranks high in their system of values. With their attention fixed on the material world, they devote great energy and effort to building a richer, more comfortable way of life. They eliminate many ideational activities that do not yield profit while taking on pursuits likely to generate wealth. Prosperity, however, is not always shared broadly. As ideational ideals atrophy and greed and egoism rise, familistic customs are discarded in favor of contractual and compulsory relationships. These prove less socially just and altruistic.

Leaders in a sensate age no longer are the clergy and owners of land, whose fortunes decline. The old aristocracy of Europe, for example, began to lose ground at the time of the crusades and never recovered. Their place was taken by the commercial bourgeoisie, the intelligentsia, and members of secular officialdom. The prosperity of a sensate phase soars highest as the culture reaches its fullest development and just before its decline.

While the link between the kind of culture in force and material wealth is clear, it is not necessarily close. Several factors prevent a precise parallel. Not the least of these is human inconsistency: people preaching one thing and practicing another, thinking one way and acting differently, failing to keep behavior in line with mentality. Added to this is a tendency of ideational leaders and institutions to grow rich unintentionally, even in spite of themselves. As such internal factors can raise ideational prosperity, so can external factors diminish wealth for other culture phases. When the black plague struck Europe in the mid-fourteenth century killing almost one-third of the population, prosperity abruptly plunged. Likewise famines, floods, and droughts set economies reeling. The Thirty Years War of the seventeenth century brought calamitous economic consequences, as did the world wars of the twentieth century. Finally, sensate cultures, by their very workings, undermine their own ambitions. For example, in an overripe sensate age, people begin to fight for a maximum slice of the economic pie. Their struggles can end up destroying order and security, leaving long-term prosperity impossible.

Leaders of the present sensate culture undercut the economic structure in other ways as well. While the capitalist class has lost virility, ability, confidence, and self-respect, its policies and acts increasingly have turned suicidal. At the same time the society's intelligentsia, though natural sensate allies of the capitalists, have attacked and denounced them unremittingly, further weakening the culture as a whole. In recent times, Sorokin pointed out, "we have witnessed a decline of both classes, the capitalists and the intelligentsia. . . .

[Their condition] is a sight as sore as that of the sacerdotal class and the landed aristocracy of the declining Ideational culture."[11] Meanwhile, the overall economy, while still uncertain in long-term trends, is doubtless in a state of deep and general crisis.

WARS AND REVOLUTIONS

Wars and revolutions are the final topics of Sorokin's vast research into social and cultural change. He first undertook the tremendous task of weighing and measuring the incidence of warfare in European cultures since the dawn of their history. With the aid of two army generals who also were professors of military science, he sought to discern how wars increase or decrease from one period to another. He studied the duration of wars, the strength of armies, and the number of soldiers killed and wounded in each century. Understanding that many of the figures are estimates, he still believed them sound enough for a broad picture of social fluctuations.

All told, he included in his study 967 important wars in ancient Greece and Rome and later European countries, including Austria and Germany, England and France, Holland and Spain, Italy and Russia, Poland and Lithuania. A list and brief description of all the conflicts filled thirty-five pages in one of *Dynamics*' lengthy appendices.

Almost every generation, with rare exceptions, has witnessed war, Sorokin found. During 375 years in ancient Greece, 213—or about 57 percent—saw armed conflicts. During 876 years in ancient Rome, 362—or some 41 percent—had wars. The story of Western European culture remains much the same. Thus, war appears to be almost as common and normal as peace.

Contrary to popular opinion, no country of Europe has shown itself consistently militant or peaceful. Russia kept the largest armies in the twelfth and thirteenth centuries, England in the fourteenth and fifteenth, Spain in the sixteenth, Austria in the seventeenth and eighteenth and France in the nineteenth century. Holland enjoyed the longest spell of unbroken peace, with more than a hundred tranquil years beginning in 1833; yet in the seventeenth and eighteenth centuries Holland was especially belligerent.

Militarism often accompanies the highest periods of cultural and scientific blossoming. Wars also accompany great cultural transitions and social decline. Likewise do armed conflicts erupt under all kinds of social conditions: in prosperity and depression, under autocratic rule and democratic regimes, in agricultural and industrial societies, among people of all religious beliefs and political creeds.

Unlike the arts, philosophy, and social relationships, the incidence of war shows no variation from ideational to sensate phases of culture. Differences exist, however, in motives for taking up arms. Ideational societies are more likely to fight for religious causes: to convert heretics, to exterminate infidels, to make their faith triumphant. Sensate societies tend to battle for sensate goals: to win territory, to gain natural resources, to assert independence, to assure or expand material standards of living. A notion held by some modern historians that economic motives underlie all wars is only ethnocentric thinking, according to Sorokin's study. Similarly, Marxism's materialist interpretation of history is irrelevant to the long stretches of ideational time that represent more than half of humankind's past.

Not only does the incidence of warfare fail to fluctuate with the two main culture phases, it appears to follow little rhyme or reason at all. Contrary to a belief held in the late nineteenth century, there is no steady trend toward diminishing warfare. Neither does war show any constant increase, as the twentieth century might suggest. In spite of many imaginative theories attributing wars to planetary influences, sunspots, climate, and other causes in an effort to identify cycles and predict future outbreaks, wars remain utterly unpredictable, coming and passing with little trend of any kind.

A single exception occurs during transitions between ideational and sensate cultures. Then armed conflicts rise in both number and size. This is a consequence of unsettled cultural and social conditions, which lead to more revolutions, crime, and suicide. When medieval culture dissolved, warfare in Europe mounted steadily, abating only when the modern sensate age became dominant and crystallized. Settled sensate days of the nineteenth century proved remarkably peaceful. Now with culture phases shifting once again, the twentieth century proved one of the cruelest and least humanitarian periods—by far the bloodiest century in all twenty-five hundred years of European history.

Modern wars, Sorokin found, have stretched longer in actual combat time than armed struggles of past ages. World War I, for example, is the first known conflict with continuous fighting for as long as four consecutive years. The total duration of combat in even the Hundred Years War between England and France was far shorter, with lengthy intervals passing between separate battles.

Wars also have grown more lethal through the ages. In the twelfth century, casualties totaled around 2.5 percent of regular fighting forces. By the fifteenth century they had more than doubled. Between then and the seventeenth century, casualties tripled again. In the twentieth century, with aircraft, bombs, and other devices of massive war, casualties leaped to 40 percent and above. For the first quarter of the century alone, the number of military wounded and dead far exceeded the total for all the centuries between the years 1101 and 1900.

Sorokin regarded as so much quackery many modern remedies proposed for war, whether limitless wealth, birth control, peace demonstrations, or this or that political regime. Wars, he wrote, "*are but logical and factual consequences of the state of disintegration of the crystallized system of relationships. . . . One of the main—and I am inclined to say even the main—weapons against war is the crystallization of the system of cultural values and of social relationships.* Until this is achieved, the efforts to prevent war are likely to be fruitless."[12]

Moving to revolutions, Sorokin examined some 1,625 uprisings in ancient Greece and Rome, in later Byzantium, in France and England, the Netherlands and Germany, Italy and Spain, Russia, Poland, and Lithuania.

Every generation is likely to see one or more internal disturbance. Revolution might be triggered by political aims, social and economic motives, national and separatist causes, religious goals, or more narrow and specific objectives, such as resistance to a law or a tax, or opposition to a government leader. Some uprisings are no more than plots involving only a few people, while others are major social conflagrations with deep and lasting effects. Most revolutions are short, with acute stages lasting only weeks, though some 15 percent of Sorokin's total raged for more than a year. On a rough average in most countries Sorokin studied, internal disturbances of one sort or another broke out every six or seven years. This led him to conclude that "inner tensions and disturbances seem to be phenomena inseparably connected with the existence and functioning of social bodies. . . . These are no less 'natural' and 'common' than storms in ordinary weather conditions."[13]

As with wars—again contrary to fairly widespread opinion—no region among those studied had internal affairs notably more tranquil or disorderly than those of other nations over time. Meanwhile, forces generating internal upheavals rarely, if ever, confine themselves to a single country. Rather, uprisings tend to spread from one country to another or to break out in several lands at once.

Also as with wars, history shows no continuous trend toward either growing peace or increasing disorder in internal affairs. Neither is there any wavelike regularity for revolutions, in spite of ingenious theories to the contrary. Thus, all attempts to forecast internal disturbances are futile.

Internal upheavals break out under all kinds of social circumstances. Disturbances of growth and cultural vitality lead people to break the fetters of old social relationships. Uprisings during decline and disorganization challenge insufferable conditions. Revolts, wrote Sorokin, "have occurred under stupid and under wise governments, under conditions of war and of peace, in monarchies and republics, in democracies and aristocracies, in prosperity and poverty, in ages of 'enlightenment' and of 'ignorance,' in urbanized and industrial as well as in rural and nonindustrialized countries; and in other most diverse circumstances."[14] Likewise, though war and revolution have coincided, evidence suggests no immediate link between the two. At the same time, both wars and revolutions have an identical underlying condition: a generally unsettled cultural or social system.

Like wars, revolutions reach a peak at times of great social and cultural transition. The most turbulent period for ancient Greece was the fifth and fourth centuries B.C., when the culture was changing from its outworn ideational form to a fresh sensate phase. In medieval Europe, disturbances increased during Charlemagne's reign in the eighth century when social, economic, and political organization underwent notable change. In the thirteenth century, when European culture was passing through its transition from ideational to sensate, from feudal to modern, from familistic to contractual and compulsory, from theocratic to secular, internal upheavals soared to a record peak.

Revolutions diminished again in the centuries that followed, reaching a low point around 1750. But drastic cultural change resumed as postmedieval social patterns were cast aside and many compulsory relationships were thrown off in favor of contractual ties. This shift started roughly with the French Revolution of 1789 and was well accomplished by the early nineteenth century. The fever of disturbance subsided through that century's second half, with the final quarter enjoying extraordinary order.

Now another age of grand and sweeping change is carrying the waning sensate culture of the modern West into its period of acute decay and ultimate disintegration. The first quarter of the twentieth century alone saw the curve of internal disturbances soar. As the century progressed, revolution reached new heights, marking the period as the most turbulent in Western history and perhaps in all the chronicles of mankind.

14

Toward a New Civilization

Sorokin detected three enormous trends unfolding in the present age. First, cultural creativity is making an epochal shift from Europe to other parts of the world. Second, modern sensate culture and the people who live by it are suffering progressive disintegration. Finally, the first early seedlings of a new cultural order are emerging and slowly growing.

From the start of history until around the fourteenth century, the creative leadership of humankind rested in Asia, northern Africa, and Mediterranean Europe—in the cultures of the Middle East and Egypt, China and India, Crete, Greece, and Rome, and the Arabic lands. Western European peoples were the latest to take up the torch of civilization. Over the past five or six centuries, they have sustained their creative mission brilliantly, especially in the arts, politics, economics, science, and technology.

Now the West's leadership is drawing to an end. The culture's power and influence has been dwindling decade by decade. Great European empires that in recent memory blanketed the earth have withered and disappeared. Centers of creative life have fled from Anglo-Saxon Europe to North America, from Spain and Portugal to South America, while in former Soviet lands the most vibrant growth occurred not in old Russia but in the Asiatic part of its former dominion. At the same time Japan, China, India, Indonesia, and Arabic countries are enjoying a cultural renascence. They are growing socially and politically, scientifically and technologically. Meanwhile, they exert new influence over international affairs and export their religions, philosophies, arts, and cultural values to the West.

If the countries of Europe had remained separate and independent, the continent would have become a provincial backwater relatively insignificant in world affairs. In political union, they can retain an important role. But in no way will the area regain the dominant position it held through the past several centuries. In the world of the future, Sorokin ventured, "I consider the vast region of the Pacific as the territorial center and the Americas, India, China, Japan, and Russia as the leading players in the coming drama of the emerging Integral or Ideational culture."[1]

CRISIS AND TRANSITION

For the meantime, until the new culture blossoms, the world will sink into deepening crisis. Some people still expect moderate, sensible, orderly progress toward the kind of terrestrial paradise envisioned in the nineteenth century: with prosperity and leisure for all, with crime, sickness, and ignorance disappearing, with cooperation and goodwill between nations, while military armaments are beaten into golf clubs and kitchen appliances. Instead of this sensate heaven on earth, Sorokin foresaw dark and violent times of bloodshed, cruelty, and misery, with humanity uprooted and the old, sweet humanist dreams swept away in a holocaust of change.

Advocates of revolutionary progress—whether Marxists, anarchists, or sensate ideologists of any other stamp—differ from moderate cultists of progress only in their impatience. Their aims are the same, and their schemes, in Sorokin's judgment, are no more than utopias of disintegrated minds and demoralized characters that typically arise in times of major cultural transition. "These mobs and their leaders are the vultures that appear when the social and cultural body is decomposing. Their eternal historical function is to pull it to pieces, and thus, though involuntarily, to clear the ground for a new life. Creation is not given to them."[2]

Many other people no longer expect a future sensate paradise but do not understand what is happening around them. They sense that present crises are not mere issues of prosperity or capitalism or democracy but reach much further in scope and significance. Crisis, after all, is shaking the foundations of almost every country on earth. It strains every tendon of civilized life, from politics to commerce, from the arts to agriculture, from religion to morality, from government to family. Even the unprecedented genius of Western science and technology, once generally productive, is increasingly poisonous.

"It is high time to realize," Sorokin wrote in *The Crisis of Our Age*, "that this is not one of the ordinary crises which happens almost every decade, but one of the greatest transitions in human history from one of its main forms of culture to another."[3] Over the past thirty centuries, only four turning points in Europe's history have compared to the present, and even these four proceeded on a smaller scale than the epoch-making crisis facing the modern age.

Sensate culture in its overripe and rotting condition has debased mankind and now is destroying him and his environment as well. Spontaneous forces inherent in the system have stripped it of fundamental values capable of commanding allegiance. This has undermined the culture's prestige and alienated from it much of humanity. The same forces have robbed the society of former security and safety, militated against freedom, and struck repeated blows at prosperity and material comfort.

"Not in the classroom but in the hard school of experience," Sorokin wrote, "people are being constantly taught by these impersonal forces an unforgettable and indelible lesson, comprehensible to the simplest mind, that the existing order has passed its creative phase and is on the verge of bankruptcy; that it spells bullets rather than bread, destruction rather than construction, misery rather than prosperity, regimentation rather than freedom; confusion rather than order; death rather than life. Its decline is not due to the murderous assault of barbarians, revolutionaries, or plotters, but to its own senility, the exhaustion of its creative forces."[4] The debilitated system might linger in agony, half alive and half dead, for decades, but its day of glory definitely is over.

Sorokin described in the pages of *Dynamics* the twilight of Western sensate culture and the dark night of transition. His predictions, published between 1937 and 1941, aroused protest, even ridicule. But the outbreak of World War II, its horrifying feast of carnage, and later trends in every aspect of society and culture more than confirmed his apprehensions. He repeated and elaborated his forecasts in later books. In the 1960s, Arnold Toynbee remarked that Sorokin's diagnosis still was being borne out by events, "and my guess is that he would not be in a hurry today to alter what he wrote. . . ."[5] Another scholar, reviewing Sorokin's auguries in the 1970s, observed, "Much of what he has predicted has already come to pass. He is, without a doubt, the most perceptive social critic of our age."[6]

Among his forewarnings:[7]

- Sensate values will become still more relative and atomistic until they lose all universal acceptance and binding power. The distinction between true and false, right and wrong, beautiful and ugly, positive values and negative values will fade to the point of producing mental, moral, social, and aesthetic anarchy.

- The culture's values, and humanity itself, will be stripped of everything divine, sacred and absolute, becoming still more material, sensual, and debased. Values will grow ever more destructive.

- The sensate mentality increasingly will interpret values and man physicochemically, reflexologically, behavioristically, mechanistically, economically, and materialistically—a universe of atoms and electron-protons with human robots enmeshed in the huge, inert web.

- Genuine, authoritative, and binding public opinion and social conscience will disappear. In their place will rise a multitude of opposing opinions thrust forward by unscrupulous factions and the pseudoconsciences of pressure groups.

- Contracts and covenants will lose binding power and contractual society will collapse. Democracy, capitalism, and the free society of free people will be swept away. Freedom will become a mere myth for the majority of people, whom centralized governments will deal with as puppets. Meanwhile, the dominant minority will turn their freedom into unbridled licentiousness.

- Might will equal right. Rude force and cynical fraud will be the only arbiters. As a consequence, wars, revolutions, and general brutality will be rampant, with nation against nation, race against race, class against class, creed against creed, person against person.

- Governments will turn increasingly fraudulent and tyrannical. They will be ever less stable and short-lived.

- The family as a sacred union of husband and wife, parents and children will continue to disintegrate. Separations and divorces will multiply until any recognized difference between marriage and illicit sexual relationship no longer exists. Children will be separated from parents at ever earlier ages. The home will become hardly more than an overnight stop.

- Private educational institutions will lose autonomy from government control and diminish in favor of public or state-controlled schools.

• Social climbing—and falling—will increase enormously. Differences between rich and poor, upper classes and common people will lessen. Monied classes will discard extravagant luxury for more modest material standards. The leisure class will approach extinction. Social inequalities will remain, but their range will diminish.

• The kind of people the society places in its upper strata will change. Inherited titles and family position will lose all importance. So will honesty and integrity. Supplanting them will be traits useful for short-run purposes, as devotion to the dominant party, manipulative skills, ruthlessness with opponents, impressive smartness, and lack of scruples.

• Voluntary and compulsory migration of peoples will uproot millions. A growing number will be refugees and human flotsam.

• Sensate culture, instead of showing unity, coherence, and inner harmony of style, will become an ethnic bazaar, a shapeless dumping ground of elements jumbled in undigested syncretism.

• The culture's creativity will continue to wane. The place of the Galileos, Leibnizes, Shakespeares, Bachs, and Rembrandts will be usurped by mediocre pseudocreators, one more vulgar than the next. Quantitative colossalism will substitute for the refinements of quality. Thought will be replaced by superficial smartness. Even the highest cultural values of the past will be degraded.

• Christianity as the society's great religion will be supplanted by a confusion of spiritual concoctions devised from fragments of science and shreds of philosophy mixed with magical beliefs and ignorant superstitions.

• The economy will deteriorate. Material standards of living will diminish. Economic depressions will worsen.

Millions of human beings will be destitute, deprived even of basic needs for survival.

- Security of possessions and of life will dwindle. People by the millions will live in constant uncertainty. Peace of mind and happiness will grow more rare. Crime and suicide will increase. A growing part of the population—though always a minority—will suffer emotional instability and depressive moods. Mental disturbances will increase. Weariness will spread over ever-larger numbers of the population. A sense of pessimism and calamity will pervade art, literature, science, philosophy, and religion. An apocalyptic mentality will develop in a sizeable part of the population.

- The society will split and polarize. One segment will be sensate cynics, hedonists, libertines, profligates, and outright criminals. These will be thoroughly materialistic, militantly atheistic, and morally depraved. A minority will evolve as stoics, ascetics, moral heroes, saints, sublime altruists, religious prophets, mystics and martyrs, all indifferent or opposed to sensate values. The latter group will form a minority in the early stages of cultural crisis. The factions will struggle against each other long and arduously as the transition wears on. Eventually, the sensate segment will diminish and fail and the rising new element will prevail.

Ordeal to Resurrection

Understandably, Sorokin's predictions were and still are distressing for "champions of the overstuffed, after-dinner utopia," as he referred to people who expect eternal sensate progress.[8] To them, his entire study could appear only direly pessimistic. But on a deeper level, as he pointed out, the work is highly optimistic. It shows social and cultural forces to be infinitely richer in creative power than the inflexible ideal of sensate utopians because they include ideational and integral creativity as well. And the study does not predict the end of Western culture as a whole. Rather, the crisis of the modern age is only a temporary stage in a process of renewal.

"I believe there is a possibility for rebirth and regeneration because of what we learn from the crises of the past," Sorokin said. "This formula describes the experience through which humanity passes: crisis, ordeal, cleansing, grace, resurrection."[9]

This chain of stages leading to cultural renewal unfolded several times in ancient Egypt; in Babylon around 1200 B.C.; in India when major crises came to an end with the revival of Hinduism or the emergence of Buddhism; in China of the sixth century B.C. when Taoism and Confucianism arose out of social disintegration; in the Hebrew nation when ordeal brought great religious prophets like Elijah, Isaiah, and Jeremiah; and in the days of ancient Rome when social decline cleared the way for the Christian faith and culture.

In the case of the modern West, the very ordeal of the passing sensate age will bring cleansing transformation. With material comforts gone, liberties vanished, pleasures dissipated, and sufferings increased; with sensate security, safety, and happiness turned into myth; with human dignity trampled; with creativity in ruins everywhere; with cities and nations erased and human blood saturating the earth; with sensate values destroyed and sensate dreams evaporated—with the overall collapse of the system—people will be forced to open their eyes to the hollowness of the worn-out culture. From disillusion with the old order will come moral awakening. Through tragedy and suffering, people are cleansed and purified.

The awakening will be stimulated by the best minds of Western society—new St. Pauls and St. Augustines, great religious and ethical leaders. Gaining momentum, it will be taken up by the masses. When this stage of catharsis arrives, the crisis will be over.

People are not left forever in a state of tragedy and suffering, Sorokin observed. "There is an element of grace in the universe, a guiding providence, that helps to lift humanity to higher levels. Many times in history we have seen proof of this creative power. And then we see society enter the period of resurrection."[10]

A new charisma and fresh release of creative forces could usher in either an ideational or an integral type of culture, Sorokin believed. The usual order suggests that an ideational culture is more likely. When sensate humanity stands at the end of its course, people are undisciplined, full of appetites and passions. They are not like the inwardly strong and self-controlled medieval humanity that emerged from an austere existence to discover the magnificent world of the senses, then easily moved into the noble and balanced integral way of life. Rather, people of an overripe and decaying sensate culture need taming and refining before spiritual and ethical values can come into their lives and culture. And they are not likely to restrain themselves willingly. In the ordinary train of events, the "policeman of history" must step in—the hard physical coercion of totalitarian rule. Then, after a strenuous period of discipline, disillusioned and chastened sensate people are strapped into the straitjacket of ideational culture for reeducation in values and reality.

However logical and historical the succession from sensate to ideational culture is, Sorokin nowhere claimed that a passing sensate phase cannot lead to a balanced integral age. "Theoretically, it is possible," he wrote in *Dynamics*, "and if other cultures are studied from this standpoint more carefully, it is probable that some other order of recurrence of these main forms can be found."[11]

By the 1960s, he seemed convinced that the West could be revived without a one-sidedly spiritual ideational age. He believed, in fact, that the harmonious blend of an integral period already was taking shape. "If human folly, assisted by destructive sensate science, does not destroy the human universe, including science itself," he wrote in that decade, "then the new sociocultural order and its science seem to be progressively shaping into what I define as integral order and science in which science and truth will again be reunited with goodness and beauty. . . . reestablishing, in St. Simon's terms, a new 'organic' order in the human world."

On the same occasion he wrote, “It is true that at the present time the new integral order or ‘positive polarization’ is just emerging, but its first fresh blades have already appeared and are slowly growing in science, philosophy, religion, ethics, fine arts, law, and even in politics and economics, as well as in other basic social institutions. To be sure, the great transition from a sensate to an integral order will take a long time (in the past similar basic transitions have required roughly one hundred and fifty years), but if mankind can avoid suicidal wars, the transition will surely be made and mankind’s creative history will enter a magnificent new era.”[12]

Like Toynbee, Sorokin saw modern warfare, with its high technology, global scale, and barbaric ruthlessness, as the preeminent threat to the future of humanity and culture. No one who attended Sorokin’s classes at Harvard before World War II was apt to forget his impassioned annual lecture announcing that one day scientists would devise a simple but tremendous explosive capable of destroying all life on earth. When that prediction came to pass with the atomic bomb, he tempered his faith in culture’s eternal renewal. If the decaying sensate order squanders its remaining energies in world incineration, he warned, the creative process of mankind can be impeded severely or ended altogether.

At the same time, Sorokin saw no reason why the modern epidemic of war had to continue. As a sociologist, he mapped out as early as the 1940s conditions for restraining armed conflict and creating an effective world organization of nations. Mere tinkering with economics and politics could not achieve lasting peace, he insisted. Deeper and more basic moves were required. The sovereignty of states should be eliminated in questions of peace and war, with countries placed on the same footing as towns and other communities. Meanwhile an international organization such the United Nations should include not only national delegates but also representatives of religion, art, science, agriculture, labor, and industry to tone down militancy and strengthen the body’s moral resources.

Eventually, he believed, countries should come under world government. Yet global union would be a long and painful process.

It posed no great difficulty in a purely mechanical sense. Any super-government under a dictatorial strongman could consolidate the world. But that kind of unity would not be necessarily good. Instead, to avert future wars and to build constructive global unity, people must be conditioned to these goals by a change in psychology and conduct—a fundamental change of morality. The same change is needed to build the creative society of the coming age.

As unworkable or otherwise unacceptable as this sort of moral solution might seem to modern sensate people, Sorokin saw it as the only one available. Efforts to patch up the crumbling system will prove useless. Humankind can be grateful to Western sensate culture for its splendid achievements. But now, when it lies contorted in agony, when it has given humanity terrible power over nature but failed to provide equal power over emotions, passions, appetites, and lusts, the culture deserves not admiration but condolences. Rather than trying to resuscitate what is hollow and increasingly barren, to revive what already is half dead, the task of the present is to make the transition to the coming phase of culture as painless as possible. This can be done by willingly abandoning the sinking ship of sensate values and working toward the spiritual values that are the only island of safety people can hope to find.

"The most urgent need of our time," Sorokin wrote in *Dynamics*, "is the man who can control himself and his lusts, who is compassionate to all his fellow men, who can see and seek for the eternal values of culture and society, and who deeply feels his unique responsibility in this universe. . . . Such a man can be trusted with the power created by the Sensate culture. Even with the present power and technique, such a man could build a society and culture with less poverty and misery, free from individual and group hatred, nobler, more just, more human, and more godly."[13]

Such people can evolve, Sorokin believed, only through altruistic ethics. One by one, they must reorganize values and behavior by rooting them in the moral truths of the kingdom of God. "This moral adjustment I regard as paramount above any technological and scientific change," Sorokin declared. "Political, economic, and technical changes should be carried out; but morality is basic to all secure social life. Without morality, there can be only struggle and hatred.

"The most radical system I know is Christianity," he continued. "If individuals could be grafted with real Christianity, there would be a reawakening. I refer specifically to the ethical ideals of the Christian religion, theological questions are of secondary importance. Matters of ritual may differ according to circumstances, but the important matter is the Golden Rule. Even Taoists, Confucianists, Buddhists, and Hindus can live up to the practice of the Golden Rule. We cannot standardize the ideas of religion, but we can standardize in terms of the Golden Rule. This ethical basis for behavior is what counts."[14]

Religion that is mainly verbal or ritualistic has not been potent, Sorokin pointed out, because of a yawning chasm it permits between preaching and practice. Yet if Christianity and other religions take the more difficult but more effective course of bringing behavior into line with ethical norms, they all can participate in laying the foundation for the age to come.

They can begin this joint effort by giving up tribal rivalries and imperialistic claims to supremacy and monopoly. "In His fullness God can hardly be adequately comprehended by any finite human mind or by any finite human beliefs. For this reason no human religion can claim to have a monopoly on an adequate comprehension of God, as God's exclusive confidant and agent."

Now that the human race has become, to a large degree, one interdependent whole, such tribalism can only interfere with the universality intended in the moral imperatives of religion. Rather, "cherishing their own beliefs, the believers of each religion can equally respect the beliefs of others as supplementary to their own, revealing additional aspects of the *mysterium tremendum et fascinosum*. Viewed so, religious differences cannot only be tolerated but genuinely welcomed and esteemed. In their totality they convey to us a fuller knowledge of the Supreme Reality than that given by a single religion."[15]

Since the main moral commands of great religions are similar, religious organizations can cooperate in transforming human behavior, social institutions, and culture through altruistic love. Sorokin defined this loftiest and most mature form of love as an active effort not to cause pain to anyone by thought, word, or deed, added to unselfish service, devotion, and sacrifice for others.

Moral teachers of every place and period would agree with his emphasis on altruistic love as the means of reconstructing culture and society and guaranteeing future creativity. From the time Sorokin completed his masterwork in mid-career until the end of his long and productive life, he continued to study, write about, and urge spiritual regeneration around the eternal principle of altruism.

"It is my firm conclusion," he wrote in one of his later books, "that without a notable altruization of individuals and groups, of social institutions and culture, neither can future wars be prevented nor a new, truly creative order be built." If, on the other hand, "humanity mobilizes all its wisdom, knowledge, beauty, and especially the all-giving and all-forgiving love or reverence for life and if a strenuous and sustaining effort of this kind is made by everyone—an effort deriving its strength from love and reverence for life—then the crisis will certainly be ended and a most magnificent new era of human history ushered in. It is up to mankind itself to decide what it will do with its future life-course."[16]

Epilogue

Civilization and the Future

THE MANY THINKERS who detect decline in Western culture differ greatly in their approach. Some come by their ideas through intuition. Others are inspired by patterns in history, economics, psychology, or sociology. A few rely on facts accumulated through empirical science.

They also differ in their range of vision. Some concentrate on imminent threats: totalitarian rule, a society turned rigid and dully noncreative, collapse into barbarism. Others picture a longer descent to a new dark age of destruction and chaos. Still others project beyond decline, speculating on the blossoming and growth of a fresh new civilization.

Some regard decline as inevitable, fulfilling a kind of natural law. Others consider it avoidable, if only enough people take steps to renew themselves and their culture.

The differences between the thinkers are many. Yet their pathways converge into significant points of agreement.

THE NATURE OF CIVILIZATIONS

The thinkers generally agree on several major factors in the study of higher cultures. They are virtually unanimous in discarding the method of dividing history into ancient, medieval, and modern periods, which relieves present social thinkers of the awkward burden of deciding where to go from there. Instead, they accept each higher culture as separate and distinct, each with its own particular rise and decline.

They also discard the notion that humankind must forever be advancing toward perfection. This linear concept of steady upward progress captured European minds for at least three hundred years. Along with the publication of Spengler's *The Decline of the West*, other theories of history emerged or reappeared. Not since World War I has a work of comparable influence supported the linear view of social development. Meanwhile, thinkers who see decline in Western culture lean toward the idea that human cultures grow and decay, rise and fall, appear and disappear in cycles.

Many of the thinkers note clear-cut stages in the process of wax and wane. They label these phases differently and interpret them in varying ways. Yet the stages themselves remain similar from one study to the next. The botanist and fishery specialist Nikolai Danilevsky, the scholar and mystical philosopher Nikolai Berdyaev, the German scholar Walter Schubart, along with Oswald Spengler, Arnold Toynbee, and Pitirim Sorokin, all map out the phases of culture, and their charts distinctly overlap. What Spengler calls cultural childhood and youth, Toynbee thinks of as the stage of growth and Sorokin classifies as ideational culture. Danilevsky writes of a culture's age of fulfillment, Schubart of the Heroic era, when people strive to alter their world, Berdyaev of a humanist-secular culture, Spengler of the phases of maturity and age, Toynbee of breakdown and disintegration, and Sorokin of the sensate cultural supersystem. In every case, the stages resemble one another.

Several of the social observers note that different cultures focus on different kinds of truth. Danilevsky, Spengler, and Sorokin point out that cultures perceive mathematics differently. In regard to world outlook, a society might follow Schubart's Messianic or Heroic viewpoints or Sorokin's ideational or sensate philosophical systems.

Similarly, each of Sorokin's three culture phases emphasizes an entirely different kind of art, music, architecture, and literature, ethics, law, economics, and social bonds. Different civilizations also specialize in different modes of creativity: the ancient Greeks excelling in the achievement of beauty, the Romans in government and law, India in spiritual sensibilities, and modern Western culture in science and technology.

The scholars in civilizational studies recognize that one culture can be transmitted to another only in certain aspects and to a strictly limited extent. They also generally agree that civilizations do not die of barbarian attacks or other outside factors, as many people have assumed; rather, they rise and fall as a consequence of forces within themselves: whether destiny, or their response to major challenges, or a natural maturing that inevitably ends in an overripe and decadent condition.

Patterns in the Past?

Not all the social thinkers who sense decline in Western culture seek evidence from patterns in the past. Yet many of them do—most notably Spengler, Toynbee, and Sorokin. Some critics challenge them severely on this point. At issue is the question: Can we really find laws, patterns, cycles, or consistencies in history?

Theories of history are in no way uncommon. They inspire and justify all great revolutions, provide the foundation for portentous human causes, underlie dynasties, uphold nations, and help explain the purpose of life. All cultures and ages have a theory of history of one kind or another, which ordinarily reflects their larger mentalities.

In past centuries, people of the West thought of history as a tale told by God. In the beginning, according to the Bible's book of Genesis, God created the world and man and woman in it, then Adam fell from grace and was banished from the Garden of Eden.

This history continues with the work of Jesus Christ redeeming humankind. It ends with a great apocalypse and the last judgment of the saved and the condemned.

The most fashionable view in the twentieth century interprets history as patternless and pointless. Its expressions range from industrialist Henry Ford's assertion in 1916 that "history is more or less bunk," to the wry comment of a modern British poet laureate that history is Odtaa, or "one damned thing after another." A classic profession of this faith is an urbane statement by the historian H.A.L. Fisher: "One intellectual excitement has . . . been denied me. Men wiser and more learned than I have discerned in history a plot, a rhythm, a predetermined pattern. These harmonies are concealed from me. I can see only one emergency following upon another as wave follows upon wave; only one great fact with respect to which, since it is unique, there can be no generalizations; only one safe rule for the historian: that he should recognize in the development of human destinies the play of the contingent and the unforeseen."[1] With the human story thus portrayed, in Shakespearean terms, as a tale told by an idiot signifying nothing, any attempt to draw a chart of history seems reckless, irresponsible, and impossible.

Yet Toynbee pointed out that advocates of a patternless past also have a chart of their own—which happens to be blank. "We all have one," he said in his 1948 radio debate with Dutch historian Pieter Geyl programmed by the British Broadcasting Corporation, "and no chart is more than one man's shot at the truth. But surely," he added in support of patterns, "the blank is the most useless and the most dangerous."[2]

Accepting the axiom that those who do not learn from the past are condemned to repeat it, many major thinkers who speak of present-day decline, and lesser ones as well, look to history for evidence of how cultures rise and fall. This only follows an ancient view of civilizations as human instruments, human contrivances, human creations. As that, cultures naturally parallel human psychology: super-confident in growth, egocentric in triumph, denying decline, haunted by fear in disintegration. If cultures are guided also by other traits of human behavior, they would be all the more predictable in their ups and downs. The main difference in the patterns that the scholars of civilization identify rests in how rigid or flexible they appear to be.

Spengler, regarding cultures as organisms, locks them into strictly fixed and predictable life cycles. Historic necessity rules cultural existence. The only human freedom in either rise or fall is to ride along, doing the necessary or doing nothing.

As a point of fact, this deterministic scheme seems to reflect what often has happened in the past, at least in times of cultural decline. As great a thinker as Plato wrote his *Republic*, a vision of an ideal political community, as an effort to salvage a failing Greece. Given a chance to put his vision into practice in the powerful Greek city of Syracuse on Sicily, he saw his political experiments fail dismally. The Roman orator and political leader Marcus Tullius Cicero and other prominent figures of his time did their utmost to preserve the integrity of old republican Rome, but to no avail. In modern times, since the French Revolution, social saviors have worked feverishly to restore, revise, reform, or salvage modern Western culture, though none of them has been able to lastingly reverse the decline they perceived.

Yet, social tendencies, however tenacious, need not be interpreted as destiny. Most critics of Spengler's deterministic scheme would favor in principle the broader human freedom proposed by the nineteenth-century Swiss historian Jacob Burckhardt. Though predicting a seemingly hopeless future of economic depression, wars, and despotism, Burckhardt never ceased believing that a few fearless people, living genuine Christianity, could suddenly and unexpectedly fertilize fresh creativity and revive the life of the society and its culture. This certainly seems likely enough. If the state of a culture reflects the condition of the souls living in it, then a culture can find renewal if its people embark on a redemptive search for true salvation. According to American anthropologist Alfred L. Kroeber, the civilization of ancient Egypt rose and fell at least four times within the same cultural framework before it finally was exhausted.

Though Toynbee was criticized for finding consistencies in history, his scheme is neither rigid nor fixed. He sometimes speaks of "laws" but more often writes of "standard patterns of development" or "tendencies." He rejects Spengler's coupling of civilizations with biological creations. He also denies that higher cultures decline by the kind of organic necessity that rules the plant and animal world. Discarding Spengler's determinism, the English historian also disregards the diagnosis that Western civilization is inescapably doomed and, as he put it, "we should fold our hands and await the inevitable blow."[3]

At the same time, he defines the growth of civilization as vanquishing material problems to grapple with spiritual ones, or "a conversion of the soul from the World, the Flesh, and the Devil, to the Kingdom of Heaven."[4] In Toynbee's view, decay is generated not by natural law but within the society itself, by human failure, with no element of necessity involved. Decline, he stresses, is a matter of choice—continued, persisting choice. "I am a believer in free will," he said, "in man's freedom to respond with all his heart and soul and mind when life presents him with a challenge."[5] Only when a civilization breaks down and skids into disintegration does Toynbee see regularities of decay hardly less rigid than Spengler's biological parallel. As with all pathologies, a culture's pattern of decline appears narrow, consistent, and predictable.

Sorokin, while finding similar patterns in the past, took issue with Toynbee on two major points. The historian's "original sin," from which other defects issued, lay in choosing "civilizations" as his field of study. As a sociologist, Sorokin found the term too loose and ill-defined: "mere congeries or conglomerations of various cultural (or civilizational) phenomena and objects adjacent in space and time but devoid of any causal or meaningful ties."[6] A second "fatal mistake" he found in Toynbee's *Study* was the historian's "acceptance of the old—from Florus to Spengler—conceptual scheme of 'genesis-growth-decline,' as a uniform pattern of change of civilizations."[7] This popular idea, he maintained, is not a formula for civilizational change but only an evaluative theory of progress or regress, of how sociocultural phenomena *should* change.

Sorokin preferred to reinterpret Toynbee's work within the more precise framework of his "cultural supersystems," made up of the fine arts, philosophy, ethics, social relationships, and other departments of culture. This done, he affirms, "many pages and chapters of Toynbee's work become illuminating, penetrating and scientifically valid."[8]

In Sorokin's scheme, unlike Spengler's and Toynbee's, a culture does not grow and decline in an evaluative sense. Rather, it changes from the spiritual-ideational phase, to the intermediate-idealistic phase, then on to the materialistic-sensate phase of development. Ripening to the limits of that phase, it changes back cataclysmically from materialistic to spiritual. Sorokin's pendulum swing is not so much about rising and falling civilizations as changing values that lead people out of one cultural paradigm and into another. Nor is his work as much an exercise in history as Spengler's *Decline* and Toynbee's *Study*. They each use history to create a grand-scale sociology of higher cultures, but Sorokin does so to the point of making history only a vehicle for defining social change.

Sorokin, like Spengler, has been called dogmatic perhaps because his system is simple and consistent and because he argued with great force. Yet more sympathetic commentators point out that he carefully avoided dogmatism, allowing that his theory need not apply to every age and place and is open to alternative conclusions. At the same time, he believed implicitly in the rhythms he found in history, and he lambasted any critic who dared to challenge them within the limits he established.

Whether patterns in history exist or not, and to what degree, can only remain open and debatable questions. Historian Christopher Dawson called Spengler and Toynbee, as representatives of metahistory, "the bugbears of the academic historian," who ordinarily is confined by the profession to far more specialized research and far narrower spans of time. Dawson might equally include Sorokin, with the free-ranging inquiries of *Dynamics*. Even social theorists like Alvin Toffler and Jeremy Rifkin who examine trends and venture forecasts work with smaller cultural groups and shorter blocks of time than Spengler, Toynbee, and Sorokin chose for their studies. Most historians and forecasters do not argue with the grand social theorists as much as look under them. Meanwhile, the grand theory studies, encompassing scores of countries and thousands of years, might naturally seem far-fetched to specialized historians and irrelevant to people who live more in the realm of the personal and present.

In the last analysis, scholars never have known quite what to do with Spengler's *Decline*. Though built upon impressive learning, the work is not a respectable performance by standards of normal scholarship. It is too intuitive, too philosophical, too metaphysical, too insistent, too poetic, too extreme. To make the matter worse, its conclusions are so powerfully disturbing that many people shrink from the work as so much "doom and gloom." Yet there it stands, after much of a century, brilliant, stimulating, still debated in the scholarly world, still instructive and, some insist, still convincing.

Toynbee's *Study* likewise is too much for many conventional scholars to bite, chew, and swallow—difficult even to read for its colossal size as the largest book of the twentieth century and a style that one critic justifiably described as "turgid and prolix." While its breathtaking scope makes the *Study* an open field for critics, its massive learning raises the work to the level of an intellectual fortress more difficult to challenge than simply to accept or dismiss.

Sorokin's *Dynamics* is no less hard to deal with. Applying scrupulous scientific empiricism to many highly subjective areas of culture, it invites critics like a barn-sized target, then deflects their judgments with meticulously quantified evidence.

Spengler, Toynbee, and Sorokin, ignoring the self-imposed limits of academic disciplines, place themselves all the more beyond the criticism of specialists with the nature of their purpose. They all ask questions bypassed by ordinary professional historians who study history for its own sake, discovering, arranging, and classifying facts but seeking no particular meaning in it all. Like historians, they gather an infinity of fragments, but then, unlike most historians, they endow the data with significance. They take what was previously formless and give it shape and meaning.

Challenges to their patterns begin with arguments about historic evidence but do not cease there. Rather, they end in the realm of personal mentalities. Ultimately the issue devolves into a shouting match between the specialist mentality that says, "You can't generalize!" and the broader mentality that says, "Yes, we can!" This is essentially an clash of vantage points—a view from the ground versus the hawk's-eye vision. In this mode of argument, each person's stand depends on cast of mind: whether inductive or deductive, thinking in particulars or seeking after broader principles. When these mentalities compete, the issue can become unresolvable. The *Manchester Guardian*, in a tribute to Toynbee on his seventieth birthday, suggested the depth of this debate by describing him as, "the philosopher-historian who has been variously hailed as one of the most remarkable minds of our age and, at the other extreme, dismissed as the author of three million words of unreadable fantasy."[9]

Meanwhile, vast and generalized studies, such as Spengler's, Toynbee's, and Sorokin's, always tend to be unnerving. Not only does the knowledge they are built upon lie beyond the grasp of most readers and critics, who cannot hope to evaluate it fully. More important, creating valid generalizations requires a special kind of mental balance, one rooted not only in broad knowledge but also in emotional maturity and dedication to truth. How can we be sure that a writer possesses these fine attributes? Particularly in an age of specialization such as our own, many people automatically go on guard against attempts to cross the cautious boundaries of what Sorokin called "Lilliputian fact-finders" who cannot bring general principles into play, much less enormous generalizations.

When a generalization is difficult to recognize, it feels safer to dismiss it than risk acceptance as an act of faith.

Ultimately the question of patterns in the past can be answered only by the individual person, who accepts or rejects them simply because they appear or do not appear likely. All grand theories of history must always lie beyond absolute proof because they encompass such vast and imperfectly known horizons of time.

Gloom or Warnings?

The presence of patterns in history, however significant, is not the ultimate point or purpose of the work of Spengler, Toynbee, Sorokin, and other social thinkers offered here. Their aim is not solely to note a phenomenon of history. They go further to raise vital issues that the majority of historians and sociologists never confront. They deal with disturbing trends that we all are dealing with and in turn are dealing with us, with issues that become ever more inescapable in a growingly turbulent world. The thinkers are sounding alarms. They are signaling dangers appearing today and looming in the near and distant future. Whatever future validity unfolding events will give to their admonitions, the warnings strike deep and are disturbing.

Virtually all the thinkers who see decline in Western culture have been accused of being pessimists, dour doomsayers living in disheartenment and despairing of the future. Some, it appears, were just that. Henry and Brooks Adams, with their "laws" of history and civilization, hold out no hope either for the present or for times to come. They see the culture dying with nothing to replace it. Likewise, the writers H.G. Wells, Aldous Huxley, and George Orwell offer bleak outlooks for the prospects of humankind.

Most of the social observers, however, deserve far less the charge of pessimism—as Spengler, for one, points out. Some, in fact, like Albert Schweitzer with his restorative ethic of reverence for life and Sorokin with his view of a rising new culture, are highly optimistic by nature, humane and full of hope, with a clear, bright view of humanity's potential. Their apparent pessimism amounts to the courage to face evils and to an earnest desire to alert people to the hazards they see. If their observations seem negative, it is only because negative issues are the topics of their work.

Yet predictions of impending troubles do not recommend themselves to a world already sated with trouble and struggling to retain what optimism it has left. As Spengler was branded an apostle of despair, Toynbee was accused of deepening the unease already prevailing in the society and fostering hopelessness. In answer, his defenders cite the historian's cautious, even exasperating, moderation. Though Toynbee detects clear symptoms of breakdown and disintegration in Western civilization, he remains noncommittal about the culture's decline. The very existence of his forty-year masterwork implies his conviction that the West is on the way down, yet he continually grants that possibly it is not. And even if decline is its present course, he presents a way for the society to escape disaster by ardent reconversion to the culture's original religious faith. "This," he spoofed one critic, "is an unnecessarily gloomy view of our situation—like the old lady who was advised to leave it to Providence and exclaimed: 'Oh dear, has it come to that?'"[10] Meanwhile, he said, "Suppose my view of history did point to a gloomy conclusion, what of it? 'Gloomy' and 'cheerful' are one thing, 'true' and 'false' quite another."[11]

A *New York Times* review of Sorokin's *Dynamics* attacked the work and its author also on grounds of undue pessimism. At once challenging, defensive, scornful, and ridiculing, the commentary stated a firm faith that the world of mankind had improved immeasurably over the centuries as a consequence of four human traits: "(1) The rational faculty, which has enabled us to look at facts as they are and use them to our advantage; (2) The inventive and scientific faculties, which have enabled us to attain a marvelous control over nature and natural resources; (3) The human sentiments, which have impelled us increasingly, and as far as we can, to drive pain and distress from the world; and (4) The human sense of personality, which has inclined us more and more to respect ourselves and to give more and more consideration to others."[12] Two years after this review appeared, World War II broke out, and Sorokin's view of the West began to seem less unduly alarmist.

All the thinkers infer that moving freely in whatever gloom of circumstance exists is better than sitting helpless in the dark of ignorance or false optimism. As Toynbee said, "How, I ask you, can one lift up one's heart and apply one's mind unless one does one's best to find out the relevant facts and to look them in the face?—the formidable facts as well as the encouraging ones."[13] The social philosophers are dealing with what they saw to be a sick society as a doctor would deal with an ailing patient. Diagnosing social and cultural malaise that many people sense but few comprehend, they reveal what they find truthfully and courageously.

Meanwhile, some of the thinkers hold out hope that the civilization might not die after all. As Burckhardt hoped for spiritual renewal, Schweitzer is emphatic that an ethical philosophy preached and practiced could restore the failing civilized order. Likewise, Toynbee never gave up hope that a declining society can rise and bloom again, if only its people meet the challenge of their time with a successful response—the challenge of the present being voluntary world unity, which he saw as best attained through the spiritual redemption of souls. Similarly, Sorokin calls out to right-minded people to renounce the materialistic, sense-based existence and embrace altruism as a way of life to save themselves from disaster and prepare the way for cultural renewal.

Even if the culture is to pass away, many of the thinkers find more reason for hope than despair. How one views the tenor of their writings—as ultimately despairing or hopeful—depends to a large extent on where one places hope: in the culture of the present or in humanity's potential to survive and thrive despite the rises and falls that mark the past and well might shape the future. In a sense, the most determinedly optimistic were those who saw an apocalyptic tide sweeping away the foundations of a hopelessly decrepit civilization.

Schubart, for example, describes the present culture as uneasy, satiated, stale, its aims not working out to anything but harm, its mood one of hatred for its own fading era coupled with a yearning for self-destruction, its immediate future a time of suicidal downfall. But the present catastrophe, he believes, will prove ultimately beneficial, clearing the way for his Messianic age of reconciliation and love.

In a similar way does Berdyaev look beyond his despair of the present to inspiring hope for the future. He perceives modern humanity as weak and empty, exhausted of creative powers, a pale shadow of enthusiastic forebears, faithless, weary, and ready to rest upon any kind of collectivism. From such people can come no renaissance. They lack the substance for rebuilding. Yet he envisions, beyond collapse of the present social order, the advent of his new Middle Ages when people, returning to ascetic living, will recover inner strength and once more rise and flourish as inwardly rich human beings.

Lasaulx and Danilevsky, Spengler and Sorokin also look beyond a period of upheaval and destruction to the rise of a vital new civilization. Most of the writings of the social observers describe the era to come as far better than the present in purely human terms. No longer will people, by following their society, spend their days slogging dully through the empty forms of a worn-out way of life, bewildered by disintegrating customs and morals, beset by a sense of striving without purpose, spiritually impoverished and morally depraved, frantically indulging swollen appetites to stave off hopelessness. Rather, they shall live and grow in a world ethically humane, unified, godly, and newly creative.

THE PROGRESS OF DECLINE

In 1683, a Polish army repulsed the Turks from their second siege of Vienna, ending once and for all the Moslem threat against Europe. That event also marked the beginning of Western hegemony over the world. In 1781, the English historian Edward Gibbon, writing in his *Decline and Fall of the Roman Empire*, questioned whether the kind of terrible catastrophe that befell Rome in the fifth century after Christ could overtake Western civilization. From the confident viewpoint of his day, he concluded that to be inconceivable. For a long time thereafter, few people found reason to contradict his verdict. Citizens of Western lands felt they were different, unique, not as other people were or ever had been. They took it for granted that their civilization would spread across the earth and prevail lastingly. Not until the concussion of the First World War shattered the culture's global domination, faith in progress, confidence in itself, and time-honored system of morality and values did thoughtful people begin to suspect that Western civilization might not be immortal.

Yet is Western civilization—or in Sorokin's terms, the modern sensate system—really declining? Can it be proven that modern Western culture as it now exists is passing away? The answer to that must be in the negative. The death of a human culture, like the demise of anything else, cannot be proven until it has occurred. We can only gather data, examine evidence, seek to gauge its condition, and make a prognosis. Yet some parallels with past patterns of decline seem obvious.

Spengler's "Period of the Contending States"— or Toynbee's "time of troubles"—appears to have blighted the twentieth century with wars matching similar events in ancient Chinese culture and other past civilizations. Sorokin, measuring the past statistically, concurred that modern wars are far from normal and signal a major cultural shift. If the social seers are correct, the period of great wars is not yet over, since a "universal state," or global government, is the final result of the spell of suicidal statecraft.

Not only massive wars but many other common schisms of cultural disintegration divide present-day world society—both Toynbee's "external proletariat" and "internal proletariat," both politically and socially. At the fringes of Western influence, many areas once reasonably stable and livable under imperial rule or Western custody are unraveling and coming apart. Southeast Asia, India, Sri Lanka, all groan with ethnic tensions. Africa's web of old colonial borders has turned to crisscrossing faultlines of present or potential separation. The label "failed states" has been invented to describe former nations now collapsed and considered irreparable. Meanwhile, as Sorokin long ago predicted, great hordes of people displaced from lands and homes wander the earth as refugees.

The Western world, as well, is turning into a messy stew of diversity. The United Kingdom sees separatist reassertions among Welsh and Scots. Catholics and Protestants have filled Ulster's streets with blood. Flemish and Walloons discriminate in Belgium; Basques and Catalans in Spain; Jurassians in Switzerland; Serbs, Croats, and Bosnians in onetime Yugoslavia; Québecois in Canada. In America the social mix that British playwright Israel Zangwill in 1914 first called *The Melting Pot* is separating out into Hispanic-Americans, African-Americans, Native-Americans, WASPS. Citizens born to the land assert that they are proud to be Italian, Irish, Polish, Greek, and Armenian, though not necessarily American. Following severe riots in Los Angeles in 1992, the *London Independent* made bold to write, "The United States is unwinding strand by strand, rather like the Soviet Union, Yugoslavia, or Northern Ireland."[14]

Hardly anyone was prepared for the breakup of the Soviet Union in 1991, but even less for vicious outbreaks of ethnic bitterness among the former union's 189 or so nationalities. As the *New York Times* reported in May 1992, "The roll call of warring nations invokes some forgotten primer on the warring tribes of the Dark Ages—Ossetians, Georgians, Abkhasians, Daghestanis, Azeris, Armenians,

Moldavians, Russians, Ukrainians, Gaugauz, Tatars, Tajiks."[15] Regarding Yugoslavia's shattering into historic subgroups, *The Economist* magazine speculated in December 1991: "Yugoslavia's may well be the war of the future, one waged by different tribes, harbouring centuries-old grudges about language, religion, and territory, and provoking bitterness for generations to come."[16]

American news correspondent and scholar Harold R. Isaacs observes, "What we have been experiencing . . . is not the shaping of new coherences but the world breaking into its bits and pieces, bursting like big and little stars from exploding galaxies, each one spinning off into its own centrifugal whirl, each one straining to hold its own small separate pieces from spinning off in their turn."[17] Isaacs continues, "We are experiencing on a massively universal scale a convulsive ingathering of people in their numberless groupings of kinds—tribal, racial, linguistic, religious, national. It is a great clustering into separateness that will, it is thought, improve, assure, or extend each group's power or place, or keep it safe or safer from the power, threat, or hostility of others."[18]

Schisms drive deep within public institutions, communities, businesses, religions, families. They are commonly expressed in weakened ethical restraints, decreasing trust, increasing crime, suicide, sexual license, divorce, and economic insecurity. No less significant are agonizing schisms sundering people's souls—a mental and emotional malaise sociologists and poets, psychologists and novelists speak of as "anomie," "social dysfunction," and various forms of alienation.

As another symptom of decline, megacities far more vast than Spengler envisioned eat into the countryside and suck the people off the land. In their decadent atmosphere of refinement and brutality, people spend lives full of high tension in work, play, and human relationships that ultimately are bereft of satisfying meaning. The Western-style megalopolis sprawls not only at the core of the culture in Rome and London, New York and Los Angeles, but also at its fringes in Bangkok and Cairo, Tokyo, Manila, and Jakarta.

The fine arts, no longer a cultural necessity, have fallen subservient to commerce, with works no longer valued for their beauty but rather as "important" or commanding high prices. We see art playing Spengler's tedious game with old forms and formlessness, producing the spectacular, the colossal, the best-seller and, above all, the transitory.

Not only in the arts but in every regard, Sorokin's sensate culture obviously is bumping up against its ultimate limits. Even sensate pleasures sate, cripple, and kill the people who embrace them most fully.

Also in line with cultural disintegration, postmodernist thinkers, many holding influential positions in universities, are losing faith in the learning of the culture. Growing skeptical about the very objectivity of knowledge, they doubt even the findings of science, still the healthiest department of the culture. Science writer John Horgan, while not disbelieving in the objectivity of science, thinks its very triumph in uncovering universal truths endangers its future. The time is approaching, he says, when the large questions science can answer will be depleted, with only details remaining as an exercise in filling smaller gaps. Sounding much like Spengler, Horton writes in his 1996 book, *The End of Science: Facing the Limits of Knowledge in the Twilight of the Scientific Age*, "Given how far science has already come, and given the physical, social, and cognitive limits constraining further research, science is unlikely to make any significant additions to the knowledge it has already generated. There will be no great revelations in the future comparable to those bestowed upon us by Darwin or Einstein or Watson and Crick."[19] Horgan grants that major challenges remain in the field, including understanding the origin of life and the nature of consciousness. He maintains, however, that those enigmas will be worked out within the limits of present theories without the need of any revolutionary discoveries in a future that for the craft is largely closed.

Historian John M. Roberts shares Horgan's mood of cultural conclusions. In his 1996 book, *A History of Europe*, he writes that

Europe's work "is done." Its knowledge and ideologies have been absorbed by non-European societies, as Toynbee predicted of the external proletariat, and turned against it. Its world-historical role is eroding away. Any claim to be the inheritor of Christendom makes no sense, he believes, in a "neo-pagan and post-Christian society." Likewise, Harvard scholar Samuel P. Huntington sees the West in decline and threatened by resurgent civilizations.

Is Toynbee's universal state being readied by a global leveling of cultures? Theodore Levitt, a marketing specialist, in a well-known article printed in the *Harvard Business Review* in 1983 predicted a world of "global markets for globally standardized products." Low-cost communication and transportation are delivering a vastly broader range of goods from everywhere to everywhere as never before. Meanwhile cyberspace, satellite hookups, television programs, and universal consumption spread cosmopolitan ideas, tastes, and behavior evenly around the world.

To be sure, such global trends are confusing, even contradictory. People are linked without being neighbors, fellow citizens, participants in a common venture, or even necessarily cordial toward each other. They might have all the devices for affiliation and still be at each other's throats. Given existing social schisms, it seems that world society is simultaneously coming together and flying apart as trends pull in opposite directions: a need to pool the earth's resources versus a longing for tribal community; the universal humanity that technology requires versus militant divisions; a need for order versus an appetites for chaos. How can a global village drawn ever closer by multinational communications, economics, ideologies, entertainment, and consumer fashions sustain such contradictions?

Caesarism, Spengler would answer: world dictatorship uniting the earth by force. Toynbee and Sorokin offer two alternatives: voluntary world union based on altruism and spiritual renewal, or dictatorship.

As another standard feature of disintegration, and a reaction as well, rediscovery of the spiritual side of life is coming on fast throughout Western culture—with the usual cosmopolitan collection of spirits: traditional and exotic, divine and demonic. This spontaneous revival has been gaining momentum at least since the 1960s, as people jaded by materialism and depleted by sensuality come to understand from their emptiness and pain that they are not merely body and intellect but also soul. Meanwhile, religious renewals and conversions are spreading rapidly over all the earth. Christians, Moslems, and other pious groups full of emotional intensity offer moral guidance and mutual support for lost souls wandering through alienated societies and in the swelling slums of big cities. To what extent the new spiritualities will unite or divide, clarify or confuse, ennoble or debase is one more matter that remains for the future to reveal.

The Future of the West

Many of the analysts compare the West's decline to that of ancient Rome, recalling the late days of the classical culture as vulgar, cosmopolitan, scientific, and groping for faith. Perhaps appropriately, readers of Spengler, Toynbee, and Sorokin have compared them to thinkers of those ancient times: the scholar St. Jerome, the theologian St. Augustine, and the Christian preacher Salvian, all of whom wrote of the decay of Roman civilization during the final few generations before its collapse.

Yet not all the observers of the modern West expect its imminent downfall. Some, like Henry Adams, Berdyaev, and Sorokin, see an end near at hand, but others, like Spengler and Toynbee, believe the culture might plod on for centuries. Meanwhile, most of the analysts agree that certain master trends measure out the stages of decline.

As disintegrations' period of chaos continues, which way the card castle of the rickety society might fall seems anyone's guess. A serious economic breakdown, which many economists fear, would have a powerful effect in a global economy. Worse is a continuance of the kind of military catastrophe that already marks the twentieth century as the bloodiest in all history. With fearsome technologies of destruction in place in countries great and small, this peril seems likely to rise repeatedly.

Though the Soviet Union and the old Cold War is gone, Russia retains the potential of a large and influential world force. China, newly powerful and confident, also can challenge present balances of power as the largest international player in history.

Through most of the twentieth century, political alignments have been defined by ideologies or superpower relations. According to leading modern thinkers, including playwright and Czech president Vaclav Havel and Harvard scholar Huntington, future global wars will hinge not on ideologies but on cultures, as many of the social thinkers in this book either state or imply. All over the world, notes Huntington, peoples and nations with similar cultures are coming together, while dissimilar peoples and cultures are splitting apart. Alignments are forming along the lines of cultural communities and seven or eight civilizations, including Western, Islamic, Chinese, Indian, and Russian-Slavic-Orthodox. Huntington hopes that countries of the declining West will band together for mutual support and greater strength. To avoid war, he advises, the world should form spheres of influence based on civilizations, with each carefully respecting the uniqueness of the others. Meanwhile, with Toynbee, he urges peoples in all civilizations to think globally, identifying and extending the values, institutions, and customs they have in common.

Permanent social breakdown, as some modern doomsday prophets envision and much popular fiction portrays, seems least likely. Almost everywhere governments remain well organized and mighty. Anyone fearing a Mad Max future need only note growing mechanisms of social control spontaneously evolving throughout society: high tech, low privacy, everybody numbered, and no place to hide.

Barring civilization's total collapse as a consequence of nuclear war or other causes, a spell of major chaos would bring down a firm hand to reinforce order—probably with the full consent of distraught citizens. The smaller breakdown of Germany's Weimar Republic in the 1920s illustrated that with the rise and broad acceptance of the Nazi party.

Spengler sees the nations of the world coming together some time after the year 2000. Judging from patterns in the past, the earth then will be writhing under warring rival Caesars. Ultimately one will triumph, striking Toynbee's knock-out blow, and merge all nations into global empire. Toynbee also judges violent union to be probable unless present nationalism, which he sees as obsolescent, gives way to voluntary world government. The English historian expected union to come soon, whether peacefully or not. In a speech at Edinburgh in 1952, he forecast that "within half a century the whole face of the planet will have been unified politically through the concentration of irresistible military power in some single set of hands."[20]

The more intense the chaos, the more likely will dictatorship arise to enforce peace and slow the progress of decline. This domination that historians call "Caesarism" might even be hailed as salvation by a frightened, weakened people welcoming their new master for bringing relief after terrifying times. Longing for security, they could even elevate him to the status of divinity.

In any case, the Caesar, the Iron Heel, the *Führer*, the Big Brother, the policeman of history should come as no surprise to modern people, who are amply forewarned in the writings of Proudhon, Burckhardt, Berdyaev, Jack London, Aldous Huxley, George Orwell, Spengler, Toynbee, Sorokin, and any number of other social seers.

The rise of a Slavic civilization occupies the speculations of many of the long-term thinkers. Schubart sees the West's hard men of action, having failed to rebuild the world to human standards, giving way in the present transition to Messianic Russians, who possess as a national characteristic a tendency to other-worldliness and will fashion a culture of the spirit. Then Russia, already a blend of East and West, will serve as a bridge for the two hemispheres to meet and merge, thus fulfilling the greatest spiritual task the human race ever has undertaken. The result will be one world-man, a fusion of the mental types of Orient and Occident.

A century earlier, Lasaulx rested hope for a new and rising culture on Eastern European Christian Slavs. In 1869, Danilevsky asserted that the Slavs were waiting on the verge of their most creative period and that a Slavic federation under Russian leadership would take up the torch of civilization from an exhausted West. Spengler, nearly fifty years later, also believed that the next great culture might arise in Russia.

Toynbee considered that the Russians might assume a dual role in shaping the future. First, he saw Russia serving as a medium for Westernizing non-Western peoples, its influence and aid helping them catch up industrially and economically. Second, he noted the Slavic country leading worldwide resistance to Western power. In various books he indicates how aggression from West to East has been going on for centuries but lately has reversed to flow the other way. Before 1917, the West was winning converts to its ideology in every corner of the globe. But after the close of the First World War, Russia, armed with Western technology and the Western political creed of Communism, placed the West on the defensive with the greatest challenge the culture had faced since the Turks withdrew from Vienna in 1683. "Considering how overwhelming the West's ascendancy over most of the rest of the World had been during the preceding quarter of a millennium, Communist Russia's feat of turning the tables on the West was impressive," Toynbee declared.[21] With the battle moving off the technological plane and onto the spiritual level, the West could not be as self-assured about its superiority.

The collapse of Communism in the 1990s could presage all the more a new era for Russia and its Slavic neighbors. As Schubart predicted, "the gray misery of the Soviet period" would pass, "as did the black night of the Tartar yoke." Russia's history has been full of false Western dawns—from Peter the Great to Catherine the Great to the revolution of 1917. Marxist Communism, one more Western light, proved contrary to the nature of the Russian people and was extinguished. Perhaps, as Schubart also predicted, the country will turn spiritually away from the West and back to the East. Possibly, as several of the thinkers foresaw, fresh spiritual beginnings among Slavic peoples will release the floodgate to their reservoir of spiritual depth and irrigate a new and unique civilization embodying the spirit of compromise and reconciliation, forgiveness and love.

Wherever its center happens to settle and whatever peoples are its leaders, the next dominant culture, according to most of the thinkers, will differ radically from the civilization that has shaped the West over the past five hundred years. Its principal concern will not lie with developing the physical environment. Rather, it will be dedicated to developing human beings.

As Albert Schweitzer hoped that Western peoples would rebuild humane ethics and halt decay in time to save the civilization, other thinkers carry the idea of human and social regeneration further, from earthly ethics to the realm of religion. Burckhardt, though less hopeful for the current social order, sees renewal of a religious spirit as the only influence that can transform the society and its people. Danilevsky foresees his future Russian-Slavic culture blossoming not only in worldly creativity but in religion as well. Schubart's Messianic age is a period of the spirit triumphant. Berdyaev, affirming "that man's creative forces cannot be regenerated or his identity reestablished except by a renewal of religious asceticism," predicts that religion will irradiate the whole of life in his new Middle Ages to come.

According to Spengler, religious renewal is the last gasp of a dying civilization, the "second religiousness" that in cultural wintertime springs from tortured consciences and spiritual hunger. Toynbee, agreeing that a valley for society tends to become a summit for religion, also sees that civilizations regularly end with a "universal church" rising from their ruin. And Toynbee carried the story further.

He showed the church preserving the vestiges of the old culture's life, then going on to serve as a womb for new civilization. Thus do Spengler and Toynbee agree with other thinkers that the future promises religious renaissance. Spengler adds that the new Russian culture which might replace the current social order will found itself upon a primitive Christianity of the Gospels to which the next millennium will belong.

Finally, Sorokin sees the present overripe and rotting sensate culture giving way to one of two alternative modes of living: either a new ideational age of faith and spiritual growth, or an integral age when life will be guided by a combination of senses, reason, and faith, with faith predominating.

In one way or another, nearly all the observers of modern culture and society see a burned-out civilization, built upon exploitation of the environment, offering its ashes to the blossoming shoots of an age of human renewal.

Living with the Future

How might we live with the future the social seers describe? If we disbelieve that the West is declining, we can simply coast ahead, trusting in the culture that tells us what to do and joining its followers in the general society. If, on the other hand, we allow that the premise of decline might be more or less correct, the patterns in the past suggest useful lessons from collective human experience.

Some four hundred years before Christ, the Greek historian Thucydides wrote that "the accurate knowledge of what has happened will be useful because according to human probability similar things will happen again." In the second century B.C., another Greek, Polybius, who compiled a history of the Mediterranean world, amplified that idea when he wrote, "The knowledge gained from the study of true history is the best of all educations for practical life. For it is history and history alone which, without involving us in actual danger, will mature our judgment and prepare us to take right views, whatever may be the crisis or posture of affairs."[22] More than two thousand years later, Toynbee echoed the same thought, remarking, "Uneasiness is a challenging call to action, and not a death sentence to paralyze our wills. Thank goodness we do know the fates of the other civilizations; such knowledge is a chart that warns us of the reefs ahead. Knowledge can be power and salvation if we have the spirit to use it."[23]

If we learn from the past as Toynbee and his fellow social thinkers saw it, can we halt the decline they have perceived in modern Western culture? Though many social thinkers agree that decay is not a matter of destiny, even the most hopeful acknowledge that restoration of the culture can occur only as a major social movement. Such a movement presently is not in evidence.

So what else can we do? How can we apply their revelations? To date, social thinkers have little to say about that. No one has presented a manual for living in the increasingly turbulent world they describe. The works condensed in this book read only like barometers warning of storms ahead. They do not even suggest methods to avoid the storms but only advise that we brace ourselves, so that if and when turbulence strikes we will not be caught off guard and hurled into helpless confusion.

Yet the writings, intentionally or not, offer keys to liberation from a questionable culture and society. They stimulate fresh thought about past and present, cause and effect, peoples, institutions, and human relationships. Also, by confirming the now-widespread suspicion that modern Western culture has gone seriously awry, they help resolve confusion and relieve anxiety born of uncertainty. More useful still, the works provide a basis for cultural comparison, which aids escape from the ethnocentric trap of regarding the culture of one's own time and place as a standard beyond doubt or question to be followed blindly. All the social thinkers imply that modern people no longer should look to their society for guidance, safety, or salvation. Such knowledge can help free us from automatic conformity to seek a better way. In these regards and others, the works of these thinkers promote a rare degree of objective cultural insight, preparing us psychologically to depend less on the culture and more on our personal integrity.

The works also carry some practical advice for living with decline. Spengler, the master doomsayer, warns modern youth that the fine arts are spurious and dead and advises them to take up technology instead of the muses, transportation rather than the paintbrush, politics instead of philosophy.

Toynbee lays out social trends of disintegrative periods like a blueprint. Understanding those, we can better find our way through the increasingly confusing labyrinth of disintegration. Having been made aware of schisms in the culture, we can work to change the course of some, sidestep others, and accept with equanimity those we cannot influence or avoid. He warns of reactions developing within souls: contrasting tendencies toward moral abandon and ascetic self-control; dropping out of the society or martyring oneself to some lofty ideal; an agonizing sense of drift or a sense of sin that leads to self-correction. Discerning these inclinations, we can fend off undesirable reactions before they begin.

Toynbee also warns of decomposition that erodes a declining civilization, eating away its cultural style and leaving promiscuity in manners and customs, art and language, philosophy and religion. Comprehending decomposition helps us to accept our losses and not rail against the inevitable and shows how people of spiritual strength can see through the chaotic promiscuity, and arrive at a sense of unity and brotherhood of man—a goal for us all.

The historian points out the avenues of escape commonly taken by people of decline as they try to flee realities they find intolerable. He shows how archaists try to slip back into the past and futurists live for times that will not come. He describes disciples of detachment withdrawing into the solitude of their souls, and then he warns that all these avenues are dead ends. The only route of escape he finds in some two dozen decaying civilizations is personal transcendence with its goal in the kingdom of God. Finally, Toynbee warns of false social saviors who emerge at times of disintegration: leaders who establish universal states, archaist and futurist saviors, saviors-by-detachment who rule as philosopher kings. Yet the sole, effective savior he finds in history he proclaims also as the only savior for the present—Almighty God and his savior-son, Jesus Christ. The agnostic scholar then advises us to pray to God for a reprieve from disaster.

Sorokin did not believe that the analysis of social change he presented in *Dynamics* offers any solution for the dilemmas and difficulties facing modern Western people. He hoped only that his findings would help people comprehend the dangers they are facing and recognize the need for a new way of living before the old way collapses into ruins. He tells us first to save ourselves by abandoning the sinking ship of sensate culture and pursuing values of the spirit, above all "creative altruism." If enough of us do that, then the dying sensate age might evolve into a well-balanced idealistic culture, which we would probably prefer to the chastening and severe ascetic ideational culture that otherwise is likely to form.

Beyond this scanty counsel, the thinkers of this book leave us to manage our own program for survival. That, perhaps, will be the subject of other books to come. Meanwhile, though the prospect of cultural collapse carries a heady fascination, it seems unwholesome to dwell upon the subject unduly. Beyond healthy constructive action, we are best advised, as the Swiss historian Jacob Burckhardt put it, to "preserve good humor and sleep at night," since "people are not made better or wiser by continually staring into chaos."[24]

Notes

1. *Progress and Doubt*

1. *Illustrated London News,* 3 August 1878, as reprinted in *History as Hot News,* ed. Leonard de Vries (New York: St. Martin's, 1973), 102.

2. *Illustrated London News,* 31 July 1897, ibid., 159.

3. *Illustrated London News,* 25 August 1894, ibid.

4. Hilaire Belloc, from his burlesque poem "Electric Light," quoted by Arnold J. Toynbee in *A Study of History,* ab. D.C. Somervell (New York: Oxford University, 1947–1957), II:99.

2. *The Alarm Sounds*

1. Quoted by Barbara W. Tuchman in *The Proud Tower* (New York: Macmillan, 1966), 55.

2. Rudyard Kipling in *Something of Myself* (Garden City, New York: Doubleday, Doran, 1937), 159.

3. "Recessional" appears in Rudyard Kipling, *The Five Nations* (Garden City, New York: Doubleday, Page, 1926), 214–5.

4. Henry Adams in *The Degradation of the Democratic Dogma,* intro. Brooks Adams (New York: Macmillan, 1919), 180.

5. E.L. Godkin, editor of the *New York Evening Post* and the *Nation,* as quoted by Barbara W. Tuchman in *The Proud Tower* (New York: Macmillan, 1966), 138–9.

6. For more of Henry Adams's social thought, see Part III of this book.

7. Max Nordau, *Degeneration* (New York: Appleton, 1895), 2.

8. Ibid., 1.

9. Ibid., 5.

10. Tuchman, *Proud Tower,* 391.

11. Charles Masterman, Under-Secretary of the Home Office, in *The Condition of England* (London: 1909), as quoted by Tuchman, ibid., 382.

12. Tolstoy quoted by Karl Lowith in *Meaning in History* (Chicago: University of Chicago, 1949), 99.

13. Quoted from Feodor Dostoyevsky's *Diary of a Writer,* August 1880, by Lowith, ibid., 98.

14. Baudelaire quoted by Lowith, ibid., 97–8.

15. From a selection entitled "Miscellany," *The Philosophical Dictionary,* in *The Portable Voltaire,* ed. B.R. Redman (New York: Viking, 1949).

16. Proudhon quoted by Erich Fromm in *The Sane Society* (New York: Rinehart, 1955), 211, trans. Erich Fromm.

17. Nobel quoted by Tuchman, *Proud Tower,* 233.

18. Ibid.

19. Ibid.

20. Burckhardt quoted by James Hastings Nichols in his introduction to Jacob Burckhardt, *Force and Freedom,* ed. James Hastings Nichols (New York: Pantheon, 1943), 20.

21. Burckhardt quoted from a letter of 26 December 1892, in Lowith, *Meaning in History,* 28.

22. Burckhardt quoted from a letter in H. Stuart Hughes, *Oswald Spengler: A Critical Estimate* (New York: Scribner's, 1952), 18.

23. Burckhardt quoted by Nichols in Burckhardt, *Force and Freedom,* 41.

24. Burckhardt quoted from a letter in Hughes, *Oswald Spenger: Critical Estimate,* 17.

25. Burckhardt quoted by Peter G. Bietenhol in "Burckhardt, Jacob," *Encyclopaedia Britannica, Macropaedia,* 15th ed. (Chicago: Encyclopaedia Brittanica, 1981), 3:483–4.

26. Burckhardt quoted from a letter of 1872, in Lowith, *Meaning in History,* 24.

27. Quoted by Nichols in Burckhardt, *Force and Freedom,* 43.

28. Ibid., 48.

29. Burckhardt quoted from a letter of 21 April 1872, in Lowith, *Meaning in History,* 27.

30. Burckhardt quoted by Lowith, ibid., 31.

31. Burckhardt quoted from a letter of 21 April 1872, ibid., 28.

32. Nordau, *Degeneration,* 16.

33. Ibid., 41–2.
34. Ibid., 42.
35. Ibid.
36. Ibid.
37. Ibid., 537.
38. Ibid., 243.
39. Ibid., 244.
40. Ibid., 254.
41. Ibid., 536.
42. Ibid.
43. Ibid., 7.
44. Ibid.
45. Ibid., 538.
46. Ibid., 538–9.
47. Ibid., 540.
48. Max Nordau, *Degeneration* (London: Heinemann, 1895), intro.
49. Quoted by Henry Adams, *Degradation of the Democratic Dogma,* 253–4.
50. R.D. Laing, *The Politics of Experience* (New York: Pantheon, 1967), 12.
51. *Reader's Digest*, May 1975, 112.
52. Pitirim A. Sorokin in *S.O.S.: The Meaning of Our Crisis* (Boston: Beacon, 1951), 109.
53. Jack London, *The Iron Heel* (New York: Macmillan, 1958), 112.
54. Ibid., 191 footnote.
55. H.G. Wells, *The Shape of Things to Come* (New York: Macmillan, 1934), 214.
56. Ibid., 212.
57. Ibid., 175–6.
58. Ibid., 245.
59. Ibid., 430.
60. H.G. Wells, *Mind at the End of Its Tether* (New York: Didier, 1946), 29–30.
61. Ibid., 8.
62. Ibid., 18.

3. *Visions of Decline*

1. Quoted by Jacob Burckhardt in *Force and Freedom*, ed. and intro. James Hastings Nichols (New York: Pantheon, 1943), 258.

2. Quoted by Nichols, ibid., 60.

3. Henry Adams, *Letters of Henry Adams* 1892–1918, ed. Worthington Chauncey Ford (Boston: Houghton Mifflin, 1938), 31 July 1896, 111.

4. Henry Adams, *The Education of Henry Adams* (New York: Modern Library, 1931), 331.

5. Henry Adams, *Letters of Henry Adams*, 111.

6. Ibid., 17 February 1896, 99.

7. Henry Adams, *The Degradation of the Democratic Dogma*, intro. Brooks Adams (New York: Macmillan, 1919), 166.

8. Noted by Lewis Mumford in *The Condition of Man* (New York: Harcourt Brace Jovanovich, 1973), 392.

9. Quoted by Timothy Paul Donovan in *Henry Adams and Brooks Adams* (Norman, Oklahoma: University of Oklahoma, 1961), 118.

10. Ibid.

11. Henry Adams, *Degradation of the Democratic Dogma*, 231.

12. Mumford, *Condition of Man*, 425.

13. Brooks Adams, *The Law of Civilization and Decay*, intro. Charles A. Beard (New York: Knopf, 1943), 349.

14. From a letter to Brooks Adams in Henry Adams, *Degradation of the Democratic Dogma*, 99.

15. Quoted by Beard in Brooks Adams, *Law of Civilization and Decay*, 48.

16. Ibid., 45.

17. Brooks Adams, ibid., dustcover.

18. Quoted from the Russian magazine *Zaria* (1869) by Pitirim A. Sorokin in *Social Philosophies in an Age of Crisis* (Boston: Beacon, 1950), 51.

19. Ibid., 52.

20. Ibid., 58.

21. Ibid., 67.

22. Ibid., 71.

23. Walter Schubart, *Russia and Western Man*, trans. Amethe von Zeppelin (New York: Ungar, 1950), 16.

24. Ibid.

25. Ibid., 286–7.

26. Ibid., 293.

27. Ibid., 26.

28. Ibid., 37.

29. Ibid., 36.

30. Ibid.

31. Ibid., 297.

32. Ibid., 295.
33. Ibid., 283.
34. Ibid.
35. Ibid., 298.
36. Ibid., 300.
37. Nicholas Berdyaev, *The End of Our Time*, trans. Donald Attwater (London: Sheed and Ward, 1933), 57–8.
38. Ibid., 12.
39. Ibid., 27.
40. Ibid., 42.
41. Ibid., 16.
42. Ibid., 33.
43. Ibid., 109.
44. Ibid., 113.
45. Ibid., 117.
46. Ibid.
47. Nicholas Berdyaev, *The Meaning of History*, trans. George Reavey (Cleveland: World, 1962), 191.
48. Berdyaev, *End of Our Time*, 119.
49. Ibid.
50. Berdyaev, *Meaning of History*, 158.
51. Albert Schweitzer, *The Philosophy of Civilization*, trans. C.T. Campion (New York: Macmillan, 1957), 1.
52. Ibid., 4.
53. Ibid., 17.
54. Ibid., 20.
55. Ibid., 39.
56. Ibid., 56.
57. Ibid., 46.
58. Ibid.
59. Ibid., 76.
60. Ibid., 281–2.
61. Ibid., 79.
62. Ibid., 310.
63. Ibid., 320.
64. Ibid., 321.
65. Ibid., 331.

4. *Spengler and Decline*

1. Quoted by H. Stuart Hughes in *Oswald Spengler: A Critical Estimate* (New York: Scribner's, 1952), 7.

2. Ibid., 92.

3. Quoted from W. Wolfradt in ibid., 89.

4. Quoted from Egon Friedell in ibid., 118.

5. Quoted from Eduard Meyer in ibid., 94.

6. Pitirim A. Sorokin in *Social Philosophies in an Age of Crisis* (Boston: Beacon, 1950), 72.

7. Ludwig von Bertalanffy in *Robots, Men and Minds* (New York: Braziller, 1967), 110.

8. Quoted by E. F. Dakin in Oswald Spengler, *Today and Destiny*, ed. E. F. Dakin (New York: Knopf, 1940), 358–9.

9. Quoted from Erich Heller by Bruce Mazlish, *The Riddle of History* (New York: Harper and Row, 1966), 308.

10. Oswald Spengler, *The Decline of the West*, trans. with notes by Charles Francis Atkinson (New York: Knopf, 1976), I:25.

11. Ibid., 22.

5. *The High Cultures*

1. Ibid., 174.
2. Ibid.
3. Ibid.
4. Ibid., 201.
5 Spengler , *Decline*, II:383.
6. Ibid., 42.
7. Spengler, *Decline,* I:183.
8. Spengler, *Decline,* II:237.
9. Spengler, *Decline,* I:172.
10. Ibid., 395.
11. Ibid., 309.
12. Ibid., 177–8.
13. Spengler, *Decline,* II:491.
14. Ibid., 492.
15. Spengler, *Decline,* I:76.
16. Ibid., 67.
17. Spengler, *Decline,* II:301.
18. Ibid., 501.

19. Ibid., 503.

6. *Culture and Civilization*

1. Ibid., 170–1.
2. Spengler, *Decline,* I, 106.
3. Spengler, *Decline,* II:334.
4. Ibid., 296–7.
5. Ibid., 304.
6. Ibid., 427 footnote.
7. Ibid., 104.
8. Ibid., 13.
9. Spengler, *Decline,* I:380.
10. Ibid., 356.
11. Ibid., 291.
12. Ibid., 294.
13. Ibid., 295.
14. Ibid., 37.
15. Spengler, *Decline,* II:170–1.
16. Spengler, *Decline,* I, 38.
17. Spengler, *Decline,* II:431.
18. Ibid., 101.
19. Ibid., 430.
20. Ibid., 454.
21. Spengler, *Decline,* I:361, 363.
22. Ibid., 231.
23. Ibid., 294.
24. Ibid., 293.
25. Ibid., 90.
26. Ibid., 424–5.
27. Spengler, *Decline,* II:83.
28. Spengler, *Decline,* I:37.
29. Spengler, *Decline,* II:465.
30. Ibid., 505.
31. Spengler, *Decline,* I:167.
32. Oswald Spengler, *Man and Technics*, trans. Charles Francis Atkinson (New York: Knopf, 1932), 103.
33. Spengler, *Decline,* II:504 footnote.
34. Spengler, *Decline,* I:40–1.
35. Spengler, *Decline,* II:507.

7. *Toynbee and History*

1. Arnold J. Toynbee, *Experiences* (New York and London: Oxford University, 1969), 14.

2. Arnold J. Toynbee, *Civilization on Trial* (New York: Oxford University, 1948), 8.

3. Arnold J. Toynbee, *The World After the Peace Conference* (London: Oxford University, 1925), 88.

4. M. F. Ashley Montagu, ed., *Toynbee and History: Critical Essays and Reviews*, (Boston: Porter Sargent, 1956), 3.

5. Pieter Geyl, longtime professor of modern history at the University of Utrecht, the Netherlands, in Geyl et al., *The Pattern of the Past: Can We Determine It?* (New York: Greenwood, 1968), 15.

6. Christian Gauss, Dean of Princeton University from 1925 to 1945, as quoted by E. F. Dakin in Oswald Spengler, *Today and Destiny*, ed. E. F. Dakin (New York: Knopf, 1940), 357.

7. Kenneth Winetrout, *Arnold Toynbee: The Ecumenical Vision* (Boston: Hall, 1975), 94.

8. Quoted from the *Observer* in *Time* magazine, 3 November 1975, 49.

9. Toynbee, *Experiences*, 127.

10. Arnold J. Toynbee, *A Study of History* (London: Oxford University, 1934–1961), X: 3.

11. Christopher Dawson, historian and writer, as quoted by Winetrout, *Toynbee: Ecumenical Vision*, 17.

12. Pitirim A. Sorokin in Geyl et al., *The Pattern of the Past: Can We Determine It?* (New York: Greenwood, 1968), 107.

13. D.C. Somervell in his note by the editor of the abridgment, in Arnold J. Toynbee, *A Study of History*, ab. D.C. Somervell (New York: Oxford University, 1947–57), 1:ix.

14. Arnold J. Toynbee, *A Study of History*, ab. D.C. Somervell (New York: Oxford University, 1947–1957), 1:80.

15. Montagu, *Toynbee and History*, 125.

16. Quoted from a letter dated 22 September 1949 to Kenneth W. Thompson of the Rockefeller Foundation, ibid., 202–3.

8. *The Civilizations*

1. Toynbee, *Study*, III:380.

2. Toynbee, *Study*, XII:279.

3. Ibid., 546–7 and 558–61.

4. Quoted from Herodotus in Toynbee, *Study,* ab. Somervell, 1: 86.
5. Toynbee, *Study,* ab. Somervell, 1:146.
6. Ibid., 165.
7. Toynbee, *Study,* III:153.
8. Ibid., 173–4.
9. Toynbee, *Study,* I:428–9.
10. Toynbee, *Study,* ab. Somervell, 1:247.
11. Toynbee, *Study,* IV:8.
12. Toynbee, *Study,* ab. Somervell, 1:248 footnote.
13. Quoted from P. Aelius Aristeides (A.D. 117–89), *In Romam,* in Toynbee, *Study,* ab. Somervell, 2:7.
14. Quoted from the Bhagavadgita in Toynbee, *Study,* VI:146.
15. Quoted from Epictetus, *Dissertationes,* in Toynbee, *Study,* VI:147 footnote.
16. Quoted from Lord Thomas Macaulay, Essay on "History," in Toynbee, *Study,* ab. Somervell, 1:362.
17. Toynbee, *Study,* ab. Somervell, 1:557.
18. Thomas Hobbes, *Leviathan* (London: Dent, 1965), 65 (originally published in 1651).
19. Toynbee, *Study,* ab. Somervell, 2:104.
20. Toynbee, *Study,* VII, 423.

9. *Prospects for the West*

1. Toynbee, *Study,* VI:320.
2. Toynbee, *Study,* IX:608.
3. Ibid., 608–9.
4. Toynbee, *Study,* XII:531.
5. Toynbee, *Study,* ab. Somervell, 1:245.
6. William Ralph Inge in *The Idea of Progress,* quoted in Toynbee, *Study,* ab. Somervell, 1:419.
7. Toynbee, *Study,* ab. Somervell, 1:259.
8. Toynbee, *Study,* VI:314.
9. Toynbee, *Study,* ab. Somervell, 2:326.
10. Toynbee, *Study,* ab. Somervell, 1:552.
11. Ibid., 554.
12. Quoted from an interview in *Playboy* magazine, April 1967, by Winetrout, *Toynbee: Ecumenical Vision,* 59.
13. Arnold J. Toynbee in Geyl et al., *The Pattern of the Past: Can We Determine It?* (New York: Greenwood, 1968), 76.

14. Toynbee, *Study*, ab. Somervell, 1:254.
15. Toynbee, *Study*, IX:411.
16. Toynbee, *Study*, VII:428.
17. Toynbee, *Study*, ab. Somervell, 2:26.

10. *Sorokin and the Crisis of the West*

1. Professor E.A. Ross in a letter to Sorokin quoted in Pitirim A. Sorokin, *A Long Journey* (New Haven, Connecticut: College and University, 1963), 223.

2. Wilbert Moore quoted in *Newsweek* magazine, 7 September 1964, 80.

3. Carle C. Zimmerman, who taught with Sorokin at Minnesota and Harvard Universities, noted that Sorokin had a photoscopic memory in Carle C. Zimmerman, *Sorokin, the World's Greatest Sociologist* (Saskatoon, Canada: University of Saskatchewan, 1968), 14.

4. John F. Cuber in *Sorokin and Sociology*, ed. G. C. Hallen and Rajeshwar Prasad (Agra, India: Satish, 1972), 155.

5. Quoted by Mexican sociologist Lucio Mendieta y Nunez in *Pitirim A. Sorokin in Review*, ed. Philip J. Allen (Durham, North Carolina: Duke University, 1963), 325.

6. Pitirim A. Sorokin in *Social and Cultural Dynamics* (New York: American Book, 1937–41), III:vii.

7. Arnold Toynbee in Hallen and Prasad, *Sorokin and Sociology*, 281.

8. Sorokin, *Long Journey*, 260.

9. Orville Prescott in the *New York Times*, quoted on the back cover of Pitirim A. Sorokin, *The Crisis of Our Age* (New York: Dutton, 1941).

10. Quoted by F.R. Cowell in *Values in Human Society* (Boston: Porter Sargent, 1970), 294.

11. Cowell, ibid., 275.

12. Sorokin, *Long Journey*, 271.

13. Ibid., 276.

14. Allen, *Sorokin in Review*, 31.

15. Toynbee in Hallen and Prasad, *Sorokin and Sociology*, 282.

16. Sorokin, *Dynamics*, I:67.

17. Sorokin in an article titled "A Survey of Cyclical Conceptions of Social and Historical Processes," *Journal of Social Forces* (Chapel Hill, North Carolina: September 1927), as quoted by Zimmerman, *Sorokin, the World's Greatest Sociologist*, 32.

18. Sorokin, *Dynamics*, IV:743.

11. *Changes in the Arts*

1. Sorokin, *Dynamics,* I:327.
2. Blaise Pascal quoted by Sorokin, *Dynamics,* I:339.
3. Sorokin, *Dynamics,* I:362.
4. Quoted from A. de Ridder and W. Deonna, *Art in Greece*, in Sorokin, *Dynamics,* I:516.
5. Quoted from F. Kimball and G.H. Edgell, *A History of Architecture,* in Sorokin, *Dynamics,* I:519.
6. Pliny, *Natural Histories*, quoted in Sorokin, *Dynamics,* I:563.
7. St. Augustine, *Confessions*, quoted in Sorokin, *Dynamics,* I:539.
8. Longinus quoted in Sorokin, *Dynamics,* I:611.
9. Quoted from J.W.H. Atkins, *English Literary Criticism: the Medieval Phase* by F.R. Cowell, *History, Civilization and Culture* (London: Thames and Hudson, 1952), 70–1.
10. Jean de Meung quoted in Sorokin, *Dynamics,* I:622.
11. Sorokin, *Dynamics,* I:649.

12. *Shifting Certainties*

1. Tommaso Campanella, Francis Bacon, and Gottfried von Leibniz quoted in Sorokin, *Dynamics,* II:109.
2. St. Augustine, *Confessions*, quoted in Sorokin, *Dynamics,* II:86.
3. Jacques Bossuet quoted in Sorokin, *Dynamics,* II:110.
4. Sorokin, *Dynamics,* II:118.
5. Ibid., 119.
6. Ibid., 201.
7. Ibid., 234–5.
8. Sir William Henry Bragg, *Electrons and Ether Waves*, quoted in Sorokin, *Dynamics,* II:462.
9. Sorokin, *Dynamics,* II:475.

13. *Shifting Human Bonds*

1. Ibid., 497.
2. John Wesley quoted from Max Weber, *The Protestant Ethic and the Spirit of Capitalism*, in Sorokin, *Dynamics,* II:505.
3. Benjamin Franklin quoted from Max Weber, *The Protestant Ethic and the Spirit of Capitalism*, in Sorokin, *Dynamics,* II:506.
4. Sorokin, *Dynamics,* II:507.

5. Ibid., 512.
6. Roman formula quoted by Sorokin, *Dynamics,* III:30–1.
7. Sorokin, *Dynamics,* III:43.
8. Epictetus, *Discourses*, quoted by Sorokin, *Dynamics,* III:166.
9. Lao-tse, *Canon on Reason and Virtue*, quoted by Sorokin, *Dynamics,* III:167.
10. Sorokin, *Dynamics,* III:256.
11. Ibid., 251.
12. Ibid., 261, 380.
13. Ibid., 503–4.
14. Ibid., 504.

14. *Toward a New Civilization*

1. Pitirim A. Sorokin, *Social Philosophies of an Age of Crisis* (Boston: Beacon, 1950), 298.
2. Sorokin, *Dynamics,* III:537.
3. Pitirim A. Sorokin, *The Crisis of Our Age* (New York: Dutton, 1941), 315.
4. Pitirim A. Sorokin, *The Reconstruction of Humanity* (Boston: Beacon, 1948), 238.
5. Arnold Toynbee in Allen, *Sorokin in Review*, 88.
6. Hallen and Prasad, *Sorokin and Sociology,* 198.
7. Sorokin, *Dynamics,* IV:775–7, and Pitirim A. Sorokin, *Man and Society in Calamity* (New York: Dutton, 1943), 308–17.
8. Sorokin, *Dynamics,* III:538.
9. R.M. Bartlett, *They Work for Tomorrow* (New York: Associated Press and Fleming H. Revell, 1943), 143–4.
10. Ibid., 144.
11. Sorokin, *Dynamics,* IV:770.
12. Sorokin in Allen, *Sorokin in Review*, 494, 473.
13. Sorokin, *Dynamics,* III:538–9.
14. Bartlett, *They Work,* 141–2.
15. Pitirim A. Sorokin, *The Basic Trends of Our Times* (New Haven, Connecticut: College and University, 1964), 155–6.
16. Sorokin, *Social Philosophies of an Age of Crisis*, 318–9.

Epilogue: Civilization and the Future

1. H.A.L. Fisher, *A History of Europe* (London: Eyre and Spottiswoode, 1935), I:vii.

2. Toynbee quoted in Geyl et al., *The Pattern of the Past: Can We Determine It?* (New York: Greenwood Press, 1968), 78.

3. Ibid., 77.

4. Arnold J. Toynbee, *A Study of History* (London: Oxford University, 1934-1961), X:192.

5. Geyl et al., *Pattern of the Past,* 76.

6. Ibid., 111.

7. Ibid., 116.

8. Ibid., 128.

9. "Dr. Toynbee at 70," *Manchester Guardian*, 16 April 1959.

10. Geyl et al., *Pattern of the Past,* 78.

11. Ibid., 76.

12. *New York Times* "Book Review," 20 June 1937.

13. Geyl et al., *Pattern of the Past,* 76–7.

14. Quoted by Daniel Patrick Moynihan in *Pandaemonium* (New York: Oxford University Press, 1993), 24.

15. Ibid., 19.

16. Ibid., 16.

17. Harold R. Isaacs, *Idols of the Tribe* (New York: Harper & Row, 1975), 11.

18. Ibid., 1.

19. John Horgan, *The End of Science: Facing the Limits of Knowledge in the Twilight of the Scientific Age*, (Helix Books/Addison-Wesley, 1996).

20. Arnold J. Toynbee quoted in J. G. de Beus, *The Future of the West* (New York: Harper & Brothers, 1953), 143.

21. Toynbee, *Study*, XII:536.

22. Thucydides and Polybius quoted in F. R. Cowell, *History, Civilization and Culture* (London: Thames and Hudson, 1952), 2.

23. Geyl et al., *Pattern of the Past,* 77.

24. Jacob Burckhardt, *Force and Freedom*, ed. James Hastings Nichols (New York: Pantheon, 1943), 49.

Bibliography and Further Readings

Adams, Brooks. *The Law of Civilization and Decay*. New York: Knopf, 1943.

Adams, Henry. *The Degradation of the Democratic Dogma*. New York: Macmillan, 1919.

_____. *The Education of Henry Adams*. New York: Modern Library, 1931.

_____. *Letters of Henry Adams 1892–1918*, ed. Worthington Chauncey Ford. Boston: Houghton Mifflin, 1938.

Allen, Philip J., ed. *Pitirim A. Sorokin in Review*. Durham, North Carolina: Duke University, 1963.

Ashley Montagu, M. F., ed. *Toynbee and History: Critical Essays and Reviews*. Boston: Porter Sargent, 1956.

Bartlett, Robert M. *They Work for Tomorrow*. New York: Associated Press and Fleming H. Revell, 1943.

Baudelaire, Charles. *Charles Baudelaire, Selected Poems*, trans. Geoffrey Wagner. London: Falcon, 1946.

Berdyaev, Nicholas. *The End of Our Time*, trans. Donald Attwater. London: Sheed & Ward, 1933.

_____. *The Meaning of History*, trans. George Reavey. Cleveland: World Publishing, 1962.

_____. *Toward a New Epoch*, trans. Oliver Fielding Clarke. London: Geoffrey Bles, 1949.

Bertalanffy, Ludwig von. *Robots, Men and Minds*. New York: Braziller, 1967.

Beus, J. G. de. *The Future of the West*. New York: Harper, 1953.

Brown, Harold O.J. *The Sensate Culture*. Dallas, Texas: Word, 1996.

Burckhardt, Jacob. *Force and Freedom*, ed. James Hastings Nichols. New York: Pantheon, 1943.

Cioran, E. M. *A Short History of Decay*. New York: Viking, 1975.

Colton, Joel G. *Twentieth Century*. New York: Time-Life, 1968.

Cowell, F. R. *History, Civilization and Culture*. London: Thames and Hudson, 1952.

_____. *Values in Human Society*. Boston: Porter Sargent, 1970.

Donovan, Timothy Paul. *Henry Adams and Brooks Adams*. Norman, Oklahoma: University of Oklahoma, 1961.

Dunan, Marcel, ed. *Larousse Encyclopedia of Modern History*. Feltham, Middlesex, England: Paul Hamlyn, 1973.

Fennelly, John F. *Twilight of the Evening Lands*. New York: Brookdale, 1972.

Fisher, H.A.L. *A History of Europe*. London, Eyre and Spottiswoode, 1935.

Fischer, K. P. *History and Prophecy: Oswald Spengler and the Decline of the West*. New York: Peter Lang, 1989.

Freud, Sigmund. *Civilization and Its Discontents*, trans. and ed. James Strachy. New York: Norton, 1961.

Fromm, Erich. *The Sane Society*. New York: Rinehart, 1955.

Gargan, Edward T., ed. *The Intent of Toynbee's History*. Chicago: Loyola University, 1961.

Geyl, Pieter. *Debates With Historians*. London: Batsford, 1955.

_____ et al. *The Pattern of the Past: Can We Determine It?* New York: Greenwood, 1968.

Hallen, G. C., and Rajeshwar Prasad, eds. *Sorokin and Sociology: Essays in Honour of Pitirim A. Sorokin*. Agra, India: Satish, 1972.

Hayes, Carlton J. H. *A Generation of Materialism 1871–1900*. New York: Harper and Row, 1941.

Herder, H. *Europe in the Nineteenth Century 1830–1880*. London: Longmans, 1966.

Horgan, John. *The End of Science: Facing the Limits of Knowledge in the Twilight of the Scientific Age*. New York: Helix Books/Addison-Wesley, 1996.

Hughes, H. Stuart. *Oswald Spengler: A Critical Estimate*. New York: Scribner's, 1952.

Huntington, Samuel P. *The Clash of Civilizations and the Remaking of World Order*. New York: Simon and Schuster, 1996.

Isaacs, Harold R. *Idols of the Tribe*. New York: Harper & Row, 1975.

Kipling, Rudyard. *The Five Nations*. Garden City, New York: Doubleday, Page, 1926.

_____. *Something of Myself*. Garden City, New York: Doubleday, Doran, 1937.

Laing, R. D. *The Politics of Experience*. New York: Pantheon, 1967.
London, Jack. *The Iron Heel*. New York: Macmillan, 1958.
Lowith, Karl. *Meaning in History*. Chicago: University of Chicago, 1949.
Lukacs, John. *The Passing of the Modern Age*. New York: Harper and Row, 1970.
Maquet, Jacques J. *The Sociology of Knowledge*. Boston: Beacon, 1951.
Marnell, William H. *The Good Life of Western Man*. New York: Herder and Herder, 1971.
Matter, Joseph Allen. *Love, Altruism, and World Crisis: The Challenge of Pitirim Sorokin*. Chicago: Nelson-Hall, 1974.
May, Rollo. *Love and Will*. New York: Norton, 1969.
Mazlish, Bruce. *The Riddle of History*. New York: Harper and Row, 1966.
McNeill, William H. *Arnold J. Toynbee: A Life*. New York: Oxford, 1989.
Moynahan, Daniel Patrick. *Pandaemonium*. New York: Oxford University Press, 1993.
Mumford, Lewis. *The Condition of Man*. New York: Harcourt Brace Jovanovich, 1973.
Nordau, Max. *Degeneration*. New York: Appleton, 1895; also London: Heinemann, 1920.
Perry, Marvin. *Arnold Toynbee and the Western Tradition*. New York: Peter Lang, 1982.
Reilly, John J. *Spengler's Future*. East Brunswick, New Jersey: Millennium, 1993.
Roberts, J.M. *A History of Europe*. London, Helicon: 1996.
Roberts, John. *Revolution and Improvement*. Berkeley and Los Angeles: University of California, 1976.
Schubart, Walter. *Russia and Western Man*, trans. Amethe von Zeppelin. New York: Ungar, 1950.
Schweitzer, Albert. *The Philosophy of Civilization*, trans. C. T. Campion. New York: Macmillan, 1957.
Sorokin, Pitirim A. *The Basic Trends of Our Times*. New Haven, Connecticut: College and University, 1964.
_____. *The Crisis of Our Age*. New York: Dutton, 1941.
_____. *A Long Journey*. New Haven, Connecticut: College and University, 1963
_____. *Man and Society in Calamity*. New York: Dutton, 1943.
_____ et al. *The Pattern of the Past: Can We Determine It?* New York: Greenwood, 1968.
_____. *The Reconstruction of Humanity*. Boston: Beacon, 1948.
_____. *Social and Cultural Dynamics*. 4 vols. New York: American Book, 1937–1941.
_____. *Social and Cultural Dynamics*, ab. Boston: Porter Sargent, 1957.

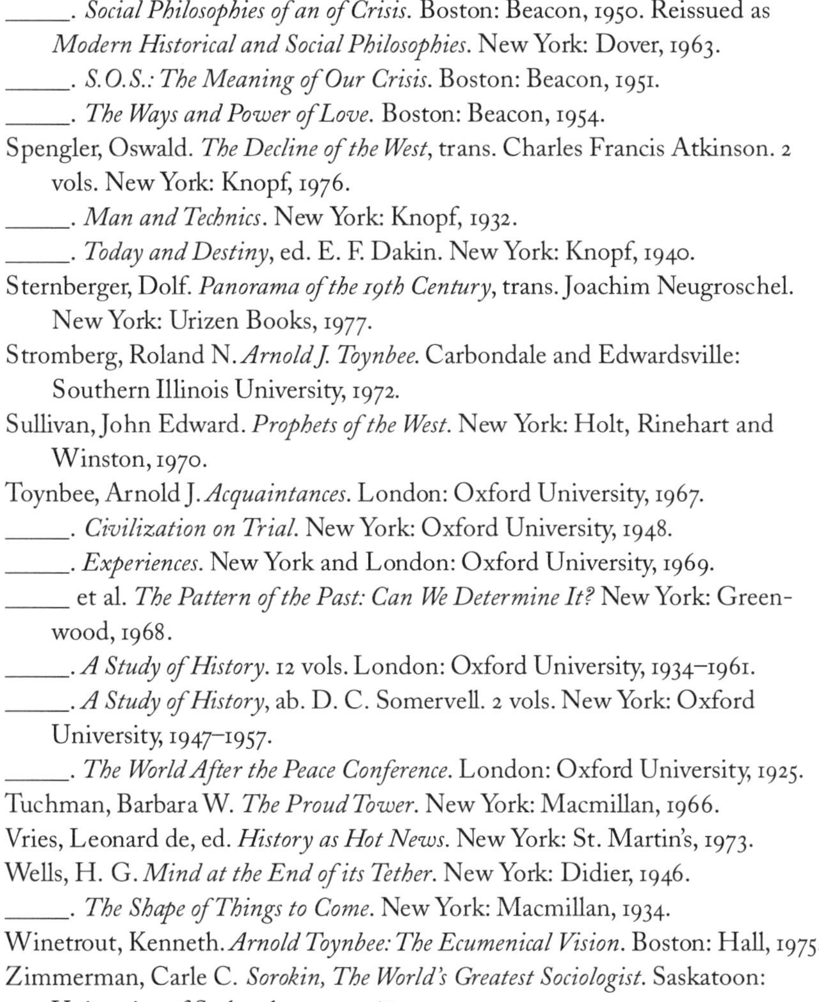

_____. *Social Philosophies of an of Crisis*. Boston: Beacon, 1950. Reissued as *Modern Historical and Social Philosophies*. New York: Dover, 1963.

_____. *S.O.S.: The Meaning of Our Crisis*. Boston: Beacon, 1951.

_____. *The Ways and Power of Love*. Boston: Beacon, 1954.

Spengler, Oswald. *The Decline of the West*, trans. Charles Francis Atkinson. 2 vols. New York: Knopf, 1976.

_____. *Man and Technics*. New York: Knopf, 1932.

_____. *Today and Destiny*, ed. E. F. Dakin. New York: Knopf, 1940.

Sternberger, Dolf. *Panorama of the 19th Century*, trans. Joachim Neugroschel. New York: Urizen Books, 1977.

Stromberg, Roland N. *Arnold J. Toynbee*. Carbondale and Edwardsville: Southern Illinois University, 1972.

Sullivan, John Edward. *Prophets of the West*. New York: Holt, Rinehart and Winston, 1970.

Toynbee, Arnold J. *Acquaintances*. London: Oxford University, 1967.

_____. *Civilization on Trial*. New York: Oxford University, 1948.

_____. *Experiences*. New York and London: Oxford University, 1969.

_____ et al. *The Pattern of the Past: Can We Determine It?* New York: Greenwood, 1968.

_____. *A Study of History*. 12 vols. London: Oxford University, 1934–1961.

_____. *A Study of History*, ab. D. C. Somervell. 2 vols. New York: Oxford University, 1947–1957.

_____. *The World After the Peace Conference*. London: Oxford University, 1925.

Tuchman, Barbara W. *The Proud Tower*. New York: Macmillan, 1966.

Vries, Leonard de, ed. *History as Hot News*. New York: St. Martin's, 1973.

Wells, H. G. *Mind at the End of its Tether*. New York: Didier, 1946.

_____. *The Shape of Things to Come*. New York: Macmillan, 1934.

Winetrout, Kenneth. *Arnold Toynbee: The Ecumenical Vision*. Boston: Hall, 1975.

Zimmerman, Carle C. *Sorokin, The World's Greatest Sociologist*. Saskatoon: University of Saskatchewan, 1968.

Index

A Note on the Author

Bruce G. Brander, a native of Milwaukee, has enjoyed an eclectic career—merchant seaman, solider, teacher, journalist, photographer, author—that has carried him to the farthest corners of the world. He has lived and worked in Austria, Ireland, France, and New Zealand, as well as the South Pacific, Canary, and Hawaiian Islands.

Mr. Brander is a former writer and editor for *National Geographic* and for the last twelve years covered international crises from Mexico to the Sudan for World Vision, a global relief agency. Now a full-time writer, he lives in Colorado Springs with his wife and their four children. *Staring into Chaos* is his fifth book.

This book was designed and set into type
by Mitchell S. Muncy
and printed and bound
by Quinn-Woodbine, Inc., Woodbine, New Jersey.

❦

On the Europe Bridge by Gustave Caillebotte
is reproduced with the gracious permission
of the Kimbell Art Museum,
Fort Worth, Texas,
on a jacket designed by Stephen J. Ott.

❦

The text face is Adobe Caslon,
designed by Carol Twombly,
based on faces cut by William Caslon, London, in the 1730s,
and issued in digital form by Adobe Systems,
Mountain View, California, in 1989.

❦

The paper is acid-free and is of archival quality.